Critical Essays on

JOHN DRYDEN

CRITICAL ESSAYS
ON
BRITISH LITERATURE

Zack Bowen, General Editor
University of Miami

◆

Critical Essays on
JOHN DRYDEN

◆

edited by

JAMES A. WINN

G. K. Hall & Co.
An Imprint of Simon & Schuster Macmillan
New York

Prentice Hall International
London   Mexico City   New Delhi   Singapore   Sydney   Toronto

G. K. Hall & Co.
An Imprint of Simon & Schuster Macmillan
1633 Broadway
New York, NY 10019

Library of Congress Cataloging-in-Publication Data

Critical essays on John Dryden / edited by James A. Winn.
     p.   cm. — (Critical essays on British literature)
    Includes bibliographical references and index.
    ISBN 0-7838-0050-9 (alk. paper)
    1. Dryden, John, 1631–1700—Criticism and interpretation.
  I. Winn, James Anderson, 1947–   . II. Series
  PR3424.C75   1997
  821'.4—dc21   97-10114
                                                CIP

The paper used in this publication meets the minimum requirements of
American National Standard for Information Sciences—Permanence of Paper
for Printed Library Materials. ANSI Z39.48-1984. ∞ ™

10 9 8 7 6 5 4 3 2 1

Printed in the United States of America

Henry Knight Miller
in memoriam

Contents

General Editor's Note

◆

The Critical Essays on British Literature series provides a variety of approaches to both classical and contemporary writers of Britain and Ireland. The formats of the volumes in the series vary with the thematic designs of individual editors, and with the amount and nature of existing reviews and criticism, augmented, where appropriate, by original essays by recognized authorities. It is hoped that each volume will be unique in developing a new overall perspective on its particular subject.

James Winn's introduction underscores the enormous variety of Dryden's literary contributions. Winn describes the critical controversies regarding the works: the split of critical opinion regarding whether the derivative nature of much of Dryden's production overshadowed its undeniable quality of expression; and whether Dryden's dependence on patronage from conflicting political sources made him a mercenary, an uncommitted turncoat, or an evolving, open-minded, honest apologist unafraid to admit changes in his own opinions. His selected essays, several of which were edited and revised especially for this volume, elaborate these critical cruxes in individual works by Dryden and reveal the extent to which even seemingly apolitical works are subtly politicized.

ZACK BOWEN
University of Miami

Publisher's Note

◆

Producing a volume that contains both newly commissioned and reprinted material presents the publisher with the challenge of balancing the desire to achieve stylistic consistency with the need to preserve the integrity of works first published elsewhere. In the Critical Essays series, essays commissioned especially for a particular volume are edited to be consistent with G. K. Hall's house style; reprinted essays appear in the style in which they were first published, with only typographical errors corrected. Consequently, shifts in style from one essay to another are the result of our efforts to be faithful to each text as it was originally published.

Introduction

JAMES A. WINN

In discussing Dryden's critical prose, Samuel Johnson praises his great predecessor for his stylistic variety:

> He who writes much, will not easily escape a manner, such a recurrence of
> particular modes as may be easily noted. Dryden is always "another and the
> same"; he does not exhibit a second time the same elegances in the same form,
> nor appears to have any art other than that of expressing with clearness what
> he thinks with vigour. His style could not easily be imitated, either seriously or
> ludicrously; for, being always equable and always varied, it has no prominent
> or discriminative characters.[1]

As Johnson trusts his readers to recognize, the quoted phrase ("another and
the same") comes from Dryden's translation of a passage from Ovid describing the mythical phoenix:

> All these receive their Birth from other Things;
> But from himself the *Phoenix* only springs:
> Self-born, begotten by the Parent Flame
> In which he burn'd, another and the same.[2]

By means of the allusion, Johnson is obliquely describing Dryden as a
phoenix—a strikingly appropriate emblem for a writer who was often reborn
from the ashes of his previous styles and opinions.[3] Adjusting readily to the
demands of different genres, Dryden wrote poems in a number of different
metrical forms, employing tones ranging from the elevated heroic to the
Baroque sublime to the wittily obscene. He translated thousands of lines of
classical literature and produced the first substantial body of critical prose in
English. His 27 plays include farces, comedies, tragi-comedies, operas, and
heroic tragedies in rhyme and blank verse. A restless thinker, he frequently
changed his positions about politics, religion, and literary theory in response

1

to the development of his own talents and the rapidly changing political and intellectual world around him. To his contemporaries (and to later critics), he sometimes seemed to change his very identity, to become *another*. Yet as Johnson reminds us, each new Dryden was inevitably a child of the old Dryden, another *and the same*.

Dryden's contemporaries recognized this aspect of his talent from the very beginning. Thomas Rymer, writing in 1674, singled out a passage from his first heroic play, *The Indian Emperour* (1665), to illustrate his "variety of matter":

> *All things are hush'd, as Nature's self lay dead,*
> *The Mountains seem to Nod their drowsie head,*
> *The little Birds in dreams their Songs repeat,*
> *And sleeping flowers beneath the Night-dew sweat,*
> *Even Lust and Envy sleep.*

> In this description, four lines yield greater variety of matter, and more choice thoughts than twice the number of any other Language. Here is something more *fortunate* than the boldest fancy has yet reached, and something more *just*, than the severest reason has observed. Here are the *flights* of *Statius* and *Marino* temper'd with a more discerning judgment, and the *judgment* of *Virgil* and *Tasso* animated with a more sprightly Wit.[4]

For Rymer, the impressive aspect of Dryden's variety is compression: he fits many "choice thoughts" into a few lines, and combines the virtues of his poetic predecessors. Although most of his contemporaries, accepting the Renaissance ideal of *copia,* took a similarly positive view of Dryden's literary variety, there were exceptions: "your Writings," wrote Martin Clifford in an unfriendly letter, "are like a Jack of all Trades Shop, they have Variety, but nothing of value."[5] Others applauded the sheer quantity of Dryden's output, linking variety and productivity: "No man hath written in our Language so much, and so various Matter, and in so various Manners, so well," wrote William Congreve. "If he had written nothing but his Prefaces, or nothing but his Songs, or his Prologues, each of them would have intituled him to the Preference and Distinction of excelling in his Kind."[6]

These comments assess the variety of Dryden's published work; the private testimony of Dr. Robert Creighton, who was the poet's contemporary at Cambridge, casts more light on the mind that imagined the work:

Dryden he said . . . was reckoned a man of good parts & Learning while in Coll[ege]: he had to his knowledge read over & very well understood all ye Greek & Latin Poets. He stayed to take his Batchelor's degree; but his head was too roving and active, or what else you'll call it, to confine himself to a College Life, & so he left it & went to London into gayer company, & set up for a Poet, wch he was as well qualified for as any man.[7]

Creighton correctly implies that Dryden's "roving and active" mind was among his qualifications as a poet. Over his long career, the mutability of that mind allowed Dryden to experience or imagine the feelings of people of different genders, religions, cultures, and political principles. When translating, he often reported that he felt a deep identification with the original writer, another assertion related to the myth of the phoenix. In the preface to *Sylvae* (1685), for example, he defended his additions to the texts he had translated for that volume:

> I desire the false Criticks wou'd not always think that those thoughts are wholly mine, but that either they are secretly in the Poet, or may be fairly deduc'd from him: or at least, if both those considerations should fail, that my own is of a piece with his, and that if he were living, and an *Englishman,* they are such, as he wou'd probably have written.
>
> (*Works,* III, 4)

In relation to his classical originals—in this case Horace, Lucretius, and Theocritus—Dryden is claiming that his thoughts are "of a piece" with those of his predecessors. In the Preface to *Fables* (1700), he develops this assertion into a full-blown theory of the transmigration of poetic souls:

> *Milton* was the Poetical Son of *Spencer,* and Mr. *Waller* of *Fairfax;* for we [poets] have our Lineal Descents and Clans, as well as other Families: *Spencer* more than once insinuates, that the Soul of *Chaucer* was transfus'd into his Body; and that he was begotten by him Two hundred Years after his Decease.
>
> (sig. A1v)

Dryden's fluid and transformative theory of literary identity should make him more attractive to modern readers than he was to Victorian scholars obsessed with ideological consistency or New Critics in search of an elusive aesthetic unity. Some of Roland Barthes's remarks in his influential essay on "The Death of the Author," though referring more directly to Balzac and Proust, seem strikingly close to Dryden's sense of literary succession:

> A text is . . . a multi-dimensional space in which a variety of writings, none of them original, blend and clash . . . a tissue of quotations drawn from the innumerable centres of culture. . . . [T]he writer can only imitate a gesture that is always anterior, never original. His only power is to mix writings, to counter the ones with the others, in such a way as never to rest on any one of them.[8]

If it is the fate of the postmodern author "never to rest" on any one statement, the "roving and active" Dryden may lay claim to being a postmodern *avant la lettre.*

The essays in this volume, all published since 1980, emphasize different aspects of Dryden's work, but none of the scholars represented here seeks to reduce him to only one of his many facets; many essays celebrate his variety; several find occasion to quote the passage on "Lineal Descents and Clans." In a wide-ranging account of "The Fabric of Dryden's Verse," Richard Luckett shows how Dryden composed some of his most enduring poems as what Barthes calls "a tissue of quotations"—and quotations not only from such famous predecessors as Spenser and Milton, but from his own contemporaries, many now forgotten. In his copy of Spenser, Luckett reminds us, Dryden jotted a revealing marginal note on the second of the *Mutabilitie Cantos:* "groundwork for a song on St. Cecilia's Day." Although he wrote his "Song for St. Cecilia's Day, 1687" without borrowing directly from Spenser, the theme of mutability appears in the emphasis on Creation and Apocalypse, the shaping of the world through music and the untuning of the sky at the end of time. As Luckett shows, Dryden deftly appropriated words and phrases for this poem from Sir John Davies, Abraham Cowley, and the forgotten poet John Norris. Using previous poetry as a "groundwork" in this way was central to his creative process. The word itself appears in his Preface to *Ovid's Epistles* (1680), where he distinguishes three kinds of translation—metaphrase, paraphrase, and imitation; in the last of these, "the Translator (if now he has not lost that Name) assumes the liberty not only to vary from the words and sence, but to forsake them both as he sees occasion: and taking only some general hints from the Original, to run division on the ground-work, as he pleases" (*Works* I, 114–15). To "run division on the ground-work," a much-admired musical skill, was to improvise variations over a repeated "ground bass"—an apt image for Dryden's way of writing, which was more likely to produce variety than consistency. Indeed, as Luckett argues in his account of the ode "To the Pious Memory of the Accomplisht Young LADY Mrs Anne Killigrew" (1686), opposing notions held in suspension often provided Dryden with striking inventions:

> The opening stanzas of the *Anne Killigrew* Ode begin by postulating two opposing notions of the history of the soul after death, and two opposing notions of the origins of poetic inspiration, resolve neither of these conundrums and, for all that, proceed unembarrassed—Dryden having from these contradictory hypotheses, to which he in no way commits himself, derived a wealth of rich and effective imagery.

Where Luckett demonstrates Dryden's engagement with other writers at the level of particular words and phrases, Earl Miner, in "The Poetics of the Critical Act: Dryden's Dealings with Rivals and Predecessors," considers the same issues thematically, as they reveal Dryden's psychology and his critical theory. His essay brings together parts of Dryden's output too often considered separately, using terms from the poet's own critical essays to illuminate his poems. From the late "Parallel of Poetry and Painting" (1695), for example, Miner concludes that "Dryden posits a freedom in imitation. . . . The artist's imitation allows for latitude in truth or goodness within a range of moral cognition while yet preserving the poet's purposes and the reader's consent." Dryden's self-consciousness about these matters made him acutely aware of his place in history; indeed, as Miner remarks, "we owe to Dryden our idea of a literary period or age." He refers to the Elizabethan poets as "the Gyant Race, before the Flood," asks the young Congreve to "Be kind to my Remains," and imagines a later writer modernizing him as he had modernized Chaucer.[9] But the man who placed himself in the lineal succession of great poets took little care to preserve his works. As Paul Hammond, the most recent editor of the poetry, reminds us, the circulation of Dryden's poems during the poet's own lifetime was contingent and haphazard; neither Dryden nor his publishers issued a "Collected Works." Hammond's thorough survey gives deep factual grounding to the common notion that Dryden and his contemporaries were always "occasional" poets, and reminds us that the circumstances of authorship in Dryden's time were quite unlike those in later centuries. Dryden's diffidence about collecting his works also confirms the restlessness of his mind. The contrast between his practice and that of such modern poets as Auden and Yeats, who issued collected works from time to time, but revised and omitted poems they no longer considered worthy of inclusion, is also instructive. Dryden was less concerned with revising (or even preserving) his past works than with expressing his present ideas.

Even without a "Collected Works," Dryden's enemies were alert to his political alterations, maliciously reprinting his verses on the death of Cromwell over 20 years later and quoting him against himself in later controversies. Perhaps because of his constant awareness of his vulnerability, Dryden's own remarks about mutability are inconsistent, some far more candid than others. In *Astraea Redux* (1660), his poem on the Restoration, he describes an important change in government as if it were a subtle artistic effect:

> Yet as wise Artists mix their colours so
> That by degrees they from each other go,
> Black steals unheeded from the neighb'ring white
> Without offending the well cous'ned sight:
> So on us stole our blessed change; while we
> Th'effect did feel but scarce the manner see.
>
> (ll. 125–30)

The "wise Artist" who was writing this poem hoped that the new King would forgive and forget his own service to the previous regime as a clerk and translator in the office of the Latin Secretary and the author of a poem on the Protector's funeral. Presenting the Restoration as aesthetic rather than political, a "blessed change" more felt than seen, he blurs distinctions that others might have wanted kept sharp and distinct. Seven years later, he was more confident of the favor of the court, and consequently more forthright about the awkwardness of changing sides: in his tragicomedy, *Secret Love,* a play particularly admired by Charles II, the character Celadon, who has been caught up in a conspiracy against the Queen, demurs when she attempts to reward him:

> I was in hope your Majesty had forgot me; therefore if you please, Madam, I onely beg a pardon for having taken up armes once to day against you; for I have a foolish kind of Conscience, which I wish many of your Subjects had, that will not let me ask a recompence for my loyalty, when I know I have been a Rebel.
>
> (V, i, 476–82)

Dryden's rivals, normally alert to opportunities for criticism, failed to notice the applicability of that speech to its author, who accepted his own "recompence" readily enough when Charles named him Poet Laureate, but they were certainly jealous of his salary, which was actually paid so infrequently that Charles II died owing him over £1200, and they tirelessly repeated the charge that he was a "mercenary," prepared to take either side of a controversy for money. Thomas Shadwell gives vent to this view in *The Medal of John Bayes* (1682):

> Now farewel wretched Mercenary *Bayes,*
> Who the *King* Libell'd and did *Cromwel* praise,
> Farewel, abandon'd Rascal! only fit
> To be abus'd by thy own scurrilous Wit.
> Which thou wouldst do, and for a Moderate Sum,
> Answer thy Medal, and thy *Absolom.*[10]

Despite the absence of any evidence that Dryden sold his talents in the way described here, the notion that he was mercenary has had a long afterlife. Eighteenth-century writers, attempting to cope with a literary marketplace in which commercial publication was replacing patronage, sneered at his dependence on his patrons; Johnson exemplifies this view when he censures Dryden's prefaces for "meanness and servility of hyperbolical adulation," though he is impressed in spite of himself with the "endless variation" of Dryden's rhetorical flattery.[11] In the nineteenth century, however, the triumph of an ethic emphasizing sincerity and consistency led to even harsher views. The low point is Macaulay's appalling portrait of Dryden as a turncoat and time-server, in which incomplete research and hostile interpretation produce the assertion that James II paid his Laureate to convert to Catholicism. Exposed as false over 60 years ago, this slander remains a part of Dryden's reputation despite the efforts of modern scholars.[12]

Although the essays reprinted here are generally more sympathetic toward Dryden, many of them necessarily consider his political mutability. In a survey of "Dryden's Public Voices," Phillip Harth studies continuities and contrasts between the political poems of the 1660s, which celebrate the Restoration as a moment of national unity, and those of the 1680s, which defend the Stuart succession in a time of partisan strain and crisis. Where others have seen the differences between these two groups of poems as reflections of fundamental changes in Dryden's own philosophy, view of history, or personality, Harth argues that the poet adapted his rhetoric to a changing political situation. "To speak of Dryden's later disillusionment," he writes, "is to imply that he earlier entertained illusions . . . that he was persuaded by his own rhetoric to believe that the English people were in reality the cohesive body of loyal subjects he portrayed in his early public poems." Thanks to book-length studies by Harth, James Garrison, Steven Zwicker, George McFadden, and Michael McKeon,[13] modern scholars are unlikely to imagine that Dryden ever "entertained illusions." Even the funeral poem for Cromwell shows restraint, discretion, and an awareness of multiple audiences; it is a poem at least as remarkable for what it does not say as for what it says. Thanks to the richness and complexity of Dryden's political writing, scholars will surely continue to disagree about the partisan resonance of particular works and particular gestures, but we are now less likely to assume that political assertions made in any of his works are the unmediated opinions of the poet himself.

Even works that make scant reference to contemporary England usually have some political resonance, and a continuing project in recent scholarship has been the recovery of political allegory and innuendo in such works. Three of the essays reprinted here find such political meanings in Dryden's plays. Katharine Eisaman Maus, in "Arcadia Lost: Politics and Revision in the Restoration *Tempest*," explains some of the surprising changes Dryden and Davenant made in their version of Shakespeare's play (1667) by appealing to the particularities of Restoration politics in the later 1660s and the larger theories that grounded the political debate. Her analysis of competing ideologies makes sense of the altered character of Prospero, the ludicrous attempts at self-government by the sailors, and even the elaborate scenery of the later operatic production of 1674. This essay is part of a welcome trend away from poking fun at this and other Restoration versions of Shakespeare. Closer attention to the fears and fixations of the Restoration theatre audience is helping us understand why the revisers felt compelled to refashion Shakespeare for their own times, and why their altered *Tempest* was a perennial favorite. In "Dryden's *Conquest of Granada* and the Dutch Wars," James Thompson establishes a political context for a play rarely thought to have contemporary reference. Drawing on primary sources, recent historical analyses of the Second and Third Dutch Naval Wars, and Dryden's forgotten propaganda piece, *Amboyna,* Thompson shows how anxieties about mercantile trade routes and colonial expansion found their way into Dryden's epic drama of the Moors and Spaniards. For its first audiences, with their "terrible immediate memories" of the Dutch burning the English fleet in the Medway, "*The Conquest of*

Granada function[ed] ideologically as a glorification of war, something along the lines of *Top Gun,* which, through its celebration of military hardware and service, serves to efface the more humiliating memories of our most recent war."

As Maus and Thompson demonstrate, the political inferences Dryden leads his audiences to draw in these plays reflect the ideology of the Stuart court, which he supported with his pen from the Restoration of 1660 to the Revolution of 1688. When Dryden returned to the theatre after losing his official posts, his skills at suggestion and implication served him at least as well in expressing opposition to William III. As James Garrison shows in "Dryden and the Birth of Hercules," the comedy *Amphitryon* (1690), despite its obvious sources in Plautus and Molière, comments wryly on the Revolution of 1688. At the end of the play, Jupiter gives a prophecy describing the heroic career of Hercules; in his version of that speech, Dryden sends a sly political message by echoing his own earlier uses of the Hercules myth in poems praising the Stuarts. For those in the audience who shared Dryden's Jacobite sentiments, these sonorous lines expressed the hope that the Revolution might be reversed, that "murm'ring Men, unwilling to be freed, [Might] be compell'd to Happiness, by need." Since he had often himself been attacked as mercenary, Dryden also enjoyed adjusting the satire on greed in his Plautine original to reflect on those who had most obviously profited from the Revolution.

When Dryden addressed the vexed issue of political change, he often appealed to the feudal values of honor and loyalty. In *Don Sebastian* (1689), for example, Benducar tries to tempt Dorax to take part in a conspiracy against the Emperor; the old soldier's reply concedes the ruler's flaws, but argues that disloyalty will lead to a complete breakdown of morality:

> He trusts us both; mark that, shall we betray him?
> A Master who reposes Life and Empire
> On our fidelity: I grant he is a Tyrant,
> That hated name my nature most abhors; . . .
> But, while he trusts me, 'twere so base a part
> To fawn and yet betray, I shou'd be hiss'd
> And whoop'd in Hell for that Ingratitude. . . .
> Is not the bread thou eat'st, the Robe thou wear'st,
> Thy Wealth, and Honours, all the pure indulgence
> Of him thou wou'dst destroy?
> And wou'd his Creature, nay his Friend betray him?
> Why then, no Bond is left on human kind:
> Distrusts, debates, immortal strifes ensue;
> Children may murder Parents, Wives their Husbands;
> All must be Rapine, Wars, and Desolation,
> When trust and gratitude no longer bind.
>
> (II, i, 288–91, 296–98, 303–11)

Similar ideas appear in Dryden's attacks on his Whig opponents in the party strife of the early 1680s. He does not criticize them for changing their allegiance from Cromwell to Charles, as he himself had done, but rather for failing to respond to Charles's forgiveness with unblinking loyalty:

> Some by their Monarch's fatal mercy grown,
> From Pardon'd Rebels, Kinsmen to the Throne;
> Were rais'd in Power and publick Office high:
> Strong Bands, if Bands ungratefull men could tye.
> (*Absalom and Achitophel,* ll. 146–149)

These lines come from Dryden's masterpiece, written in defence of the Stuart succession and in resistance to those urging a change in the Constitution. The crisis in which Dryden composed that poem was rife with moral and political ambiguity: he was defending a king whose flaws and excesses were a matter of public knowledge. Howard Weinbrot pursues these issues in " 'Nature's Holy Bands' in *Absalom and Achitophel:* Fathers and Sons, Satire and Change." Carefully teasing out the strands of Dryden's rhetoric, and drawing usefully on pious seventeenth-century theories of patriarchy and scabrous poems of sexual insult, Weinbrot argues that his "alliance with the king's mercy and filial piety allows Dryden room respectfully to satirize the king himself." Among the Laureate's strategies was a slippery and creative approach to genre, as A. E. Wallace Maurer demonstrates in an amusing and learned account of "The Form of Dryden's *Absalom and Achitophel,* Once More." Maurer surveys the many attempts to settle the poem's genre and divide it into sections, a critical confusion that began with Dryden's wonderfully laconic title page: "*Absolom and Achitophel. A Poem.*" Playfully concealing his own identity, which was soon obvious from the virtuosity of the poem, Dryden also refused to supply a generic signpost. As the inadequacy of various proposed labels shows, the poem draws on many genres without becoming a recognizable example of any. "Dryden's generative power," writes Maurer, "produced an amalgam of something authoritatively and appropriately fire-new"—imagery that readers of this essay may want to connect to the myth of the phoenix.

The Medall (1681), composed a few months later, is a more direct attack on Anthony Ashley Cooper, Earl of Shaftesbury, leader of the Whig opposition. At one point, Dryden employs the imagery of prostitution and venereal disease to excoriate Shaftesbury:

> But thou, the Pander of the Peoples hearts,
> (O Crooked Soul, and Serpentine in Arts,)
> Whose blandishments a Loyal Land have whor'd
> And broke the Bonds she plighted to her Lord;
> What Curses on thy blasted Name will fall!
> Which Age to Age their Legacy shall call;

> For all must curse the Woes that must descend on all.
> Religion thou hast none: thy *Mercury*
> Has pass'd through every Sect, or theirs through Thee.
> But what thou giv'st, that Venom still remains;
> And the pox'd Nation feels Thee in their Brains.
>
> (ll. 256–66)

In this little allegory, England appears as a weak woman, unable to keep her vows when seduced by the blandishments of Shaftesbury, and the idea of mutability often involved the politics of gender.[14] In *The State of Innocence,* his rhyming operatic version of *Paradise Lost* (written 1674, published 1677), Dryden gave Adam a speech associating Eve with restless change:

> ADAM: Add that she's proud, fantastick, apt to change;
> Restless at home; and ever prone to range:
> With shows delighted, and so vain is she,
> She'll meet the Devil; rather than not see.
>
> (Act V, p. 39)

Yet despite his ability to express the period's stock misogyny, Dryden knew that being "apt to change" and "prone to range" were not qualities unique to women. In 1675, he assigned similar sentiments and words to a woman accusing a man of infidelity. Quarreling with her husband in *Aureng-Zebe,* the empress Nourmahal claims that men call women mutable in order to conceal their own restlessness:

> Your own wild appetites are prone to range;
> And then you tax our humours with your change.
>
> (Act II, p. 23)

The repetition of the rhyme pair and of one complete phrase ("prone to range") reveals the later passage as a recasting of the first. Dryden regenders the accusation of mutability without altering the basic materials. The hermaphroditic phoenix, which he treats as female in some poems, male in others, is a perfect emblem for this kind of gesture.[15]

    If his period, like centuries before and after, casually coded mutability as a feminine weakness, Dryden recognized it as an essential part of the human condition. He argues that case in the dedication to *Aureng-Zebe,* obliquely defending his decision to abandon rhymed drama, a form he had championed vigorously for 13 years:

> As I am a Man, I must be changeable: and sometimes the gravest of us all are so, even upon ridiculous accidents. Our minds are perpetually wrought on by the temperament of our Bodies: which makes me suspect, they are nearer alli'd, than either our Philosophers or School-Divines will allow them to be. . . .

An ill Dream, or a Cloudy day, has the power to change this wretched Creature, who is so proud of a reasonable Soul, and make him think what he thought not yesterday.

(sig. a1r-v)

Dryden also candidly admits changing his mind about the theory of tragedy in "The Grounds of Criticism in Tragedy," which he published with *Troilus and Cressida* in 1679: "I doubt not but I have contradicted some of my former opinions, in my loose Essays" (*Works*, XIII, 224). And in the "Epistle Dedicatory" to *The Spanish Fryar* (1681), he disarmingly criticizes the excesses of his earlier heroic plays:

I remember some Verses of my own *Maximin* and *Almanzor* which cry, Vengeance upon me for their Extravagance, and which I wish heartily in the same fire with *Statius* and *Chapman:* All I can say for those passages, which are I hope not many, is, that I knew they were bad enough to please, even when I writ them: But I repent of them amongst my sins.

(sig. A2v)

The religious language here is ironic and self-deprecating, but Dryden soon had occasion to write more seriously about his religious beliefs. In *Religio Laici* (1682), he defended the Anglican "middle way," arguing against deists, Roman Catholics, and unlettered Dissenters, and taking pains to emphasize the personal nature of faith. "*MY* Salvation must its Doom receive," he wrote, "Not from what *OTHERS,* but what *I* believe" (ll. 303–04). The opening lines employ the powerful Christian imagery of light shining in the darkness to stress the limits of human reason:

Dim, as the borrow'd beams of Moon and Stars
To *lonely, weary, wandring* Travellers,
Is *Reason* to the *Soul:* And as on high,
Those rowling Fires *discover* but the Sky
Not light us *here;* So *Reason*'s glimmering Ray
Was lent, not to *assure* our *doubtfull* way,
But *guide* us upward to a *better* Day.
And as those nightly Tapers disappear
When Day's bright Lord ascends our Hemisphere;
So pale grows *Reason* at *Religions* sight;
So *dyes,* and so *dissolves* in *Supernatural Light.*

(ll. 1–11)

Five years later, in an obscure and elaborate beast fable, Dryden undertook the task of defending his conversion to Roman Catholicism, knowing full well that both the conversion and the poem were certain to be ridiculed. *The Hind and the Panther* was widely parodied and attacked on its first appearance in 1687; Swift later called it "a compleat Abstract of sixteen thousand Schoolmen from *Scotus* to *Bellarmin*";[16] and few commentators before our own century have attempted analyses. Most damning of all is Keith Walker's decision to eliminate the poem entirely from his recent Oxford edition, as if Dryden's longest and most complex original poem could be arbitrarily excluded from his corpus. The difficulty of the poem is surely one reason for such disdain, caution, and silence, but in recent years some critics have risen to the challenge. Steven Zwicker's essay, "The Paradoxes of Tender Conscience," is an instance of this welcome trend. Taking on the notoriously obscure fables of birds with which the Hind and the Panther entertain and criticize each other in Part III of the poem, Zwicker outlines the awkward and contradictory positions in which James II and his Laureate found themselves, and points to paradox as the best available rhetorical strategy: "paradox allowed Dryden to celebrate the mysteries of Christianity and ally them with the institutional tenets and practices of Roman Catholicism. Paradox also allowed Dryden to soften the obvious contradictions between the language and spiritual program of toleration and the closeting, politicking, and bullying of this king and his closest advisors."

Perhaps because of the strain of the situation, the passages on mutability in *The Hind and the Panther* are among Dryden's finest. He lists the powerful forces that might dissuade anyone from a conversion—"picque of honour to maintain a cause, / And shame of change, and fear of future ill" (III, 401–02)—all emotions he must have been experiencing at the time. And in an overtly confessional passage, he connects false belief to his poet's pride in his creativity and imagination:

> My thoughtless youth was wing'd with vain desires,
> My manhood, long misled by wandring fires,
> Follow'd false lights; and when their glimps was gone,
> My pride struck out new sparkles of her own.
> Such was I, such by nature still I am,
> Be thine the glory, and be mine the shame.
>
> (I, 72–77)

Dryden's formula here—"Such was I, such by nature still I am"—comes very close to the idea Johnson borrowed from his later translation: he knew that he was "always 'another and the same,' " that his conversion to Rome had not altered his essential personality or his poetic practice, including his habit of revisiting his own metaphorical language.[17] This very passage, though dramatizing the most notorious change in a lifetime of changes, draws directly on the poem he now sought to contradict: many readers would remember that the imagery of wandering fires and false lights had also appeared in *Religio Laici*. In this case as in many others, Dryden describes his new belief by recasting words and images he had already used to describe his previous opinion. A poet less radically honest, or more averse to risk, would surely have avoided reminding his readers of his earlier work, but returning to rhymes, images, and ideas he had previously employed and making them serve quite different argumentative purposes was Dryden's characteristic mode of revision. Where Pope, a generation later, fussed endlessly with his poems, revising their language and even their typefaces with each new edition, Dryden, who rarely altered any published work, revised *himself* by writing new works; by reusing the "fabric" of his earlier writing, he dramatized the unceasing development and alteration of his mind.

Memory was central to this process, and Congreve informs us that Dryden was "happy in a Memory tenacious of every thing that he had read."[18] Not only could he readily recall lines and images from his own works and those of others, but he had meditated deeply on the meaning of memory, as David Morris shows in "Writing/Reading/Remembering: Dryden and the Poetics of Memory." The brief poem "To the Memory of Mr. Oldham" (1684) is one of Dryden's most personal utterances, and Morris's essay on that poem is the most personal of the essays reprinted here. Morris draws inspiration from figures as diverse as Virgil, Keats, George Bellows, Freud, and Heidegger, but he also has the courage to relate this poem, in which an older poet laments the loss of a promising younger one, to the psychological dynamics of the modern classroom. This essay accomplishes something theorists frequently posit as a possibility for criticism: it evokes an elegiac mood with a power not unlike the power of the poem itself.

In explaining how Dryden and his contemporaries "constructed an aesthetics built upon memory," Morris invokes a letter Hobbes wrote to Sir William Davenant in 1650, when Dryden was an undergraduate: "Time and Education begets experience; Experience begets memory; Memory begets Judgement and Fancy: Judgment begets the strength and structure, and Fancy begets the ornaments of a Poem. The Ancients therefore fabled not absurdly in making memory the Mother of the Muses." Forty years later, the issues raised in that genealogy were still important to Dryden, who dramatized them memorably in the opera *King Arthur* (1691), for which he had Henry Purcell as a collaborator. A full context for this rich work would include the politics of the early 1680s, when Dryden wrote his first version of the libretto (now lost); the politics of the early 1690s, for which he doubtless made adjustments; the tangled history of heroic drama and opera throughout the period;[19] and the empiricism of Hobbes and Locke, as Eric Jager demonstrates in "Educating the Senses: Empiricism in Dryden's *King Arthur.*" In this version of the story, Arthur's beloved is the blind princess Emmeline; her attempts to understand vision through touch and hearing give dramatic shape to controversies about sense impressions and knowledge that were currently urgent for Dryden's contemporaries. Though possessed of all his senses, Arthur undergoes a parallel process of moral education, in which he learns that his eyes may often deceive him. As Robert P. MacCubbin points out in "The Ironies of Dryden's 'Alexander's Feast; or the Power of Musique':

Text and Contexts," similar issues inform that work: "During the seventeenth century the Platonic explanation of musical effects on the innately harmonic soul was supplanted by empirical study of the more mundane operation of sound impulses on the body." In both these late works, we may observe Dryden drawing upon both the latest scientific knowledge and the ancient traditions linking music with emotions and morality. MacCubbin also shows how Dryden's recasting of the myth of Alexander and Timotheus expresses the poet's skepticism about William's military policies. This willingness to live simultaneously in the world of ancient Pythagorean lore and modern science, ancient myth and modern politics is yet another instance of Dryden's capacity to assimilate materials from a wide variety of sources, yet make them his own. "He appears," wrote Johnson, "to have had a mind very comprehensive by nature, and much enriched with acquired knowledge. His compositions are the effects of a vigorous genius operating upon large materials" (*Lives of the English Poets,* I, 457).

So comprehensive was that mind that no one-volume collection of essays can fairly represent the range of Dryden's career and output. The emphasis on poetry and drama in this collection reflects the emphases of recent scholarship; a new generation of scholars would help us by exploring those parts of Dryden's corpus not much studied by currently active researchers. Unfortunately, the preponderance of male scholars in this collection also reflects the current state of Dryden scholarship. Our female colleagues working in this period have contributed pioneering studies of such authors as Margaret Cavendish, Katherine Philips, and Aphra Behn, expanding and complicating our sense of the politics of gender in the later seventeenth century; a challenge to the next generation is the incorporation of insights gained from those studies into our view of Dryden.[20]

Dryden has been a central figure in my own studies for the last 20 years. Not least among the pleasures he has afforded me has been the opportunity to know others who share my enthusiasm for him. Scholars long established as experts, including Earl Miner and Phillip Harth, answered my queries and gave me encouragement as I began work on the biography. Howard Weinbrot, Steven Zwicker, Robert MacCubbin, and Wallace Maurer have been frequent and stimulating correspondents; Paul Hammond and Richard Luckett have often and generously shared the fruits of their own researches, sustaining a transatlantic conversation. Eric Jager, the youngest scholar included here, wrote the first version of his paper in the first graduate seminar I taught at Michigan. Indeed, I am delighted to say that I count all the authors represented here as friendly colleagues. United in defense of an oft-maligned poet, Dryden scholars have tried to avoid acrimony among ourselves. Our disagreements—and we have them, of course—are generally expressed with wit and civility. Although much of our conversation now takes place by electronic mail, I like to think it catches some of the spirit that Dryden praised in the dedication of *The Assignation* to Sir Charles Sedley, where he compares the poets of his own age to those who flourished under the emperor Augustus:

> We have, like them, our Genial Nights; where our discourse is neither too serious, nor too light; but alwayes pleasant, and, for the most part, instructive: the raillery neither too sharp upon the present, nor too censorious on the absent; and the Cups onely such as will raise the Conversation of the Night, without disturbing the business of the Morrow.
>
> (*Works* XI, 321)

My fondest hope for this collection is that it may attract more students and scholars into that pleasant company, so that more glasses will be raised to the memory of John Dryden.

Notes

1. "Dryden," in *Lives of the English Poets,* ed. G. B. Hill, 3 vols. (Oxford: Clarendon, 1905), 1:418.

2. "Of the Pythagorean Philosophy," *Fables,* pp. 502–503. Wherever possible, quotations from Dryden follow *The Works of John Dryden,* ed. Edward Niles Hooker, H. T. Swedenberg et al. (Berkeley: University of California Press, 1955–), here cited as *Works.* I refer to poems by line number; to plays by act, scene, and line; and to prose by volume and page. For works not yet published in the California edition, I follow the first London editions, citing by page number.

3. Hill and other editors of Johnson have missed this allusion, citing instead a similar phrase—"another, yet the same"—from Pope's *Dunciad,* in a passage describing the ghost of Elkanah Settle:

> Wond'ring he gaz'd: When lo! a Sage appears,
> By his broad shoulders known, and length of ears
> Known by the band and suit which Settle wore
> (His only suit) for twice three years before:
> All as the vest, appear'd the wearer's frame,
> Old in new state, another yet the same.
>
> (III, 35–40)

I follow the text given in *The Twickenham Edition of the Works of Alexander Pope,* ed. John Butt et al. (London: Methuen, 1950–67). Pope is probably remembering Dryden's phrase; his notes refer to the controversy between Dryden and Settle.

4. From the Preface to Rymer's translation of *Rapin's Reflections on Aristotle's Treatise of Poesie,* excerpted in *Dryden: The Critical Heritage,* edited by James and Helen Kinsley (London: Routledge, 1971), pp. 115–16.

5. From Clifford's *Notes upon Mr. Dryden's Poems in Four Letters* (written c. 1671–72, published 1687), printed in full in Kinsley and Kinsley, pp. 175–189, here quoting p. 175.

6. From the Epistle Dedicatory to Congreve's edition of *The Dramatick Works of John Dryden* (1717), excerpted in Kinsley and Kinsley, p. 265.

7. Trinity College Muniments, "Great Volume of Miscellany Papers III," no. 42.

8. Roland Barthes, "The Death of the Author" (1968), in *Image—Music—Text,* translated by Stephen Heath (New York: Hill and Wang, 1977), p. 146.

9. "Another Poet, in another Age, may take the same Liberty with my Writings; if at least they live long enough to deserve Correction" (Preface to *Fables,* sig. b1r-v). For the other phrases, see "To my Dear Friend, Mr. Congreve," ll. 5, 73.

10. From *The Medal of John Bayes,* usually attributed to Shadwell, printed in full in Kinsley and Kinsley, pp. 143–150, here quoting p. 150.

11. *Lives of the Poets,* I, 399. The famous imagery of perfume in this passage may also be obliquely derived from Dryden's lines on the phoenix. Johnson writes: "As many odoriferous bodies are observed to diffuse perfumes from year to year without sensible diminution of bulk or weight, [Dryden] appears never to have impoverished his mint of flattery by his expenses, however lavish." Compare Dryden's lines on the death of the phoenix:

> Of *Casia, Cynamon,* and Stems of *Nard,*
> (For softness strew'd beneath,) his Fun'ral Bed is rear'd:
> Fun'ral and Bridal both; and all around
> The Borders with corruptless Myrrh are crowned:
> On this incumbent, till aetherial Flame
> First catches, then consumes the costly Frame:
> Consumes him too, as on the Pile he lies;
> He lived on Odours, and in Odours dies.
>
> (*Fables,* p. 503)

12. Macaulay examined the Privy Seal order of 1685 renewing Dryden's patent as Poet Laureate, a routine document. Without checking earlier records, he leapt to the conclusion that Dryden's supplementary pension of £100, awarded to him by Charles II in 1677 (and rarely paid), was a bribe from James to encourage Dryden to convert. See Macaulay's *History of England* (1865), 6 vols. (London: Macmillan, 1914), 2:850–52. Louis Bredvold set the record straight in "Notes on John Dryden's Pension," *Modern Philology* 30 (1933): 267–74. For a complete record of Dryden's financial dealings with the court, see James A. Winn, *John Dryden and his World* (New Haven: Yale University Press, 1987), Appendix C, pp. 525–31.

13. See Phillip Harth, *Pen for a Party: Dryden's Tory Propaganda in its Contexts* (Princeton: Princeton University Press, 1993); James D. Garrison, *Dryden and the Tradition of Panegyric* (Berkeley: University of California Press, 1975); Steven N. Zwicker, *Dryden's Political Poetry; The Typology of King and Nation* (Providence: Brown University Press, 1972); *Politics and Language in Dryden's Poetry* (Princeton: Princeton University Press, 1984); and *Lines of Authority: Politics and English Literary Culture, 1649–1689* (Ithaca: Cornell University Press, 1993); George McFadden, *Dryden the Public Writer, 1660–1685* (Princeton: Princeton University Press, 1978); and Michael McKeon, *Politics and Poetry in Restoration England: The Case of Dryden's Annus Mirabilis* (Cambridge: Harvard University Press, 1975).

14. Dryden frequently treated the relations between the King and the nation in erotic terms, portraying political rivals to the Stuarts as seducers or rapists of London or England. For examples from "To Sir Robert Howard," *Astraea Redux, Annus Mirabilis,* and *Albion and Albanius,* see James A. Winn, *"When Beauty Fires the Blood": Love and the Arts in the Age of Dryden* (Ann Arbor: University of Michigan Press, 1992), pp. 155–60.

15. In his first published poem, "Upon the death of the Lord HASTINGS" (1649), Dryden laments the fact that Hastings, who died at 18, was childless: "Thus, without Young, this Phoenix dies, new born" (l. 80). In his verses to the Duchess of York on her husband's naval victory at Lowestoft, published in the front matter to *Annus Mirabilis* (1667), he describes his patroness as a "new-born *Phoenix*" (l. 52); in his poem on the death of Charles II, *Threnodia Augustalis* (1685), he uses a similar passage to describe Charles as a male phoenix attended by female muses (ll. 364–72); in the Killigrew ode (1686), Maria Beatrice is "our

Phenix Queen" (l. 134). There are also references to the phoenix in *The Rival Ladies, The Conquest of Granada, Aureng-Zebe,* and *Don Sebastian.*

16.   "Introduction" to *A Tale of a Tub,* quoted in Kinsley and Kinsley, p. 245.

17.   The twentieth-century revival of serious attention to Dryden began with Louis Bredvold's influential study of *The Intellectual Milieu of John Dryden* (Ann Arbor: University of Michigan Press, 1934), which employs impressive learning and ingenuity to argue that Dryden's shift from the Anglican position outlined in *Religio Laici* to the Roman Catholic apologetics of *The Hind and the Panther* was in fact part of a consistent philosophical development, but that position cannot possibly be sustained, as later scholarship has shown. See especially Phillip Harth, *Contexts of Dryden's Thought* (Chicago: University of Chicago Press, 1968). I am arguing here for the continuity of Dryden's poetic technique, not the consistency of his thought.

18.   Kinsley and Kinsley, p. 264.

19.   See my essay, "Heroic Song: A Proposal for a Revised History of English Theatre and Opera, 1656–1711," *Eighteenth-Century Studies* 30 (1997), in press.

20.   I have attempted to begin this process in *"When Beauty Fires the Blood."* See especially chapter 7, " 'That Language their Converse Refines': Dryden and Women of Letters."

The Fabric of Dryden's Verse

RICHARD LUCKETT

The modern and the seventeenth-century meanings of "fabric" have common elements, disparate emphases. When Dr Johnson wrote of Pope that "he used almost always the same fabrick of verse" he meant that he wrote almost exclusively in the heroic couplet.[1] Johnson's sense is the modern sense, the manufactured material of which an object, most usually a building or a dress, is made. I shall have something to say about that aspect of Dryden's verse, but my aim is to try to go beyond it, to suggest its relation to what I believe to be the principal seventeenth-century sense of fabric: that is, the building itself, the sum of the parts. The seventeenth-century sense and the modern sense are not obviously exclusive; it is precisely their interrelation that is useful for my argument.

I shall begin with prophecy, a device about which Dryden was certainly as dubious as you may be, but which, once he had hedged his bets, he never hesitated to use. As he wrote in his *To Sir Robert Howard,* of 1660:

> Yet let me take your Mantle up, and I
> Will venture in your right to prophesy.
>
> 'This Work, by merit first of Fame secure,
> 'Is likewise happy in its Geniture:
> 'For since 'tis born when *Charls* ascends the Throne,
> 'It shares at once his Fortune and its own.'

I shall hedge my own bets by modifying the word to "prediction." I anticipate, if only because of the inadequacies of the available editions, that in the field of Dryden scholarship more and more evidence will come to light of his borrowings of words, of phrases, images, and procedures, but particularly the first two, from his immediate predecessors, and from his contemporaries amongst the English poets. I think, that is to say, that the convenient and prevalent notion of "common stock," which is in itself testimony to the situation that I am about to outline, will disappear, and that scholars will find increasing numbers of sources for Dryden in which it seems probable that he has drawn directly on particular poems because they had a relation to his immediate concern in composition—in other words, an exploration of what Eliot was describing when he said, with a sufficiency which is in itself a criti-

Richard Luckett, "The Fabric of Dryden's Verse." © The British Academy 1982. Reproduced by permission from *Proceedings of the British Academy,* Vol. LXVII, *1981 Lectures and Memoirs,* 289–305.

cal challenge: "The capacity of assimilation, and the consequent extent of range, are conspicuous qualities of Dryden."[2] In fact, this process is already under way, and it is its bearing on criticism that to an extent I want to anticipate.

The kind of thing I have in mind can best be illustrated by attempting a reconstruction of the way Dryden may have worked in writing one of his most famous odes. I cannot demonstrate that he did work in quite the sequence I propose; I think also that one obvious question—was he consciously or unconsciously proceeding in such a manner?—does not answer to the circumstances of the kind of process of creation that I hope will emerge from this account. But that is something I must endeavour to substantiate in the description.

When Dryden accepted the commission to write an ode for the 1687 feast of the Gentlemen Lovers of Musick he was dealing with a genre established as recently as 1683, and having for its exemplars a contemptible piece by Christopher Fishbourn, an even more contemptible piece by Nahum Tate (which has the distinction, remarkable in criticism, of being described as "sugary, simpering, and mincing with almost incredibly bad taste" by so latitudinarian a commentator as Montague Summers), and a workmanlike poem, which Dryden would certainly have known, by John Oldham.[3] What is at once evident in these poems, even in the Oldham, is a lack of structure. That the need for an appropriate structure for a Cecilian Ode concerned Dryden we know from his copy (now in the library of Trinity College, Cambridge) of Spenser. Stanza 12 of the second of the Mutabilitie Cantos contains a reference to how, at the marriage of Peleus and Thetis:

> . . . *Phoebus* self, that god of Poets hight,
>   They say did sing the spousall hymne full cleere,
>   That all the Gods were ravisht with delight
> Of his celestiall song, and Musicks wondrous might.

Against this, Dryden wrote: "groundwork for a song on St. Cecilia's Day." He never used it, though the "Power of Musick" is of course the theme of *Alexander's Feast*. But what is suggestive is the subject of the Canto as a whole: Dame Mutabilitie's plea to

> This great Grandmother of all creatures bred
> Great *Nature,* ever young yet full of eld,
> Still mooving, yet unmoved from her sted

and Spenser's extraordinary extended exploration of, and meditation upon, change, time, immortality, eternity, and the universe, which raises so many of the questions that were to preoccupy philosophers and theologians (and, of course, poets) for the next century. It is no great jump from the Mutabilitie

Cantos to Sir John Davies's discussion in *Nosce Teipsum* of the proposal "That the Soule cannot be destroyed":

> *Perhaps* her *cause* may cease and she may die;
>   God is her *cause,* his *word* her maker was,
>   Which shall stand fixt for all eternitie,
>   When heaven and earth shall like a shadow passe.
>
> *Perhaps* some thing repugnant to her kind
>   By strong *Antipathy* the *Soule* may kill;
>   But what can be *contrarie* to the mind,
>   Which holds all *contraries* in concord still?
>
> She lodgeth heate, and cold, and moist and drye,
>   And life, and death, and peace, and warre, together.

Which brings us to the actual language of the *Song:*

> Then cold, and hot, and moist, and dry,
> In order to their stations leap,
>   And MUSICK'S pow'r obey . . .

as well as back to that paradox of uncreation to which Spenser had alluded with: "And *Natur*'s selfe did vanish, whither no man wist." We are in contact with both the actual language of the *Song* and with its form when we turn to Cowley's Pindarick on "The Resurrection," which would unavoidably have come to Dryden's mind since its second stanza was drawn on quite directly by John Oldham in his *Ode* for 1684, "Begin the Song." Oldham, however, used only the opening of the stanza, which tells how the years

> All hand in hand do decently advance,
> And to my *Song* with smooth and equal measures *dance.*

It was the continuation of Cowley's stanza which stirred Dryden's imagination:

> Whilst the *dance lasts,* how long so e're it be,
> My *Musicks* voice shall bear it companie,
>   Till all *gentle Notes* be drown'd
>   In the *last Trumpets* dreadful sound;
> That to the *Spheres* themselves shall *silence* bring,
>   Untune the *Universal String.*
>   Then all the wide extended *Skie*
>   And all th' *harmonious Worlds* on high
>   And *Virgil*'s sacred *work* shall dy . . .

We are also in contact with the essential dramatic device of the *Song*, a point that can be made more explicit by turning to another Pindarick on "Nature's great solemn Funeral," John Norris's *The Consummation*. Norris was a friend of Dryden's, and his ode was published shortly before the composition of *A Song*. It is an ambitious, not very successful, piece. It draws, as it could scarcely avoid doing, on the Cowley. And so there are good ideas in it. Norris gets Cowley's "untun'd" into his last line, the position that it occupies in Dryden's poem, thus terminating his creation with uncreation:

> And now the World's *untun'd,* let down thy *high-set* string.

It also introduces one important new device: Time, by means of a somewhat drastic pun, becomes an actor, "The Antient Stager of the Day," and the image of the theatre stays in Norris's mind:

> See how the Elements resign
> Their numerous charge, the scatter'd Atoms home repair . . .
> They know the great Alarm,
> And in confus'd mixt numbers swarm,
> Till rang'd, and sever'd by the *Chymistry* divine,
> The Father of Mankind's amaz'd to see
> The Globe too narrow for his Progeny.
> But 'tis the *closing* of the Age
> And *all* the *Actors* now at once must grace the *Stage.*

The theatre evidently stayed in Dryden's mind also, and I do not think it fanciful to suggest that Norris's "globe" may have triggered a recollection of a passage which he had once had occasion to excise from *The Tempest*—the pageant becoming not "insubstantial" but "crumbling," the transformations ultimate, the ending of the revels final, the Globe, the theatre, itself the operative image. For the essential dramatic device of *A Song* is functional, turning, just as Shakespeare does, the occasion, the gathering in Stationers' Hall, into a part of the poem's imagery. The last trumpet becomes a real trumpet, the assembly of the Gentlemen Lovers of Music becomes "This crumbling pageant," and a synecdoche of the Last Judgement. The literalism is stark; the equation, "trumpet" "last trumpet," almost naïvely obvious, if not brazen; the effect is totally shocking. Dr Johnson thought the use of the image of the Day of Judgement "so awful in itself, that it can owe little to poetry"; but the Cowley and Norris Odes by their comparative insignificance (though Johnson admired part of the Cowley) show that it owes everything to poetry.[4] Dryden even manages to extend what we might normally presume to be the scope of the art itself; and yet: "owes everything to poetry"? Norris, Oldham, Cowley, Davies, are all drawn upon directly; from a distance, Spenser and Shakespeare make their contributions. But what is so striking is the unlikeness of Dryden's material, animated in his poem, as compared to what we might think of as its inert form in his sources—the radical reformation that it has undergone. Dryden has contrived simultaneously to find in the occasion itself his principal image, to use this image of the creation and uncreation of the world as his plot, to introduce as the logical subplot the history of music—Jubal, Orpheus, and Cecilia are each progressively more gifted exponents of the art—and then within this double frame to create a series of character parts which comes, again with an irresistible logic, directly out of an account of the invention of the first musical instrument, and ends its passage from the profane to the sacred with a further movement, where no further movement had seemed possible, into the most awful dimension of the sublime. The affects of the viol (Jubal's chorded shell, the *testudo*), the trumpet and drum, flute, lute, violin, and organ, provide a conspectus of the primary human emotions. In perceiving this Dryden not only found but fixed the form of the Cecilian Ode in perpetuity, and it is as much a musical as a literary innovation, a feat of design which, if it does not impress as such, only fails to do so because it appears so obvious; a kind of "Try sparrowhawks, Ma'am," which makes a perfect order in a field where disorder doubly prevailed, should we allow Pushkin's opinion that "Ecstasy does not require any intellectual power capable of relating the parts to the whole. . . . Homer is immeasurably greater than Pindar, the ode . . . stands on the lowest rungs of poetry . . ."[5] and take in addition Dryden's own view of English Pindaricks. These he appears to have recognized for what they were: an invention of the "happy genius of Mr. Cowley," which gave an apparent classical license for something wholly unclassical, a poem "like a vast tract of land newly discovered. The soil wonderfully fruitful . . . overstocked with inhabitants, but almost all salvages, without laws or policy."[6]

I believe that similar accounts could be given of the creation of many of Dryden's poems: of *To the Pious Memory of Mistress Anne Killigrew,* for example, of which Jonson's *To the Immortall Memory . . . of Sir Lucius Cary and Sir H. Morison* is an obvious source, contributing a strategy (in that both poems are not about the historical characters of their subjects, but about the virtues that those characters could be taken to illustrate), a fundamental structural device (the introduction of the poet's person into the poem), and verbal echoes. Less anticipatable as a source is Anne Killigrew's own verse, which Dryden had evidently read with attention and which gave him the basis for:

> Mean time her Warlike Brother on the Seas
> His waving Streamers to the Winds displays,
> And vows for his Return, with vain Devotion, pays.
> Ah, Generous Youth, that Wish forbear,
> The Winds too soon will waft thee here!
> Slack all thy Sailes, and fear to come,
> Alas, thou know'st not, Thou art wreck'd at home!

The *Dies Irae* in Roscommon's translation, Nathaniel Lee's *Theodosius* (where the Dioscuri also appear), which provided the image of

'Twas *Cupid* bathing in *Diana*'s Stream,

besides two poems by Cowley on the matchless Orinda, together with some others of the poems prefaced to Katherine Philips's works—a connection obvious enough, but topically strengthened because both Katherine Philips and Anne Killigrew died of smallpox—also play their part. Nor does Dryden hesitate to borrow from himself, making extensive use of motifs (the comparison of poetry and painting, the Last Judgement), and details from his earlier work—indeed, even from his earliest work, his *Upon the Death of the Lord Hastings* of 1649. These things all come together in what Johnson called, with reason, "undoubtedly the noblest ode that our language has ever produced," and are united and transformed by Dryden's development of a dominant theme: an attempt to answer the question "How shall the poet be saved?" which Anne Killigrew's life, death, and innocence are all made insistently to demand.[7] Jonson's strategy is carried a stage further, and the problem of writing an acceptably panegyrical elegy on a young lady who practised, with at best a modest talent, the "two Sister-Arts of Poësie, and Painting" is resolved by writing a poem overtly introducing Dryden himself, as practitioner of the arts of poetry and playwriting, and the reflections prompted by the idealization of Anne Killigrew that her death has made incumbent upon him. But this very issue is explicit in the first stanza of James Tyrell's *To the Memory of the excellent Orinda* which, like Dryden's canonization of Anne Killigrew, sees Katherine Phillips as a saint, yet in the order of the poets, and which suggests the problem of the pure tribute from the impure vessel. Moreover, in a manner almost alarming in the context of my argument, the second stanza of Tyrell's poem raises abruptly the whole question of design, of scheme, in the Pindarick. What Dryden has done is to implement the notion structurally, and this is the aspect of his poetic gift that I am now concerned to urge.

This is not just a way of looking at Dryden: it is an identification of a method of composition to which he himself admits, and which attracted comment (albeit in an oblique and sometimes disparaging form) from his contemporaries, the most notable, since it cannot disguise a qualified admiration despite its disapproval, being Gerard Langbaine's description of Dryden as the "skilful Lapidary." Dryden was fascinated by the process of creation, to the extent that the *Epistle Dedicatory of the Rival Ladies* is sometimes cited, a little implausibly (since it neglects Hobbes, and, of course, Shakespeare) as the first account in English of the psychology of composition:

This worthless present was designed you, long before it was a play; when it was only a confused mass of thoughts, tumbling over one another in the dark;

when the fancy was yet in its first work, moving the sleeping images of things towards the light, there to be distinguished, and then either chosen or rejected by the judgment. . . . And, I confess, in that first tumult of my thoughts, there appeared a disorderly kind of beauty in some of them, which gave me hope, something worthy my Lord of Orrery might be drawn from them.

"Judgment" is the operative faculty, "distinguishing" the instrumental process, "order" (and here I think we should recollect the French *ordonnance*) the principle of Beauty. Or we can turn to the first prologue to *Secret Love:*

> He who writ this, not without pains and thought
> From *French* and *English* Theaters has brought
> Th' exactest Rules by which a play is wrought.
>
> The Unities of Action, Place, and Time;
> The Scenes unbroken; and a mingled chime
> Of *Johnsons* humour, with *Corneilles* rhyme.
>
> But while dead colours he with care did lay,
> He fears his Wit, or Plot he did not weigh,
> Which are the living Beauties of a Play . . .

to *To my Dear Friend Mr. Congreve, On His Comedy, call'd The Double-Dealer,* where a sustained architectural analogy with a precise allusion to what was contemporaneously happening at the top of Ludgate Hill introduces a listing of the excellencies of Congreve's predecessors which concludes with his sub-sumation of their virtues, to the *Essay on Dramatic Poesy,* and Crites on Ben Jonson, the "greatest man of the last age," who was willing "to give way" to the Ancients "in all things":

he was not only a professt Imitator of *Horace,* but a learned Plagiary of all the others; you track him every where in their Snow: if *Horace, Lucan, Petronius Arbiter, Seneca,* and *Juvenal* had their own from him, there are few serious Thoughts which are new in him; you will pardon me, therefore, if I presume he lov'd their fashion, when he wore their Cloaths.

Tracking Dryden, but in the snow of his contemporaries, is precisely the tendency in Dryden scholarship that I am predicting and that I have endeav-oured, in a particular instance, to demonstrate; and it is an activity for which I now wish to suggest a perspective, a perspective in perhaps a distressingly literal sense, since it has to do with the architectural proclivity of the Restora-tion, with which I am anxious to associate the underlying processes that seem to me the common factors in the fabrication of Dryden's verse. These processes have it in common that they are structural; and this I take to be an element in English poetry that is both uncommon and, to a certain extent, unpopular. It is certainly untypical.

The architectural proclivity of the Restoration is neatly summed up by Evelyn, who in his diary entry for 4 February 1685, which is, in effect, an obituary for the King, wrote that Charles II loved "Planting, building, & brought in a politer way of living, which passed to Luxurie & intollerable expense." Did Evelyn then reflect that on 28 October 1664 he had recorded a conversation with Charles, occasioned by his presentation to the King of his *Sylvae* and his translation of Roland de Fréart's *Parallèle de l'Architecture?* My point is not that Evelyn might have done more than a little to whet that appetite the effects of which he subsequently deplored, but that the irony reveals the way in which the two concerns, which have as their common factor the necessity of design, imbued the culture of the Restoration, a culture with which Dryden quite consciously identified himself, of which he was, to an extraordinary degree, the deliberate emissary, a culture which had to it a quiddity, a sense of its own particularity, perhaps unique in English history. "All, all, of a piece throughout": Dryden's summary in *The Secular Masque* from *The Pilgrim* reveals his absolute awareness of the way he had come to adumbrate a period; and in a sense this is what his poems do too.[8] My account of *A Song for St. Cecilia's Day* may have suggested the manner in which that poem made a number of other poems redundant. "Who now reads Cowley?" Few people, since what Cowley did was better done by Dryden. Why should Pope have tried to suppress his *Ode on St. Cecilia's Day?* One reason must be that he had come to see that there was nothing in it that had not been better done by Dryden. But *The Secular Masque* is not, as it happens, merely inspired hindsight. It was the Restoration itself that enabled Dryden to speak as a poet. At that time, by which he was twenty-eight, he had, so far as we know, written only four poems. From 1660 onwards until his death in 1700 there is not a year in which he fails to publish. And here I must return to my beginning and bring the poem *To Sir Robert Howard* back into play: his prophecy is in fact far apter for his own career than for Howard's, and the poem tells us why:

> this is a piece too fair
> To be the child of Chance, and not of Care.
> No Atoms casually together hurl'd
> Could e're produce so beautifull a world.
> Nor dare I such a doctrine here admit,
> As would destroy the providence of wit.

No event in English history was ever more witty than the providential Restoration, and when that Restoration was jeopardized Dryden used the model of wit-writing established by Davenant in *Gondibert* to indicate why. *Annus Mirabilis,* which follows *Gondibert* not only in its stanzas and manner, but also in its latent five-act organization (I cannot at all assent to Ker's description of it as a "series of fragments, with no more than an accidental unity"), confounds prophecy with wit.[9] The Republicans had claimed that God was with them, and saw in the course of history their justification of that claim. The year 1660 had turned their proposition to dead sea fruit, and was, consummately, a witty providence. But 1666, when England suffered the aftermath of plague, the Dutch in the Medway, and the Great Fire, threatened to be, and was represented by adherents of the Old Cause as being, its reversal. In *Annus Mirabilis* Dryden propounded a possible way of seeing the events of that year, a year of darkness, or, if you consented to his vision, of wonders, interpreting it on the same principle, in a poem which was a triumph of design.

The poet as architect is sufficiently familiar as both a topos of debate with which Plato and Quintilian made play, and as a subject of debate which no reader of Ben Jonson could ignore. I am not now concerned with the metaphor, but the particular status of architecture in the Restoration, a status demonstrated, in its poetic context, by John Webb's complaint when John Denham was appointed Surveyor General of the King's Works in 1660: "Though Mr Denham may, as most gentry, have some knowledge of the theory of architecture, he can have none of the practice, but must employ another."[10] It is as gentleman, not as poet, that Denham has some knowledge of the theory of architecture, and it is to this aspect of Webb's assumption, the assumption equally attested to by Sir Roger Pratt's observation: "if you be not able to handsomely contrive it yourself, get some ingenious gentleman who has seen much of that kind abroad . . . to do it for you," that I want to draw attention.[11] The tardiness of Sir Christopher Wren's discovery of his avocation as architect is as striking as the tardiness of Dryden's discovery of his avocation as poet. What is more, Wren had himself, in his translation of Horace's *Epistle to Lollius,* essayed poetry, and in 1663 in conversation expressed views on wit sufficiently striking for his friend Thomas Sprat to write them down, develop them, and then report them back to their originator: the Wit of Discourse

> uses the best and easiest Words, is not the first that takes up new ones, nor the last that lays down old ones. But above all, its chiefest Dominion is in forming new Significations, and Images of Things and Persons. And this may be so suddenly practised, that I have known in one Afternoon, new Stamps, and Proverbs, and Fashions of Speech raised, which were never thought of before, and yet gave Occasion to most delightful Imaginations . . . Wit consists in a right ordering of Things and Words for Delight.

Sprat ends by lamenting, in verse wittily symptomatic of the disease he describes, the fact that "All the World are at present Poets," and by asking "What is to be done with this furious Generation of Wits and Writers?"[12]

I think this offers a clue as to Dryden's discovery of himself as a poet, and his practice as a writer. It is debatable whether Sir John Denham was ever the architect of a building, but there has never been any question that he was the architect of a poem in which the two senses of fabric coinhere. The achievement of *Cooper's Hill*, which opens with an allusion, by means of Waller's poem on the occasion, to Inigo Jones's beautifying and regularizing of Old St. Paul's, is the stance of the poet, independent of Royal Windsor and rebellious Runnymeade, who equates himself with the river upon which both places stand:

> O could I flow like thee, and make thy stream
> My great example, as it is my theme!
> Though deep, yet clear, though gentle, yet not dull,
> Strong without rage, without o'erflowing full;

lines which Dryden both commended in his criticism, and, in his poem *To Sir Robert Howard*, imitated:

> Yet as when mighty Rivers gently creep,
> Their even calmnesse does suppose them deep,
> Such is your Muse: no Metaphor swell'd high
> With dangerous boldnesse lifts her to the sky . . .
> So firm a strength, and yet withall so sweet,
> Did never but in *Sampson*'s Riddle meet.

It is Dryden's prompt perception of the importance of this, rather than his imitation, that signifies. This is not to deny that he responded to the fabric of the heroic couplet as it was employed by Denham: he manifestly did so, to the extent of writing blank verse which is really disguised couplets, and using broken couplets, as the normative and restraining form, in his Pindarick Odes. But what I think him to have found far more compelling was Denham's equation of viewpoint and Archimedean point; the balance of the couplet inherent in the balance of the composition.

In his *Dedication of the Aeneis* to the Marquess of Normanby Dryden recounts that he

> had also studied *Virgil*'s Design, his disposition of it, his Manners, his judicious management of the Figures, the sober retrenchments of his Sense, which always leaves somewhat to gratifie our imagination, on which it may enlarge at pleasure; but above all, the Elegance of his Expressions, and the harmony of his Numbers. For . . . the words are in Poetry, what the Colours are in Painting. If the Design be good, and the Draught be true, the Colouring is the first Beauty that strikes the Eye.

"If the Design be good, and the Draught be true"; it is the essential precondition, and the metaphor runs throughout Dryden's criticism: "But in a room contrived for state, the height of the roof should bear a proportion to the area: so in the heightenings of poetry, the strength and vehemence of figures should be suited to the occasion, the subject, and the persons." Dryden's admission in his dedication to *Troilus and Cressida* (1679) that he was "often put to a stand, in considering whether what I write be the Idiom of the Tongue . . . And have no other way to clear my Doubts, but by translating my English into Latine, and thereby trying what sense the words will beare in a more stable Language," is interesting not so much for what it may or may not have to tell us about the state of English, or Dryden's Latinity, as for what it reveals about Dryden's reflex of thought, his capacity for an immediate shift into another mode of conceptualizing the matter. Dryden's translations also signify here, first in their quantity, the extent to which they are his preferred mode (over half his published verse, it has been estimated, is translation), secondly in their customary procedures—the use of a multiplicity of texts, commentaries, and existing English versions. There is, in this process, an assumption of an underlying recoverable form, which is equally the assumption that could cause him, in the *Fables,* to make a passage of Chaucer comprehend a passage of Lucretius—and the effect is not of anything applied, not of superimposition, but of something derived from the essence of the concerns which Aristotle, Lucretius, Chaucer, Robert Burton, and Dryden had in common. And I must emphasize that I consider this as much a matter of the ectomorph as of the endomorph, of the perception of the space created by a structure as of the scaffolding itself, the space implied by Dryden when he said of "piety" in its Virgilian application to Aeneas, that "the word in Latin is more full than it can possibly be expressed in any modern language" and which he himself consistently exploited, as when, in *To the Pious Memory* he described Anne Killigrew as ". . . yet a young Probationer, / And Candidate of Heav'n."

This radical cast of mind in Dryden emerges in many different ways: in the way he takes over existing mythologies or devices and inverts them: the prophecies of doom (and the title of the poem itself) in *Annus Mirabilis,* Shadwell's claim to the Jonsonian inheritance in *Mac Flecknoe,* Marvell's sardonic glimpse of Charles as Saul in *Absalom and Achitophel,* the Whigs' emblematic token in *The Medall,* the title of Lord Herbert's deistical tract in *Religio Laici,* the fable out of a low church pamphlet in *The Hind and the Panther,* in the mordant critique of empire ("Here let my sorrow give my satyr place") in the same poem.[13] It finds expression in his recurrent concern with origins—of painting in *To Sir Godfrey Kneller,* of poetry in *To the Earl of Roscommon,* of music (as we have seen) in *A Song for St. Cecilia's Day*—a concern that is as naturally extended to scriptural text as to Stonehenge. This same radicalism has a clear relation to the aspect of Dryden which must have some bearing on the psychology of his conceptual brilliance: that is, his taking of risks.

Such a taking of risks can assume many forms. A fascination with the subject is in any case implicit in the recurrent images of gambling and trade as in the superficially unlikely contest of *Threnodia Augustalis,* where we find both the assertion that

> Never was losing game with better conduct plaid . . .

and the equivocal

> The vain *Insurancers* of Life,
> And He who most perform'd and promis'd less,
> Even *Short* himself forsook th'unequal strife.

Money is a constant topic in Dryden, but it is never far removed from the question of chance. In *Annus Mirabilis* we have the possibility that 1667 will reverse 1666, the King's prayers be denied, the Dutch enter the Thames, the plague break out anew. In *Absalom and Achitophel* the risk is that the mockery of Charles would not, by its subject, be regarded as worth the end that it achieves (after all, what would James have said had Dryden chosen to treat him in such terms?). In *Religio Laici* the risk is that the acceptance of the critique of scriptural texts will lead to an entire dependence on embodied tradition, and here, of course, for Dryden, it ultimately did. Dryden's Catholicism, in *The Hind and the Panther,* and the position of political absolutism (however humane and qualified) set out in the postscript to the translation of *The History of the League,* are both in a sense compensatory, symptomatic of a desire for certainty impelled by that almost involuntary clarity of vision that could make Dryden in his first play, *The Wild Gallant,* anticipate virtually every argument for the rights of women that would be advanced in the next three centuries, and in his penultimate, *Amphitryon,* present as bleak a view of the human condition and the nature of human happiness as the context of comedy has ever allowed. It is this vision, too, that informs Dryden's conditionality, his tendency to say, in criticism, "on the one hand there is this, on the other that," and to plump for neither, just as the opening stanzas of the *Anne Killigrew* Ode begin by postulating two opposing notions of the history of the soul after death, and two opposing notions of the origins of poetic inspiration, resolve neither of these conundrums and, for all that, proceed unembarrassed—Dryden having from these contradictory hypotheses, to which he in no way commits himself, derived a wealth of rich and effective imagery. Hence also, I suspect, the appeal for Dryden of *The Knightes Tale,* that fable in which, so notably, events occur, but in which the moral questions seem deliberately unresolved, are indeed challenged as the kind of questions that we might assume them to be, and which has, as Dryden handles it, that acutely uncomfortable emphasis, so disconsolatory, on the fact of tragedy as, in fact, tragedy. And who, in the seventeenth century, but Dryden would think to compare Virgil to a tightrope walker, even though the image has its precedent in Horace?

Some kind of insight into this state of mind is to be obtained from a reading of Joseph Glanvill, whose sermons, particularly that on "Catholic Charity," so aided and influenced Dryden in the composition of *Religio Laici:*

> He that is extreme in his Principles, must needs be narrow in his Affections: whereas he that stands on the middle path, may extend the arms of his Charity to those both sides: It is indeed very natural to most, to run into extremes: and when men are faln Out with a Practice, or Opinion, they think they can never remove to too great a distance from it, being frighted by the steep before them, they run so far back, till they fall into a precipice behind them. *Every Truth is near an Errour:* for it lies between two Falshoods.[14]

This awareness of not at all an easy or comfortable middle way (the emphasis is Glanvill's) seems to touch a particular chord in Dryden, and Glanvill continues:

> The Apostle tells us, that we *know but in part,* and makes Confidence an Argument of Ignorance. If any man think that he knoweth any thing, he knoweth nothing yet, as he ought to know. And *Solomon* reckons it as an argument of Folly; *The Fool rageth and is confident:* and there is nothing that discovers it more.

So we have in Dryden this architectonic tendency, his faculty for strong design, and at the same time a characteristic which might seem to point in quite another direction, though it is repeatedly an essential part of the plotting of his poems: the instant of absolute seriousness that is most frequently achieved by introducing the poet in his proper person, but is also often an apartness, an abstraction, as in the recurrent songs for aerial spirits, or the pellucidity of

> Hark, hark, the Waters fall, fall, fall;
> And with a Murmuring sound
> Dash, dash upon the ground,
>   To gentle slumbers call.

The moment itself can be illustrated by the King's prayer in *Annus Mirabilis,* when any notion of wit-writing is abruptly damped down, or by the elegy for the Earl of Ossery in *Absalom and Achitophel;* or by the introduction of the poet through the way in which *Annus Mirabilis* is submitted as the offering of a non-combatant who nevertheless, as a gentleman, should have been in the war—"a due expiation for my not serving my King and Country in it. All gentlemen are almost oblig'd to it. . . ." In *Mac Flecknoe* he uses his own creation of Maximin (from *Tyrannick Love*) against himself, just as in the same poem he sardonically inverts his own triumphant naming of London as Augusta, which has been the apogee of *Annus Mirabilis.* In *Religio Laici* the repudiation of Dryden's own poetic gift which is the climax—or rather the climactic humility—of the poem, is clinched in terms of the invocation of *"Tom Shadwell's Rhimes,"* the shabbiness of which it has been one of the major achievements of the exercise of that gift to establish. In the Oldham elegy he attaches to his criticism of his subject's poems a criticism of his own, the two in conjunction substantiating each other in a manner that confirms the seriousness of feeling, precision of sentiment and absence of hyperbole in the poem. In *To the Pious Memory of . . . Anne Killigrew* he assesses the moral worth of his dramatic writings in terms that go beyond anything that Jeremy Collier was to suggest. In the Prologue and Epilogue to *All for Love* he makes as devastating a self-criticism in terms of craftsmanship. In *The Cock and the Fox* he introduces a disrespectful reference to *Alexander's Feast.* His radical eye was always turned upon himself (some of the self-criticisms in the prose are quite as remarkable); that it could be so was in large measure a consequence of his adoption of, proclivity for, underlying designs independent of the patterns of human volition and of emotional fulfillment in the sense of the gratification of appetite. When he perceives the "groundwork" of a *Song for St. Cecilia's Day* it is significant that he sees it as that, as a foundation, as the artist's draught: such a scheme is the necessary armature of his imagination. Indeed, in the *Dedication of the Aeneis* we can discover Dryden discerning his own manner of composition in another poet:

> I have already told your Lordship my Opinion of *Virgil;* that he was no Arbitrary Man. Oblig'd he was to his Master for his Bounty, and he repays him with good Counsel. . . . From this Consideration it is, that he chose, for the ground-work of his Poem, one Empire destroy'd, and another rais'd from the Ruins of it. This was just the Parallel.

Saintsbury attributed "the frantic rage which Dryden's satire provoked in his opponents" to "a coolness always to be discovered at the centre of his scorn"—an opinion which is quoted where one might least expect to find Saintsbury approved, in the first of Wyndham Lewis's Enemy Pamphlets, *Satire and Fiction.* Yet it is a context that I find revealing. Lewis, in his practice of two arts, aimed for a similar coolness (and it is worth pointing out that the word is Dryden's own: he refers, in the Preface to *The Fall of Man,* to "the Coolness and Discretion which is necessary to a Poet"). In literature, at least, Lewis seldom achieved this. But when he did it was because of a perception of a form, a structure, the allegedly "abstract" form upon the necessity of which post-Impressionist theory (not at all, ultimately, a theory of abstraction) so forcefully insisted.

I want to end by postulating two further parallels. Picasso's saddle and handlebars of a racing bicycle that have become a bull seems to me to have been inadequately discussed in the available criticism. There is a way in which the object speaks rather than looks. It is a statement about Picasso's mixed allegiances, to Paris and the north (the land where the bicycle race is a predominant passion) and to the South and Tauromachy. It is also a political statement, since it was made in 1943 in a France divided politically along just such a line as the device, in its construction, premisses, and denies. My second parallel is quite simply Handel's setting of *A Song for St. Cecilia's Day 1687* where Handel drew on a recently published volume of keyboard music by Gottlieb Muffat, the *Componimenti . . . per il cembalo,* to an extent breathtaking even for the hardened student of Handel as a borrower. Yet the work is magnificent, no part more so than the elaborate fugato of the final chorus, which Handel has constructed simply by orchestrating a conjunction of Muffat's (unaltered) music, and Dryden's words. As with the poems, the act of composition is the perception of this conjunction, the fabrication a transformation. Matthew Arnold, who of course claimed Dryden for prose, nevertheless said something, if unwittingly, for the other side, when he reminded readers of the Preface to the 1853 edition of his *Poems* that:

> What distinguishes the artist from the mere amateur, says Goethe, is *Architectonicè* in the highest sense; that power of execution, which creates, forms, and constitutes: not the profoundness of single thoughts, not the richness of imagery, not the abundance of illustration.

In just such a way Dryden created—and often with an economy comparable to that of Picasso and Handel—from fabric, a fabric.

Notes

1.   Samuel Johnson, *Lives of the English Poets,* int. Arthur Waugh, 2 vols., London, 1906 (1952), ii. 305. Johnson's *Life* also provides another relevant usage; of the *Essay on Man* he observes that it "plainly appears the fabrick of a poet" (ibid., p. 274).
2.   T. S. Eliot, *Selected Essays* (London, 1951), p. 312.
3.   Thomas Shadwell, *Complete Works,* ed. Montague Summers, 5 vols. (London, 1927), i., p. ccxi.
4.   Johnson, op. cit. i. 311.
5.   Tatiana Wolff (ed.), *Pushkin on Literature* (London, 1971), p. 170.
6.   *Letters upon Several Occasions* (London, 1696), pp. 55–6.
7.   Johnson, op. cit. i. 310.
8.   Thomas Rymer makes the necessary point quite explicitly when he writes, in his *Tragedies of the Last Age* (1678): "I have thought our Poetry of the last Age as rude as our Architecture. . . ."
9.   John Dryden, *Essays,* ed. W. P. Ker, 2 vols. (Oxford, 1900), i. p. xxxiii.
10.   Howard Colvin, *A Biographical Dictionary of British Architects and Craftsmen* (London, 1978), p. 258.
11.   Sir Roger Pratt, *The Architect,* ed. R. T. Gunther (Oxford, 1928), p. 60.
12.   Stephen Wren, *Parentalia* (London, 1750), pp. 258–9.
13.   For *The Hind and the Panther,* cf. Paul Hammond, *Notes and Queries,* 29, no. 1 (February 1982), pp. 55–7.
14.   Joseph Glanvill, *Some Discourses, Sermons and Remains,* ed. Anthony Horneck (London, 1681), p. 119.

The Poetics of the Critical Act: Dryden's Dealings with Rivals and Predecessors

EARL MINER

> Perhaps no nation ever produced a writer that enriched his language with such a variety of models. To him we owe the improvement, perhaps the completion of our metre, the refinement of our language, and much of the correctness of our sentiments. By him we were taught "sapere at fari," to think naturally and express forcibly.
>
> —Johnson, *Life of Dryden*

Arnold's dream that poetry would replace religion had its premiss in religious disbelief. Not surprisingly, the dream has gone unfulfilled. Today some theorists doubt poetry sufficiently to suppose that criticism must replace literature: Arnold's dream now beckons as a critical nightmare. But if this is the modern critical condition, it is not the modern poetic condition. Nor has it always been so for critics. Even today, most of us know in our hearts that all creation is the most fundamental if also usually implicit criticism. This is where Dryden enters. He constantly engaged with other writers, wrote in an astonishing range of translations, of sorts of nondramatic poetry, of drama, and of prose styles. He was the first English writer aware that he was prosecuting a critical career in which poetic practice and critical precept were counterparts.

To Dryden we owe the realization for English literature that what we can know involves defining self in relation to world, world to self; and that the process of definition involves remembered versions of both, presently understood versions of both, and hitherto unknown versions. The last is the creative part in which poets excel. But it is infeasible without the other two. We see this congeries of definitions in Dryden's prefaces. His explicitness, like Shakespeare's silence, is a personal trait. He constantly joins features of our

Earl Miner, "The Poetics of the Critical Act: Dryden's Dealings with Rivals and Predecessors." © Oxford University Press 1979. Reprinted from *Evidence in Literary Scholarship: Essays in Memory of James Marshall Osborn*, edited by René Wellek and Alvaro Ribeiro (1979), by permission of Oxford University Press.

understanding of the world that usually are thought discrete: literature, other arts, politics, history, religion, science. One of the most public of poets, he is also one of the most personal of critics. In both roles, he is extraordinary innovative. But he made no pretence to have invented everything, and his translations, allusions, and adaptations show him involved in "influence" or "reception," what in the end is best understood as concomitant creation, criticism, and self-definition.[1]

The demonstration of these matters requires an intimate knowledge of the writings of any poet treated, and the simplest writing with which to begin, at least for Dryden, is his prose criticism. In a late essay, *A Parallel Betwixt Poetry and Painting,* he insists that art is founded on imitation of nature and must please (including "what ought to please" as a norm).[2] This typical Renaissance neo-Aristotelianism and neo-Horatianism is remarkable because he seeks to harmonize two premises whose relation came about quite accidentally. His discussion makes something else clear. Mimesis pervades Western literature because it assumes not just that nature is imitable, but that it is real, knowable, and shareable. The assumption induces great confidence. Disagreeing with Aristotle over why imitation pleases (*Poetics,* ch. 5), he argues that it involves cognitive and ethical matters: truth through our reasoning and good by exercise of our will. On that basis, "The imitation of nature is therefore justly constituted as the general, and indeed, the only, rule of pleasing, both in poetry and painting" (Watson, ii. 193).

Dryden posits a freedom in imitation. In portraying character, "there is a better or worse likeness to be taken: the better is panegyric, if it be not false, and the worse is a [satire]." He recalls a passage in the *Poetics* where three writers are said to have depicted people better, worse, and like (Watson, ii. 202). The artist's imitation allows for latitude in truth or goodness within a range of moral cognition while yet preserving the poet's purposes and the reader's consent.

These important issues seem never to have been aired adequately. Their centrality to Dryden can be shown in the earlier "Account" prefixed to *Annus Mirabilis.* Discussing "descriptions or images," he declares that "historic and panegyric" poetry are "branches" of "epic poesy" (Watson, i. 101). Panegyric clearly also implies its obverse, worse likeness, satire. All this relates very clearly to Dryden's non-dramatic practice, in which varieties of narrative predominate. Wonder and grandeur, the high mimesis, involve a world of time and history, of large numbers of people, and of strong personalities defined by shared values. In this public world, Dryden and Milton found what they believed truly real. By serving supernal ends beyond the contingent, the true narrative, the real heroic of these poets offered a species of theodicy and asserted divine providence. Such narrative allowed for subsidiary branches of praise and blame for better or worse likenesses, as Milton's Satan shows to perfection. The historical filled the distant heroic with the matter of time and place.

Two of Dryden's historical concepts have redirected our thought. One deserves a name, Crites's Question. In *An Essay of Dramatic Poesy,* Crites asks: "Is it not evident in these last hundred years (when the study of philosophy [i.e. science] has been the business of all the virtuosi in Christendom), that almost a new nature has been revealed to us?" (Watson, i. 26.) This echoes, and alters, Sidney's remark on the poet's disdaining to be bound to reality and growing "in effect another nature."[3] Sidney has in mind centaurs and the like. Dryden has in mind a concept far more radical: a changing nature. Crites's "almost" (like Sidney's "in effect") betrays some hesitation. And well it might, since such historicism would ultimately jeopardize Dryden's beliefs in the uniformity of human nature, the comparability of historical episodes (cyclicity), and mimesis itself.

The other, closely related, historical concept is so familiar as to seem always to have existed. But we owe to Dryden our idea of a literary period or age.

> Well then; the promis'd hour is come at last;
> The present Age of Wit obscures the past:
> Strong were our Syres; and as they Fought they Writ,
> Conqu'ring with force of Arms, and dint of Wit;
> Theirs was the Gyant Race, before the Flood;
> And thus, when *Charles* Return'd, our Empire stood.

So Dryden to Congreve (ll. 1–6). This is akin to talk of the dramatists of "the former age" in *An Essay of Dramatic Poesy* and elsewhere. This conception of a period made possible a genuine historical view of literature and other human enterprises, something Dryden deals with in terms of progress pieces on an art such as painting (*To Sir Godfrey Kneller*) or a technology such as navigation and shipping (*Annus Mirabilis*). With these ideas Dryden laid the basis for historical understanding of literature. They also made him a genuine comparatist. He considered for drama the ancients and, among the moderns, the Spanish, French, and English. He compared Chaucer with Ovid and Boccaccio. In comparing Horace and Juvenal, he declared: "'Tis generally said that those enormous vices which were practised under the reign of Domitian were unknown in the time of Augustus Caesar; that therefore Juvenal had a larger field [as satirist] than Horace" (Watson, ii. 132). From this we see that the historical element helps to distinguish difference and the theoretical helps to identify common elements, as they have tended to do ever since Dryden.

The distinction between differentiating historicism and homogenizing theory is sufficiently clear to allow for some joining of the two for greater effect. In his poetry, the one implies the other in his constant preoccupation with likening, combining. The standard example of congruence between prose and poetry must be *Religio Laici,* whose prose preface covers the very topics of the poem in their order, ending with just the same concern over the poem's style. Yet we read the poem in preference to the prose, for the reasons we return to *Mac Flecknoe*. Poetry matters more than prose, at least when prose attempts the same thing as poetry. When poems give better or worse likeness, each version of the truth holds interest.

It seems agreed that *Mac Flecknoe* uses a theatrical coronation progress for its situation, and that it weaves three major strands: monarchy or politics involving a slight plot; art and especially drama, clearly committing the poem to a critical act; and religion, validating politics and art. The combination is presided over by an implicit heroic standard, with history, panegyric, and satire made immediate. The princes are Richard Flecknoe and Thomas Shadwell, historical characters who inhabit a real world, alive with art; or rather they rule over "all the Realms of Non-sense" (l. 6), a barbarous Ireland or, more idyllically, "Some peaceful Province in Acrostick Land" (l. 206). The old topos of the epic poet as king has a new day, especially since the ruler is also a divine, "As King by Office, and as Priest by Trade" (l. 119). So art becomes politics becomes religion becomes art once more in ceaseless combinatory play.

The additional crucial element in *Mac Flecknoe,* human relationship of father and son, has counterparts in "To the Memory of Mr. Oldham." The analogies for the Dryden–Oldham relation begin with heroic *amicitia* as the older and younger poets are compared with Nisus and Euryalus in the *Aeneid.* But the poem ends by assimilating Virgil's Augustus–Marcellus relation to Dryden and Oldham, thereby making Dryden the monarch and Oldham the lost successor. In few words, this poem takes a better likeness to the worse of *Mac Flecknoe* even while sharing many concerns and analogies. Examination would show that various of these elements recur in the Killigrew and Purcell odes, *A Song for St. Cecilia's Day, Alexander's Feast,* as well as the addresses to Kneller and Southerne. Of course there are also real distinctions, since Dryden honours the historical integrity in each instance. But the poem to Congreve astonishingly resembles *Mac Flecknoe* in subject and analogy. Again a father–king–artist is unseasonably deposed. Again he addresses his most promising son, a dramatist, with charges. Again different ages are involved. But a far better likeness is taken in the assessment by heroic metaphor of "Dryden's poetic kingdoms."

Connections such as those between father and son, ruler and inheritor, artist and king gave him ways to define his relations with his fellow poets. He differs from the Elizabethans in feeling no need to *defend* poesy.[4] But since poesy required doing, he had to consider other doers. As Shakespeare fussed a little over the rival poet, and as Jonson and others fulminated in theatrical wars, he had to consider contemporaries who sometimes had to be thought enemies. For him, this was the arena where self-definition became most heated, problematical.

In recent years much has been made of the anxiety or repression a poet undergoes in trying to overgo a strong predecessor. As Ďurišin says, quoting the Russian Formalist, Tynyanov: "literary continuity represents . . . a struggle, a tension, often between contradictory developmental trends. 'Every literary continuity is, above all, a contest, a disruption of an old compactness and a new alignment of old elements.' "5 As Duriš̌in himself puts it better still, "in every process of reception of literary values, the dominant feature is the act of completion, of finishing, of overcoming, a differentiating act" (p. 54). As we have seen, for Dryden differentiation was to a large extent historical, a matter involving the character of writers in one age as against those in another. This is another way of saying that the writers that create a poet's alarms and arouse the liveliest limbic activity are those in one's own age rather than one's dead predecessors or as yet unborn successors.

We know that he got on unusually well with most of his contemporaries. Was there ever another poet who dealt so warmly with younger contemporaries? Although he owed to truth certain important qualifications in taking a better likeness, what generosity is there in his poems on the dead John Oldham and the dead Anne Killigrew! He could expect no gain from such tributes. But as with Milton in *Lycidas* or Shelley in *Adonais,* he did pay tribute to poets of his time who were lost before they could achieve what they might have. If there were contemporaries who were enemies, there was also that last reviewer, Death, whom any ambitious writer had most to fear.

Of all these poems on artists who were his contemporaries, the most handsome must be the one to his young friend Congreve. Dryden hailed him as a "promis'd" superior in comedy. He said that Congreve's first play was the best maiden effort he had ever seen. In the poem to Congreve he asserted that *The Double Dealer* proved that at last their age had someone on whom Nature had bestowed a genius equal to Shakespeare's. Before we dismiss this assertion as hyperbolic nonsense, we may ponder a couple of things. For one, a comparison of Congreve's first two plays with Shakespeare's initial pair would more readily suggest what Dryden claims than the opposite. For another, and especially considering that in *All for Love* Dryden had essayed the Shakespearian topic, such praise of a fellow poet over oneself is as rare as the Phoenix. After all, he is talking about an individual's promise in a new era taking on its character as he enters old age. He is addressing a contemporary of genius, one whose promise might have put him in the class of Shakespeare, Purcell, or Dryden himself. The event shows that Will. Congreve was happier with a sinecure than as a writer. If that is a kind of satire or worse likeness, Congreve rather than Dryden suffers.

In considering his relations with his contemporaries, a double distinction must be held in mind. He mentioned, or is mentioned by, many contemporaries, although he actually addressed or commemorated relatively few. On the other hand, his address to few is relatively many by comparison with most other poets. Together the distinctions imply several things of importance. In general, he proves in the liveliest fashion that any poet understands himself most clearly by taking a relation to contemporaries. In addition, for good or ill, for better or worse likeness, certain writers matter more than others. Such basic matters pertain to all writers. What beyond them distinguishes him is his explicit understanding of his contemporaries, which is to say his explicit self-definition by relation to them. Only a poet who is also an explicit critic and is comfortable in himself and his world could have such composure as his. It is also a feature of his poetic self-portraits that they involve the same kind of comparative exercise, albeit implicit, that we remember from his prose criticism, in which Juvenal is compared with Horace in different ages or Jonson with Shakespeare in the same. He was generous, and in treating his contemporaries was handsomely willing to take a better likeness, to praise.

From Dr. Johnson on, Dryden's praise of his contemporaries in his prose, especially his dedications, has usually seemed beyond comprehension when it has not seemed fulsome and self-serving. Let us say that there is excess, and then let us ask how often poets err in generosity to their contemporaries. But let us also examine his fine print. Amid the excess, and especially in the poetry, there will also be found a closer likeness of the truth than is supposed. Congreve provided us with a positive instance. Anyone attending to the poems on such writers as Oldham and Killigrew will see that they are quite carefully placed by the end of Dryden's tribute. A less well known example, the poem to Thomas Southerne, consoles him for the failure of one of the finest comedies of the time, *The Wives Excuse*. The consolation is genuine. And so is the advice: imitate, he says, Etherege in style and Wycherley in wit.

> Learn after both, to draw some just Design,
> And the next Age will learn to Copy thine.
> (ll. 30–1)

Advice direct mingles with comfort, setting Southerne in a context of earlier poets, so that the present may yield to a happy future, so that the present may be better understood in terms of past and future, so that indeed there may be some historical continuity in genuine literary quality.

The poetic evidence of his relation with his contemporaries includes a number of matters involving Milton. Here was a great poet with whom he might have felt uneasy, but in fact did not. Within a decade or so of the publication of *Paradise Lost* and *Paradise Regained,* he treated them as classics, as fonts for borrowing and allusion. He essayed what Milton had planned, a dramatic version of *Paradise Lost.* Like Milton, he found it a mistake and only published *The State of Innocence* when a corrupt text appeared. In 1688 Jacob Tonson the bookseller wished to make something special of *Paradise Lost,* so that besides the illustrations he introduced he asked Dryden for commendatory verses. The contribution is at once stiff and uninteresting. Like their subject, Dryden required more room for manoeuvre. But he knew what he was doing. He put into English a distich written by the Italian Selvaggi, honouring Milton's visit to Rome. Milton was so proud of his being compared favourably to Homer and Virgil (and by an Italian no less) that he included the verses in his 1645 *Poems.* Dryden connects his version with *Paradise Lost,* a poem the Italian never knew. Mediterranean flattery has been translated into just if not very remarkable criticism.

The poem to Kneller offers a somewhat different definition of art and life by consideration of a contemporary. Although it has resemblances with various other poems, its chief interest lies in the quite unusual, dyspeptic tone. The progress of painting turns out to be as dispiriting as his other progress pieces are optimistic. Painting improved through Grecian times. The Romans kept it alive, but in lesser state. Then came the "*Goths* and *Vandals,* a rude Northern Race" (l. 47). Thereafter the art slept with the ruins of poetry until Raphael and Titian. This leads to Kneller's gift to the poet, a painted version of the Chandos portrait of Shakespeare. Defining himself by Shakespeare (rather pointedly choosing him rather than Kneller as a positive model), he is "Proud to be less; but of his Godlike Race" (l. 76). That race excels the other one of painters.

> Our Arts are Sisters; though not Twins in Birth;
> For Hymns were sung in *Edens* happy Earth,
> By the first Pair; while *Eve* was yet a Saint;
> Before she fell with Pride, and learn'd to paint.
> Forgive th' allusion; 'twas not meant to bite;
> But Satire will have room, where e're I write.
>
> (ll. 89–94)

The last line is very true, if we allow also for the presence of panegyric as the obverse, for history as part of the public world, and hopes for heroic endeavour. He is also playing a role, Mr. Satirist. The year before he had had fresh access of fame from his translation of Persius and much of Juvenal. As Juvenalis Britannicus he "bites." Yet more is involved. He is worried about both arts, about monarchy (the topos for both kinds of artists), and his usual complex of values in "this Age," "these Inferiour Times" (ll. 117, 118). Historical insight breeds pessimism in the artist caught like ravished Rome in another "stupid Military State" (l. 51), the time of King William and his wars, rebellion in Ireland and protest at home, taxes, and harassment of Catholics. His grumpiness over 1688 and All That quite strikingly resembles Milton's in 1660, with the fuming over England's choosing "a captain back to Egypt."

The times are not, however, deterministic. If Kneller depresses Dryden, in the same year Congreve buoys him. Many of the same motifs are used: historical development in a progress piece, a monarchy of politics and a kingdom of art in disarray. The people addressed differ. When the vain Kneller had his poem republished after the poet's death, certain questioning passages were omitted. When Congreve published Dryden's plays in 1717, he said very simply, "I loved Mr. *Dryden.*" Dryden is engaged with his contemporaries all right, and his use of any one of them in a poem both reflects and defines his concerns.

The likeness taken need not be simply positive or negative, as many poems show, although none better than *Mac Flecknoe*. In this satire presented as panegyric, Dryden unhistorically bestows upon Flecknoe and Shadwell a love like that between him and Congreve. Actually, the son of Flecknoe was originally probably Elkanah Settle.[6] Whether to Settle or Shadwell, the love given is that Dryden felt for his own real and artistic sons. The king and Prince of Dulness absolute possess their ranks, because monarchy and art define each other positively to Dryden. The filial and paternal relation, the royalty and succession, the art and praise comically supposed join with prophecy to aid in defining the nature of the poet. In this ebullient and positive, if therefore more deadly praise in a worse likeness, Dryden composedly defines himself as an artist with an assured laughter derived from comic versions of his own ideals.

Certain other contemporaries were such that he would not fit them into that scheme of art–politics–religion. One can only assume of these people, especially as we find them in *Absalom and Achitophel,* that they seemed important enough to offer genuine danger of some kind. One such was Buckingham, whom he refuses to allow a son, as by contrast are Ormonde (Barzillai) and even Shaftesbury (Achitophel) after a sort, as also notoriously the king. It is not a little interesting that Dryden's quarrels with the profligate nobleman (Rochester serves as another example) do not lead him to accusation of grievous sins and crimes. It would be impossible to infer from his character of Zimri that the Duke of Buckingham had deserted his wife for a double adultery and the killing of his partner's husband. Since Dryden left out these things, we must assume that he did not choose to define his own *character* against such corruption. He chooses rather to consider Buckingham and Rochester as rival *poets,* challengers to his art. *The Rehearsal* is not the worst parody of what is not the best dramatic kind, the heroic play. But Buckingham and Rochester must have seemed to be getting up a party against him to deny him an audience. As we can see, in defining himself against his contemporaries, he responded differently within a range of a number of motifs and situations. As it happens, he responded well to good people and, with the exception of Shadwell and possibly Rochester, duly acknowledged the talents of those whom he opposed. He managed the writer's most difficult critical passage, relation with contemporaries.

As all writers, or anyone acquainted with them, know, their basic concern in taking relation is with their contemporaries. No writer of the past can exert the emotional pressure, good or bad, on a writer that living friends or enemies do. That said, there is of course a proper subject of concern in the less important relation taken by a writer with other writers of some distance in time or space. When Pound extolled the haiku, or Yeats the nō, both arts were being practised in Japan. It is striking that our "classical" writers have been definitively dead since the sack of Rome, whereas the "classical past" of the Japanese involved a literary culture across the sea that continued to evolve. No wonder that the Japanese felt the Chinese "classics" to be almost contemporaneous as well as classical, and no wonder that from time to time they would reject what might seem a contemporary rival.

Dryden is typical of English poets in his dealings with earlier writers. In the Renaissance way, he draws on some with indifference to what we would term plagiarism. He uses some as positive models, others as cautionary examples. But like all artists, he was most interested in qualities that might live for his own purposes. Here is a process of assimilation, an effort to contemporize the past through adaptation, rejection, and all that goes on in a revisionary use of what one wants to one's own ends. A small but telling example occurs in *Mac Flecknoe,* where he dismisses Thomas Dekker (l. 87) along with Thomas Heywood, James Shirley, and one contemporary, John Ogilby (l. 102). No one has bothered to ask why that is the order, but the death years of the four authors are successively 1632, 1641, 1666, and 1676. The past stretching back to a Dekker is brought, as negative example, into temporal line with a present Ogilby.

Translation illustrates the contemporizing best. Dryden was involved in this art from his rendering of Persius and other authors as a schoolboy to his *Fables* in 1700. In nothing else must a poet submit to a predecessor as much as in translation, and it is very significant indeed which poets find translation uncongenial, which give up their own work to translate, and which are at home in both. As we have seen, Dryden poses as the English Satirist after rendering Persius and much of Juvenal. But he is always finding the poet he is engrossed in possessed of a soul most like his own. Homer, the first book of whose *Iliad* appears in *Fables,* is merely the last example: "My thoughts are at present fixed on Homer; and by my translation of the first Iliad I find him a poet more according to my genius than Virgil" (Watson, ii. 266). What we call translation represents only the most obvious use of writers in another language or, like Dryden's Chaucer, in an earlier version of one's own tongue. He even speaks of transfusion, which perhaps we can relate to other appropriations ranging from translation and plagiarism to allusion or echo. He was aware of these varieties, and spoke of distinctions between metaphrase, paraphrase, and imitation as progressively "looser" kinds of translation. The point is important, but for some reason he has been over-credited for it, even as his most profound remark of this kind has gone unappreciated: "I have endeavoured to make Virgil speak such English as he would himself have spoken, if he had been born in England, and in this present age." (Watson, ii. 247.) The difficulties of that enterprise are daunting. But any attempt to understand the past without acknowledging one's own presence as understander is less daunting than doomed. He was well aware of the difficulties, adding to the old saying that Virgil was the torture of the grammarian that he was the plague of the translator. Yet he assumes translation to be necessary and that it involves bringing an author into one's own present language.

The obvious purpose of translation, as for any kind of writing, is that it is meant to be read, to have readers. England at that present age consists not solely of John Dryden but also of numerous readers ranging from excellent judges to "mob readers" who prefer the flashy to "solid sense and elegant expression" (Watson, ii. 243). The universal stylistic premiss is decorum, engaging the writer with the subject (for translation, another writer's creation) and the audience. To consider only the former is to ignore half the matter of a writer's self-definition. In fact, the audience often matters more than the author translated, just as rival contemporary poets certainly account for more of a writer's concern than does a predecessor.

Dryden's concern with his audience involves so much of his writing in prose and verse as to require a book. Congreve is both subject and part of the audience of the poem addressed to him. Shadwell is part of the audience of real readers and also, as Mac Flecknoe, an audience in the poem. This complicated, rich subject can be reduced to compass only by some such means as considering Dryden's advocacy of Horatian affectivism, teaching and delight. By comparison with critical predecessors and contemporaries, he is generally more liberal in assigning greater importance to pleasure. The liberality implies an easy faith in his relation to his audience. In 1666, he allowed that delight is "one intention of a play" (Watson, i. 38: the earliest critical use of "intention"?). Two years later, he argues that "delight is the chief if not the only end of poesy . . . for poesy only instructs as it delights" (Watson, i. 113–14), distinguishing such pleasure from what may take with audiences of mob readers. In 1670, he allows delight a larger role still (Watson, i. 152), and in 1677 he argues against the redoubtable Rymer that although "The great end of the poem is to instruct . . . by making pleasure the vehicle of that instruction," "The chief end of the poet is to please" if the poet is to have an audience (Watson, i. 219). Here we see a writer confident in his art and his age growing yet more certain that he can carry his audience with him in new ventures.

The stresses of the 1680s altered such assurance. The epistle to the reader prefixed to *Absalom and Achitophel* (1681) envisioned an audience harsh or friendly as they are Whig or Tory. In the next year he set before *The Medal* a defiant "Epistle to the Whigs." In 1682 he also published his first religious confession, *Religio Laici,* stressing the personal nature of his beliefs: "For *MY* Salvation must its Doom receive/Not from what *OTHERS,* but what *I* believe" (ll. 303–4). Such self-assertion increases in the poems until 1688, but often as expressions of confidence in himself as man and poet rather than in his audience. By the time he wrote *The Hind and the Panther,* he deliberately wrote above the heads of an audience he expected to be largely hostile to a Catholic poem: "Much malice mingl'd with a little wit/Perhaps may censure this mysterious writ" (Pt. III, ll. 1–2). Here is a change that has not been discussed but that reveals a great deal about how an author must define self by audience. For Dryden the change can be characterized as a shift from a Protestant insistence on faith (the "what *I* believe" of *Religio Laici*) to a Catholic stress on good works ("Good life be now my task" in *The Hind and the Panther*, I. 78).

The shift in self-definition by relation to his audience led him to numerous adjustments. These became crucial with the 1688 Revolution, after which he shows a new interest in instructing his audience. In the preface to *Don Sebastian* (1690), he tells us that, in addition to the general moral, there are others "couched under every one of the principal parts and characters" (Watson, ii. 50). Here is the general moral in the last four lines of the play.

> And let *Sebastian* and *Almeyda*'s Fate,
> This dreadfull Sentence to the World relate.
> That unrepented Crimes of Parents dead,
> Are justly punish'd on their Childrens head.

Let it be declared that such morals seem unbearably reductive of a great play like *Don Sebastian*. Let it be asked if, or how, Dryden meant them.

Fables Ancient and Modern is to some of us his finest achievement, and certainly it is his last work of great scale. In it he is busy supplying morals. This is done by shading, by adding to the offences of the guilty in versions of Ovid to make their punishment more appropriate. He adds emphatic morals where Boccaccio had none. And in translating *The Nun's Priest's Tale*, he extends Chaucer by separating the concluding lines into a labelled "Moral."

> The Cock and Fox, the Fool and Knave imply;
> The Truth is moral, though the Tale a Lie.
> Who spoke in Parables, I dare not say;
> But sure, he knew it was a pleasing way,
> Sound Sense, by plain Example, to convey.
> And in a Heathen Author we may find,
> That Pleasure with Instruction should be join'd:
> So take the Corn, and leave the Chaff behind.
> (ll. 814–21)

In a shift of emphasis that has not been studied, Dryden alters his early emphasis on religious typology to a dominant religious tropology, moving from what is to be believed to what is to be done, from faith to works, as we have seen in contrasting *Religio Laici* with *The Hind and the Panther*. But for Dryden, if not for Bunyan, tropology signals an alteration of his definition of his relation to his audience. After years of sufficient faith in that relation, he gradually found it necessary to instruct his readers. He does add Horatian affectivism to Chaucer's passage, but teaching has grown more important than delight.

That is too simple. It seems to be accepted that the *Fables* is an integrated collection in which the poems are linked one to the next and, more importantly, are integrated by variations on a number of topics related to the search for the good life: valour, love, parents and children, husbands and wives, politics, history, philosophy, and religion. These are not new in his writing, but they have now been fitted to an easy narrative, rather than absorbed by metaphorical forces that may exchange with each other, as in *Mac Flecknoe.* The art is at once simpler in the foreground and more complex in the larger background. For example, the work opens with *To the Dutchess of Ormond,* which gives a very positive version of love, wife and husband, parents and children, valour, history, and religion. The set becomes highly problematical in the next poem, *Palamon and Arcite,* where in Chaucerian or Robertsonian fashion he emphasizes the results of concupiscence and wrath, especially in a pagan setting. He also places his poems not based on works by other poets toward the beginning and end of the collection, so that their ideal, Christian versions set off the imperfect or heathen in a kind of personal testimony, an ethical proof of his own.

If Dryden feels it necessary to underscore the moral import of his writing, it seems fair to assume two things. He must now think that ethical-religious-philosophical matters are of greater importance than the aesthetic-political-religious complex he had dealt with before. The balance of his interests has altered. It must also be true that he doubts the capacity of all his audience to understand as he wishes them to do without such guidance. Without sifting a great deal of evidence, it is impossible to do more than suggest what is happening. One thing is the enlargement of his audience, and the addition to it of a larger component of women readers, for whom his respect seems to have been less than it was for men educated at the schools and the universities. In the last poem in *Fables, Cymon and Iphigenia,* he begins with a *poëta loquitur* to the Duchess of Ormonde, telling her that this is written for her and "all the Fair" so that they may discover, "When Beauty fires the Blood, how Love exalts the Mind" (ll. 38, 40). Here is the old topos of love as education. The hero, Cymon (whose name means "brute"), awakens to reason as he sees and then loves Iphigenia. The tale goes on to very different things, however, ending with his seizing her from her promised husband at the marriage altar and subsequently running off with her amid violent homicide.

The moral of love as education proves to be drastically insufficient, and the *Fables* ends bleakly for our possibility of finding the good life in other than religious terms. The discrepancy between the simple moral foreground and the more complex moral background suggests that in the last ten or fifteen years of his life Dryden sought to instruct what he thought the larger portion of his audience, giving them both simpler morals and more explicit guidance.

For the choicer few, a far more complicated view of human life is provided by indirection or implication, whether in *Don Sebastian* or in *Fables*. The two audiences are not absolutely distinguished after the earlier Renaissance method of supposed veiled truths for the initiate. Dryden seems careful to make the morals and the simplicities sufficiently inadequate to beckon an attentive reader toward what is more profoundly meaningful.

It must have been important to him, however, that he could assume a saving remnant of a knowing audience. His faith lies in them, in himself, and in the great authors he was, after all, drawing on in *Fables*. Late in life he found security in the sense that he belonged with them, and they with him, even if after 1688 he necessarily felt cut off from the easy relation with his audience that he had enjoyed as playwright, poet, and critic in his earlier years.

This example of a single poet cannot apply in detail to all other writers. It does show, however, that matters of "reception" or "influence" belong to a larger class of understanding by definition of self with world. And the relation taken between self and world, involves not merely earlier writers but also contemporary writers and one's audience. Of these three, the last two are immeasurably more important than the first. A writer relates to earlier writers only as they are manifested in their works. Allusion, imitation, appropriation, and translation are the typical symptoms of the relation. Relation to contemporary writers involves something far more emotional—rivalry or at least what can only be termed personality. One may not actually know as a person some contemporary writer, although of course Dryden knew all of importance to some degree. But one feels that they live, and that their writings are not a canon but an evolving career like one's own. Relation to one's audience is less personal, except of course in special instances, particularly including contemporary writers or people for or about whom one writes. Audiences also change in identity and taste, just as accidents such as sudden political changes can alter one's own position. These matters seem so obvious as to make one wonder if their evident truth has led the ingenious to search out more fanciful explanations.[7]

There is, of course, the historical possibility that what was true for writers of Dryden's time and before was not true for writers of Blake's time and after. It could be argued that the ambition of a Dryden to excel is fundamentally different from the ambition of a Blake to be original. Let us pursue this. We may say that the Romantics sought to free themselves from the tyranny of the past, only to find themselves aboriginal in the strict sense. To begin all over is to have to re-create the past without its faults. To such writers the past becomes a burden only because the present is so terrifyingly free and the future so unpromising.

Yet this interpretation, which may have something to it, does not have enough. In his "Memorial Verses," Arnold spoke in a definitive phrase of "Wordsworth's healing power," and we have the testimony of Mill to prove that that was no idle expression. If that was true of Wordsworth with his sorrows over our gradual separation from nature, it was certainly true of the other great Romantic poets. They were all well aware of problems and failure, because they had looked at life. But they got on well with the great poets except those immediately preceding them, as is shown for example by Keats's sudden efflorescence after his discovery of Dryden's odes. The problems they had to deal with and that concerned them most were their fellow poets (even when Wordsworth was Coleridge's friend) and their audiences, which involved the exile of Shelley and Byron. Does one need to dwell on what inhibitions of subject matter Victorian audiences imposed on a Dickens?

The idea that the crucial relation is one between a poet and a predecessor seems to be no more than an allegory for the strains felt by contemporary critics. For no good reason, the idea has got abroad that critics understand literature better than do poets. That also has a limited truth, since critics have as their business making explicit for other readers. But that truth has placed unnecessary burdens on the critic and imperilled two truths of greater importance. Every critic must bow to the fact that the poet is the radical, if only implicit, critic, who best understands what is of import in what has gone before and what can be made of what exists at present. It is preposterous to assume that any critic has ideas remotely as original as Milton's about the epic, Swift's about satire, or Joyce's about the novel. It is much healthier to think of the critic as a reader in Sunday Best than as a Mad Scientist seeking to re-do creation. It is exciting to enter on to theoretical heights, but the blood of literary life has difficulty there in keeping pace, and rather than enable us to see farther, that vantage-point too often puts us among clouds of obscurity or induces in the critic pains of high-altitude sickness. When we can all participate as readers in the great literatures of the world, there is no indignity in doing so. In writing about what we discover, about the nature of what is discovered, or even about the nature of discovery, we play as critics in a no-loss enterprise. To confuse that play with the enterprise of poets is to enter a game in which the chance of winning is only illusory, and in which the most intelligent people are sure to suffer from knowledge of self-inflicted loss. One example of Dryden's "variety of models," to recall Johnson, appears when he describes his translation of Virgil. He describes that version of one great predecessor by alluding to another.

> Lay by Virgil, I beseech your Lordship and all my better sort of judges, when you take up my version; and it will appear a passable beauty when the original Muse is absent. But, like Spenser's false Florimel made of snow, it melts and vanishes when the true one comes in sight.
>
> (Watson, ii. 252)

This model of how "to think naturally and express forcibly" is as "just and lively" today as it was when it appeared in 1697.

Notes

1. The fashions of words sometimes make us look silly when the fashion passes. My Ph.D. dissertation was accurately entitled "The Japanese Influence on British and American Literature" (1955). But "influence" was then such a disreputable term that for a book the title became pretentious: *The Japanese Tradition in British and American Literature* (1958). Thirteen years later Claudio Guillén, or common sense, had made the word tolerable, as in "The Aesthetics of Literary Influence," chs. 1 and 2 of *Literature as System* (Princeton: Princeton University Press, 1971). The idea that there is a problem in the transactions between modern and older writers derives from the Romantics, as I have shown in "The Double Truth of Modern Poetic Criticism" in *Sense and Sensibility in Twentieth-Century Writing*, ed. Brom Weber (Carbondale and Edwardsville: Southern Illinois University Press, 1970), pp. 16–25. After such blame of past writers was translated into the notion of 'dissociation of sensibility' by T. S. Eliot and others, it became, in the fine phrase of Walter Jackson Bate's title. *The Burden of the Past* (Cambridge, Mass.: Belknap Press, 1970). The idea has been greatly extended to a general theory of literary genesis by Harold Bloom in *The Anxiety of Influence* (New York: Oxford University Press, 1973) and later studies. My preferences run more to Dionýz Durišin, *Sources and Systematics of Comparative Literature* (Bratislava: Univerzita Komenského, 1974), wooden as its English is; and *Rezeptionsästhetik*, ed. Rainer Warning (Munich: Fink Verlag, 1976); and Wolfgang Iser, *Der Akt des Lesens* (ibid. 1977).

2. Dryden, *Of Dramatic Poesy and Other Essays*, ed. George Watson, 2 vols. (London: Dent, 1962), ii. 181–208, especially 193–200. Hereafter cited as "Watson."

3. G. Gregory Smith, ed., *Elizabethan Critical Essays*, 2 vols. (Oxford: Clarendon Press, 1904), i. 156.

4. See Smith's introduction to *Elizabethan Critical Essays*, i, pp. xxi–xxxi, on "The Defence" essential to Elizabethan criticism.

5. Durišin, op. cit., p. 53.

6. See George McFadden, "Elkanah Settle and the Genesis of *Mac Flecknoe*," *Philological Quarterly*, xliii (1964), 55–72.

7. Hazlitt has, however, put it succinctly on contemporary poets: "I cannot say that I ever learnt much about Shakespeare or Milton, Spenser or Chaucer, from these professed guides; for I never heard them say much about them. They were always talking of themselves and one another" ("On the Living Poets," third paragraph).

The Circulation of Dryden's Poetry

PAUL HAMMOND

I. CONTINGENCY AND THE CANON

When we read the poems of Dryden in a collected edition, it is easy to forget that this is not how his contemporaries would have encountered his work.[1] Even if an edition arranges the poetry in the chronological order of its publication, and provides ample details about its bibliographical history, it is still difficult to make an imaginative leap back to a period before the canon was completed and ordered, before the occasional and fugitive pieces were bound up with the major public masterpieces. Modern editors cannot avoid creating an anachronistic canon by reason of their very fidelity in collecting all that was written, with an assiduity far beyond anything that Dryden himself ever envisaged. It is the purpose of this article to attempt to recover a sense of the fragmentary, haphazard, and contingent character of the circulation of Dryden's poetry, and to suggest what a late seventeenth-century reader would have understood by the phrase "Dryden's poems." This article will chart the pattern of publication across Dryden's career, investigating which form of publication he thought suitable for particular kinds of poems; which pieces he collected and reprinted, and which were forgotten; and which were given circulation in manuscript, either by Dryden himself, or by his readers. Building on the information presented by Hugh Macdonald and Peter Beal in their invaluable bibliographies,[2] the present essay will seek to interpret this and other evidence so as to reconstruct both Dryden's attitude to the publication of his poetry, and the extent of the opportunities available to contemporary readers who were interested in following his work.

It is an elementary fact, but one which is nevertheless both remarkable and rarely remarked upon, that Dryden did not issue collections of his work. There were no volumes from him called *Poems Written upon Several Occasions*. It was not that the Restoration publishing trade eschewed such collections: notable examples of that kind of book include Denham's *Poems and Translations* (1668), Tate's *Poems* (1677), Marvell's posthumous *Miscellaneous Poems*

Paul Hammond, "The Circulation of Dryden's Poetry," *Papers of the Bibliographical Society of America* 86 (1992): 379–409. Reprinted by kind permission of the author.

(1681), Oldham's *Some New Pieces* (1681) and *Poems, and Translations* (1683), and Behn's *Poems upon Several Occasions* (1684). It is clear that the collection of miscellaneous poems by a single writer was a familiar form of book in the Restoration, yet Dryden chose not to publish in this way. Virtually all his poems are occasional pieces, called forth by some public event or private obligation, and he seems to have been generally content with the form of publication which they received on the occasion for which they were designed: a prologue to a colleague's play, a prefatory poem for a friend's book, an intervention in a political crisis; moreover, many of the translations seem to have been commissioned rather than volunteered. When Dryden did gather some of his pieces together for the first of Tonson's miscellanies—the *Miscellany Poems* of 1684—he was quite self-effacing. His name does not appear on the title-page, and although the volume begins with his three most celebrated and controversial poems, *Mac Flecknoe, Absalom and Achitophel,* and *The Medall,* they are anonymous. Later in the volume comes a selection of Dryden's prologues and epilogues, but although most of them are attributed to him they are not marked out in any way from the miscellaneous poems by other hands which surround them. The conclusion which one draws from this is that Dryden was generally content with the contingency of publication for a specific purpose, and had no desire to assemble an oeuvre under his name, as modern editors do on his behalf.

This raises the question of Dryden's use of anonymity. There were good reasons why *Mac Flecknoe, Absalom and Achitophel,* and *The Medall* appeared anonymously. The two political poems were outspoken attacks on the Whig leaders, and violent physical retaliation was a possibility, although this was more likely in 1681–82 when they were first published than in 1684 when the political crisis was over. In fact, anonymity did not prevent the first readers of *Absalom and Achitophel* from guessing its authorship very quickly, and no one seems to have attributed it to anyone other than Dryden. Only five days after its publication one potential reader had heard of it, and wrote: "Tis Dreydon's they say; and no doubt, upon ye presumption, somebody will fall upon him."[3] Somebody had already fallen upon him in Rose Alley on 18 December 1679, upon the presumption that he had written the anonymous *An Essay upon Satire,* which was probably the work of the Earl of Mulgrave alone. The anonymity of *Mac Flecknoe* might likewise have stemmed from a fear of retribution, but may also be attributable to a form of delicacy in not forcing an open, public breach with Shadwell. The two men had in fact been punctilious in not referring to each other by name in the critical debates which led up to the poem.

Added to this calculated anonymity is the accidental anonymity which attended the publication of many of Dryden's works. We do not know whether the prologues and epilogues which he wrote for other men's plays, or for special occasions such as a performance before the King and Queen, were announced as being by Dryden when they were spoken in the theatre; they did not always carry his name when they were printed or when they circulated in manuscript. When Dryden's songs were printed in anthologies or copied in manuscript, they too were often anonymous. Doubts over authorship even attached sometimes to plays. In some cases the authorship was divided or disputed: *The Indian Queen* was probably a collaboration between Dryden and Sir Robert Howard, but was printed without any mention of Dryden in Howard's *Four New Plays* (1665).[4] *Sir Martin Mar-all* was probably written by Dryden based on some materials by the Duke of Newcastle; it was printed anonymously in 1668, but as Dryden's in 1691.[5] Pepys refers to the play as "made by my Lord Duke of Newcastle, but as everybody says corrected by Dryden": evidently in some cases one's view of a play's authorship depended on what one heard. In another instance Pepys seems to have attributed to Dryden a play which was actually by Flecknoe—a beautifully ironic misattribution.[6] Anonymity, both deliberate and accidental, concealed the authorship of many of Dryden's works from his readers.[7]

Positive misattribution, the crediting to Dryden of work which was not his, also had an effect on his reputation. Even a well-intentioned deception proved unfortunate when the commendatory verses which Tonson wrote in Dryden's style for Creech's translation of Lucretius were accepted as Dryden's not only by the grateful Creech but also by the malevolent Tom Brown, who turned them into evidence of Dryden's treachery towards Creech.[8] More unfortunate was the misattribution of *An Essay upon Satire,* which may have been associated with Dryden by readers who knew about his authorship of *Mac Flecknoe;*[9] otherwise there was nothing in what we now perceive to be Dryden's poetic oeuvre by 1679 to suggest that he had an inclination either for verse satire or verse criticism. But misattribution can also be mischievous, and in the hands of his opponents in 1682 and 1689 Dryden's supposed authorship of the *Essay* became another charge against him.[10] Nevertheless, a significant number of satirical verses are attributed to Dryden by contemporaries from 1677 onwards, which suggests that the circulation of *Mac Flecknoe* in manuscript in 1676 may have prompted some readers to believe that Dryden had joined the semi-clandestine world in which political and literary satire circulated in handwritten copies. Amongst the satires and epigrams attributed to Dryden during his own lifetime, and excluded from modern editions, are verses on the Duchess of Portsmouth's picture (*c.* 1677);[11] a satire in 1677 on Robert Julian, the "secretary to the muses" who masterminded much of the manuscript circulation of unprintable verses;[12] the verses "On the Young Statesmen" (1680);[13] a ballad on Sir Robert Peyton (1680);[14] *An Heroic Poem* lampooning various victims (1681);[15] lines on Count Konigsmark (1682);[16] an epigram on Lawrence Hyde, Earl of Rochester (1687);[17] the anticlerical satire *The Tribe of Levi* (1691);[18] an epigram on Louis XIV (1692);[19] and a satirical epitaph on Queen Mary (1694).[20] Whether or not Dryden actually wrote any of these, the fact that contemporaries thought it likely is a significant (and now neglected) element in how his poetic oeuvre was imagined. Of course, some of these spurious attributions may have been made mischievously or maliciously by readers who wished to cause trouble for him. There were also obviously malevolent misattributions which were actually a form of ventriloquism, such as *The Address of John Dryden, Laureat to His Highness the Prince of Orange* (1689), and the *Satyr upon Romish Confessors* and *Satyr upon the Dutch* which were fabricated by sly editing of his genuine prologues and epilogues.[21] That readers also fathered on him several prologues, epilogues, and songs is less significant: these were forms which Dryden regularly employed, whereas the association of him with clandestine satires shows that at least some of his early readers assumed him to have quite another kind of literary role from the ones which he was prepared to claim in public. With hindsight editors can reject such accretions to and distortions of the pure, authorially-based canon, but we need to remind ourselves that such purity is anachronistic, and that Dryden's contemporary readers would have known a canon and a reputation which was to some extent reworked and reimagined by others, generally for political reasons.

It is not only the public perception of Dryden's oeuvre which was shaped by such factors: the oeuvre itself, the poetry which he actually wrote and published, was also determined partly by political and economic constraints. Dryden was never in a position socially or financially to ignore the practicalities which attended the career of a professional writer. Indeed, to support himself and his family simply from the writing of poetry was not an option, at least not until the arrival of Tonson. Given the dearth of documentary evidence for the relations between Dryden and his chief publishers, Herringman and Tonson, it is difficult to assess their influence on his work, but a brief discussion must be attempted here. Dryden was probably employed by Herringman in the late 1650s and early 1660s to write prefaces for some of his publications, and no doubt to assist generally in preparing books for the press.[22] It was Herringman who entered on the Stationers' Register the volume containing Dryden's *Heroique Stanza's* on the death of Cromwell, and Herringman who published Dryden's first major poems after the Restoration, *Astraea Redux, To His Sacred Majesty, To My Lord Chancellor,* and *Annus Mirabilis*. Herringman also published two books to which Dryden contributed commendatory poems—Robert Howard's *Poems* and Walter Charleton's *Chorea Gigantum*. Herringman's list provided good company for Dryden, for he was also publishing Cowley, Davenant, Denham, Killigrew, and Waller. But Herringman does not appear to have been an adventurous publisher, and it is noticeable that, particularly after 1680, he survived on classic stock rather than by breaking new ground.[23] Dryden's poems of the 1660s look entirely appropriate in a list which includes Davenant's *A Panegyrick to Generall Monck* (1659), Cowley's *Ode, upon the Blessed Restoration* (1660), and Waller's *Instructions to a Painter* (1666), but his publications after 1680 seem to reflect the interests of a different publishing house, and almost of a different writer. The long hiatus in Dryden's publication of non-dramatic poetry between 1667 and 1680 is explicable in one way because of his concentration on drama (an economic necessity, quite apart from Dryden's artistic preferences), but it may be no coincidence that his resumption of nondramatic poetry began soon after he met Jacob Tonson.[24] Tonson published *Troilus and Cressida* in the autumn of 1679, and *Ovid's Epistles* in the spring of 1680. We do not know who organised *Ovid's Epistles;* Dryden no doubt played a leading role, but it is worth noting that Tonson (or his brother) had previously published work by four of the contributors—Behn, Otway, Rymer, and Tate—so that he already had his own literary contacts. *Miscellany Poems* (1684) and *Sylvae* (1685) seem to have been put together chiefly by Tonson, with some indecision and improvisation on his part,[25] and although Dryden wrote to Tonson that in *Sylvae* he was "resolvd we will have nothing but good, whomever we disoblige"[26] he did not see all the contributions.[27] Tonson's preface to *Examen Poeticum* (1693) indicates that he organised both that volume and the translation of Juvenal and Persius,[28] while the complete Virgil was a commission from Tonson which Dryden accepted with misgivings that grew as the project wore on. Whatever the dynamics of their relationship, it is clear at least that Tonson took a leading role in the promotion of classical translation in the 1680s and 1690s, and provided Dryden with a financial incentive to pursue that side of his interests. Moreover, the form of publication which Tonson developed— the miscellany and the composite translation—allowed Dryden to be selective in his translating, and to concentrate on those mutually complementary and contrasting portions of the classics which appealed to his philosophical interests.

II. THE OCCASIONAL POEMS 1658–85

Most of Dryden's non-dramatic writing from the reign of Charles II is occasional, composed for a particular event or person and published in an appropriate form for that occasion. There is a small group of political poems from the early years of the reign which were all published as separate items: *Astraea Redux* (1660) on the Restoration, *To His Sacred Majesty* (1661) on the coronation, *To My Lord Chancellor* (1662), and the more substantial *Annus Mirabilis* (1667) on the Dutch War and the Fire of London which occurred together in 1666. The separately published topical poem was a recognised contemporary form, and one which is well represented in Herringman's list.[29] A single printing of each of these poems seems to have satisfied public interest. *To His Sacred Majesty* was reprinted in 1662 in *Complementum Fortunatarum Insularum,*[30] but this was probably to help fill out a volume of "Peeces relating to the present Times" rather than to satisfy any public clamour for more copies of Dryden's poem. *Annus Mirabilis* was pirated in 1668,[31] at a time when the handling of the Dutch War was growing increasingly controversial, and further poems on the subject—notably the *Advice to a Painter* series—were stimulating interest among readers. It is difficult to know at this distance how much respect was accorded to *Annus Mirabilis* in its own right: Pepys thought it "a very good poem" but did not choose to keep it in his library;[32] on the other hand the poem was preserved in a verse miscellany bound up in 1667.[33] Manuscript copies of *To His Sacred Majesty* and *To My Lord Chancellor* survive in British Library MS Burney 390, but they were probably not transcribed until the mid-1670s.[34] These four poems on public occasions were reprinted together in 1688 as Tonson's first attempt to create a "Collected Poems" by issuing Dryden's poems in a uniform format ready for binding together,[35] but prior to that reprint readers would have had access only to the original pamphlets, supposing they survived. It is unlikely that a reader whose interest had been caught by *Absalom and Achitophel* in 1681 would have had much success if he had enquired for Dryden's earlier poems in booksellers' shops.

However, there is one public poem from this early period which proved to be an exceptional case: the *Heroique Stanza's* on the death of Cromwell. Dryden himself prepared a fair copy of the poem,[36] perhaps for presentation to an influential politician, around the time of Cromwell's funeral in 1658: as a member of the Cromwellian civil service it might have been a useful way for him to draw attention to his talents at a time of upheavals in government. The poem was first printed in 1659 along with pieces by Waller and Sprat, and was not reissued by Dryden until 1691 or 1692 when Tonson reprinted it to add to the four which he had already produced in a uniform format in 1688. However, the poem was reprinted by Dryden's enemies in 1681, twice in 1682, and again in 1687, in an attempt to embarrass the poet laureate with his former allegiance. Moreover, fourteen other manuscript copies of the poem survive, an unusually large number for one of Dryden's poems.[37] One copy seems to date from 1667, another from 1673, and a third from 1681, while others may belong to the later 1680s and 1690s.[38] This evidence suggests that the poem retained its political sensitivity and interest right through Dryden's career, though it was brought back to public attention at a period of national crisis when his role as a Tory polemicist made this poem too much of a hostage to fortune for it to be forgotten.

There is another group of occasional pieces to be considered, those which were written to or for fellow–writers, and published as part of the prefatory material to their books. Dryden contributed complimentary verses to Sir Robert Howard's *Poems* (1660), Walter Charleton's *Chorea Gigantum* (1663), Nathaniel Lee's *The Rival Queens* (1677), the Earl of Roscommon's *An Essay on Translated Verse* (1684), John Oldham's *Remains* (1684), and John Northleigh's *The Parallel* (1685). In addition to these there is one commendatory poem which stayed in manuscript: "To Mr L. Maidwell on his new method" was written *circa* 1684 to promote Maidwell's Latin grammar, and survives in a manuscript copy of that work.[39] Dryden never collected any of these pieces, and the only circulation which they had was in the books which they were designed to promote. The fact that Dryden published some of his most important reflections on the English language, translation, the classical heritage, and the role of the poet in these occasional and uncollected pieces suggests several inferences about his self-understanding and his use of publication. First, it points to a generosity and diffidence which is content that these poems should work to promote the books of his friends. Dryden's writing *circa* 1684 is particularly concerned with the art of the poet and translator (besides the poems to Roscommon, Oldham, and Maidwell, there is the translation of Virgil's *Eclogue* IX and the Preface to *Sylvae*), but he does not build these various statements into a single volume which would carry his name and assert his status: he eschews any Jonsonian ambition to definitiveness and personal importance. This attitude seems to fit with the reticence about his authorial voice which one observes elsewhere in Dryden's work, in his liking for dialogue, allegory, and translation.[40] On the other hand, Dryden is not simply conferring favours through these commendatory poems: the gains are often reciprocal, for his association with these addressees helps to establish his own poetic status and cultural role. Though hindsight (which includes our perception of the significance of Dryden's completed oeuvre compared with that of his self-important aristocratic contemporaries) may suggest that Dryden was the dominant literary figure of his age, it is important to recall his vulnerability—his financial dependence on the theatre, on the King, and on Tonson, his social need for the goodwill of aristocratic patrons, his political danger as a Tory partisan and, later, as a Catholic, and his artistic need to differentiate himself from the mass of "holiday writers" and hacks. In such circumstances his commendation of Roscommon (like his dedication of two Horatian translations in *Sylvae* to Roscommon and Rochester) makes a self-protective social and literary claim.[41] These poems also form part of a refashioning of his poetic role for the mid-1680s after the literary battles of the Exclusion Crisis, for in the poems to Roscommon, Oldham, and Maidwell, Dryden is establishing his credentials as a classical poet and translator, both through what the poems themselves say and through the associations which they establish for him—the links to Roscommon the theorist of translation, to Oldham the successful practitioner, and to Maidwell the classical grammarian. But as well as helping Dryden to rework his own image and role, these poems also map out a collaborative project to promote translation, one in which Tonson was a leading figure. In this respect there is a reciprocity involved here, with Roscommon himself in his *Essay* singling out some of Tonson's translators for commendation.

In the case of the major public poems of the early 1680s, the pattern of publication is relatively simple. *Absalom and Achitophel* was published in 1681 and rapidly reprinted both by Tonson and by pirates. Approximately nine editions were published in 1681–82: the number depends somewhat on how one defines "editions," since there seems to have been some very rapid partial resetting and reprinting in the early stages,[42] but it is clear that a large number of copies were printed in the first year of the poem's life, possibly six to eight thousand if the normal size of an edition was a thousand copies. There were also two Latin translations, which were presumably undertaken primarily to advance the translators' own careers politically, though it is possible that they were also designed as Tory propaganda for foreign readers. Thereafter the poem appeared again in *Miscellany Poems* (1684) and in 1692 in Tonson's uniform format. In this case, demand seems to have been satisfied by the printed texts without recourse to manuscript circulation. Only two manuscripts survive, and these probably testify to the prestige value of a manuscript rather than to any difficulty in obtaining a printed copy. This is not surprising, since it was in both the political and commercial interests of Dryden and Tonson that the poem should achieve the widest possible circulation.[43] Indeed, its publishing history shows that it probably reached a larger audience than Dryden had ever previously achieved for his poems, or would ever achieve again.

The pattern in the case of *The Medall* is similar, though less spectacular: two issues of Tonson's edition, an Edinburgh edition, and a Dublin edition; there is no complete manuscript copy. As with *Absalom and Achitophel,* republication in *Miscellany Poems* seems to have sufficed until the 1692 reprint. *Religio Laici* went through two editions in 1682, and a third in 1683, but was never subsequently reprinted in Dryden's lifetime. However, a letter from Dryden to Tonson which probably dates from August or September 1684[44] shows that at that stage he thought of including it in *Sylvae* (1685), which indicates that he had no serious theological reservations about the poem at that date. Its exclusion from the 1692 collection suggests that after his conversion Dryden wanted to suppress this embarrassing product of his Anglican years—though it is interesting that he did not feel the same way about the commitment expressed in the *Heroique Stanza's. Threnodia Augustalis,* Dryden's poem on the death of Charles II, went through three London editions and one Dublin edition in the first year, but was not reprinted subsequently. In this case the reason for its neglect is unclear: perhaps there was simply no interest in Charles once history had moved on.

In the cases discussed so far, the circulation of poems in manuscript is merely a minor adjunct to the primary mode of publication through print. But there are three poems from this period for which manuscript was the chief mode of publication because of the very nature of the poems themselves.[45] The "Verses to her Highness the Dutchess" which Dryden printed in the prefatory material to *Annus Mirabilis* had evidently circulated in manuscript in 1665, for he records criticism of them; perhaps a fair copy had been presented to the Duchess and other copies had been passed around the coffee houses.[46] No separate manuscript now survives. Presumably the verses *To the*

Lady Castlemain had originally been presented to that lady in manuscript at some time around 1667. The poem first reached print in John Bulteel's *A New Collection of Poems and Songs* (1674), but since five manuscripts survive, all of which derive from a source independent of *A New Collection,* there was evidently sufficient interest in the poem (or in its addressee) for a small manuscript circulation to have been created.[47] At least three of the extant manuscript copies can be dated approximately. That in British Library MS Burney 390 ff. 12^v–13^r dates from the mid-1670s,[48] while the one in Bodleian Library MS Eng. Poet. e 4 was probably transcribed late in 1672.[49] The copy in the Society of Antiquaries MS 330 likewise probably dates from 1672.[50] Dryden did not collect the poem himself until he included it, with some revisions to remove youthful excesses and awkwardnesses, in *Examen Poeticum* (1693). It seems likely that the poem served its purpose as a piece of flattery to the King's mistress in the late 1660s, and there was no point in Dryden reprinting it—indeed, it could have caused him embarrassment—once her liaison with the King had ended in 1670, and Dryden had become established as a dramatist. By 1693, however, it was merely of historical (perhaps even nostalgic) interest.

The most remarkable instance of a poem being published solely and deliberately in manuscript is *Mac Flecknoe.* After writing it in the summer of 1676[51] Dryden probably released a manuscript copy into circulation in the London literary world.[52] Fifteen manuscript copies now survive,[53] which is a remarkably high number for a poem by Dryden, though not particularly unusual for a popular Restoration satire. The manuscripts are of two kinds. Some are single leaves or small booklets, and it must have been in this form that the poem was originally passed from hand to hand; they generally survive now only because they have been bound up with other papers. An example is the transcript made by John Oldham (now Bodleian Library MS Rawl. Poet. 123). The other copies are found in large manuscript miscellanies, usually along with other Restoration satires; these were either commonplace books compiled by individual readers, or anthologies written by a professional scribe for commercial sale. Examples of this kind of manuscript are the Gyldenstolpe and Robinson miscellanies.[54] But how popular was *Mac Flecknoe,* and how widespread a circulation did it achieve before an opportunistic pirate printed it in 1682? John Oldham's transcript is dated 1678; three of the scribally produced miscellanies can be dated to 1680.[55] These are the only four manuscripts which can certainly be shown to predate the poem's appearance in print. Six more are assigned by Peter Beal to "1678–80s," while he assigns the remaining five simply to the late seventeenth century. But even if as many as ten of the extant manuscripts predate 1682, what does that tell us about the extent of the poem's circulation? A significant (but unquantifiable) number of copies must have perished, for David M. Vieth has established that none of the extant manuscripts was copied from any of the others; we might therefore easily double the number of extant copies to estimate the number which originally existed. Perhaps twenty or thirty were in existence before 1682, each being read by a small group of friends. However conjectural these figures may be, they suggest a relatively small readership of perhaps a hundred or two in the poem's first six years. That may have been all the attention which Dryden wanted for his poem, so long as its readers were knowledgeable and influential in the contemporary literary and theatrical world—as, indeed, they would have to be if they were to appreciate its rich allusiveness. A few allusions to and borrowings from *Mac Flecknoe* before 1682 show that the poem was known to a select group,[56] but the rarity of these allusions points to that group being small. *Mac Flecknoe* had nothing like the enormous contemporary impact of *Absalom and Achitophel* which is so evident both from its publishing history and from the number of replies and allusions which the poem generated. Moreover, not only did *Mac Flecknoe* circulate in manuscript, it circulated anonymously. Only two manuscripts attribute it to Dryden, and only one of these (Yale Osborn Collection b 105) can be dated before 1682: only the select few would know its authorship.

The pirated publication of *Mac Flecknoe* in 1682 by the mysterious "D. Green" turned the poem from a semi-private literary satire into a public, political satire, for its new (and unauthorised) subtitle "A Satyr upon the *True-Blew-Protestant* Poet, T.S. By the Author of *Absalom & Achitophel*" clearly relocates the poem within the series of verse satires generated by the Exclusion Crisis, and specifically as part of the very bitter personal and political exchange between Dryden and Shadwell. This started with Shadwell's savage *The Medal of John Bayes,* which had appeared by 15 May 1682; though anonymous, it was attributed to Shadwell by some contemporaries. Presumably Dryden reached the same conclusion, for he contributed the outspoken lines on Shadwell as Og to *The Second Part of Absalom and Achitophel;* the passage was probably written in May, though the poem was not published until about 10 November. Green's edition of *Mac Flecknoe* was available by 4 October. Meanwhile, Green had already published the lampoon on Dryden called the *Satyr to his Muse,* which appeared in late July. Green's publication of *Mac Flecknoe* materially altered the poem's purpose, and in so doing altered the public's conception of the kind of poet that Dryden was, thwarting any intentions which Dryden may have had of confining Shadwell's humiliation to a select audience rather than parading it before the general public. Of course, after *The Medal of John Bayes* Dryden may not have been sorry to see *Mac Flecknoe* in print, though the fact that the text of the 1682 edition derives from the manuscripts currently in circulation[57] indicates that he did not personally arrange its publication. After the deterioration in their public relationship which all this occasioned, Dryden presumably had no reason not to issue a correct text of the poem in *Miscellany Poems* in 1684 along with *Absalom and Achitophel* and *The Medall.* By that date he was clearly on the winning side of the political debate, while the literary dispute which had originally occasioned *Mac Flecknoe* (centering on Ben Jonson, the function of comedy, plagiarism, and Shadwell's classical pretensions) had lost its edge. Moreover, by printing *Mac Flecknoe, Absalom and Achitophel,* and *The Medall* in that sequence, Dryden was engaging in a retrospective revision of *Mac Flecknoe*'s significance: placing it in its correct chronological order, yet acquiescing in the now prevailing association of it with the two political satires.

III. Songs, Prologues, and Epilogues from the Plays, 1665–85

The songs from Dryden's plays had a life which was quite independent of the plays themselves.[58] They circulated in various forms: as words only, in printed miscellanies or in manuscript; and as musical settings, generally in print but sometimes also in manuscript. A fashion for printing the texts of songs in miscellanies seems to have been a particular feature of the 1670s, and there are some seventeen anthologies from this decade which include songs by Dryden. The popularity of the songs varied, but most of Dryden's songs found their way into at least one printed anthology, and many had a manuscript circulation as well. This pattern may be illustrated by a few examples.

The song "Ah fading joy" from *The Indian Emperour* (1665) exists in three anthologies, two manuscripts, and a setting by Pelham Humphrey. "I feed a flame" from *Secret Love* (1667) survives in one anthology and four manuscripts. One song from *Sir Martin Mar-all* (1667) is included in three anthologies and the other in two. But particularly popular were the songs from *An Evening's Love* (1668). "After the pangs of a desperate lover" is found in five anthologies (two with music) and two manuscripts; "Calm was the evening" in nine anthologies (three with music) and four manuscripts; and "Celimena, of my heart" in three anthologies and two manuscripts. It is notable that only one manuscript has all three songs, which testifies to the eclecticism of those who compiled these manuscripts, particularly the commonplace books. The songs from *An Evening's Love* also inspired adaptations. "Calm was the evening" acquired two extra stanzas in some texts, while five different imitations and parodies were penned.[59] "Celimena" also prompted two parodies.[60] Similarly popular were the songs from *The Conquest of Granada* (1670–71): "Beneath a myrtle shade" is found in five anthologies (three with music) and four manuscripts; "Wherever I am" in seven anthologies (three with music) and five manuscripts; "How unhappy a lover am I" in six anthologies (three with music) and five manuscripts (one with music). Rapid quotation and parody once again testify to the popularity and familiarity of these songs:[61] the first four lines of "Wherever I am" are quoted in Joseph Kepple's novel *The Maiden'head lost by Moonlight* (1672),[62] while in Edward Ravenscroft's *The Citizen Turn'd Gentleman* (1672) Mr. Jordan sings an adaptation of Dryden's song, "How happy a lover am I." *Marriage A-la-mode* (1671) also provided a popular song, for "Whilst Alexis lay prest" found its way into seven anthologies (two with music) and three manuscripts. Most of the songs from Dryden's subsequent plays had some after-life in anthologies, but it is the songs from the period 1668–71 which seem to have been most successful in catching the public's attention. It is worth remarking, however, that when they were thus reprinted or transcribed, these songs almost always appeared without any attribution.

Sometimes the appearance of songs in printed anthologies seems to have preceded the printing of the play itself. (It is hardly ever possible to ascertain more about the date of these anthologies than the year given on their title-pages.) *An Evening's Love* was not printed until 1671, but two songs from it appear in *Merry Drollery, Complete,* whose title-page is dated 1670 (as well as in *The New Academy of Compliments,* dated 1671). Songs from *The Conquest of Granada* (printed in 1672) appear in *Westminster Drollery* (1671) and *The New Academy of Compliments.* It is clear that the songs must have circulated in copies which were obtained either from the author or (whether licitly or illicitly) from the playhouse.

In the light of this evidence that Dryden's songs were well known, and sometimes parodied, it is interesting to turn to the curious case of the song "Farewell, fair Armeda," where the evidence for Dryden's authorship rests entirely upon allusion and parody. The song appeared anonymously in four miscellanies in 1672, three more in subsequent years, and survives in two manuscripts. Malone attributed it to Dryden on the basis of references in *The Rehearsal* which associate it with Mr Bayes.[63] It was evidently a popular piece, for there is a reply "Blame not your Armida," and no fewer than three parodies, one of which seems to refer to Dryden's mistress Anne Reeves.[64] Thus the song is associated with Dryden once through allusion and once through parody, but nowhere directly.

Dryden's prologues and epilogues also had an existence which was independent of the printed texts of the plays for which they were written. Dryden almost always composed both a prologue and an epilogue for his own plays, and these were printed with the play. It was rare for any of Dryden's prologues and epilogues to appear in printed miscellanies (other than Tonson's *Miscellany Poems* and *Examen Poeticum*). The only significant exception is *Covent Garden Drolery* (1672), which prints the Prologue to *Albumazar* (from 1668), the Prologue and Epilogue to *Marriage A-la-mode* (from 1671), the Prologue and Epilogue to *Secret Love* performed by the women (1672), and the Prologue to *Wit without Money* (also 1672).[65] It is clear from the textual problems of the Prologue and Epilogue to *Marriage A-la-mode* that these texts originated in the playhouse.[66] This exceptional appearance of a group of Dryden's prologues and epilogues in a miscellany may be associated with the exceptional plight of the King's Company at this particular juncture. After the fire which destroyed their theatre they were thrown back upon improvised resources and upon the loyalty of their audience: both the Prologue to *Secret*

Love and Prologue to *Wit without Money* reflect these exigencies. Perhaps the company was glad of the extra publicity which it received from the publication of these pieces in *Covent Garden Drolery.*

Dryden's prologues and epilogues may not have been published much in the printed anthologies, but beginning with the Prologue to *Albumazar* some of them enjoyed a limited circulation in manuscript. It is difficult to discern a pattern in this circulation. Two dozen manuscripts contain prologues or epilogues from the period 1668–85; most of the interest was taken in those from the years 1670–76, and, to a lesser extent, in the political prologues and epilogues from 1680–82. The prologues spoken at Oxford during the annual visit of the King's Company in July are well represented. However, because the number of extant texts is small, it is not clear whether the pattern of distribution among the surviving manuscripts provides a reliable index to the original popularity of the pieces, or is simply attributable to the chances which attend the survival or disappearance of manuscripts. The latter must surely weigh heavily. At least two of the manuscripts which include the Oxford prologues have an Oxford provenance,[67] suggesting a local source for the text. The Epilogue to *The Man of Mode* (1676) is the piece most frequently represented in the manuscripts, though even here the number of copies is only five. As with *Mac Flecknoe,* the extant manuscripts probably represent only a fraction of those which once existed, the interest taken in prologues and epilogues being to a large extent topical and ephemeral. In most cases the playhouse seems the most likely provenance for the text of these manuscript copies.

Instances of manuscript circulation for which there is no longer any direct evidence can be inferred from the papers of John Oldham. He evidently knew Dryden's 1673 "Prologue to the University of Oxford," for he echoes it in a manuscript draft from *c.* 1678;[68] the prologue did not reach print until the publication of *Miscellany Poems* in 1684, several months after Oldham's death in December 1683. Oldham therefore had access to a manuscript of the poem, though none now survives amongst his papers. Indeed, since Oldham was an undergraduate at Oxford in 1673 it is quite likely that he heard the prologue spoken, and either made notes from it himself in the theatre or obtained a copy from the players. Oldham's papers furnish a second example, for in his sketches for *A Letter from the Country* (begun in late March 1678 and finished in July) he uses an idea from Dryden's Prologue to Shadwell's *A True Widow.*[69] The play was staged in March 1678 but not printed until early 1679, after Oldham's *Letter* was finished, so once again Oldham is recalling what he heard in the theatre, or using a manuscript copy. No manuscript of that prologue now survives. Similarly, Oldham echoes Dryden's *To the Lady Castlemain* in *A Letter from the Country,*[70] and therefore knew that poem either in manuscript or in John Bulteel's *A New Collection of Poems and Songs* (1674).

While the prologues and epilogues which Dryden composed for particular plays (whether his own or those of his colleagues) were almost invariably printed with those plays, the pieces which he composed for specific occasions (such as the opening of the new playhouse, or the summer visit to Oxford) were not put into print. Dryden, as a man of the theatre, seems to have thought that they served their purpose if they were successful on the occasion for which they were designed: they were not poems to be accorded the permanence of print. It was not until the prologue as a form acquired a polemical political function with the onset of the Exclusion Crisis that it became something which he thought should be printed as a poem in its own right. Previously, prologues and epilogues were part of the bantering relationship between dramatist, actors, and audience; they were written for a particular play or performance, a specific theatre with its regular audience, and they had a tone of voice which marked them out as essentially spoken pieces. The first of Dryden's prologues to be printed separately was his "Epilogue Spoken to the King," which was performed in March 1681 during the critical session of parliament at Oxford. An ostensibly eirenical and patriotic poem, it was effectively a partisan intervention in the crisis on behalf of the King's position. It was important for the King to sway public opinion, and in this the epilogue may have had a small part to play. It was no doubt to this end that it was printed rapidly in Oxford (the lack of an imprint suggests a hasty and even a clandestine arrangement, while the subtitle "Spoken . . . on Saturday last" indicates its immediacy), and also published in London (by Richard Royston, the royalist bookseller). Next came the printing of the "Prologue and Epilogue Spoken at *Mithridates,*" controversial pieces which were evidently being talked about around London, for both Whig and Tory newspapers quoted them.[71] In 1682 Dryden's "Prologue and Epilogue to *The Loyal Brother,*" "Prologue to His Royal Highness," "Prologue to the Duchess," "Prologue and Epilogue to the King and Queen," and "Prologue and Epilogue to *The Duke of Guise*" were all put into print as separate pamphlets, each of them making its contribution to the management of public opinion. Each was published by Tonson.[72] These were followed by the "Epilogue to *Constantine,*" "Prologue to *The Disappointment,*" and "Prologue and Epilogue to *Albion and Albanius.*" In the case of the politically controversial "Epilogue to *Constantine,*" Tonson's publication was a riposte to a pirated printing by "C. Tebroc" (i.e. "C. Corbet"), a text whose errors may have originated in a shorthand copy made during a performance.[73] The pattern of publication therefore changes as the function of prologues and epilogues alters with the political climate.

It was only after public events had conferred this significance on his prologues and epilogues that Dryden made an effort to collect them. There are nineteen prologues and epilogues included in *Miscellany Poems* (1684), arranged in a group.[74] When preparing the volume Dryden must have made a careful review of his work, for he can be seen to have followed a coherent pattern when selecting from amongst his many pieces in this genre. He did not reprint those which had already appeared with his own plays or the plays of his colleagues (except for one recent, topical piece, the "Epilogue to *The Unhappy Favourite*"). But he did reprint all his occasional pieces, except for those prologues from the 1680s which had already appeared in pamphlet form, and with the further anomalous exception of the Oxford prologue of July 1681, which was first collected in *Examen Poeticum* in 1693. From the evidence which survives, it seems that Dryden generally did not revise these pieces, though the text of the Epilogue to Banks's *The Unhappy Favourite* as printed in *Miscellany Poems* is less colloquial than that originally printed with the play, and also tends to move the printed text away from its original theatrical occasion by substituting "they" for "you" in references to the audience.[75] By 1684, then, all but one of Dryden's prologues and epilogues which we now know about had been printed, either in the plays to which they refer, or as separate pieces, or in *Miscellany Poems*. In the latter volume they were printed together in a single group, offered for the first time as a coherent body of work in their own right.

IV. THE MISCELLANIES AND TRANSLATIONS: 1684–1700

The publication of *Miscellany Poems*[76] in 1684 gave Dryden the opportunity to collect *Mac Flecknoe, Absalom and Achitophel,* and *The Medall* (though not *Religio Laici,* perhaps because Tonson still had copies on his hands), together with many of his prologues and epilogues. But the volume gives no special prominence to Dryden. Even if Tonson had begun by reprinting Dryden's three satires in octavo format to provide a collection of his public poems, that aim was not carried through, and *Miscellany Poems* as published has a different emphasis. Dryden is not named on the title-page, and the three satires are anonymous. Indeed, it is the presence of classical translations which is given prominence, and, as Stuart Gillespie has argued,[77] *Miscellany Poems* seems to have been inspired by Tonson's desire to build on the success of his *Ovid's Epistles* by publishing several other collections of classical translations by various hands. The title-page of the volume indicates this clearly enough: *Miscellany Poems. Containing a New Translation of Virgills Eclogues, Ovid's Love Elegies, Odes of Horace, and Other Authors; with Several Original Poems. By the most Eminent Hands.* Typographically the most striking word on the title-page is "TRANSLATION." The same is true of the joint title-page which Tonson produced for *Miscellany Poems* and its sequel *Sylvae;* this reads: *Miscellany Poems, In two Parts, Containing New Translations of Virgil's Eclogues, Ovid's Love-Elegies, Several Parts of Virgil's Aeneids, Lucretius, Theocritus, Horace, &c. With Several Original Poems, Never before Printed. By the most Eminent Hands.* The contents page of *Miscellany Poems* draws the reader's attention to the constituent parts of the volume: Dryden's three satires appear first, but without any collective heading; then come "Several of *Ovids* Elegies," arranged in order, book by book, and occupying ninety pages; then follows a heading "Odes of *Horace*" and a list of ten odes and one epode. Miscellaneous poems come next without any separate heading, a mixture of other classical translations (from Propertius, Petronius, Theocritus, and Virgil), with a batch of Dryden's prologues and epilogues. Finally there is another separate heading, "*Virgils* Eclogues, Translated by several Hands"; all ten eclogues are translated, with numbers II, VIII, and X being offered in two different versions. Since this section of Virgil's *Eclogues* is separately paginated and has its own title-page, it seems likely that Tonson originally intended this an independent collection.[78]

So, far from a reader of *Miscellany Poems* registering Dryden as being specially prominent in the collection, it is likely that the connoisseur of translation, at whom the volume seems to have been aimed, would have been attracted by other names whose reputation in this field had already been established. The Earl of Roscommon contributed translations of Horace's *Odes* I xx and III vi, and Virgil's *Eclogue* VI (as well as a poem in praise of *Religio Laici*). Roscommon was already presiding over an informal academy with an interest in translation,[79] and his version of Horace's *Ars Poetica* had been published in 1680 (by Herringman, whose subsequent loss of Roscommon to Tonson is worth noting); it was reprinted in 1684, the year which also saw the publication by Tonson of his *Essay on Translated Verse*. Thomas Creech, whose translation of Lucretius had been published in 1682 and reprinted three times in 1683, contributed versions of five of Ovid's *Elegies* and two of Virgil's *Eclogues*. His complete translations of Horace and of Theocritus would appear later in 1684. Other names which might impress the potential purchaser were Sir Car Scroope, Sir Charles Sedley, the Earl of Rochester, Thomas Rymer, Nahum Tate, the Earl of Mulgrave, Richard Duke, and Thomas Otway.

While *Miscellany Poems* gave Dryden the chance to collect some fugitive pieces, and to contribute to Tonson's aim of producing more-or-less co-ordinated sets of classical translations, the second miscellany, *Sylvae* (1685), was conceived differently. Six months after the publication of *Miscellany Poems* in February 1684 Dryden was writing to Tonson about the compilation of its sequel.[80] They agreed that *Religio Laici* would not be included, and that the collection would consist wholly of new material. *Sylvae* does not attempt to offer groups of translations from a particular classical corpus, though there are small groups of translations from Theocritus, Catullus, Ovid, and Horace. The most coherent section of the volume is Dryden's opening sequence of translations from Virgil, Lucretius, Theocritus, and Horace, prefaced by a substantial critical essay; there are thematic links between the translations (notably the topics of death, sexuality, and retirement from the life of city and court), but Dryden does not attempt to draw out these connections in his preface, nor does he reprint in *Sylvae* those of his contemporary poems which have strong links with these translations, particularly "To the Memory of Mr Oldham" and "To the Earl of Roscommon." Once again, it seems that Dryden is declining the opportunity to create an oeuvre for himself by bringing together those poems which speak to related issues.

Examen Poeticum (1693),[81] the third of the miscellanies, mixes classical translation with the rounding up of strays from earlier in Dryden's career, though in this volume the work of other named contributors dominates. Even so, Dryden's translation of the first book of Ovid's *Metamorphoses* is accorded special prominence, coming first in the volume and being given its own half-title. It is followed by other fables from books IX and XIII. There is an episode from Homer, but otherwise Dryden's activities as a translator seem to have been devoted chiefly to his Juvenal and Persius, which were published separately that same year. *Examen Poeticum* reprints several pieces which had previously not been collected by Dryden: the "Prologue to the Duchess" (separately printed in 1682); the "Song for St Cecilia's Day" (separately printed in 1687); "To the Lady Castlemain," now revised; "To Anne Killigrew" (published in her *Poems* of 1686); and the "Epitaph on Sir Palmes Fairborne" (printed in *Poetical Recreations* [1688]). To these Dryden added some previously unpublished items: two prologues, two songs, a hymn, and an epitaph. Once again, however, these pieces do not add up to an installment of a "Collected Poems," for they are scattered through the volume. Dryden's contribution to the fourth miscellany, *The Annual Miscellany for the Year 1694,* was minor: a translation of Virgil's *Georgics* III, and "To Sir Godfrey Kneller." Dryden had already planned his complete translation of Virgil (he had determined upon it by December 1693) and *Georgics* III was evidently a trailer for the larger collection, however much it may have appealed to Dryden in its own right.

The major volumes of translations which were the product of Dryden's last decade—the Juvenal and Persius of 1693, the Virgil of 1697, and the *Fables* of 1700—are relatively straightforward from the point of view of the present inquiry. The Juvenal reached a second edition in 1697, and the Virgil a second edition in 1698. Lines which Dryden translated from Juvenal's *Satire* VI but which were omitted from the printed text for reasons of decency, had a very limited circulation in manuscript, since they survive in the margins of Dryden's presentation copy of the book to Thomas Monson, and on the endpapers of another copy.[82] A few passages from the Juvenal, Persius, and Virgil translations survive in manuscript copies,[83] but they are of minor interest. There was no reason for any circulation of the translations outside the printed editions, though some readers did transcribe passages which they considered specially fine.[84]

V. The Occasional Poems 1685–1700

In one respect the circulation of Dryden's poetry in the reigns of James II and William III followed a pattern which is now familiar. Dryden generally made no effort to collect the poems which he had written to or for his friends and colleagues: like the earlier poems to Roscommon, Oldham, and Maidwell, his poems introducing books by John Northleigh, Henry Higden, Thomas Southerne, William Congreve, George Granville, and Peter Motteux were left to work for the benefit of their addressees. Dryden did, however, reprint his poem to Anne Killigrew in *Examen Poeticum.* The separately published memorial poems *Eleonora* (1692) and *An Ode, on the Death of Mr. Henry Purcell* (1696) were not reprinted, though *Alexander's Feast* (1697) was included in *Fables* (1700).

Dryden may have regarded his verse letter to Sir George Etherege, written in 1686, as a private poem with no business in the public domain, but (along with Etherege's verse correspondence with the Earl of Middleton) it achieved a comparatively wide circulation in manuscript: eleven copies now survive, some of them quite close to the date of composition.[85] Others are assigned by Dr. Beal to the period *c.* 1690, which is the point at which the poem was put into print in *The History of Adolphus* (1691)—presumably no more than an opportunistic piece of publishing which had nothing to do with Dryden himself.

But the major factor which affected the circulation of Dryden's poetry in this period was the political climate. The publication of *The Hind and the Panther* in 1687 was an event which had a considerable political importance, in that it was the first public account of his new Catholic faith by the Poet Laureate to the new Catholic King.[86] The poem went through three London editions in 1687, and was printed in the same year at Edinburgh, in Holyrood House, by James Watson, "Printer to His Most Excellent Majesties Royal Family and Houshold"; it was also printed in 1687 in Dublin. Evidently the poem was important to the court. It was not, however, reprinted after 1687, either because there was no commercial demand, or because after the Revolution in 1688–89 it was thought too provocative to the new régime. Two manuscripts of *The Hind and the Panther* are extant, one of which, the Traquair copy, testifies to Jacobite interest in the poem.[87]

Three of Dryden's poems from this period had a significant manuscript circulation because of their political character. "The Lady's Song," a Jacobite piece, was not printed until after Dryden's death (in *Poetical Miscellanies: the Fifth Part* [1704]), but five manuscripts from the late seventeenth century survive.[88] In Bodleian Library MS Don. c 55 the song is dated 1691, and that is also the probable date at which it was copied into University of Leeds Brotherton Collection MS Lt 54.[89] The song must have circulated in manuscript in the early 1690s amongst sympathetic readers, but was too provocative to be printed. The "Prologue to *The Prophetess*" included lines critical of William III's expensive preparations for war in Ireland, and was banned after the first night. Although it was printed with the play in 1690, most copies lack the separate leaf on which the prologue appeared.[90] The person who copied out the prologue for a Mr. Charlett of Trinity College Oxford wrote:

"This Prologue was spoken but once & after forbid by y^eL^d Chamberlain, which I suppose will encrease the value with persons of y^r Curiosity."[91] Not surprisingly, the prologue circulated widely in manuscript: seventeen copies are known.[92] All date approximately from the last decade of the seventeenth century, and the text in Brotherton Collection MS Lt 54 was almost certainly transcribed in 1691.[93] Finally, Dryden's lines "Upon the Death of the Earl of Dundee," translated from the Latin verses by Dr. Archibald Pitcairne, were likewise accorded an extensive circulation in manuscript. (They too were first printed in *Poetical Miscellanies* in 1704.) Nineteen manuscripts are known to survive, the largest number of extant manuscript copies of any poem by Dryden.[94] In several copies the poem is dated 1689, and most of the surviving manuscripts were apparently written in the 1690s. In the last decade of his life, Dryden evidently found that even mildly oppositional verse could only be circulated in this clandestine manner.

VI. The Changing Perception of Dryden's Oeuvre

This article has considered the circulation of Dryden's poetry from the point of view of the author, his publishers, and scribes. But what would his readers have had available to them at different stages in Dryden's career? Let us finally consider briefly what interested (but not especially privileged) readers of contemporary poetry might know of Dryden's work at five-year intervals.

In 1660 there would be no reason to single Dryden out from the crowd of versifiers who greeted the King's return. His *Heroique Stanza's* on the death of Cromwell had appeared in print in 1659, but a year later had probably been forgotten (albeit only temporarily). Hardly any reader in 1665 would consider asking his bookseller for poems by Dryden: the few occasional pieces from the early 1660s had probably disappeared. By 1670, however, Dryden was an established playwright. Theatre-goers would have come across Dryden's prologues, epilogues, and songs in the playhouse; they might have bought play quartos and read the poems there; they would be likely purchasers for *Covent Garden Drolery* and its rivals when they appeared in the early 1670s. *Annus Mirabilis,* along with the oppositional "Advice to a Painter" poems which followed it, may already have been forgotten, though the compiler of MS Burney 390 in the early 1670s was sufficiently interested in Dryden's panegyrics from the early 1660s to copy them out (which may suggest that no printed copies were available at that date). Five years later, in 1675, the perception of Dryden as a poet would be much the same: almost exclusively as a successful dramatist, with a talent for songs and a pleasing line in prologues. By 1680 little would have changed, for although other writers had poured out verses on the Popish Plot and the Exclusion Crisis, Dryden was keeping a discreet distance from these political squabbles, except for some barbed references in occasional prologues and epilogues. Readers who moved in exclusive literary circles might have come across a manuscript copy of *Mac Flecknoe*, and made themselves a transcript; the wealthier ones could have commissioned a handsome manuscript anthology of unprintable poems on contemporary affairs: 1680 is the year when several of these were being produced for connoisseurs. Readers might have seen other manuscript satires attributed to Dryden, and wondered whether the attributions were correct. In 1680 one could also have purchased *Ovid's Epistles,* with its rather indifferent poems redeemed by Dryden's sharp and confident essay on translation.

By 1685 everything had changed. The publications of 1681–82 had quite suddenly revealed a remarkably diverse and astringent poetic talent, equally adept at literary demolition, political invective, and religious controversy. The prologues and epilogues had become more polemical, and had been appearing as printed leaflets as well as turning up in manuscript copies: they were now poems for the streets and the coffeehouses as well as for the theatre, pieces to read as well as to hear. *Miscellany Poems* had gathered a lot of Dryden's poetry together rather conveniently, and though the major satires were still anonymous the pretence at concealment did not fool many; even so, there was no "Collected Poems," and Dryden's early work was hard to come by (except for the maliciously reprinted *Heroique Stanza's*). The promise which had been held out by *Ovid's Epistles* that Dryden was turning his attention to translation was confirmed briefly in *Miscellany Poems* and impressively in *Sylvae*, though many of his most important statements about the writer's art and the state of contemporary language and literature had been made in passing in commendatory poems which were only accessible if one bought the books of his friends.

By 1690 everything had changed again. The flood of major publications in the early 1680s had dried up. *The Hind and the Panther* had made an impact in 1687, but the Revolution seemed to have silenced him. Soon Dryden's work would begin to be seen in surreptitious manuscript copies passed round in Jacobite circles. His position was awkward, perhaps dangerous, and it was hard to foresee what kind of role Dryden would make for himself as a writer under this new regime. Meanwhile Tonson was reprinting Dryden's earlier work in a uniform format, so that the interested reader could have the major poems bound up together: *Annus Mirabilis, To His Sacred Majesty,* and *To My Lord Chancellor* were reissued in 1688, *Heroique Stanza's* in 1691 or 1692, *Britannia Rediviva, Mac Flecknoe, Absalom and Achitophel,* and *The Medall* appeared in 1692. Sets of Dryden's poems were made available with suitable title-pages.[95] Demand for Dryden's earlier work clearly continued.

By 1695 it was clear that Dryden had decided to devote himself to translation: readers had seen from *Examen Poeticum* and the Juvenal and Persius that his gifts were undiminished, and there were promises of a great literary event in the offing, the publication of Dryden's complete Virgil. By 1700, the year of Dryden's death, the Virgil of 1697 had been followed, and his career crowned, by the publication of *Fables Ancient and Modern*. After Dryden's death Tonson collected a few stray pieces in his continuing series of Miscellany Poems (which he promoted by advertising the first four parts as having been "Publish'd by Mr. *Dryden*"[96]); those rescued in this way included the Jacobite pieces and some Ovidian translations left over from an attempt in the 1690s to produce a composite *Metamorphoses*.[97]

To follow the course of Dryden's career in this way is, in however summary a form, to reconstruct the contingencies of publication which our easy overview of the completed canon so often obscures. It also reminds us that Dryden was a very different kind of writer from Pope; whereas Pope paid scrupulous attention to the promotion of his work and the construction of his image from an early date, self-consciously fashioning his persona and his oeuvre, Dryden left his poetry to work for itself, to fulfil the functions for which it was composed, and only sought for it to live beyond its first occasion if there was a real demand. In this attitude to his writing there is both the professionalism which we associate with him, and a modesty which the slanders of his enemies have sometimes encouraged us to forget.

Notes

1. I am grateful to Professor John Barnard and Dr. David Hopkins for their comments on a draft of this essay.
2. Hugh Macdonald, *John Dryden: A Bibliography of Early Editions and of Drydeniana* (Oxford, 1939); Peter Beal, *Index of English Literary Manuscripts*, vol. 2: 1625–1700, Part I (London, 1987).
3. Macdonald, p. 20.
4. Macdonald, pp. 89–91.
5. Macdonald, pp. 97–99; *The Works of John Dryden*, ed. H. T. Swedenberg et al., 20 vols. (Berkeley, 1956–), IX, 354–55, and see the facsimile of the title-page (of an unidentified copy) on IX, 206, which carries a manuscript note attributing the play to Newcastle.
6. *The Diary of Samuel Pepys*, ed. Robert Latham and William Matthews, 11 vols. (1970–83), VIII, 387; IX, 307.
7. The question of the anonymity of Dryden's prose lies outside the scope of this article, but it may be mentioned that Dryden did not put his name to *Notes and Observations on the Empress of Morocco* (1674), or *His Majesties Declaration Defended* (1681): see Macdonald, pp. 166–67.
8. For Tonson's deception, see G. Thorn-Drury, "Some Notes on Dryden," *Review of English Studies*, 1 (1925), 197; for Brown, see his *The Late Converts Exposed* (1690), pp. 53–54.
9. For contemporaries' assumptions about the authorship of the *Essay upon Satire*, see *The Gyldenstolpe Manuscript Miscellany of Poems by John Wilmot, Earl of Rochester, and other Restoration Authors*, ed. Bror Danielsson and David M. Vieth, Stockholm Studies in English, 17 (Stockholm, 1967), pp. 350–51.
10. Macdonald, p. 217.
11. Attributed to Dryden in British Library MS Harley 6914, and in Victoria and Albert Museum MS Dyce 43.
12. See *Poems on Affairs of State*, vol. I: 1660–78, ed. George deF. Lord (New Haven, 1963), pp. 387–91. Four manuscripts attribute this poem to Dryden: see p. 477.

13.   See *Poems on Affairs of State,* vol. 2: 1678–81, ed. Elias F. Mengel, Jr. (New Haven, 1965), pp. 339–41, 537.

14.   See *Poems on Affairs of State,* II, 305–11. No attributions are recorded here, but the poem is attributed to Dryden in Nottingham University Library MS PwV 199.

15.   See *Poems on Affairs of State,* II, 228–34; attributed to Dryden in British Library MS Harley 7317.

16.   See James M. Osborn, *John Dryden: Some Biographical Facts and Problems,* rev. ed. (Gainesville, Fla., 1965), pp. 269–70.

17.   "Here lies a creature of indulgent fate" (*c.* 1687) is attributed to Dryden in British Library MS Harley 6914 and MS Add 27408, and in Bodleian Library MS Firth c 15; see also Macdonald, p. 319.

18.   Attributed to Dryden by Anthony Wood: see Macdonald, p. 269, n. 4.

19.   Attributed to Dryden in Bodleian Library MS Rawl. Poet. 173.

20.   English translation attributed to Dryden in Bodleian Library MS Eng. Poet. f 13.

21.   Macdonald, pp. 265, 320; for other examples, see pp. 319–21.

22.   See Osborn, pp. 184–99.

23.   For a sense of Herringman's output I am indebted to C. William Miller, "Henry Herringman Imprints: A Preliminary Checklist" (mimeographed by the Bibliographical Society of the University of Virginia, University Library, Charlottesville, Va., 1949).

24.   For Dryden and Tonson generally, see Kathleen M. Lynch, *Jacob Tonson: KitCat Publisher* (Knoxville, 1971), pp. 17–30; see also note 77 below. There is a somewhat rudimentary list of Tonson's publications in G. F. Papali, *Jacob Tonson, Publisher: His Life and Work* (1656–1736) (Auckland, 1968), pp. 144–213.

25.   For a discussion of the preparation and printing of this volume, see Paul Hammond, "The Printing of the Dryden–Tonson *Miscellany Poems* (1684) and *Sylvae* (1685)," *PSBA,* 84 (1990), 405–12.

26.   *The Letters of John Dryden,* ed. Charles E. Ward (Durham, N.C., 1942), p. 23.

27.   *Sylvae* (1685), sig. a8ᵛ.

28.   "Having formerly Printed two Parts of Miscellany Poems, they were so very kindly receiv'd, that I had long before now Endeavour'd to obtain a Third, had I not almost ever since the Publishing of the Second been Solliciting the Translating of *Juvenal,* and *Persius.* Soon after the Publishing of that Book I waited upon several Gentlemen to ask their Opinion of a Third Miscellany, who encourag'd me to endeavour it, and have considerably help'd me in it." (*Examen Poeticum* [1693], sig. B7ʳ.)

29.   For example: Sir William Davenant, *A Panegyrick to Generall Monck* (1659), and *Poem, upon His Sacred Majesties Most Happy return* (1660); Abraham Cowley, *Ode, Upon the Blessed Restoration* (1660); Sir Thomas Higgons, *A Panegyrick to the King* (1660); Edmund Waller, *To the King Upon his Majesties Happy Return* (1660).

30.   Macdonald, p. 10.

31.   Macdonald, pp. 14–15.

32.   *The Diary of Samuel Pepys,* VIII, 40 and note.

33.   Beal, pp. 392, 398–99. This MS is now British Library MS Add 69823. It was transcribed from a copy of the second issue of the first edition of *Annus Mirabilis* (Macdonald 9 a ii): it has the revised text of the lines on Prince Rupert (ll. 419–20), but the unrevised text of the line on Berkeley (l. 267). It fails to take account of the errata listed in all known copies of the first edition.

34.   *To His Sacred Majesty* occurs on ff. 9ʳ–10ʳ, *To My Lord Chancellor* on ff. 11ᵛ–12ʳ, and *To the Lady Castlemaine* on ff. 12ᵛ–13ʳ; all are attributed to Dryden. They are preceded on ff. 6ʳ–7ᵛ by Rochester's *A Satire against Reason and Mankind,* which was probably composed in 1674, and thus provides a *terminus a quo* for the transcription of the three poems by Dryden.

35.   Macdonald, p. 15.

36.   British Library MS Lansdowne 1045, ff. 101ʳ–103ᵛ.

37.   For the printed texts, see Macdonald, pp. 3–7, and for the manuscripts, see Beal, pp. 403–04.

38.   The copy in British Library MS Egerton 669 (which Beal dates "late 17th century") probably dates from 1667, as a note on f. 2ʳ indicates that the MS was bound on 16 March 1667; Dryden's poem appears along with Waller's elegy and other material from 1651–63. The copy in British Library MS Add. 18220 (dated "1672–3" by Beal) was probably transcribed in the early summer of 1673, as it follows items dated March, April, and May 1673. It is possible that the copy in British Library MS Harley 7315 (*c.* 1703, according to Beal) may date from the Exclusion Crisis, as it follows a list of items for auction on 9 January 1680 (which probably means 1680/1).

39.   See John Barnard and Paul Hammond, "Dryden and a Poem for Lewis Maidwell," *TLS,* 25 May 1984, p. 586.

40.   I have discussed this extensively in *John Dryden: A Literary Life* (Basingstoke, 1991).

41.   Dryden was one of the members of the informal academy around the Earl of Roscommon (see Carl Niemeyer, "The Earl of Roscommon's Academy," *Modern Language Notes,* 49 [1934], 432–37). For an instance of Dryden emphasising his aristocratic literary connections, see his account of genial evenings in the company of Sir Charles Sedley in the dedication to *The Assignation* (1673) (*Works of John Dryden,* XI, 319–23).

42.   Macdonald (pp. 21–24) indicates the rapidity with which the early editions were produced, though his account is incomplete. The treatment of the printing of *Absalom and Achitophel* in *The Works of John Dryden,* II, 411–13, is seriously defective. I hope to clarify this problem in a future article.

43.   Tonson's political position at this date is unclear; after 1688 he certainly had Whig sympathies.

44.   *Letters,* p. 23.

45.   For a general discussion of the manuscript circulation of works in the seventeenth century, see Harold Love, "Scribal Publication in Seventeenth-Century England," *Transactions of the Cambridge Bibliographical Society,* 9 (1987), 130–54.

46.   "Some who have seen a paper of Verses which I wrote last year to her Highness the *Dutchess,* have accus'd them of that onely thing I could defend in them; they have said I did *humi serpere*" ("An Account of the ensuing Poem," ll. 202–04, in *The Poems of John Dryden,* ed. James Kinsley, 4 vols. [Oxford, 1958]).

47.   I have discussed the manuscript circulation of this poem in "Dryden's Revision of *To the Lady Castlemain,*" *PBSA,* 78 (1984), 81–90. Since then Peter Beal has discovered a fifth manuscript of the poem: Society of Antiquaries MS 330. The readings of this manuscript place it firmly within the manuscript tradition identified in my article, and associate it particularly closely with Bodleian Library MS Eng. Poet. e 4.

48.   See the evidence in note 34.

49.   The poem occurs on pp. 173–74. It is preceded by two datable poems: on p. 167 lines on "Michaelmas Term 1672," and on pp. 172–73 Dryden's "Prologue to *Albumazar*" (spoken February 1668; printed in *Covent Garden Drolery* [1672]). It is followed on p. 175 by Dryden's *"Prologue to Wit without Money"* (spoken February 1672; printed in *Covent Garden Drolery*), on pp. 176–77 by an Oxford prologue from July 1671, and on pp. 177–78 by the prologue to *Cambyses* (1672).

50.   The poem occurs on f. 44ʳ⁻ᵛ. It is preceded on f. 42ʳ⁻ᵛ by the "Prologue to *An Evening's Love*" (spoken June 1668, printed 1671), and followed by the "Prologue to *Wit without Money*" and the Oxford prologue of 1671.

51.   The date is established by David M. Vieth, "The Discovery of the Date of *Mac Flecknoe*" in *Evidence in Literary Scholarship,* ed. René Wellek and Alvaro Ribiero (Oxford, 1979), pp. 63–87.

52.   For the manuscript transmission of *Mac Flecknoe,* see David M. Vieth, "Dryden's *Mac Flecknoe:* The Case against Editorial Confusion," *Harvard Library Bulletin,* 24 (1976),

204–45; supplemented by Paul Hammond, "The Robinson Manuscript Miscellany of Restoration Verse in the Brotherton Collection, Leeds," in *Proceedings of the Leeds Philosophical and Literary Society: Literary and Historical Section,* 18 (1982), 275–324. None of the extant manuscripts is particularly close to the archetype, so the evidence from the manuscript tradition does not allow us to connect the circulation directly with Dryden.

53.   Beal lists fourteen manuscripts. I am informed by Professor Harold Love that a further manuscript copy exists in National Library of Ireland MS 2093, but I have been unable to verify this since the library does not answer letters.

54.   See *The Gyldenstolpe Manuscript Miscellany;* Hammond, "The Robinson Manuscript Miscellany." The Robinson Manuscript is Leeds University Library Brotherton Collection MS Lt 54.

55.   These are Gyldenstolpe, Robinson, and Yale University Library MS Osborn Collection b 105.

56.   Examples are collected by Vieth in "The Discovery of the Date of *Mac Flecknoe,*" pp. 67–69.

57.   Vieth, "Dryden's *Mac Flecknoe.*"

58.   Unless separately documented, the following information about the circulation of Dryden's songs depends upon *The Songs of John Dryden,* ed. Cyrus Lawrence Day (Cambridge, Mass., 1932) for their appearance in print, and Beal for their circulation in manuscript.

59.   The version in *The New Academy of Compliments* (1671), pp. 192–93, adds two further stanzas; the imitation "Green was the garden and pleasant the walk" is found in the same volume, pp. 289–90; "Fair was my mistress, and fine as a bride" is found in *Covent Garden Drolery,* pp. 38–39; "Sharp was the air, and cold was the ground" in *Mock Songs and Joking Poems* (1675), pp. 129–30; "Bright was the morning, clear the air" in British Library MS Add 30303; and "Serene was the air, and unpearled the fields" in *Holborn-Drollery* (1673), pp. 50–53.

60.   Both in *Mock Songs and Joking Poems,* pp. 107–08 and 133.

61.   The following is new information.

62.   The context indicates that the reader was expected to recognise the song; after quoting the first four lines, the narrator says: "Now you'l say this is very like a modern Song of ours, but I assure you what follows, could I but remember it, was not at all like it, and it was only by chance, that he thought of the first Stave, for it is certain there are common notions, which are obvious to all that make upon the same Subject" (*Restoration Prose Fiction 1666–1700,* ed. Charles C. Mish [Lincoln, Nebr., 1970], p. 169).

63.   "BAYES: If I am to write familiar things, as Sonnets to *Armida,* and the like, I make use of Stew'd Prunes only" (George Villiers, Duke of Buckingham, *The Rehearsal,* ed. D. E. L. Crane [Durham, England, 1976], II. i. 114–16).

64.   "Farewell dear *Revechia*" appeared in *Covent Garden Drolery,* pp. 39–40; other parodies are found in *Mock Songs and Joking Poems,* pp. 79–80; British Library MS Egerton 2623; *Roxburghe Ballads,* vol. 4, ed. J. W. Ebsworth (Hertford, 1881), p. 82.

65.   The volume also contains the "Prologue to *Julius Caesar,*" but I have argued that the attribution of this to Dryden by modern scholars is mistaken (see Paul Hammond, "Did Dryden write the *Prologue to 'Julius Caesar'?*", *English Studies,* 65 [1984], 409–19).

66.   See Paul Hammond, "The Prologue and Epilogue to Dryden's *Marriage A-la-mode* and the Problem of *Covent Garden Drolery,*" *PBSA,* 81 (1987), 155–72.

67.   Bodleian Library MS Don. f 29 (compiled by William Doble at Trinity College *c.* 1669–74); British Library MS Add. 14047.

68.   *The Poems of John Oldham,* ed. Harold F. Brooks with the collaboration of Raman Selden (Oxford, 1987), p. 545.

69.   *Ibid.,* p. 543.

70.   *Ibid.,* p. 430.

71.   See John Harrington Smith, "Dryden's Prologue and Epilogue to *Mithridates,* Revived," *PMLA,* 68 (1953), 251–67.

72.　Tonson and others were also printing a number of politically topical prologues and epilogues by Otway at this date: *Prologue. By Mr. Otway to his Play call'd Venice preserv'd* (A. Green, 1681); *Prologue To a New Play, called Venice Preserv'd* (A. Banks, 1682); *Epilogue to Venice Preserv'd on the Duke's coming to the Theatre* (Hindmarsh, 1682); *Prologue to the City-Heiress* (Tonson, 1682); *Epilogue to Her Royal Highness* (Tonson, 1682). For other instances of topical prologues being published in broadside form in the crisis years 1681–83, see *The Prologues and Epilogues of the Restoration 1660–1700,* ed. Pierre Danchin, Part II: 1677–1690 (Nancy, 1984), pp. xviii–xx and nos. 315, 319, 320, 321, 324, 326, 328, 332, and 334.

73.　Smith, p. 287, n. 8. The only Corbet who is known to have been a publisher at this date is Charles Corbet, who published a poetical broadside on the Plot in 1683, and two ballads on the frost in 1683–84 (Henry R. Plomer, *A Dictionary of the Printers and Booksellers . . . from 1668 to 1725* [London, 1922], p. 81). He seems to have been just the kind of small, opportunistic operator who would have cashed in on a topical poem, while at the same time trying to conceal his identity.

74.　For this section, and the anomalous place of the "Prologue intended for *Calisto,*" see Hammond, "Printing."

75.　*The Works of John Dryden,* II, 457–58.

76.　For the preparation and printing of this volume, see Hammond, "Printing."

77.　Stuart Gillespie, "The Early Years of the Dryden-Tonson Partnership: The Background to their Composite Translations and Miscellanies of the 1680s," *Restoration,* 12 (1988), 10–19.

78.　Gillespie, p. 15; Hammond, "Printing."

79.　See Niemeyer.

80.　*Letters of John Dryden,* p. 23.

81.　For the circumstances of the publication of *Examen Poeticum,* see Tonson's preface (B7^r–B8^r), partly quoted in note 28 above.

82.　*The Works of John Dryden,* IV, 781–82.

83.　Beal, pp. 416, 422–23.

84.　Beal, pp. 396–97.

85.　Peter Beal dates British Library MS Add 11513 *c.* 1687, which is also a likely date for the transcription of the copy in University of Leeds Brotherton Collection MS Lt 54 (see Paul Hammond, "Robinson Manuscript," pp. 318–19). For the circumstances in which these verse letters circulated, see Beal p. 448.

86.　Interest in the poem is attested by the replies which it provoked (see Macdonald, pp. 253–63); see also Peter Beal, " 'The most constant and best entertainment': Sir George Etherege's Reading in Ratisbon," *The Library,* 6th ser., 10 (1988), 122–44, especially pp. 131–32.

87.　Beal, p. 405; Richard Eversole, "The Traquair Manuscript of Dryden's *The Hind and the Panther,*" *PBSA,* 75 (1981), 179–91.

88.　Beal, p. 406. See also Anne Barbeau Gardiner, "A Jacobite Song by John Dryden," *Yale University Library Gazette,* 61 (1986), 49–54.

89.　Hammond, "Robinson Manuscript," p. 321; it is preceded and followed by material from 1691.

90.　Macdonald, pp. 161–62.

91.　Bodleian Library MS Ballard 47, ff. 83–84; Beal, p. 412.

92.　Beal, pp. 412–13.

93.　Hammond, "Robinson Manuscript," p. 323.

94.　Beal, pp. 421–22.

95.　Macdonald, pp. 15–16.

96.　Macdonald, p. 75.

97.　David Hopkins, "Dryden and the Garth-Tonson *Metamorphoses,*" *Review of English Studies,* 39 (1988), 64–74.

Arcadia Lost: Politics and Revision in the Restoration *Tempest*

KATHARINE EISAMAN MAUS

I

The most popular play on the Restoration stage was *The Tempest,* as revised by John Dryden and William D'Avenant in 1667. Pepys thought it was "good, above ordinary plays" when he saw it on its opening night; he was to attend eight performances in the next two years. "After dinner, to the Duke of York's house to see the play, *The Tempest,* which we have often seen; but yet I am pleased again, and shall be again to see it."[1] In 1674 the revised *Tempest* was staged for the first time as an "opera," with elaborate scenery and several new songs. According to John Downes, "All things were perform'd in it so exceedingly well, that not any succeeding Opera got more money."[2] The play was more often revived than any other between 1660 and 1700; innumerable contemporary allusions indicate that virtually everyone was familiar with it. It continued to be received favorably through the eighteenth century, and into the nineteenth.

Modern critics, however, have not shared the enthusiasm of the Restoration audience. "To appraise this wretched stuff in the light of critical rules would be absurd," Hazelton Spencer fumes, calling the play "the worst, as it was the most successful, of the Restoration adaptations prior to 1700."[3] Allardyce Nicoll complains that it panders to "the immoral, degenerate qualities of the age."[4] The Dryden-D'Avenant *Tempest* has received more sympathetic, or at least more tactful, attention from a few critics who see the revision as an attempt to render Shakespeare's dense language more immediately comprehensible in performance, to reshape the play according to neoclassic norms, to make Shakespeare's improbable fictions more acceptable to a scientifically minded audience, or to exploit the new scenic resources of the Restoration stage.[5] I will argue, however, that the revised *Tempest* is best understood in terms of sociopolitical issues which were of primary practical importance in the latter half of the seventeenth century. The new play redefines the limits and uses of sovereignty.

Katharine Eisaman Maus, "Arcadia Lost: Politics and Revision in the Restoration *Tempest*." Reprinted from *Renaissance Drama* 13 (1982): 189–209. Reproduced by permission of Northwestern University Press.

II

It certainly seems plausible enough to assume that the collaborators undertook the revision with more-or-less coherent goals in mind. Dryden and D'Avenant alter *The Tempest* far more than *Troilus and Cressida* or *Macbeth*—they take only about a third of their material from the original play, displacing and rearranging the Shakespearean material to serve the demands of a substantially new plot.[6] A brief summary will suggest the extent of the alteration.

Like Shakespeare, Dryden and D'Avenant begin their play with a storm and a shipwreck. Shortly thereafter, however, the adaptation diverges from the original. As the revised *Tempest* begins, Prospero has managed to raise his two daughters, Miranda and Dorinda, to adolescence in ignorance of his foster-child Hippolito, whom he also brought as an infant to the island. Hippolito is the rightful Duke of Mantua, disinherited in the same coup that overthrew Prospero himself. Hippolito is doomed, according to his horoscope, if he ever beholds a woman; Prospero therefore keeps the young people apart by threats. The girls, however, finally disobey their father's injunctions. Dorinda begins a conversation with Hippolito; infatuation ensues. When Prospero chides his daughters for their insubordination he quickly discovers Dorinda's passion, and wonders why Hippolito remains unharmed.

Meanwhile, Prospero sends Ariel to bring Ferdinand to Miranda. They fall in love but, as in the Shakespearean version, Prospero refuses to allow an unimpeded courtship. He sends Ferdinand to a cave in which he has sequestered Hippolito. From Ferdinand, Hippolito learns that there is more than one woman in the world, and inductively reasons that if one is good, more are better. The four young people assiduously pursue their courtships—but inevitably, given the inexperience and guileless volubility of the participants, misunderstandings arise on all sides. Eventually a jealous Ferdinand challenges Hippolito to a duel. Hippolito, ignorant of the martial arts, is badly wounded and falls unconscious. Furious, Prospero dismisses Ariel to find Gonzalo, Alonzo, and Antonio, whom he has been tormenting with ingenious apparitions. When the shipwrecked courtiers arrive, Prospero declares his intention to execute Ferdinand at daybreak for Hippolito's murder.

The next day, Prospero rejects Miranda's last-minute efforts to save her lover's life. Ariel, however, announces that he has revived Hippolito by a combination of medicine and magic. The still-groggy Hippolito claims that he is no longer promiscuously inclined—but more misunderstandings among the lovers nearly lead to another fight at the bedside. All difficulties, though, soon resolve themselves. Alonzo, Antonio, and Prospero are already reconciled by the happy circumstances of Hippolito's recovery and Ferdinand's pardon. The couples prepare to be wed, though Hippolito, Miranda, and Dorinda are still ignorant of their marital responsibilities.

In the revised *Tempest* the low characters—Stephano, Mustacho, Ventoso, and Trincalo—are all sailors, and like their Shakespearean counterparts they quickly find each other once ashore. Stephano proclaims himself duke, Mustacho and Ventoso viceroys. Trincalo rejects their pretensions, and attempts to gain a title himself by marrying Caliban's sister Sycorax. Stephano arrives on an ambassadorial mission, ostensibly to make peace with Trincalo, but actually to seduce Sycorax. The scene ends in uproar. The low characters do not reappear until the end of the final scene, when they and the rest of the company watch Ariel and his lover Milcha perform a saraband.

The script of the operatic *Tempest* differs little from the Dryden-D'Avenant play. Scenes are sometimes rearranged and speeches cut to allow room for new songs and special stage effects; the text includes elaborate descriptions of scenery and other mechanical devices. The initial storm scene features witches who fly about on wires, as does Ariel, throughout the play, at every opportunity. Tables vanish, and holes open onstage to give the guilty courtiers a view of the hell that awaits them. The fifth act includes a nuptial masque, and ends with a choral version of "Where the bee sucks, there suck I." Although D'Avenant had died in 1668, and Dryden did not help with the operatic version, the Restoration *Tempest* was understandably still considered their play. The text of the 1674 opera continued to be ascribed to them on the title pages of subsequent editions.

III

What are we to make of all this? The plot alterations inaugurated by Dryden and D'Avenant react in very significant ways upon the character of Prospero. Shakespeare's Prospero is, by his own account at least, an educator, a dealer in revelatory illusion, who would prefer not to acknowledge the coercive implications of his power. In Milan he puts "the manage of his state," the sordid business of day-to-day politics, in the hands of his practical, opportunistic brother; though he fiercely resents his overthrow, his forced isolation on the island really only completes his retirement, and gives him an opportunity to construct his own Arcadia.[7] In the masque he has performed for Miranda and Ferdinand at the end of Act IV, his imagination need not be constrained by the imperfections of reality. He is free to recreate the golden world:

> Earth's increase, foison plenty,
> Barns and garners never empty.
> Vines with clust'ring branches growing,
> Plants with goodly burden bowing;
> Spring come to you at the farthest
> In the very end of harvest.
>
> (ll. 110–116)[8]

Gonzalo, Prospero's good-hearted, foolish old supporter, is intuitively sensitive to his lord's version of the marvelous island—he is the only one to notice the miraculous freshness of his salt-drenched clothes—and in his plans for the island he effectively articulates Prospero's ideal:

> All things in common nature should produce
> Without sweat or endeavor. Treason, felony,
> Sword, pike, knife, gun, or need of any engine
> Would I not have; but nature should bring forth,
> Of its own kind, all foison, all abundance
> To feed my innocent people.
>
> (II.i.155–160)

Gonzalo would "with such perfection govern, sir / T'excel the golden age." His fellows ridicule his guileless refusal to recognize the necessity of labor or the demands of sexuality. "The latter end of his commonwealth forgets the beginning," exclaims the worldly wise Antonio, who understands the contradiction implicit in the idea of a governing power which never asserts itself against the subject's will.

Not surprisingly, the pastoral ambitions of Shakespeare's Prospero render him profoundly suspicious of anything unteachable or unassimilable—anything which, by demanding to be repressed, sets limits upon his power or calls his benevolence into question. He must resort to force or threats of force with Caliban, who rejects his tutelage; with Ariel, who forgets his debt of gratitude; with Alonso and Antonio before they repent of their usurpation; with Trinculo and Stephano when they attempt to overthrow him. Prospero never really need fear that these intransigent elements will successfully displace him from his position of power on the island. He resents them so violently because they force him to realize that his pastoral vision is anomalously managerial and competitive, that it can be enacted only at the expense of Caliban's or Ariel's version of Arcadia.

Miranda, the apt student, presents no problem until the arrival of Ferdinand divides her loyalties; when she protests against Prospero's treatment of her beloved, she elicits a violent outburst of rage. "What, my foot my tutor? . . . One word more shall make me chide thee, if not hate thee" (I.ii.467–476). Shakespeare's Prospero is anxious about sexuality, particularly female sexuality. The only mother on the island has been a witch whose pregnancy changed her sentence from death to exile, rendered her indestructible. For Prospero the mother is necessary but also stubbornly unassimilable, a potential competitor, and so he fears that Sycorax might be typical. When Miranda asks innocently, "Are you not my father?," he answers with peculiar insistence upon his wife's chastity.

Early in Shakespeare's play, Prospero reacts to all these "things of darkness" by repressing them—enslaving Caliban, subduing Ferdinand, threatening to peg a sullen Ariel in the entrails of an oak. In the Shakespearean version, though, Prospero's repressive impulses are eventually modified and overcome; thus many critics see him as a white magician, or even as a version of the author himself. For Prospero's power is essentially transformational; he aims to alter reality rather than fix it in some eternal shape. He must therefore be acutely conscious of time, of the need to seize the appropriate day. "I find my zenith doth attend upon / A most auspicious star" (I.ii.181–182). He accepts the limits set upon him by fate and by his contract with Ariel, and begins to interpret his own activity in terms of timely revelation, of fruition, rather than as the maintenance of a static order. He supervises the courtship of Miranda and Ferdinand by both encouraging and restraining it, forbidding premature indulgence in the interests of a decorous and fertile consummation. Eventually Prospero's acceptance of the relation between change and creativity modifies his vision of a timeless Arcadia, and leads him to a reconciliation with the un-Arcadian elements he initially finds most threatening. He forgives the courtiers, blesses the daughter he has lost, and acknowledges Caliban as his own.

The Dryden-D'Avenant Prospero begins with the same obsessions and anxieties; the second scene of the play, in which Prospero talks to Miranda, Ariel, and Caliban, is reproduced almost word for word. But Prospero's repressive tendencies are here exaggerated. He is kin to the neurotic and domineering father of a farce. While Shakespeare's Prospero selectively represses the intransigent elements of his world, the Dryden-D'Avenant Prospero makes no such discrimination. Hippolito, Dorinda, and Miranda, who "murmur not . . . but wonder" are kept in caves like Caliban, their freedom of movement severely restricted. Furthermore, the sexual aspects of Prospero's anxiety are developed at much greater length. Instead of dealing frankly with Hippolito or his daughters, he misrepresents vital information; the extreme sexual naïveté of the young people in the revised *Tempest* is the source of much of its comic humor as well as its near-tragedy. Knowing that the children will take metaphor for literal fact, this Prospero employs satiric tropes which betray his own state of mind. He tells his daughters that men are "all that you can imagine ill," more dreadful than "the curled Lion or the rugged Bear."

DORINDA: Do they run wild about the Woods?

PROSPERO: No, they are wild within Doors, in Chambers
And in Closets.

(II.iv.106–108)

To Hippolito, the new Prospero describes women as "the dangerous enemies of man":

> Their voices charm beyond the Nightingales;
> They are all enchantment, those who once behold 'em
> Are made their slaves forever.
>
> (II.iv.47–49)

The magic of sexual attraction competes with Prospero's art, and (like his own "enchantment") it seems to his mind a negative process, enslavement rather than liberation.

Dorinda, Miranda, and Hippolito discover their sexuality despite Prospero's injunctions: "I find it in my Nature," says Dorinda, "because my father has forbidden me" (II.iv.132–133). The new Prospero deals not in revelation, but in concealment; the progress of the plot toward marriage and forgiveness represents a violation rather than an expression of his will. D'Avenant and Dryden part company more and more drastically with the Shakespearean text, as they delimit a fundamentally static and beseiged character, without the means to cope with or reconcile himself to the manifold threats he perceives in his world. Their Prospero can never acknowledge his relationship to Caliban; at the end of the new play he merely orders the savage back into the cave.

In the fifth act of the original *Tempest,* Shakespeare's Prospero struggles to overcome his resentment against his brother and his brother's accomplices.

> Though with their high wrongs I am struck to th' quick,
> Yet with my nobler reason 'gainst my fury
> Do I take part. The rarer action is
> In virtue than in vengeance. They being penitent,
> The sole drift of my purpose doth extend
> Not a frown further.
>
> (V.i.25–30)

Conversion, not persecution, is now his aim. In the revised *Tempest,* on the other hand, the D'Avenant-Dryden Prospero struggles not to outgrow his anxieties and obsessions, but rather to reify them—to impose them on the people he controls. This Prospero torments people who are conscious of their sin from the outset. "Alas, I suffer justly for my crimes," Alonzo exclaims in the first scene, when he believes the ship will sink. Antonio ascribes the shipwreck to divine justice:

> Indeed we first broke truce with Heav'n;
> You to the waves an Infant Prince expos'd,
> And on the waves have lost an only Son;
> I did usurp my Brother's fertile lands, and now
> Am cast upon this desert Isle.
>
> (II.i.21–25)

The new Prospero's persecution of the sinners—much more relentless than in the Shakespearean *Tempest*—thus has no particular moral or educational purpose. His power is essentially sinister, as he admits when he calls upon his spirits in a crisis. "I thought no more to use their aids; (I'm curs'd because I us'd it)" (IV.iii.159–160). He is not inclined to forgiveness even as the play begins to close; after Ferdinand has wounded Hippolito he tells Alonzo:

> Blood calls for blood; your Ferdinand shall dye,
> And I in bitterness have sent for you,
> To have the sudden joy of seeing him alive,
> And then the greater grief to see him die.
> (IV.iii.150–153)

Not Prospero's will, but the "blessed day," the miraculous and unanticipated circumstance of Hippolito's recovery, transforms the Restoration *Tempest* from revenge tragedy to comic romance.

It is possible to imagine a play in which the new Prospero's primitive and unself-conscious moral nature would become the occasion for satire, but this does not seem to be the point of the Dryden-D'Avenant *Tempest*. In Shakespeare's version Prospero's Arcadian ideal is not idiosyncratic; Ariel, Gonzalo, Caliban, Miranda, and Ferdinand all articulate some version of it. In the D'Avenant-Dryden adaptation, though, the pastoral no longer constitutes a shared ideal—indeed, it does not seem available as an ideal at all. Gonzalo's speeches are cut, Ariel's songs deleted or shortened. Caliban is no longer mysteriously susceptible to beauty, but prefers his sister Sycorax because she is bigger than Prospero's daughters. Lacking the Arcadian vision, which calls into question the competitive, coercive, and manipulative aspects of power, the ruler has no impulse to reconcile his activity with factors that limit and define it.

In the Shakespearean *Tempest* the courtiers are returning from the marriage of Alonso's daughter, Claribel, and the king of Tunis. Gonzalo, spokesman for Arcadia, identifies Tunis with ancient Carthage, and compares Claribel with "the widow Dido." The Virgilian reference is important, because Aeneas's conquest in Italy depends upon his rejection of the distraction Dido represents. He must repress the demands of his sexuality in order to found his city—a city which, in later years, will come into its own as it once again resists the Punic threat. Against such a background, the marriage of Claribel represents a new sort of foreign relations—a political strategy no longer repressive or competitive. Tunis-Carthage is now accepted rather than resisted; it is the solution of romantic comedy rather than of tragedy or epic. It is not surprising that the shallow cynics Antonio and Sebastian, who mock Gonzalo's naïve pastoral vision, reject also his identification of Tunis with Carthage, and all the consequences implicit in that identification. And it is not surprising that in the D'Avenant-Dryden *Tempest,* the goal of the sea voyage has changed. These courtiers, "in defense of Christianity," have been fighting to drive the Moors out of Portugal—not to wed but to war with Africans upon the competitive Virgilian principle.

In other words, the revised *Tempest* contains no model for the Shakespearean Prospero's ultimate gesture of acceptance and reconciliation. There is no process by which love might be related to death, or poetry to passion; all change is thus of necessity revolutionary or destructive. The Shakespearean Ariel sings "Full fathom five thy father lies" to Ferdinand as he leads him to Miranda, so that the prince decides that she must be "the goddess / On whom these airs attend." In the revised version the funeral song no longer leads to Miranda, and the new Ferdinand unlike the earlier one finds the song simply "mournful." The link between death and sexuality is severed, and Ferdinand cannot now find the rich and strange metamorphoses of his father's drowned body either wonderful or reassuring.

It is, therefore, highly significant that Dryden and D'Avenant omit in their revision the masque of Ceres with which Shakespeare's Prospero celebrates his daughter's betrothal. In the original *Tempest,* Prospero attempts to supply a heretofore missing maternal principle, which in the first act he had been prone to regard as competitive with his own creative and procreative power. The heroine of the masque is the fertile grain goddess, the original patroness of the unproblematic golden world over which Prospero wishes he could preside. Ceres' productivity, though, is dependent upon her daughter, Persephone, and limited by her daughter's affiliation with the king of the underworld, the principle of death. Early in the masque, Juno and Ceres banish Venus and Cupid, the rival mother and child, who represent the darker, uncontrolled aspects of sexuality; and Ceres excludes winter and death from the blessing she gives Miranda and Ferdinand: "Spring come to you at the farthest / In the very end of harvest" (IV.i.115–116). Ceres does not mention her absence. But the proximity of love and death, creation and destruction, is reasserted in the harvest dance which follows.

The nymphs who were cold and chaste at the beginning of the masque are made "fresh" by their encounter with the phallic sicklemen, whose death-dealing "grim reaper" aspect is inseparable from their virile and life-giving sexuality. The sweaty reapers represent all the "things of darkness" which threaten Prospero's Arcadian vision—the necessity of labor, the necessity of death, the necessity of passion—and also the ultimate inseparability of the things of darkness from the things of light. In this scene the proximity of nymphs and reapers reminds Prospero of Caliban's proximity, and of the plot to usurp his kingly power. The same proximity of idealism and necessity, creativity and destructiveness, will also lead Prospero, finally, to acknowledge Caliban as his own.

The Shakespearean Prospero thus uses pastoral to transcend pastoral— or at least to achieve a more mature and comprehensive vision than Gonzalo's naïve utopianism will permit. But while the original Prospero dreams of a world in which repression is unnecessary, the Restoration Prospero, entirely devoid of the Arcadian impulse, dreams instead of a world in which repression is merely unproblematic. In the 1674 operatic *Tempest* he, too, stages a masque—the festivities upon which the play ends.[9] Not surprisingly, its symbolism differs markedly from Shakespeare's. The new masque begins as Amphitrite asks her husband Neptune for calm seas. Good weather is described entirely in negative terms: "Tethys no furrows now shall wear, / Oceanus no wrinkles on his brow." Neptune's control over the elements clearly depends upon sheer power—"You I'll obey," sings Aeolus, "Who at one stroke can make / With your dread trident, the whole earth to shake." Authority here takes the same form as Prospero's did in the first act. All the obstreperous winds are "boistrous prisoners" safe in their "dark caverns," just as Miranda, Dorinda, Hippolito, and Caliban were once sequestered. "To your prisons below / Down, down you must go," Aeolus commands; "We / Will soon obey you cheerfully," reply the tritons and nereids, acquiescing with a thoroughness that Dorinda, Hippolito, Miranda, Caliban, and even Ariel have been unable to match. The Dryden-D'Avenant Prospero learns nothing in the course of the play; in the operatic version, the masque at the end of the fifth act only emphasizes his intransigence.

<h1 style="text-align:center">IV</h1>

The Restoration audience could not have preferred the revised version of *The Tempest* because it was more poetic, complex, or imaginative than the original. It is tempting to think, in light of the foregoing analysis, that they did find it more plausible. The D'Avenant-Dryden adaptation is much more explicitly and exclusively political than the Shakespeare play. The puns on "art" in I.ii. are cut, and so are the two speeches in Shakespeare's *Tempest* most obviously concerned with artistry—the address to Ferdinand after the masque ("we are such stuff as dreams are made on"), and Prospero's renunciation speech, his promise to break his rod and drown his book. In the Restoration adaptation, however, Prospero's expanded political role compensates somewhat for his lack of artistic self-consciousness. As he tells Alonzo when he resolves to execute Ferdinand:

> Here I am plac'd by Heav'n, here I am Prince,
> Though you have dispossessed me of my *Millain*.
> (IV.iii.148–149)

He has seven subjects to the Shakespearean Prospero's three—seven subjects whose interaction constantly threatens to overwhelm his authority. In the Restoration *Tempest,* though a political role is no longer synonymous with an artistic or priestly role, politics alone is enough to keep one busy.

Since the revised play is so determinedly a play about government, current political theory might help illuminate reasons for the differences between the two Prospero's, and for the appeal of the later conception to Restoration audiences. In 1612, when Shakespeare's *Tempest* was first performed, James I's earliest theoretical tracts on kingship were little more than a decade old. In *Basilikon Doron* and *The Trew Law of Free Monarchy,* both published at the end of the sixteenth century, James had maintained that he held his royal position by divine right. He used as a supplementary argument a patriarchal theory of kingship which derived the state from the family, and conceived of kingly authority as an extension of fatherly power. Patriarchalists take a limited view of the subject's freedom, maintaining that he has no more right to choose his ruler than children have to choose their fathers. This restriction need not be irksome, however, since the king's fatherly care is originally and ideally loving, and only incidentally coercive. Thus Shakespeare's Prospero, with his vision of an unoppressive golden age, resents Caliban's refusal to accept the role of adoptive child.

The idea that the origin of states is familial was in fact a very old one.[10] But in this particular form it became an important polemical weapon in the seventeenth century, when the Stuarts and their supporters found patriarchalism an attractive basis for their absolutist claims. The theory retained adherents until the end of the century, when the Whiggish John Locke dealt it a death blow,[11] but it had met with fierce opposition even before the Civil War. Populists like Winstanley, and even some absolutists like Hobbes and Digges, wanted to replace the patriarchalist doctrine with a theory of a conventional state—a government based upon a contract among free individuals, rather than one based upon naturally occurring hierarchical relationships.[12] The notion of the father-king came increasingly under attack in the war years and after, and patriarchal theorists became increasingly defensive in their pronouncements. As the century wore on, patriarchalism seemed increasingly nostalgic—an attempt to recover the lost monarchical privilege enjoyed by the early Stuarts.

Clearly, when a theory like this one is current and controversial, a political reading of *The Tempest* would make Prospero a version of the patriarchalist father-king. But in the 1660s, when Dryden and D'Avenant are collaborating on their revision of *The Tempest,* the figure of the father-king—at least in its more extravagant or extreme forms—is already becoming anachronistic. It is not surprising that the D'Avenant-Dryden Prospero seems so threatened by change, so willing to employ repressive tactics in order to maintain his shaky authority.

Shakespeare's Prospero learns to allow for and accept unassimilable and potentially competitive elements—the maternal principle, for example, omitted by patriarchal theorists like James Maxwell, who render the fifth commandment as "Honora patrem etc."[13] But he can afford to be generous. Trinculo and Stephano, or villains like Sebastian, think in terms of usurpation; they implicitly accept a monarchical system of government even while they attempt to subvert the individual in charge. Kingship as an institution is taken for granted.

The low characters in the Dryden-D'Avenant *Tempest* are not even aware of Prospero's existence until the end of the fifth act. Instead, they make their own arrangements among themselves:

> MUSTACHO: Our ship is sunk, and we can never get home agen: We must e'en turn Salvages, and the next that catches his Fellow may eat him.
>
> VENTOSO: No, no, let us have a Government.
>
> (II.iii.48–51)

Stephano appoints himself duke, and makes Mustacho and Ventoso his viceroys. "Agreed, agreed!" they shout together. Although their pre-governmental state of nature is a sham, since their relations on the island are based on prior relations aboard ship, the low characters obviously believe they are constituting a state on contractual grounds.[14] They immediately and hilariously encounter the difficulties contractual theorists always take pains to treat: the problem of who could "speak for the people" in the absence of any constituted authority or procedures, and the problem of a person who refuses to accept the contract. "I'll have no laws," Trincalo declares, and goes off to form his own government with Caliban as his subject and Caliban's sister as his queen. Main plot and subplot in the Restoration *Tempest* seem curiously exclusive, at least when compared with the tightly constructed Shakespearean model. In fact, though, the very detachment of the low characters constitutes a threat more subtle, but also more dangerous, than the threat of usurpation in the Shakespeare play. The Dryden-D'Avenant Prospero is besieged, not in his person, as is the Shakespearean Prospero, but in his role. The ideological basis of his authority is subverted by the possibility that the patriarchal conception of monarchy is bankrupt.

The utter failure of the sailors' attempts at self-government is important, though, because it helps define sources for the conservatism of post-war monarchists like Dryden and D'Avenant. The revised *Tempest* is not in the least subversive of the monarchical principle; it merely refuses to grant to the king and father special prerogatives in other kinds of endeavor. Prospero with all his faults is a just and orderly ruler, and the postwar royalists consider justice and order the primary virtues of the good sovereign. The conception of a Prospero who is limited but nonetheless efficient is typical of Dryden's pessimistic conservatism.[15] In *Absalom and Achitophel* and *The Hind and the Panther* he argues for traditional forms not because he has illusions about their transcendent goodness, but because he believes that radical change necessarily brings about worse evils. Any tradition, any constituted authority, is better than none. Like his Prospero, he has a lively suspicion of lurking chaos; the source of satiric vigor in poems like *MacFlecknoe* and *The Medall* lies largely in the tension between immoral disorder and a justly repressive authority.

Dryden sides with the forces of order, but he defines that order carefully; Charles II is no omnipotent Shakespearean Prospero, but "a king, who is just and moderate in his nature, and who rules according to the laws, whom God has made happy by joining the temper of his soul to the Constitution of his government."[16] Charles's virtue, for Dryden, lies not in his extravagant assertions of power, but in his willingness to limit that assertion. Shakespeare throughout his long career is fascinated by the managerial personality, whether good or evil; in Dryden's plays absolutist aspirations are inevitably and unmistakably foul both in their sources and their effects.

This is not to say that Dryden is insensitive to a conception of authority which is both more ambitious and less coercive. His prologue begins with a recognition, somewhat like the Shakespearean Prospero's, that creative and destructive potentials are inseparable:

> As when a Tree's cut down, the secret root
> Lives under ground, and thence new branches shoot,
> So, from old *Shakespeare's* honoured dust, this day
> Springs up and buds a new reviving Play.
>
> (ll. 1–4)

Shakespeare, not Prospero, is the ultimate patriarchalist authority figure, embodying the monarch, the father, the artist, and the magician all at once:

> *Shakespeare,* who (taught by none) did first impart
> To Fletcher wit, to labouring Jonson art,
> He, Monarch-like, gave those his subjects law,
> And is the nature which they paint and draw.
> But *Shakespeare's* Magick could not copy'd be,
> Within that Circle none durst walk but he.
>
> (ll. 6–9, 19–20)

This kind of omnipotence, however, is both unique—an attribute of the creatively heroic ancestor—and archaic, inimitable in a self-conscious modern world.

> I must confess t'was bold nor would you now
> That liberty to vulgar wits allow
> Which works by Magick supernatural things:
> But *Shakespeare's* pow'r is sacred as a Kings.
> Those legends from old Priesthood were received,
> And he then writ, as people then believed.
>
> (ll. 21–26)

Modern artist and audience lack the confident vision conferred by the old unquestioning belief—they can recapture it, if at all, only in a prologue's moment of sentimental nostalgia. Perhaps a sense of loss always accompanies the evocation of traditional simplicity, but here that loss seems so absolute and irrevocable that the naïve golden world of fifty years ago lacks any contemporary urgency at all. However, regretfully, the adapters find that they must shoulder aside Shakespeare's central concerns, or at best grant them a marginal status. The fundamental problems are different now, and demand a new, if in some ways inferior, treatment.

In fact, though, when D'Avenant and Dryden separate Prospero's kingly authority from any special innovative genius, they do not so much repudiate the possibility of political creativity as relocate it. The real hero of the Dryden-D'Avenant *Tempest* is Ariel, who believes that Prospero's power over him is unjust. "Why should a mortal by Enchantments hold / In chains a spirit of aetherial mold?" (IV.iii.274–275). Nevertheless, he obeys Prospero in very trying circumstances. Finally, when Prospero assumes that Hippolito is dead, and resolves to execute Ferdinand, Ariel on his own initiative succeeds in resurrecting the wounded boy. Ariel, not Prospero, is responsible for the happy denouement; Ariel, not Prospero, learns to exploit repressive circumstances in productive ways. The potential for a creative political order resides not with the benevolent monarch, but with the loyal, resourceful subject.

Like the treatment of Prospero, the new emphasis on Ariel in the revised *Tempest* has parallels in Dryden's other work. In the Shakespearean *Tempest*, Prospero's sense of his imaginative resources is bound up with his sense of control over other people. Dryden, however, characteristically makes a sharp distinction between political power and creative potency, and locates the latter not with the monarch but with the subject. In *Astraea Redux, Annus Mirabilis, Absalom and Achitophel,* and *Britannia Redivivia,* poetic vocation finds its best and fullest employment in the celebration of the sovereign. The panegyric in *Annus Mirabilis* becomes an alternative to "serving King and Country" in the wars;[17] it is the literary version of a service required of all loyal and capable subjects. Poets are not kings, nor kings poets; Flecknoe's pretenses to sovereignty only emphasize his creative bankruptcy, and in the preface to *All for Love* Dionysius and Nero (bad kings both) render themselves ridiculous by aspiring to poetic laurels.[18] Ariel, whose creative initiative preserves the comic ending to the revised *Tempest,* is a type of the imaginatively loyal subject so crucial to Dryden's sense of himself as a citizen and, eventually, as laureate.

The revised *Tempest,* in other words, is the product of a staunch but distinctively Restoration brand of conservatism. Politicized by the traumatic events of the mid-seventeenth century, D'Avenant and Dryden believe that between Shakespeare and themselves, 1612 and 1667, there is a great gulf set. They find themselves forced to reconceive Prospero and his subjects, in order to bring them into line with their version of a well-run state. This kind of preoccupation cannot have seemed anomalous or unintelligible to contemporaries. Certainly the published script of the operatic version indicates that the set designer, at least, was fully aware of the play's political implications. The published text of the opera lovingly describes the new scenery:

> the Curtain rises, and discovers a new Frontispiece, join'd to the great Pilasters, on each side of the Stage. This frontispiece is a noble Arch, supported by large wreathed Columns of the Corinthian order; the wreathings of the Columns are beautifi'd with Roses wound round them, and several Cupids flying about them. On the Cornice, just over the Capitals, sits a Figure with a Trumpet in one hand, and a Palm in the other, representing *Fame*. A little further on the same Cornice, on each side of the Compass-pediment, lie a Lion and a Unicorn, the supporters of the Royal Arms of *England*. In the middle of the arch are several Angels, holding the King's Arms, as if they were placing them in the midst of that Compasspediment. Behind this is the Scene, which represents a thick Cloudy Sky, a very Rocky Coast, and a Tempestuous Sea in perpetual Agitation.[19]

This explicit reference to England's real king must be intended as a sort of defense, as a way of pointing out the differences where art and life might otherwise seem uncomfortably close. Charles II is *not* Prospero, the frontispiece claims. Its tranquil, symmetrical design flatly contradicts the scene behind it, which depicts nature confused, dangerous, "in perpetual Agitation." The frontispiece makes traditional claims for the king's stable, central position in the natural and divine order of things. Its iconology recalls precisely those myths of royal omnipotence central to the prewar court masque—the myths so conscientiously purged from the revised *Tempest*.

As the description indicates, this frontispiece acts as a sort of visual frame for the dramatic action. It is, on one hand, a way of containing and limiting the significance of the play—a warning to the audience not to confuse the impotent, repressive Restoration Prospero with the real powers that be. Mediating between the play and the audience, it emphasizes the unreality of the dramatic spectacle, and thus keeps the potentially frightening implications of the fiction within reassuring bounds. However, the frontispiece is also (like the prologue celebrating Shakespeare) a marginal, nostalgic element, subverted by the action at center stage. The frame can seem not more true or reliable than the dramatic fiction, but less—a sort of *de post facto* window dressing which unfortunately stresses just those analogies it was apparently designed to defeat.

One suspects, in fact, that the ambivalence of this new scenery, which denied and at the same time emphasized the contemporary relevance of the Restoration *Tempest,* constituted part of its appeal. In an era when the Stuart mythology seemed increasingly inappropriate, as well as indispensable, the average Restoration playgoer must have been keenly—even painfully—sensitive to the various claims of competing ideologies. A play which acknowledged such difficulties, but which also transmuted them into gorgeous and apparently escapist spectacle, must have been extraordinarily compelling. If the Restoration audience greeted the revised *Tempest* with unparalleled enthusiasm, it is probably because Dryden and D'Avenant, and the operatic producers after them, managed to address the hopes and fears of large numbers of their contemporaries.

Notes

1. *The Diary of Samuel Pepys,* ed. R. Latham and W. Matthews (London, 1970), IX, 48 (3 February 1668).
2. John Downes, *Roscius Anglicanus* (London, 1708), p. 34. A Restoration "opera" was not entirely sung; it was usually a lavishly staged production involving vocal and instrumental music, and spoken dialogue as well. In its proportion of speech to song it was more like a modern musical than like a modern opera.
3. *Shakespeare Improved* (Cambridge, Mass., 1927), pp. 201, 203.
4. *Dryden as an Adapter of Shakespeare* (London, 1922), p. 17.
5. The best discussion is in the introduction to the 1667 *Tempest* in Maximilian Novak and George Guffey, eds., *The Works of John Dryden* (Berkeley, Calif., 1970), X, 319–343. All line references to the D'Avenant-Dryden *Tempest* are to this edition. Montague Summers, in *Shakespeare Adaptations* (London, 1922), p. cvii, describes the way the revised *Tempest* makes use of the Restoration stage. While helpful, some of the claims these critics make raise new questions. If D'Avenant and Dryden are writing neoclassic comedy, why do they observe the unities of time and action so much more loosely than Shakespeare does in his very tightly constructed play? If their audience is too sophisticated to accept Shakespeare's implausibilities, why does it applaud the far greater offense to reason represented by Ariel's magical cure of a mortally wounded boy, or the devils impersonating Fraud, Pride, Rapine, and Murther who dance before the guilty courtiers? If the collaborators wish to take advantage of the new scenic resources of the Restoration stage, why do they omit Shakespeare's masque of Ceres, a fine opportunity for the display of theatrical magnificence?
6. Roughly, the Shakespearean material is disposed as follows: the second half of Shakespeare's I.ii becomes II.ii and III.v in the Dryden-D'Avenant version; Shakespearean material from II.ii and V.i is incorporated with considerable variation into II.iii, III.i, and V.ii of the adapted play. Four scenes (I.i, I.ii, II.i, and II.ii) begin in the same way as their Shakespearean counterparts, but diverge from the earlier play as they proceed. Acts II and IV of the Shakespearean *Tempest* have no equivalent in the Dryden-D'Avenant version. II.iv, II.v, III.iii, III.iv, III.vi, V.i, most of V.ii, and all of the Act IV in the revision have no equivalent in Shakespeare.
7. The importance of pastoral to *The Tempest* has received considerable attention. The major treatments are: Frank Kermode, Introduction to *The Tempest,* Arden Shakespeare (London, 1964), xiv–lxiii. This introduction was first published in 1954. Stephen Orgel, "New Uses of Adversity: Tragic Experience in *The Tempest,*" *In Defense of Reading,* ed. R. Poirier and R. Brower (New York, 1962), pp. 110–132. Northrop Frye, *A Natural Perspective* (New York, 1965), pp. 149–159. Frye also expounds his views on pastoral in *The Tempest* in his introduction to the play in *The Pelican Shakespeare,* ed. Alfred Harbage (London, 1969), pp. 1369–1372. Harry Berger, "Miraculous Harp: A Reading of Shakespeare's *Tempest,*" *ShStud,* V (1969), 253–283. David Young, *The Heart's Forest: A Study of Shakespeare's Pastoral Plays* (New Haven, Conn., 1972), pp. 148–191. Thomas McFarland, *Shakespeare's Pastoral Comedy* (Chapel Hill, N.C., 1972), pp. 146–175. Kermode, Frye, and McFarland emphasize the positive aspects of the pastoral vision and are extremely sympathetic to Prospero. Berger, who stresses the neurotic element in Prospero's constitution, makes a good case for a "darker" reading of *The Tempest,* but I think he misreads the final act. Orgel perceptively distinguishes between Prospero's

experience and the experience of the other characters in *The Tempest,* and shows how Prospero's perspective differs from the perspective of the audience. Young is more interested in the theatrical self-consciousness of *The Tempest* than in the issues that directly concern me here, but he agrees that the play moves toward a recognition that "apparently unalterable opposites . . . are mutually complementary, aspects of the same thing" (p. 170).

8.   All line references to the Shakespeare play are to *The Pelican Shakespeare,* ed. Alfred Harbage (London, 1969).

9.   The masque of Amphitrite and Neptune is printed in all seventeenth-century editions of the revised *Tempest* after 1674. It is most easily available to the modern scholar in *The Complete Works of Thomas Shadwell,* ed. Montague Summers (London, 1927), II, 265–267. Shadwell was probably responsible for the additions to the D'Avenant-Dryden script made for the operatic production.

10.   See, for example, Aristotle, who begins his *Politics* with a discussion of the household, arguing that the "elementary relationships" of husband and wife, parent and child, master and servant precede both logically and temporally the more complicated relations among the citizens of the *polis.* But Aristotle considers patriarchal kingship only one of several kinds (see III.xiv.14). For an account of the fortunes of patriarchalism during the Civil War, Commonwealth, and Restoration, see Gordon Schochet, *Patriarchalism in Political Thought* (New York, 1975), pp. 159–224.

11.   John Locke, *The First Treatise of Government* (London, 1690).

12.   Thomas Hobbes, *Leviathan, or the Matter, Form, and Power of a Commonwealth, ecclesiastical and civil* (London, 1651), pts. I and II. Dudley Digges,*The Unlawfulness of subjects taking up armes against their soveraigne . . .* (Oxford, 1643).

13.   *Sacro Sancta Regem Majestas, or, the Sacred and Royal Prerogative of Christian Kings* (Oxford, 1644), p. 161.

14.   For more information on Dryden and Hobbes, see Louis Teeter, "The Dramatic Use of Hobbes' Political Ideas," pp. 341–373, and John A. Winterbottom, "The Place of Hobbesian Ideas in Dryden's Tragedies," pp. 374–396, in *Essential Articles for the Study of John Dryden,* ed. H. T. Swedenberg (Hamden, Conn., 1966).

15.   I will concentrate on Dryden in the following few pages, partly because his work is more familiar to the general reader, and also because, according to his introduction to the revised *Tempest,* D'Avenant was concerned less with adapting the main plot than with devising scenes for the low characters. The prologue on Shakespeare is entirely Dryden's work. However, the ideas that I attribute to Dryden here are commonplace enough in the later seventeenth century; they are shared not only by D'Avenant but by many Restoration conservatives—including, most likely, the majority of playgoers in the 1660s and '70s. For D'Avenant's simultaneous loyalty to, and disenchantment with, Charles II, see Alfred Harbage, *Sir William D'Avenant: Poet Venturer 1606–1668* (Philadelphia, 1935), pp. 135–141. David Ogg, in *England in the Reign of Charles II* (Oxford, 1934), gives a thorough and entertaining account of the way political and theoretical issues intersect during the later part of the seventeenth century. See particularly I. 139–141, and II.450–523. The importance of Dryden's politics for his literary practice has received a great deal of attention. See, e.g., Bernard Schilling, *Dryden and the Conservative Myth: A Reading of Absalom and Achitophel* (New Haven, Conn., 1961), pp. 1–95; Alan Roper, *Dryden's Poetic Kingdom* (London, 1965), pp. 50–103; Ann T. Barbeau, *The Intellectual Design of John Dryden's Heroic Plays* (New Haven, Conn., 1970), pp. 3–54; Stephen N. Zwicker, *Dryden's Political Poetry* (Providence, R.I., 1972); Isabel Rivers, *The Poetry of Conservatism 1600–1745* (Cambridge, Eng., 1973), pp. 127–174; Sanford Budick, *The Poetry of Civilization* (New Haven, Conn., 1974), pp. 81–110.

16.   Dedication to *All for Love,* a play not yet available in the California Dryden. It is reproduced in *Dryden: The Dramatic Works,* ed. Montague Summers (London, 1932), IV, 177.

17.   *The Works of John Dryden,* I, 50.

18.   Preface to *All for Love, Dryden: The Dramatic Works,* IV, 185.

19.   *The Complete Works of Thomas Shadwell,* ed. Montague Summers, II, 199.

Dryden's *Conquest of Granada* and the Dutch Wars

JAMES THOMPSON

In "Of Heroic Plays," John Dryden proposes that "an Heroick Play ought to be an imitation, in little of an Heroick Poem" (11:10),[1] and accordingly Eugene Waith writes that "The design of *The Conquest of Granada,* then, belongs squarely in a tradition of heroic poem which has been importantly modified by romance."[2] I want to argue that the accustomed context of epic is a misleading frame in which to understand Dryden's play. Instead of employing a universal model of heroism, we need to historicize more particularly the concept of heroism in this play.[3] Almanzor is neither a generic epic hero, as in the traditional reading, nor is he an embodiment of a Hobbesian man in a state of nature who is socialized to Christian culture, as in the other conventional treatment; rather, he functions as an emblem of the military conquistador who, under the demands of a budding colonial empire, must be replaced with or translated into a new type of hero, a prototype of the colonial administrator.

That is to say, I do not want to read this play within its accustomed context of epic; rather than connect *The Conquest of Granada* to the *Aeneid* or the later variants in Tasso and Ariosto, I would rather connect it to Dryden's own, more immediate work, *Amboyna, or the cruelties of the Dutch to the English merchants* (1673).[4] The later play, as its title suggests, reads like transparent war propaganda, but the two plays raise some elementary questions of literary history: what has the grand and heroic *Conquest* to do with the crude and topical *Amboyna*? Is the one simply shameless and embarrassing propaganda while the other aspires to epic grandeur? Do the vulgar *Amboyna* and the Virgilian *Conquest* share the same moment in political and literary history? By reading both of these plays, not just the nakedly topical one, within the context of the Dutch wars, we will be in a position to evaluate the nature of heroism in Dryden's best known heroic play, *The Conquest of Granada.*

The Conquest of Granada revolves around the Spanish defeat of the Moors in the fifteenth century, an event long celebrated by English and European

Reprinted with permission from "Dryden's *Conquest of Granada* and the Dutch Wars," *The Eighteenth Century: Theory and Interpretation,* vol. 31, Texas Tech University Press (1990), pp. 211–225.

historians as the final conquest of Islam, a vanquishing forever of the military power of Moorish culture which had threatened European stability for centuries. This conquest is presented as a making the world safe for Christianity, a defeat, not just of a rival military power, but rather a defeat of the pagan barbarians, in effect, a kind of reversal or repair of the fall of Rome. In the words of Anne Barbeau, "The larger historical design of *The Conquest,* therefore, involves the expansion of Christianity in Europe, this time at the expense of Islam instead of heathendom."[5] The conquest of Granada, then, served to mark for a second time the extension of European hegemony, a conquest, not just of the Iberian peninsula, but of the world—a making of the world safe for European Empire, just as the Roman Empire had once before. All of this, so far, is obvious enough in Dryden's play: its hero is restored as a lost Christian son, while the barbaric world of the infidels is reclaimed by its rightful and righteous rulers, Ferdinand and Isabella, the true Christian monarchs. The opening of Part II of *The Conquest of Granada* foregrounds all of these issues of conquest, empire, and religious hegemony. King Ferdinand celebrates his conquest as the historical origin of empire:

> At length the time is come, when *Spain* shall be
> From the long Yoke of *Moorish* Tyrants free.
> All Causes seem to second our design;
> And Heav'n and Earth in their destruction join.
> When Empire in its Childhood first appears,
> A watchful Fate o'resees its tender years;
> Till, grown more strong, it thrusts and stretches out,
> And Elbows all the Kingdoms round about:
> The place thus made for its first breathing free,
> It moves again for ease and Luxury:
> Till, swelling by degrees, it has possest
> The greater space; and now crowds up the rest.
> When from behind, there starts some petty State;
> And pushes on its now unwieldy fate:
> Then, down the precipice of time it goes,
> And sinks in minutes, which in Ages rose.
>
> (1.1.1–16; 11:105–6)

Queen Isabella responds, not in terms of the temporal and temporary rule of military conquest, of the cyclical rise and fall of empire, but rather in terms of the eternal sway of Christian empire:

> Should bold *Columbus* in his search succeed,
> And find those Beds in which bright Metals Breed;
> Tracing the Sun, who seems to steal away,
> That Miser-like, he might alone survey
> The Wealth, which he in Western Mines did lay;
> Not all that shining Ore could give my heart

> The joy, this Conquer'd Kingdom will impart:
> Which, rescu'd from these Misbelievers hands;
> Shall now, at once shake off its double bands:
> At once to freedom and true faith restor'd:
> Its old Religion, and its antient Lord.
>
> (1.1.1–36; 11:106)[6]

To what purpose does Dryden, a didactic and political writer in every-thing he undertook, put these visions of the restoration of empire? And why, we might want to ask, would Dryden have turned to this fifteenth-century event in 1670? Why this siege of 1492, and furthermore, why in 1670 and not 1665 or 1675 or 1685? The events of the early 1670s suggest that Dry-den may have had a more immediate empire in mind, for the two parts of *The Conquest of Granada* appeared in between the second and third Dutch wars, in fact, on the eve of the third Dutch War, another war involving the Spanish Empire's claim to another small possession, Holland. The First Part of *The Conquest of Granada* was actually composed nearer to the occasion of the sec-ond Dutch war than its first production indicates, for the play was ready a full year earlier, in 1669, but was put off on account of pregnancy among the King's Company's actresses.[7] Dryden draws the explicit comparison between his characters and the events of the second Dutch war in his Dedication to the Duke of York, imaging him as the very "patern" of Almanzor and heroism (11:7), on the basis of his recent valiant performance at the battle of Lowest-oft.[8] Indeed, this Dedication deliberately places the play between the two wars, looking backwards to the last war while anticipating future conflict with the same antagonists:

> When the *Hollanders,* not contented to withdraw themselves from the obedi-ence which they ow'd their lawful Sovereign, affronted those by whose Charity they were first protected: and, (being swell'd up to a preheminence of Trade, by a supine negligence on our side, and a sordid parsimony on their own,) dar'd to dispute the Sovereignty of the Seas; the eyes of three nations were then cast on you: and, by the joynt suffrage of King and People, you were chosen to revenge their common injuries . . . and when our former enemies again provoke us, you will again solicite fate to provide you another Navy to overcome.
>
> (11:4–5)

Taken by itself, however, this passage and this dedication are somewhat misleading, for they represent the last conflict as a glorious victory. But the immediate memory of the second Anglo-Dutch war was anything but heroic, coinciding with the plague and the London fire, and ending with the humili-ating raid by the Dutch admiral de Ruyter and his burning of the English fleet on the Medway.[9] For Londoners and play-goers, this was no distant war: both Dryden, in the *Essay of Dramatick Poesie,* and Samuel Pepys, in his *Diary,* write that Londoners could hear the guns from the battle of Lowestoft. Pepys reports, "All this day, by all people upon the River and almost everywhere else hereabout, were heard the Guns, our two fleets for certain being engaged" (June 3, 1666; 6:116).[10] Furthermore, the evidence of the effects of war still lay about on the streets: Pepys, our best known play-goer of the period, was intimately acquainted with the miseries visited on the workers of the Dutch wars: "Did business, though not much, at the office, because of the horrible Crowd and lamentable moan of the poor seamen that lie starving in the streets for lack of money—which doth trouble and perplex me to the heart. And more at noon, when we were to go through them; for then a whole hundred of them fallowed us—some cursing, some swearing, and some praying to us" (Oct. 7, 1665; 6:255).[11] This play, however, offers a very different vision of war in Almanzor's military prowess as noble sport:

> We have not fought enough; they fly too soon:
> And I am griev'd the noble sport is done.
> This onely man of all whom chance did bring
> [Pointing to Ozmyn.]
> To meet my Arms, was worth the Conquering.
> (3.1.270–72; 11:53–4)

In the face of what must have been terrible immediate memories, *The Conquest of Granada* functions ideologically as a glorification of war, something along the lines of *Top Gun,* which, through its celebration of military hardware and service, serves to efface the more humiliating memories of our most recent war. In essence, then, *The Conquest* seeks to reheroize military action, rehabilitating it after the humiliations of the second Dutch war.

Dryden's next serious play after *Conquest II* is *Amboyna, or the cruelties of the Dutch to the English merchants* (1673). Only *The Assignation, or Love in a Nunnery* (1672) intervenes; this is an anti-Catholic and, by extension, an anti-French farce, in which the nunnery, a *"Seraglio* of the Godly" (4.1.11; 11:366), and Catholic authority are consistently sexualized and thereby trivialized. But even *The Assignation* is relatively subtle compared to *Amboyna,* a play which resuscitates the memory of a sixty-year-old injury by the Dutch to English trade in the East Indies, a call to remember a long forgotten *Maine.* With its violent and hostile nationalism, *Amboyna* glorifies war in more obvious ways than does *The Conquest:* "Who ever beheld so noble a sight / As this so brave, so bloody Sea Fight" (376).[12] The glorious and heroic visions of empire in *The Conquest* need to be compared with the more gritty and mercantile topicality of *Amboyna.* The latter is a straightforward play produced to fan the flames of war hysteria by representing the "Barb'rous, ungrateful Dutch" (392) as treacherous, greedy, and cruel, especially to their English benefactors. Their Protestant solidarity not withstanding, all antagonism between the Dutch and the English stems from rivalry over trade. In the opening exposition, one Dutchman, Van Herring, shows some reluctance to support a plan "to cut all of their [English] throats, and seize all of their Effects within this Island," because "they were the first discovers of this Isle, first Traded hither, and show'd us the way." Two other Dutchmen, Fiscal and Harman, celebrate Dutch perfidy to the English:

FISCAL: I grant you that, nay more, that by composition, made after many long and tedious quarrels, they were to have a third part of the Traffick, we to build Forts, and they to contribute to the charge.

HARMAN: Which we have so increas'd each year upon 'em, we being in power, and therefore Judges of the Cost, that we exact what e're we please, still more then half the charge, and on pretence of their Non-payment, or the least delay, do often stop their Ships, detain their Goods, and drag 'em into Prisons, while our Commodities go on before, and still forestall their Markets.

FISCAL: These I confess are pretty tricks, but will not do our business, we must our selves be ruin'd at long run, if they have any Trade here; I know our charge at length will eat us out; I wou'd not let these *English* from this Isle, have Cloves enough to stick an Orange with, not one to throw into their bottle-Ale.

(354–5)

The point of contention here is not military might per se, but its end: trade and commodities, spice and cloves. Towerson, the heroic English sea captain (played by Charles Hart, who played Almanzor two years earlier) is martyred by the Dutch in the end, and as he is led off to his execution, he exits praising his employers in blank verse:

Tell my friends, I dy'd so as
Became a Christian and a Man; give to my brave
Employers of the *East India* Company,
The last remembrance of my faithful service;
Tell 'em, I seal that Service with my Blood;
And dying, wish to all their Factories,
And all the famous Merchants of our Isle,
That Wealth their gen'rous Industry deserves;
But dare not hope it with Dutch partnership.
(403)

Compared to the more familiar heroic verse of *The Conquest of Granada,* this play may appear laughable, but we need to ask how they may be related. Is it only an author which these plays have in common? Does the patent topicality and political or propagandistic nature of *Amboyna* suggest that this is fundamentally a different form of play than the *Conquest,* which we have categorized as heroic drama; in short, is mercantile heroism a variant of military heroism? Do these two plays share the same moment in political and literary history? One of these plays occupies a well known role in our narrative of literary history, while the other has been dismissed, remembered, if at all, only because we value other works by Dryden, such as the *Conquest*. These two plays, then, present us with many vexedly familiar problems of relating literature to history, and the question of relation, precedence, and determination amongst literary, economic, and political history. We can try to resolve these issues by working with a coherent theoretical model of history and interpretation a model set out in Fredric Jameson's *The Political Unconscious;* Jameson argues that interpretation

> of a particular text must take place within three concentric frameworks, which mark a widening out of the sense of the social ground of a text through the notions, first, of a political history, in the narrow sense of punctual event and a chroniclelike sequence of happenings in time; then of society, in the now already less diachronic and time-bound sense of a constitutive tension and struggle between social classes; and, ultimately, of history now conceived in its vastest sense of the sequence of modes of production.[13]

By connecting these two plays with the immediate historical conditions of empire, and a mercantilist understanding of trade, we can begin to see the larger sense in which Dryden's drama is historically determined. That is to say, Dryden's *Conquest of Granada* and *Amboyna* are plays written at least partly in response to and reflecting or mediating the conditions of the contemporary hostilities of the second and third Dutch wars. But more significantly, both the plays and the wars themselves are inextricably part of an historical formation in which the most far-reaching economic changes involve the capitalizing of foreign trade and the expansion of empire. Marx provides an effective summary of this historical formation:

> The different mementa of primitive accumulation distribute themselves now, more or less in chronological order, particularly over Spain, Portugal, Holland, France, and England. In England at the end of the 17th century, they arrive at a systematical combination, embracing the colonies, the national debt, the modern mode of taxation, and the protectionist system. These methods depend in part on brute force, *e.g.,* the colonial system. But they all employ the power of the State, the concentrated and organised force of society, to hasten, hothouse fashion, the process of transformation of the feudal mode of production into the capitalist mode, and to shorten the transition. Force is the midwife of every old society pregnant with a new one. It is itself an economic power.[14]

Let us look first at the political history, in the narrow sense of punctual event and a chroniclelike sequence of happenings in time, as Jameson puts it. To begin with, these two plays can be seen in terms of their differing relation to the Dutch wars: the two Parts of *The Conquest* function to close off the second Dutch war and to efface its humiliation with mythic heroism, while *Amboyna* works to initiate or to sustain a new round of hostilities, to summon up support for the third Anglo-Dutch war by arousing anti-Dutch sentiment. According to James Winn, Dryden's most recent biographer, *Amboyna* may in fact have been produced in the spring of 1673, at which time "propaganda was even more urgent during the meeting of Parliament than at the outset of the war."[15] The connection between *Amboyna* and the Anglo-Dutch wars is hardly subtle, but the connection between *The Conquest* and the wars is, on the contrary, far from clear; most obviously, *The Conquest* does not represent a contemporary sea battle, but a distant historical event. The fifteenth-century event that *The Conquest* presents would, however, have been less distant to theater goers on account of the contemporary English conflict with Moors over the building of the mole or breakwater in Tangier. Charles's marriage in 1661 to the Portuguese princess, Catherine of Braganza, brought Charles the possession of Bombay and Tangier, and by building a breakwater in Tangier, the government hoped to extend their shipping and trade into the Mediterranean by protecting the sea lanes from African piracy. England held possession of Tangier from 1661 until it was evacuated and abandoned in 1684, during all of which time it was under siege by Moors. This marriage also embroiled Charles and England in Spain and France's disputes over the possession of the Netherlands. English alliance with Portugal (through marriage to Catherine) implicitly set them against the Dutch who were at war with Portugal, for the Dutch were principally responsible for breaking up the Portuguese empire. If in this period, Spain and France were still recognized as the two great European powers (with France growing more powerful over a waning Spain), and as such overshadowing the small quarrels of England and Holland, the remarkable success of Dutch and later English trade was nevertheless transforming these two smaller nations into serious potential rivals to the imperial giants.

It was acknowledged then and now that the real issue at stake in the Second Dutch war of 1664–1667 was England's commercial rivalry with the Dutch—trade with the East and West Indies. Samuel Pepys records the opinion of his friend Captain Cocke, who "discoursed well of the good effects in some kind of a Duch war and conquest (which I did not consider before but the contrary); that is, that the trade of the world is too little for us two, therefore one must down" (Feb. 2, 1664; 5:35). Sir George Clark sums up the situation rather baldly: "This second Anglo-Dutch war is the clearest case in our history of a purely commercial war. It was a war of which the purpose was simply to take by force material places and things, especially ships; for once the question hardly arises whether the military means accorded well with the political aims."[16] Dutch trade had profited from the decay of Spanish and Portuguese power; the Dutch advantage lay in their efficiency: cheap credit, banking innovations at the Bank of Amsterdam, low tariffs, religious toleration, and, above all, free trade. Holland, in short, was pictured as the new model state which encouraged and fostered trade. Holland's success in trade very plainly did not come from military conquest or prowess, but rather from the power of capital per se—in the trade of commodities, not in their manufacture—in exchange, not production.

The economic miracle of United Provinces was a subject of constant discussion in seventeenth- and eighteenth-century English political economy, from tariffs and the conditions of trade, to low interest, to the innovations of the Bank of Amsterdam, which was regularly presented as the appropriate model in proposals for a Bank of England. In pamphlets on interest, banking, trade, and political economy in general, from Rice Vaughan through John Locke and on up through Sir James Steuart and Adam Smith, Holland was *the* foreign example held out for English instruction. Locke's influential *Some Considerations of the Consequences of the Lowering of Interest and the Raising of the Value of Money* (published in 1691 but written in the 1670s) is peppered with praise of the Dutch economy and Dutch trade: "In *Holland* it self, where Trade is so Loaded"; "the *Dutch,* Skilfull in all Arts of promoting Trade; *Holland* is a Country where the Land makes a very little part of the Stock of the Country. Trade is their great Fund; and their Estates lie generally in Money."[17] Much later, in Adam Smith's *The Wealth of Nations* (1776), praise of the Dutch economy is central to his argument: "that trade which, without force or constraint, is naturally and regularly carried on between any two places, is always advantageous. . . . Though there are in Europe, indeed a few towns which in some respects deserve the name of free ports, there is no country which does so. Holland, perhaps, approaches the nearest to this character of any, though still very remote from it; and Holland, it is acknowledged, not only derives its whole wealth, but a great part to its necessary subsistence from foreign trade."[18]

The Dutch wars were fought over trade, and they should be seen as an official extension or a systematic venture above and beyond ordinary competition and the normal preying upon shipping and one another's outposts in the East and West Indies and along the West African coast. An analogy can be drawn here between the last phase of enclosure, as E. P. Thompson presents it in *Whigs and Hunters, the Origins of the Black Act,* and the struggle over navigation, maritime law, and fishing rights—the official pretexts for the Dutch wars (see Ogg here, 234–45); in both cases, what we see is a bourgeois process of systematizing exploitation by legitimating it. The same process is at work in the struggle over the use of privateers and pirates: colonization is the legitimating and the systematizing of a formerly episodic rapine. Similarly, the seemingly endless struggles over maritime law can also be seen as part of the long-term effort to systematize trade or exploitation, in short to consolidate empire in the East Indies and in North America. The treaty of Breda, which concluded the second Dutch war, as David Ogg puts it, "may be said to have intensified the commercial rivalry between the two nations and to have led directly to the Third and last Dutch War."[19] Ogg observes of the aftermath of the three Anglo-Dutch wars:

> Thus, in the four years of neutrality secured by the peace of 1674, England was able to make up for the handicaps with which she had entered the race for maritime supremacy, and in those years our French and Dutch rivals were weakened by prolonged war. A striking contrast of motives was thereupon illustrated. The Dutch were left struggling for their national independence and security; Louis was fighting for glory and revenge, while the peacable English were profiting by a policy of penetration and development.[20]

While Dryden's *The Conquest of Granada* explicitly represents the originary defeat of religious rivals, the Moors, the play implicitly represents the more immediate defeat of economic rivals, the Dutch. The religious victory of the distant empire in historical Granada promotes the immediate, commercial ends of the immediate empire, as Dryden's play celebrates both the origin and the extension of European hegemony over the third world. From this perspective then, King Ferdinand's remarks about the cyclical nature of history make more sense:

> Till, swelling by degrees, it [Empire] has possest
> The greater space; and now crowds up the rest.
> When from behind, there starts some petty State;
> And pushes on its now unwieldy fate:
> Then, down the precipice of time it goes,
> And sinks in minutes, which in Ages rose.
> (1.1.11–16; 11:106)

The aged Empire is not Moorish, but the Moorish conquerors, Portugal, Spain, and by extension, France, whose hegemony will shortly be overrun by "some petty State," the maritime nation and future commercial giant, England. Restoration England regularly presented itself as having to choose between Spain and France on the one side and Holland on the other, and in part, this choice is one between military and mercantile conquest. The financial disasters which accompanied the second Dutch war only served to press home this lesson; Pepys reports of a meeting with the King, Coventry, and the Navy Board: "Sir G. Ascu, he chiefly spoke that the warr and trade could not be supported together—and therefore, that trade must stand still to give way to that" (Feb. 15, 1665; 6:11).[21]

It is perhaps farfetched to imagine that in 1670 the economically and politically farsighted were poised to see the global expansion of empire and capital. (This is, after all, the argument of Lenin's *Imperialism, the Highest Form of Capitalism.*) Nevertheless, to English observers, the Portuguese and the Spanish model of empire was plainly in a state of decay, while the new, innovative Dutch model was clearly ascendent. From our perspective, it is clear which of the models, old or new, feudal or bourgeois, military or commercial, England took. Just like the Progress of the Renaissance, capitalism follows a northwest vector, from the Venetian Bank of the Rialto, to the Bank of Amsterdam, to the Bank of England, and the struggles between England and Holland in the second half of the seventeenth century are struggles over market control, struggles over credit and exchange. In all manner of political discourse in this period, the proper European model on which to base England's future development was posed as a choice between Holland's William of Orange and France's Louis. This choice is not only a choice between Catholic or Protestant model governments, but it is also a choice, on the one hand, between the French example of crude and brutal exploitation of feudal adventurism—primitive accumulation at its crudest—and, on the other hand, the highly efficient and systematic colonization of Holland. From the benefit of hindsight, and England's colonial expansion across the eighteenth century, it is clear that the Dutch model was the wave of the future.

What Dryden may have thought of old style conquest may be inferred from his earlier play, *The Indian Emperour* (1665), in which the Spanish conquistadors are presented as brutal, rapacious, and exploitive, "A Nation loving Gold" (2.1.45; 9:47). Though the Indians are violent, they are nevertheless noble; in his preface, Dryden describes the Indian Emperor as "great and glorious," in a play about "the sufferings and constancy of *Montezuma*" (9:27–28). The Spaniards, however, are all duplicitous and appetitive: Cortez himself admits, "By noble ways we Conquest will prepare, / First offer peace, and that refus'd make war" (1.1.51–52; 9:31). Once again, the brutality of imperialist conquest is intertwined with a kind of "natural" Catholic/Spanish sadism, a combination of rapacity and violence which comes to a head in the climactic scene in which "a Christian Priest" and Pizarro torture Montezuma on the rack:

PIZ.:   Thou has not yet discover'd all thy store.

MONT.:   I neither can nor will discover more:
    The gods will Punish you if they be Just;
    The gods will Plague your Sacrilegious Lust.

CHR. PRIEST.:   Mark how this impious Heathen justifies
    His own false gods, and our true God denies:
    How wickedly he has refus'd his wealth,
    And hid his Gold, from Christian hands, by stealth:
    Down with him, Kill him, merit Heaven thereby.

IND. HIGH PR.:   Can Heaven be Author of such Cruelty?

(5.2.1–10; 9:98)

And again, military prowess has been stripped of its glory, for it is presented as a mere means to an end, the power of imperial accumulation and exploitation.

The historical moment of these plays, which I have described in political, economic, and imperial terms has some literary consequences which can be seen in the different representations of heroism in these three plays, *The Indian Emperour, The Conquest of Granada,* and *Amboyna.* Almanzor, a kind of unregenerate *High Plains Drifter* ("I cannot stay to ask which cause is best; / But this is so to me because opprest" [1.1.127–28; 11:27]), is innately noble, and, as such, untouched by the brutality and cruelty evident in the earlier play.[22] But Almanzor still has to be turned from martial conquest and socialized to a new type of conquest, a new type of empire, for eventually he will become the manager of colonial trade. The English saw a choice before them between military and mercantile conquest, a choice presented in *The Conquest of Granada,* which domesticates the violently heroic, retraining the Almanzors of the future empire, not to conquest, but rather to service as colonial administrators. Traditionally, the shift is interpreted in terms of redemptive love, a necessary turn in the love/honor plot so common to Restoration serious drama; as Eric Rothstein puts it, "Almanzor begins fiercely and ends in gentility."[23] But, as I have tried to argue, this civilizing process from ferocity to gentility is not merely a function of plot; it is rather an historical shift, determined by the advent of capital and its consequent transformation of the dominant form of imperial power from the sword to the commodity.

This shift in heroism, from military to mercantile can be related to the whole problematic of heroism in the Restoration, and to the redefinition of the heroic in Samuel Butler's parodic *Hudibras* as well as in Milton's *Paradise Lost.* Whether we attribute these changes to the final decline of the Renaissance and aristocratic cult of honor or to a cultural hangover from the civil wars, the literary status of military valor was gradually but distinctly being redefined. In the invocation to the Muse which opens Book IX of *Paradise Lost,* Milton rejects as a fit subject

> Wars, hitherto the only Argument
> Heroic deem, chief maistry to dissect
> With long and tedious havoc fabl'd Knights
> In Battles feign'd.
>
> (9:28–31)

These changes in the representation of heroism have been the subject of much discussion about Restoration serious drama, especially the shift from heroic drama to other forms of tragedy. Laura Brown in particular has demonstrated how, increasingly across this period, tragedy comes to focus on feminine, passive, and defenseless characters, feminine figures of indistinct social status, who serve as a literary bridge between earlier aristocratic notions of honor and later bourgeois notions of personal virtue.[24] More commonly, however, *The Conquest of Granada* is read as the persistence of an older, classical heroism, modified as it is by a tradition of romance. But even in *The Con-*

quest, heroism is contradictory, for even Almanzor shows signs of newer forms. In his influential essay on Restoration comedy, John Traugott argues of this period, "The age seems to say that it is the human fate neither to believe nor to give up idealism, and the age's literature has it both ways, a never-never land of love and honor and a local habitation where lust and will and manners are the reality."[25] I want to attribute this complexity to historical contradictions: between military and mercantile heroism, between the military force of the Royal Navy and the economic force of the East India Company, between the persistence of feudal and aristocratic conceptions of personal honor and the emergence of a nascent morality of improvement more suited to a fully capitalized economy and its bourgeois society.

In Dryden and later, the relation between military and mercantile heroism is seen as temporal and causal, presented under the trope or the name of progress and civilization: colonies must be conquered before they can be managed and improved. And so Almanzor is presented as an exemplification of the civilizing process. Yet from our post-colonial perspective, we can see that the relation, military conquest being replaced by colonial administration, is not so simply successive. The relation is rather more complicated and dialectical: the colonial administrator must continue to use coercion and force; that is to say, the colonial administrator absorbs and retains all of the functions of the military conqueror, though those functions are obscured by a different social and historical formation. All of these contradictions are evident in incipient form in Dryden's *Conquest of Granada.* I do not mean to read this play as a prototype of *Lord Jim* or "The Man who would be King," but from the perspective just outlined, it is clear that neither of these successive roles, conqueror or administrator, military or mercantile hero, is simple and uncontradictory, for the conqueror prefigures the administrator, just as the administrator preserves the conqueror.

These contradictions are most glaring in the character of Almanzor, who enacts the civilizing process. Using the romance plot of familial recognition, the enemy warrior Almanzor is incorporated within the conquering family:

KING FERDINAND: I'me now secure this Sceptre, which I gain,
Shall be continued in the power of *Spain;*
Since he, who could alone my foes defend,
By birth and honour is become my friend.

(Part II, 5.3.272–75; 9:198)

Almanzor, in short, functions as both the conquered and the conquering, effacing the contradictions of colonial rule by serving successively as colonial subject and colonizer. The union of the two is evident in the very last lines of the play, lines of the King to his new colonialist, to pursue and subdue the conquered, in short to maintain and to administer, to perpetuate the conquest:

KING FERDINAND: Mean time, you shall my Victories pursue;
          The Moors in woods and mountains to subdue.

ALMANZOR: The toyles of war shall help to wear each day;
        And dreams of love shall drive my nights away.
        Our Banners to the *Alhambra*'s turrets bear;
        Then, wave our Conqu'ring Crosses in the Aire;
        And Cry, with showts of Triumph; Live and raign,
        Great *Ferdinand* and *Isabel* of *Spain.*

(Part II, 5.3.341–48; 9:200)

Conquest is not a state like siege, as it is pictured in Part I of this play, but is rather an ongoing relation of dominance, as it is pictured at the end of Part II. *The Conquest of Granada* works through a shift in the function of empire, from a state to an ongoing action or relation, from inert conquest to market.

Notes

I would like to thank James Winn for his advice with this essay.

1.   With the exception of *Amboyna,* references to Dryden are from *The Works of John Dryden,* ed. Edward Niles Hooker and H. T. Swedenberg, Jr. (Berkeley and Los Angeles, 1956—); citations to volume and page will be preceded by act, scene, and line when appropriate.

2.   Eugene Waith, *Ideas of Greatness, Heroic Drama in England* (London, 1971), 217.

3.   Laura Brown has begun the process of historicizing heroism in these plays; see *English Dramatic Form 1660–1760* (New Haven, 1981), 10–22. For the racist and imperialist dimensions of the sense of European greatness or heroism as compared to Eastern inferiority, see Edward Said, *Orientalism* (New York, 1978).

4.   Michael McKeon has treated these matters at length in connection with *Annus Mirabilis:* we have valued the transcendent in Dryden, not the historically specific and topical, in effect replicating his ideological and political argument, his celebration of England's eternal greatness and strength of will, which rise above and dwarf the local and temporary setbacks of 1666 (*Politics and Poetry in Restoration England, The Case of Dryden's Annus Mirabilis* [Cambridge, Mass., 1975]). Topicality enters discussions of the *Conquest* with the rivalry between the Zegrys and the Abencerrages, which is commonly interpreted as an allegory of contemporary factionalism. The editors of the *California Dryden* also connect the remarks about funding in Part II to the second Dutch war (11:453, n. 31–34). An opposition is drawn between the minor, local or topical issues and the larger, more important themes of law, faith and justice, and so after topical issues are identified and elucidated, they are dismissed. By the terms of this opposition, the political is therefore necessarily topical and minor—mere factionalism. The impulse to minimize topicality and the historicity of this play is exemplified by Geoffrey Marshall, who writes, "War is then metaphorically appropriate as a means to show passions in action—wars international, civil, interpersonal, psychological. In a play like *The Conquest of Granada* all four types of war take place, and all four are related" (*Restoration Serious Drama* [Norman, OK., 1975]), 67. Rather than studying the relation of the poem to the specific war, Marshall shifts the discussion to war in general and the theory behind war.

5.   Anne T. Barbeau, *The Intellectual Design of John Dryden's Heroic Plays* (New Haven, 1970), 111. Barbeau's is a discussion of the political theory at work in these plays, as a play of

ideas, a working through of the conflict of ideas exemplified by Sir Robert Filmer and Thomas Hobbes, and problems of royal authority and succession: "The 'laws of justice' are carried out in this play because all of the virtuous inhabitants of Granada find their way to the Christian court. . . . Dryden thus shows that the change from Muslim tyranny to Christian rule has occurred in such a way that justice has prevailed" (126); "*The Conquest* is one of the best examples of Dryden's fusion of apparently turbulent historical change with the actually 'immutable' 'laws of justice' " (125). Susan Staves provides the fullest exposition of the political theory represented in *The Conquest of Granada* in *Players' Scepters: Fictions of Authority in the Restoration* (Lincoln, Neb., 1979), 66–70, 126–29. In general, commentators on Dryden's heroic plays are either interested in ideas, as are Barbeau and Staves, or in character; the latter approach is illustrated by Michael M. Alssid, *Dryden's Rhymed Heroic Tragedies* (Salzburg Studies in English Literature, 1974), 190–224, who describes Almanzor at the end of Part I as "ashamed and depressed" (205).

    6.   This notion of the organic generation of gold appears in another text of Dryden's on the Dutch wars, stanza 139 of *Annus Mirabilis,* where gold is also connected with empire, conquest, and potential wealth:

> As those who unripe veins in Mines explore,
> On the rich bed again the warm turf lay,
> Till time digests the yet imperfect Ore,
> And know it will be Gold another day.
> (553–56; 1:80)

    7.   See the Epilogue to Part I, ll. 25–32. James A. Winn argues that the play was begun in the winter of 1668/69; see *John Dryden and His World* (New Haven, 1987), 200.

    8.   In *Dryden the Public Writer 1660–1685* (Princeton, 1978), 88–94, George McFadden argues for a serious analogy between Almanzor and the Duke of York, not just as typical dedicatory exaggeration: "Dryden's boldness, even effrontery, in weaving these critical characterizations [of James and Charles] into the texture of his play should not prevent us from recognizing them for what they were: the faithful fulfillment of his duty as poet, and especially as Laureate, not only to please but to instruct and correct the great: in this case, Charles and James Stuart" (94).

    9.   For the fullest narrative of the second Dutch war, and the problems of financing it, see Ronald Hutton, *The Restoration: A Political and Religious History of England and Wales 1658–1667* (Oxford, 1985), 214–75.

    10.   *The Diary of Samuel Pepys,* ed. Robert Latham and William Matthews, 11 vols. (Berkeley, 1970–1983). References will be noted in the text.

    11.   See David Ogg for a description of the appalling working conditions amongst sailors and shipyard workers, their starvation and exploitation: *England in the Reign of Charles II* (Oxford, 1955), 1:261.

    12.   *Amboyna* is quoted from Montague Summers's edition of *Dryden: the Dramatic Works* (London, 1932), Vol. 3.

    13.   Fredric Jameson, *The Political Unconscious* (Ithaca, N.Y., 1981), 75.

    14.   *Capital,* vol. I, ed. Frederick Engels, trans. Samuel Moore and Edward Aveling (New York, 1967), 751. See also the *Grundrisse.* "The tendency to create the *world market* is directly given in the concept of capital itself. Every limit appears as a barrier to be overcome. Initially, to subjugate every moment of production itself to exchange and to suspend production of direct use values not entering into exchange, i.e. precisely to posit production based on capital in place of earlier modes of production which appear primitive from its standpoint" (Karl Marx, *Grundrisse,* trans. Martin Nicolaus [Harmondsworth, 1973], 408).

    15.   Winn, *John Dryden,* 580–81, n. 86.

    16.   Sir George Clark, *The Later Stuarts 1660–1714* (Oxford, 1956), 63.

17. John Locke, *Several Papers relating to Money, Interest and Trade* (1696; rpt. New York, 1968), 98, 107, and 109.

18. Adam Smith, *The Wealth of Nations,* ed. Edwin Cannon (Chicago, 1976), 1:514 and 1:523.

19. Ogg, *England,* 314.

20. *Ibid.,* 388.

21. Noted in Hutton, *Restoration,* 237; Ascu here is Sir George Ayscue, naval commander.

22. If Almanzor's constant switching of sides seems strange or exaggerated to a twentieth-century reader, a little reading in seventeenth-century diplomatic history will soon familiarize one with the pattern. In between the second and third Dutch wars, Sir William Temple negotiated the Triple Alliance between England, Holland and Sweden, ostensibly against or in the face of France's great power. That alliance did not long withstand Charles's inclination to France and the Cabal (his ministers, Clifford, Arlington, Buckingham, Ashley [Anthony Ashley Cooper-Shaftesbury], and Lauderdale): their foreign policy was dictated by the terms of Charles infamous secret treaty with Louis XIV. The Third Dutch war was prompted by this secret treaty of Dover with Louis (1670), in which the French and the English were allied against the Dutch; the war proved to be extremely unpopular at home, stirring up sympathy for the Dutch and considerable popular anti-French sentiment. The war, as usual, came to a stalemate, and Charles was hampered by substantial anti-Catholic resentment in Commons. Commons forced Charles to retract his Declaration of Indulgence and in turn passed the Test Act; the Commons then proceeded to attack his ministers, the Cabal. Peace was signed in 1674. See Ogg for a full account of the second Anglo-Dutch war, *England,* 283–321; and for the third, see 357–88.

23. *Restoration Tragedy: Form and the Process of Change* (Madison, Wisc., 1967), 57. John Winterbottom, "The Development of the Hero in Dryden's Tragedies," *Journal of English and Germanic Philology* 52 (1953): 161–73, is the first to explore thoroughly the theme of redemptive love and Almahide's socializing of Almanzor.

24. Laura Brown, "The Defenseless Woman and the Development of English Tragedy," *Studies in English Literature* 22 (1982): 429–43. In "An Few Kind Words for the Fop," Susan Staves similarly argues that the fop of Restoration comedy prefigures more "feminine," male protagonists typical of later eighteenth-century drama (*Studies in English Literature* 22 [1982]: 413–28).

25. John Traugott, "The Rake's Progress from Court to Comedy," *Studies in English Literature* 6 (1966): 395. Bruce King's argument that the restoration audience laughed at its Heroic plays is an extreme version of this position, as is Derek Hughes's, who argues that Dryden's heroic plays "are studies of the disparity between Herculean aspiration and human reality" (*Dryden's Heroic Plays* [Lincoln, Neb., 1981], 2). In an earlier discussion of the *Conquest,* Bruce King writes, "The play is a clever double satire in which idealistic sentiments are subverted by naturalistic associations, while the latter are satirized by the comic-heroic rhetoric in which they are presented" (*Dryden's Major Plays* [New York, 1966], 60).

Dryden's Public Voices

PHILLIP HARTH

Dryden's career as a poet spanned some forty years, and during all that time there was scarcely a year in which he did not deal in one way or another with public issues. In recent years, critics have discovered plentiful signs of Dryden's persistent concern with matters of public importance in his plays, his translations, and of course "To My Honour'd Kinsman," which he called "a Memorial of my own Principles to all Posterity."[1] To a very real degree, therefore, Dryden was always a public poet. What I am going to talk about, however, is Dryden's public poetry in a more narrow sense: poems which respond to some immediate public issue and seek to influence the attitude of his contemporaries toward that issue. Poems of this kind are always occasional in the best sense of the word, for they are usually initiated by some public event—the restoration, coronation, death, or accession of a king, the birth of a prince, a war or great calamity such as the Fire of London, a popular furor which threatens to tear the nation apart, as did the excitement over the Popish Plot and the Exclusion Crisis. Now while Dryden wrote a fair number of such poems, they all belong to two widely separated periods of his poetic career. The first such period is a seven-year span beginning with *Astraea Redux* in the year of the Restoration and ending with *Annus Mirabilis* in 1667. A long interval of fourteen years follows in which Dryden was occupied with writing plays and criticism and in which he produced no public poems. It is succeeded by the second period, another seven-year span which begins with *Absalom and Achitophel* in 1681 and ends with *Britannia Rediviva* on the very eve of the Revolution which brought Dryden's public poetry to an untimely close.

The striking differences between these two groups of public poems have attracted a fair amount of attention in recent years, while the long interval of Dryden's life which separates the two has understandably suggested to most critics who have considered the matter that these differences reflect the poet's changing beliefs, feelings, and attitudes on public questions. Therefore we have had studies of Dryden's changing idea of history, of his changing con-

Phillip Harth, "Dryden's Public Voices." Originally published in *New Homage to John Dryden* (William Andrews Clark Memorial Library, University of California, Los Angeles, 1983). Reprinted by permission.

ception of heroism, of his changing attitude toward prophecy, and of his changing views on various other subjects. Many of these studies consider some of Dryden's other poems of the 1690s as well, but they see his public poems of the 1680s as marking the beginning of important changes in his beliefs and attitudes which are described by such phrases as "increasingly pessimistic vision," "implicit repudiation of earlier views," "failure of idealism," "estrangement," "despair," and, most frequently, "deep" or "bitter disillusionment."[2]

I believe, however, that to read these poems as chapters in the biography of Dryden's mind overlooks their function as political poems designed primarily to influence public attitudes and which, if they are to have any chance of succeeding, must be constantly adapted to changing conditions. If this is the case, then the divergences between Dryden's early public poems and his later ones may indicate not that his beliefs and feelings have changed, but that in each case he is speaking in different public voices. I want to consider this possibility by comparing the two groups of Dryden's public poems, limiting my attention, however, to those public poems which he wrote during the reign of Charles II. In the process of comparing them, I hope to show that their differences in theme and technique, while certainly important, are not as radical as they are sometimes assumed to be.

Dryden's public poems written in the aftermath of the Restoration have been the subject of some remarkably good criticism in recent years, but they have not been considered together as a coherent group. James D. Garrison's *Dryden and the Tradition of Panegyric,* which appeared in 1975, analyzes *Astraea Redux, To His Sacred Majesty,* and *To My Lord Chancellor* as outstanding examples of the genre he is considering, while Michael McKeon's *Politics and Poetry in Restoration England,* published the same year, studies *Annus Mirabilis* in much greater detail. Working independently, and discussing different poems written in the early and middle years of the same decade, these two critics have discovered certain themes and techniques in these individual poems which prove to be closely complementary and reveal the presence of a consistent public voice in Dryden's poetic oratory of the 1660s.[3]

The pervasive theme of "national harmony and reconciliation" which Garrison finds in the panegyrics of 1660, 1661, and 1662 is the exact complement of the theme of "mutual interest," "mutual love," and "unity" which McKeon discovers in *Annus Mirabilis* later in the decade. Their only difference reflects the changing conditions appropriate to the immediate aftermath of the Restoration in which we are shown the forging of a close alliance between the King and his people, and a slightly later period in which the fusion of their interests has become so complete that it seems always to have existed. The most prominent characteristic of this vision of national harmony is its insistent emphasis on unanimity, on a popular expression of love and loyalty toward the King unflawed by the presence of individual dissent or misgiving. In *Astraea Redux,*

> those Crowds on *Dovers* Strand
> Who in their hast to welcome you to Land
> Choak'd up the Beach with their still growing store,
> And made a wilder Torrent on the shore
> (276–79)

are the popular manifestation of public rejoicing at Charles's return which is shared by all Englishmen practically without exception.[4] With one heart and one voice they express their love and loyalty to their restored monarch. A year later, in *To His Sacred Majesty,* the people's emotions are undiminished. The same host of loyal subjects flock to the King's coronation, "Loud shouts the Nations happiness proclaim / And Heav'n this day is feasted with your name" (35–36). English harmony has become so universal that now, Dryden tells the King, even

> The jealous Sects that dare not trust their cause
> So farre from their own will as to the Laws,
> You for their Umpire and their Synod take,
> And their appeal alone to *Caesar* make.
> (81–84)

Each of these public poems confirms its predecessor's picture of lasting concord by showing the bonds between prince and people strengthened by the passage of time, and reaching a climax in *Annus Mirabilis* where it is the citizens of London, that former scene of popular disaffection, who now, working in perfect unison "Like labouring Bees on a long Summers day" (574), symbolize their affections by building a ship appropriately christened the *Loyal London:*

> This martial Present, piously design'd,
>   The Loyal City give their best-lov'd King:
> And with a bounty ample as the wind,
>   Built, fitted and maintain'd to aid him bring.
> (613–16)

Dryden's portrait in these early public poems of a cohesive body of Englishmen united behind their beloved monarch is, of course, a political myth which substitutes the ideal for the actual. As McKeon has shown, the reality was quite different; the English people in the early years of the Restoration period were sorely divided over a number of important issues.[5] No more in 1660–1662, the time of the panegyrics we are considering, than in 1666, "the year of wonders" celebrated in *Annus Mirabilis,* were Englishmen a united people all of whom gave the King their unqualified support and identified his interests with their own. But in an era preceding the growth of parties these dissident issues were sufficiently fragmented to prevent their capturing national attention to anything like the extent that was to be the case some fifteen years later, and the fiction Dryden creates in his early public poems has, therefore, a minimal plausibility which could not have been maintained very long beyond this decade. By ignoring national differences and implicitly denying them, Dryden promotes a group psychology as yet unrealized by picturing it as already in existence. It would never be realized, of course, but that was more than Englishmen could know at the time.

Nothing serves quite as well to submerge individual differences and deflect attention from them as does a foreign war, and a great part of *Annus Mirabilis* is taken up with war, and preparations for war, against the Dutch. As McKeon perceptively comments, "A foreign enemy is an obvious means of defining a national collectivity because it characterizes what is common to the group by exhibiting, in itself, what is alien to it." For this reason, "in Dryden's Anglo-Dutch War, all of England is galvanized against the foreigners, the outsiders, the 'foe.' "[6] Every other interest must yield priority to the single aim of defeating the Dutch. Time enough to consider other national goals once this immediate purpose has been achieved:

> But first the toils of war we must endure,
>   And, from th' Injurious *Dutch* redeem the Seas.
> War makes the valiant of his right secure,
>   And gives up fraud to be chastis'd with ease.
>   (665–68)

In the early panegyrics, written at a time when England was at peace, Dryden might seem to be deprived of any opportunity of deflecting latent hostilities toward a foreign foe. Yet as G. M. MacLean has persuasively argued in a recent article, even the earliest of these poems, *Astraea Redux,* stresses an imperialist theme which he interprets as "a call for a just and necessary war against England's mercantile and maritime competitors, especially Holland" implying a belief on Dryden's part, even at this early date, that "a war against the Dutch for purposes of expanding trade and sea power would forestall and divert attention away from any domestic problems following the king's return to power."[7] Dryden certainly expresses the hope, in *Astraea Redux,* that English animosities will hereafter be directed exclusively against a foreign enemy:

> Tremble ye Nations who secure before
> Laught at those Armes that 'gainst our selves we bore;
> Rous'd by the lash of his own stubborn tail
> Our Lyon now will forraign Foes assail.
>   (115–18)

And by identifying the mutual interests of prince and people as commercial rivalry with other countries and the expansion of foreign trade at the expense of England's neighbors, Dryden promotes a policy which must inevitably lead to a maritime war:

> Our Nation with united Int'rest blest
> Not now content to poize, shall sway the rest.
> Abroad your Empire shall no Limits know,
> But like the Sea in boundless Circles flow.
> Your much lov'd Fleet shall with a wide Command
> Besiege the petty Monarchs of the Land.
>
> (296–301)

In *Annus Mirabilis,* therefore, Dryden presents the Anglo-Dutch War as a consequence of legitimate English interests in foreign trade which require them to break the Dutch monopoly:

> Trade, which like bloud should circularly flow,
>   Stop'd in their Channels, found its freedom lost:
> Thither the wealth of all the world did go,
>   And seem'd but shipwrack'd on so base a Coast.
>
> (5–8)

If prince and people are now joined in a harmonious union which allows them to recognize their mutual interests and to pursue a cohesive policy, this is because each side brings to their relationship the proper dispositions. These dispositions to harmony are not the same in the early panegyrics as they are in *Annus Mirabilis,* since they are appropriate in each case to changing conditions, but they exactly complement each other. In the early panegyrics, written in the immediate aftermath of the Restoration, the nation's well-being depends on reconciliation between the English people and their monarch, at last recalled from a long exile. On the part of the people, this reconciliation depends on their exhibiting dispositions of repentance, reparation, and reformation—the very qualities which Dryden stresses in the early panegyrics. In *Astraea Redux,* "The Land returns, and in the white it wears / The marks of penitence and sorrow bears" (254–55). Moved by their repentance, the people hasten to make reparation by recalling and welcoming their injured prince: "So tears of joy for your returning spilt, / Work out and expiate our former guilt" (274–75). Finally, they turn to reformation, a chastened people who have taken to heart the lessons of their turbulent past: "But since reform'd by what we did amiss, / We by our suff'rings learn to prize our bliss" (209–10). On the part of the prince, his reconciliation with his people depends on dispositions of forgiveness, mercy, and a willingness to forget the former wrongs he suffered at their hands. For the King too has learned valuable lessons from the past: "Inur'd to suffer ere he came to raigne / No rash procedure will his actions stain" (87–88). As a result, Dryden reminds the

King in *Astraea Redux*, "you find / Revenge less sweet then a forgiving mind" (260–61), while in *To His Sacred Majesty* he declares:

> Kind Heav'n so rare a temper did provide
> That guilt repenting might in it confide.
> Among our crimes oblivion may be set,
> But 'tis our Kings perfection to forget.
> Virtues unknown to these rough Northern climes
> From milder heav'ns you bring, without their crimes:
> Your calmnesse does no after storms provide,
> Nor seeming patience mortal anger hide.
>
> (85–92)

Yet these peaceful dispositions of repentance on one side and of mercy on the other do not suggest an apathetic people and a listless prince. Just as the English people have lost none of their warlike spirit in laying down the arms they bore against themselves, since they will soon take them up against a foreign foe, so the King's mildness is reserved for his own subjects alone. In *To His Sacred Majesty*, Dryden tells the King that "It was your Love before made discord cease: / Your love is destin'd to your Countries peace" (121–22), but at the same time declares: "In stately Frigats most delight you find, / Where well-drawn Battels fire your martial mind" (107–8).

In *Annus Mirabilis* we are shown these opposite but complementary dispositions coming into play: a prince and people joined in loving alliance to make war against their common enemy, the Dutch. But the era of necessary reconciliation has now passed, the King has indeed forgotten his subjects' former crimes, and new dispositions on either side have succeeded those which Dryden stressed in the early panegyrics. On the people's part, love, gratitude, and loyalty have replaced repentance, while in place of forgiveness the King now exercises paternal care:

> The Father of the people open'd wide
>   His stores, and all the poor with plenty fed:
> Thus God's Annointed God's own place suppli'd,
>   And fill'd the empty with his daily bread.
>
> (1141–44)

On each side, these new dispositions confirm the truth of those which Dryden had presented earlier. The people's love and gratitude are evoked by a king who truly proved to be a forgiving father; their continued reformation has earned his paternal trust.

The pervasive optimism of Dryden's early public poems derives its power from the assumption that this reformation will last indefinitely because the English are a naturally loyal people whose recent sins were a temporary aberration from their normal behavior. In fact, his references in these poems to the late rebellion carefully deflect much of the guilt from the English people and place it squarely on a few traitors, a small minority who form the only exception to the general rejoicing at the King's Restoration in *Astraea Redux,* and whose numbers are steadily dwindling:

> The discontented now are only they
> Whose Crimes before did your Just Cause betray:
> Of those your Edicts some reclaim from sins,
> But most your Life and Blest Example wins.
> (314–17)

It is these "designing Leaders" whom Dryden holds responsible for the public disorders of recent years, while "the Vulgar" were only "gull'd into Rebellion."

> For by example most we sinn'd before,
> And, glass-like, clearness mixt with frailty bore.
> (207–8)

Momentarily misled by the force of bad example, the English shortly repented their mistake and repined for their exiled monarch even before his return:

> While Our' cross Stars deny'd us *Charles* his Bed
> Whom Our first Flames and Virgin Love did wed.
> (19–20)

This image of the English as a loving bride who longs for the return of her royal spouse is repeated in the dedication to *Annus Mirabilis,* where it is applied to the citizens of London in particular: "Never had Prince or People more mutual reason to love each other, if suffering for each other can indear affection. You have come together a pair of matchless Lovers, through many difficulties; He, through a long Exile, various traverses of Fortune, and the interposition of many Rivals, who violently ravish'd and with-held You from Him: And certainly you have had your share in sufferings."[8] Whether thwarted by their stars or ravished and withheld from their lover by rivals, the English people as a whole remained loyal to Charles in their hearts in spite of a separation for which they bear only a passive responsibility.

Dryden seems to go out of his way, in fact, to emphasize the security of English loyalty after the Restoration by referring in two of his early public poems to the "fatal mercy" of the King's father. This was potentially a sore subject, since the mildness of Charles I at the start of his troubles had been cited many times as a fatal mistake in policy which had unwittingly encouraged the growth of the rebellion. Consequently it had come to be accepted as a warning which his son would be well advised to heed. Yet in *Astraea Redux,* Dryden praises Charles II for possessing the same temperament as his father, and encourages him to exercise it:

> But you, whose goodness your discent doth show,
> Your Heav'nly Parentage and earthly too;
> By that same mildness which your Fathers Crown
> Before did ravish, shall secure your own.
>
> (256–59)

The explanation of this paradox lies in the change of conditions between 1640 and 1660. The same mildness which ravished his father's crown will secure his son's because the temporary aberration of English loyalty which cost Charles I his crown and his life has now faded into history. What was a fatal weakness in the father will be a saving grace in the son. Speaking of the quality of mercy in *To My Lord Chancellor,* Dryden returns to the same example:

> Heav'n would your Royal Master should exceed
> Most in that Vertue which we most did need,
> And his mild Father (who too late did find
> All mercy vain but what with pow'r was joyn'd,)
> His fatal goodnesse left to fitter times,
> Not to increase but to absolve our Crimes.
>
> (55–60)

Again it is the appearance of fitter times and an altered people which will insure opposite effects from the same family trait. Under different circumstances, the "fatal goodness" of the martyred monarch becomes a life-giving quality to be emulated rather than shunned.

The prophecies which conclude the first and last of Dryden's early public poems carry into the future his picture of prince and people united by a lasting bond of reciprocal love and mutual interest. McKeon's demonstration that the vision at the close of *Annus Mirabilis* exploits commonplaces of prophecy and eschatology can be applied to *Astraea Redux* as well.[9] But these prophecies also depend for their credibility on the extent to which Dryden has made the accompanying picture of a prince and people already joined in the harmonious pursuit of mutual interests a convincing one. For his prophecies are glowing visions of greater commercial prosperity which will ultimately crown a pursuit whose auspicious beginnings are described by Dryden in the body of each poem. It is good to remember that his early public poems are political oratory, and that most political oratory in every age employs prophecies which are redolent with hope, offering a bright prospect of the future. Most political prophecies share certain characteristics. In the first place, they are extraordinarily sanguine, often unrealistic, and seldom realized. Second, political prophecies are really conditional promises: they depend for their fulfillment on the public's adopting or adhering to certain policies. Essentially, therefore, they are a persuasive technique for enticing people into pursuing a particular course by offering them a reward. The prophecies which play so prominent a part in Dryden's early public poems exhibit both these characteristics. By telling the English people again and again that they are a loyal and obedient race whose interests are those of their monarch and whose future is a glorious prospect, he would persuade them to accept his fiction as reality, and to make life imitate art. As Mandeville was later to observe in his "Enquiry into the Origin of Moral Virtue," the "Moralists and Philosophers of all Ages"—the poets too, he might have added—having "thoroughly examin'd all the Strength and Frailties of our Nature, and observing that none were either so savage as not to be charm'd with Praise, or so despicable as patiently to bear Contempt, justly concluded, that Flattery must be the most powerful Argument that could be used to Human Creatures."[10]

When Dryden returned to the writing of public poetry after an interval of some fourteen years, the state of the nation, never as bright as he had pictured it in his early career, had worsened considerably, and he was now to paint it in colors so dark that *Absalom and Achitophel* and *The Medal* present a striking contrast to his early public poems. In fact, so many of the same themes reappear in these later poems, but in such a fashion as to exhibit their differences, that we seem to be looking at England from an opposite perspective. If the earlier picture was a fiction, may we say that the later one is more realistic? Only to the extent that it now admits the presence of divisions in what had never been a seamless society. But Dryden goes far beyond simply recognizing the existence of political differences in his later public poems. He exploits, intensifies, and exaggerates them, and in the process creates another fiction to replace his earlier one. Instead of saying that Dryden's later public poetry is more realistic than the earlier, it would be more accurate to say that he now employs new strategies to deal with altered conditions.

If the pervasive theme of the early public poems had been national harmony, group cohesiveness, and a spirit of unanimity, that of these later poems is fragmentation, mutual antagonism, and a state of disorder. England has become a nation rent by divisions, suffering from "publick Lunacy" and "Fumes of Madness," and plunged in a mad pursuit after "wild desires." Mutual interests have given way to divided aims, not only between the two parties but among the Whigs themselves, who are not a real party in any sense, but a "Trait'rous Combination" of selfish and conflicting interests who accept Shaftesbury's leadership and

> Whose differing Parties he could wisely Joyn,
> For several Ends, to serve the same Design.
>   (493–94)

On two separate occasions in *Absalom and Achitophel* Dryden offers a catalogue of the "several Factions" within the Whig coalition which underscores their divergent interests and shows that the only common factor among them is that all are "Rebels who base Ends pursue" (806).

In *Annus Mirabilis,* Dryden had turned England's war with the Dutch to advantage by stressing the mutual interest shared by all Englishmen in defeating the nation's enemy. In *Absalom and Achitophel* and *The Medal* he pictures Shaftesbury and the other Whig leaders as an insidious and far more dangerous enemy within their midst. Dryden's phrase for one of the Whig factions, "Pretending publick Good, to serve their own" (504), is true to some extent of all; for under cover of "pretended frights" and "Hypocritique Zeal," they are promoting various ends which, though artfully disguised, are inimical to the nation's interests. Again, what Dryden says of the Enthusiasts applies to all the Whig factions:

> 'Gainst Form and Order they their Power employ;
> Nothing to Build and all things to Destroy.
>   (531–32)

By isolating, identifying, and excluding a part of English society as "the enemy" in *Absalom and Achitophel* and *The Medal,* Dryden employs a strategy which is similar in some respects to his treatment of the Dutch and other foreign rivals in his early public poems. It is true that in order to do so he must abandon once and for all the earlier fiction of national cohesiveness, but the very process of cutting off a certain segment from the community and making it alien to the rest of society provides him with the opportunity of trying to restore a sense of mutual interest among the remainder and of creating the kind of group psychology engendered by most wars, whether foreign or civil. In fact, Dryden deliberately darkens his picture of this already turbulent period, portraying a violent political struggle in terms usually reserved for armed combat, and describing the state of the nation as one in which "Peace it self is War in Masquerade" (752). This picture may seem to come somewhat closer to the truth than his earlier portrait of a harmonious England, but it is nevertheless a myth which refashions the actual state of affairs to serve Dryden's purpose of identifying the King's opponents as the nation's enemies. In his dedication to the King of *The History of the League,* written after public excitement over the Exclusion Crisis had abated, Dryden explicitly compares the recent political turmoil to a foreign war in order to argue that in this case the nation had been confronted with an even more dangerous enemy. Congratulating the King on having weathered the "Storm" and overcome "all this violence of Your Enemies," he declares that "You have perform'd a Greater and more Glorious work than all the Conquests of Your Neighbours. For 'tis not difficult for a Great Monarchy well united and making use of Advantages, to extend its Limits; but . . . to Govern a Kingdom which was either possess'd, or turn'd into a *Bedlam,* and yet in the midst of ruine to stand firm, undaunted, and resolv'd, and at last to break through all these difficulties, and dispell them, this is indeed an Action which is worthy the Grandson of *Henry* the Great."[11] What Henri IV of France had weathered, of course, was an actual civil war of the greatest magnitude against a professed enemy fighting under its own colors. His grandson, struggling against a hypocritical enemy in a situation where "Peace it self is War in Masquerade," has performed an exploit requiring equal courage, even if no blows were struck.

If the English people in Dryden's early public poems are distinguished by their steadfast loyalty to their beloved monarch, in these later poems they "estrange their alter'd Hearts / From *David*'s Rule" (290–91). The same volatile people "Who banisht *David* did from *Hebron* bring, / And, with a Generall Shout, proclaim'd him King" (59–60) have repented their decision and "Now, wondred why, so long, they had obey'd / An Idoll Monarch which their hands had made" (63–64). In fact, Dryden emphasizes the complete reversal of the people's former disposition by echoing in *Absalom and Achitophel* the words he had used in *Astraea Redux* to describe "those Crowds on *Dovers* Strand / Who in their hast to welcome you to Land / Choak'd up the Beach with their still growing store." It is Achitophel who on this occasion recalls the day

> when on *Jordan*'s Sand
> The Joyfull People throng'd to see him Land,
> Cov'ring the *Beach,* and blackning all the *Strand*
> (270–72)

in order to contrast it with the present time when we see "Those heaps of People which one Sheaf did bind, / Blown off and scatter'd by a puff of Wind" (277–78).

In presenting the English in these later poems as a "People easie to Rebell" (215), Dryden exaggerates as far in the opposite direction as he had done in portraying their fidelity to the King in his early public poems. They are now

> a Headstrong, Moody, Murmuring race,
> As ever try'd th' extent and stretch of grace;
> God's pamper'd people whom, debauch'd with ease,
> No King could govern, nor no God could please.
> (45–48)

But this is hyperbole. The English are not really a people whom "no King could govern," even in *Absalom and Achitophel,* for if they were, the happy resolution which brings that poem to a close would be impossible. Furthermore, like other racial slurs, it is an unwarranted generalization which in this case ignores "the sober part of *Israel*" (69) who remain steadfast in their loyalty. But just as Dryden exacerbates the nation's divisions as a means of healing them, so he pictures the English as a people in the most scornful terms in order to shame a considerable sector of them out of their disloyalty. As Mandeville was later to imply, contempt is the mirror image of praise, each of them an exaggerated reflection of reality which can serve the same purpose of correction. The dominant impression Dryden creates of the English in his later public poems is not that they cannot be governed, but that as a nation they cannot be depended upon because they possess an unstable temperament. They are "a fickle rout" whose political alignments are nothing but "humours," dependent on the climate and therefore unpredictable. Their periodic disquiets are not the effect of any reasonable apprehension about their liberties, but simply occasions when

> every hostile Humour, which before
> Slept quiet in its Channels, bubbles o'r.
> (138–39)

Similarly, their intermittent resumptions of allegiance to their monarch are not the sign of a steadfast affection, for they are a people

> who, at their very best,
> Their Humour more than Loyalty exprest.
> (61–62)

The later poems do not deny, therefore, the nation's enthusiasm for their returning king which was celebrated in the earlier poems. They deny its permanence, reinterpret its motivation, and take away its lustre.

This is a dark picture, but it is not a hopeless one. If English loyalty now proves to be an unstable humor, English rebelliousness is also a humor of no greater permanence. The oscillation of the people's temper proves that if their allegiance will not hold for long, neither will their disaffection. As Dryden remarks in *The Medal,*

> to both extremes they run;
> To kill the Father, and recall the Son.
> (99–100)

It is true that in one of his most scathing characterizations of the English in *Absalom and Achitophel,* Dryden portrays them as an unsteady race "govern'd by the *Moon*" who

> Tread the same track when she the Prime renews:
> And once in twenty Years, their Scribes Record,
> By natural Instinct they change their Lord.
>
> (217–19)

But this, like the scornful words "No King could govern," is hyperbole belied by the rest of the poem, in which the people murmur but do not rebel or change their lord, are restored to tranquility in less than three years, and behold the inauguration of a different era:

> Henceforth a Series of new time began,
> The mighty Years in long Procession ran:
> Once more the Godlike *David* was Restor'd,
> And willing Nations knew their Lawfull Lord.
>
> (1028–31)

There is some consolation to be found in the fact that the people are governed by their humors, indeed, for as Dryden explains in *The Medal*, those humors are subject to an English climate which favors returning tranquility:

> Our Temp'rate Isle will no extremes sustain,
> Of pop'lar Sway, or Arbitrary Reign:
> But slides between them both into the best;
> Secure in freedom, in a Monarch blest.
> And though the Clymate, vex't with various Winds,
> Works through our yielding Bodies, on our Minds,
> The wholsome Tempest purges what it breeds;
> To recommend the Calmness that succeeds.
>
> (248–55)

The prophecy that concludes *The Medal* is a literal application of this climatic cycle to English public affairs, and although it is filled with political storms, it ends in the same succeeding calm. In contrast to the prophecies that conclude the early public poems, it deliberately eschews any visionary appeal, for

> Without a Vision Poets can fore-show
> What all but Fools, by common Sense may know,
>
> (287–88)

and it is filled with dark forebodings instead of bright promises. But it is a prophecy like Jonah's, which does not foretell what must inevitably take place but warns the people of what will follow from a course of action which can still be abandoned in time to avert its evil consequences. Dryden's prophecy describes what would ensue

> If true Succession from our Isle shou'd fail,
> And Crowds profane, with impious Arms prevail.
>
> (289–90)

This contingent picture, an exact replica of the years 1640 to 1660, confirms Dryden's words in *Absalom and Achitophel:*

> Yet, grant our Lords the People Kings can make,
> What Prudent men a setled Throne would shake?
> For whatsoe'r their Sufferings were before,
> That Change they Covet makes them suffer more.
> All other Errors but disturb a State;
> But Innovation is the Blow of Fate.
>
> (795–800)

Yet what is most dissuasive about Dryden's picture of an England torn once again by civil war is not the sufferings it would entail, for a nation's people have often been willing to endure the greatest sufferings for the sake of an important goal. What Dryden emphasizes is the uselessness of suffering for the sake of changes which will prove impermanent, and in pursuit of innovation which for this people is only an idle dream. Often as they forget their allegiance, they eventually return to it, "Secure in freedom, in a Monarch blest." Therefore Dryden's description of where a successful rebellion would ultimately lead brings *The Medal* to exactly the same conclusion as his narrative of an aborted revolution in *Absalom and Achitophel:*

> And our wild Labours, wearied into Rest,
> Reclin'd us on a rightfull Monarch's Breast.
>
> (321–22)

Absalom and Achitophel and *The Medal* describe, therefore, two entirely different paths which lead to the same destination. The road not taken is the one depicted in *The Medal,* where the English people, once they abandon the monarchy, must wander aimlessly along dark byways without a guide, pursuing a long and arduous journey which proves to be a circle, and ends at last where it began. The road taken is the one described in *Absalom and Achitophel,* where the English people have strayed again into the wilderness, but the King rescues his lost flock, leading them out of the desert by the shortest route back to safety. The crucial difference in this latter journey is supplied by the presence of the King, displaying the qualities of leadership required in such an emergency.

For this reason, *Absalom and Achitophel* offers a striking contrast to Dryden's early public poems in its picture not only of the dispositions exhibited by the English people, but of the dispositions appropriate to the King. Those qualities of mildness, mercy, and forgiveness which figure as the King's most important attributes in the early public poems reappear in *Absalom and Achitophel,* for they are essential elements of Charles's nature, which has not altered with advancing age. He is still a man who, as even Absalom must privately admit, is

> Mild, Easy, Humble, Studious of our Good;
> Enclin'd to Mercy, and averse from Blood.
> (325–26)

Until the hysteria over the Plot begins, these gentle qualities promote concord among the people,

> And *David*'s mildness manag'd it so well,
> The Bad found no occasion to Rebell.
> (77–78)

But once civil fury has overtaken the land, Charles's easygoing disposition ceases to be beneficent and begins to have an opposite effect on the nation. Dryden now refers to Charles's attributes in the same terms he had applied earlier to these family traits as exhibited by the King's father, whose "fatal goodnesse" had cost him his crown. Describing the rebel leaders, he refers to

> Some, by their Monarch's fatall mercy grown,
> From Pardon'd Rebels, Kinsmen to the Throne.
> (146–47)

Later he exclaims, "How Fatall 'tis to be too good a King!" (812). Achitophel explains to Absalom how the King's disposition is working to his own advantage:

> Not that your Father's Mildness I condemn;
> But Manly Force becomes the Diadem.
> 'Tis true, he grants the People all they crave;
> And more perhaps than Subjects ought to have:
> For Lavish grants suppose a Monarch tame,
> And more his Goodness than his Wit proclaim.
> But when shoud People strive their Bonds to break,
> If not when Kings are Negligent or Weak?
> (381–88)

   The striking difference in the way Dryden now portrays the King's mercy and mildness appears when we compare his portrayal of Charles as David in *Absalom and Achitophel* with his earlier use of this image in *Astraea Redux.* In this first public poem after Charles's return, Dryden describes the young king's wanderings before his Restoration:

> Forc'd into exile from his rightful Throne
> He made all Countries where he came his own.
> And viewing Monarchs secret Arts of sway
> A Royal Factor for their Kingdomes lay.
> Thus banish'd *David* spent abroad his time,
> When to be Gods Anointed was his Crime,
> And when restor'd made his proud Neighbours rue
> Those choise Remarques he from his Travels drew,
> Nor is he onely by afflictions shown
> To conquer others Realms but rule his own.
>
> (75–84)

All Dryden's modern editors without exception have interpreted these lines as his earliest allusion to Second Samuel and to David's brief exile during Absalom's rebellion. But Dryden's image here is that of the young David of First Samuel, like Charles an anointed king driven into long exile before he had yet mounted his throne, forced to settle for a time in Gath among the Philistines, and, once he was restored to his own people, leading them successfully against his former hosts. This is the David whose most prominent characteristics as a youth were his gentleness toward his own countrymen—grieving for them in exile, sparing Saul when he had him in his power and forgiving his persecution—and, at the same time, his vehemence toward Israel's foes: the same combination of different but complementary qualities Dryden attributes to the young Charles, who has learned "to conquer others Realms but rule his own."

The image of David which Dryden uses for Charles in *Absalom and Achitophel,* taken from Second Samuel, carries very different implications. This is the "indulgent *David,*" older but not wiser, whose fondness for his rebellious son leads him to close his eyes to the young man's designs, neglect his own safety, and allow the kingdom to drift to the brink of disaster. Charles's similar behavior threatens to have similar consequences for England. The King's mercy, mildness, and forgiveness are still virtues in the abstract, but changing conditions have made them as inopportune in 1680 and 1681 as they were for his father in 1640 and 1641, and if continued they will lead to the same outcome Dryden had referred to in his early public poems, where the martyred king's "fatal goodnesse" had increased instead of absolving the rebels' crimes, until his mildness had at length ravished instead of securing his crown.

Therefore in *Absalom and Achitophel* David's "faithful Band of Worthies" convince him at last

> That no Concessions from the Throne woud please,
> But Lenitives fomented the Disease.
>
> (925–26)

David heeds their advice before it is too late, and his speech from the throne at the end of *Absalom and Achitophel* shows him reluctantly setting aside, one by one, the very qualities for which Dryden had praised Charles in his early public poems. The same king who in *Astraea Redux* found "Revenge less sweet then a forgiving mind" now declares:

> Thus long have I, by native mercy sway'd,
> My wrongs dissembl'd, my revenge delay'd:
> So willing to forgive th' Offending Age,
> So much the Father did the King asswage.
> But now so far my Clemency they slight,
> Th' Offenders question my Forgiving Right.
> . . . .
> Yet, since they will divert my Native course,
> 'Tis time to shew I am not Good by Force.
>
> (939–50)

The same king whom Dryden had praised in *To His Sacred Majesty* because "Your calmnesse does no after storms provide, / Nor seeming patience mortal anger hide" now exclaims:

> Must I at Length the Sword of Justice draw?
> Oh curst Effects of necessary Law!
> How ill my Fear they by my Mercy scan,
> Beware the Fury of a Patient Man.
>
> (1002–5)

Thus the King, on the advice of "the sober part of *Israel*" and with the consent of Heaven, adopts at last those qualities of rigor toward his enemies and of resolution toward his deluded subjects to which he is disinclined by nature, but which he has come to see as indispensable in this national emergency. Since Dryden wants to make this appear to be the solution to England's present difficulties, the suddenness of the poem's happy resolution, and its brevity, once the King has announced his new policy, are entirely appropriate.

The very fact that this solution applies to a particular crisis in English affairs, however, ought to discourage us from seeing it in absolute terms as a sign that Dryden has changed his views on the proper relations between prince and people and the qualities a monarch ought to exhibit, or that the later public poems represent a repudiation of the attitudes he had expressed on these questions in his early public poems. Following Charles's death, Dryden offered a retrospective view of his reign in the tenth stanza of *Threnodia Augustalis* which celebrates its greatest achievements. It begins:

> For all those Joys thy Restauration brought,
> For all the Miracles it wrought,

> For all the healing Balm thy Mercy pour'd
> Into the Nations bleeding Wound,
> . . . .
> For these and more, accept our Pious Praise.
> (292–304)

And it ends:

> Not Faction, when it shook thy Regal Seat,
>   Not Senates, insolently loud,
>   (Those Ecchoes of a thoughtless Croud,)
> Not Foreign or Domestick Treachery,
> Could warp thy Soul to their Unjust Decree.
> So much thy Foes thy manly Mind mistook,
> Who judg'd it by the Mildness of thy look:
> Like a well-temper'd Sword, it bent at will;
> But kept the Native toughness of the Steel.
> (318–26)

These two passages, praising Charles for different, but not inconsistent, qualities which distinguished the opening and the closing years of his reign, could pass for fair descriptions of Dryden's early public poems and his later ones respectively, and they can stand together without any contradiction.

In acknowledging that under different circumstances the King must adopt different roles toward his people, therefore, Dryden's later public poems betray no significant alteration in his basic political principles. But what of the other beliefs and attitudes which figure in both these groups of poems? Can we say that Dryden's views of heroism have changed in *Absalom and Achitophel,* that he displays a different attitude toward prophecy and history in *The Medal,* that he reveals in both poems a deepening pessimism with the English people and a growing disillusionment with the prospects for his country? Not, I think, on the evidence of these two poems, nor on that of the early public poems either. To speak of Dryden's later disillusionment is to imply that he earlier entertained illusions. It is to assume that he was persuaded by his own rhetoric to believe that the English people were in reality the cohesive body of loyal subjects he portrayed in his early public poems, that, carried away by visionary enthusiasm, he embraced his prophecies in those poems as actual forecasts of the nation's future. On the other side it is to assume that he came to accept the darker fictions of his later public poems as literal representations of reality, to believe himself a historian rather than a poet, and to forget his angry question in *The Vindication of "The Duke of Guise,"* "Am I ty'd in *Poetry,* to the strict rules of *History?*"[12] But neither of those assumptions is warranted by Dryden's public poems. What unquestionably did change between the decade of the 1660s and that of the 1680s was the state of the nation, and Dryden was realistic enough not only to recognize that change—as who could ignore it?—but to realize that changing conditions require different remedies, as well as different strategies to recommend them.

Notes

1. *The Letters of John Dryden,* ed. Charles E. Ward (Durham, N.C.: Duke University Press, 1942), p. 120.

2. See, for example, Achsah Guibbory, "Dryden's Views of History," *PQ,* 52 (1973), 187–204; Michael West, "Shifting Concepts of Heroism in Dryden's Panegyrics," *PLL,* 10 (1974), 378–93; James D. Garrison, *Dryden and the Tradition of Panegyric* (Berkeley and Los Angeles: University of California Press, 1975), pp. 175–97; Garrison, "Dryden and the Birth of Hercules," *SP,* 77 (1980), 180–201.

3. See Garrison, *Dryden and the Tradition of Panegyric,* pp. 147–75; McKeon, *Politics and Poetry in Restoration England: The Case of Dryden's "Annus Mirabilis"* (Cambridge, Mass.: Harvard University Press, 1975), pp. 47–78.

4. All quotations from Dryden are taken from the California edition of *The Works of John Dryden* (Berkeley and Los Angeles: University of California Press, 1956—).

5. See McKeon, *Politics and Poetry,* pp. 79–147.

6. Ibid., p. 69.

7. See G. M. MacLean, "Poetry as History: The Argumentative Design of Dryden's *Astraea Redux," Restoration,* 4 (1980), 54–64.

8. *Works,* I, 48.

9. See McKeon, *Politics and Poetry,* pp. 151–266.

10. Bernard Mandeville, *The Fable of the Bees,* ed. F. B. Kaye (Oxford: Clarendon Press, 1924), I, 42–43.

11. *Works,* XVIII, 6.

12. Ibid., XIV, 318.

The Form of Dryden's *Absalom and Achitophel,* Once More

A. E. WALLACE MAURER

In notes, articles, and books in our century, well over a hundred writers have treated the form of *Absalom and Achitophel* either as central in their study or as integral to it. While they have augmented our understanding of this profoundly occasional work, they have not concurred on its form, as is evident in the array of considerations of it as epic, epyllion, epic episode, satire, epic satire, Varronian satire, formal verse satire, classical oration, Jonsonian masque, political pamphlet, painting, biblical allegory, narrative, drama, chronology, music, typology, folklore, "Poem," and varying combinations of some of these. The disagreement among scholars is further ramified, in that some affirm single-form hypotheses, some venture clustered-design hypotheses, some propose varying numbers of divisions, and almost all respond with differing structural conceptions to defend or reject Samuel Johnson's charge of defective structure in the work.

What ultimately underlies this search for form is awareness that the fullest sense of Dryden's incentive and of the scope of his art and mind in *Absalom and Achitophel* would come with discovery of its form, since in its central signification form relates to any organized act and the impulsion behind it. What this paper accordingly aims to achieve is, first, to mark the reach of accumulated scholarship on the form of *Absalom and Achitophel* and, second, to locate and apply, with some ineluctable guesswork used where facts end, Dryden's conception of form to the work, keeping in view the indisputable perceptions about its form in the accumulated commentary. Doing that provides light, I believe, for discernment of the organic and governing form of *Absalom and Achitophel.*

A. E. Wallace Maurer, "The Form of Dryden's *Absalom and Achitophel,* Once More." Originally published in *PLL: Papers on Language and Literature,* Volume 27, No. 3, Summer 1991. Copyright © 1991 By the Board of Trustees, Southern Illinois University. Printed by permission.

1

The single-form theories, of which we will distinguish four, are the most numerous, showing by that very frequency how procrustean problems inherent in each or revealed in juxtaposition of two or more render their authority problematic. Consider, first, epic. The work was early called an *"epyllion, or epic in miniature, comprising satiric elements."* Epic predominated, accommodating satire ad libitum. Fifty years later, the same work became "a powerful imaginative transformation of *Paradise Lost"* into satire, enlisting epic. These opposed conceptions originated in the poem's presumed connections with epic and then built on different selective grounds.[1]

Classical oration has figured as a second single-form theory. Its most elaborated exposition first set up Dryden's conception of Varronian satire (Dryden 4: 47. 2–6) as preliminary structural groundwork. This accounted for the "multifold" and "disparate" elements in the poem: biblical role; conventional literary parallels; epic features; Satanic and Messianic echoes from Milton's epics; characters; dramatic dialogue; analyses of events; eulogy; allusions to recent history; contacts with contemporary pamphlets and with contemporary poems like *Naboth's Vineyard* (1679) and "Advice to Painter" poems (Thomas 170–71). Varronian satire, however, needed "a unifying structural principle" (Thomas 172; Dryden 4: 80. 19). The theory located this in the classical oration, identifying its parts—exordium, narratio, propositio and partitio, confirmatio (with digressio), peroratio—with designated segments of *Absalom and Achitophel.*[2]

A third single-form theory has centered on painting. The conceivable transference of the grand tensions in Renaissance painting to *Absalom and Achitophel* had by midcentury seemed quite likely (Wallerstein 448–49). The subsequent groundwork of Professor Jean Hagstrum, revealing the Pantheon of paintings borne in the minds of Restoration and eighteenth-century writers (xvii–xxii, 181–82), confirmed this intuition and opened up connections between painting and the structure of this poem. Very recently one such investigation accounted for an *Absalom and Achitophel* of five sections when read in conjunction with a viewing of Rubens's allegorical cycle, the *Banqueting House Ceiling,* in Whitehall (Copeland 34–36).

Finally, a fourth single-form (or, more properly, single-mode) theory— *Absalom and Achitophel* as satire—has evoked inquiry as extensive as the range of Restoration use of satire.

Unresolved difficulties inherent in all four theories preclude their acceptance: in the first, the need to reconcile categorically opposed formal claims; in the second, room for difference of view on the place and kind of oratorical parts in the poem; and in the third, the related questions of Dryden's knowledge of the Rubens painting and of its universal recognition by his readers.[3] To accept the fourth, one would have to reconcile claims for the general influence of satire, for the subtly diffuse influence of formal satire, for the dominance of formal satire, for English adaptation of satire, and for an applied view of satire as control over chaos and over forms necessary to effect that control.[4] Beyond resolution of those claims, readers would also have to face the fact that Dryden's own use of the term "satire" as applied to *Absalom and Achitophel* encompassed less than the whole work.[5]

Given the radical variety of suggested forms, none entirely disconnected from some aspect of the poem, it is not surprising that a few scholars have conceived of the work as a composite of forms, a kind of *Gesamtkunstwerk*. They do not, however, favor that theory without mixed feelings. Upon insisting on "the poem's elusive but unified genre," inferring that "the poem is allegorical," that Dryden as "*Historian*" "considered the poem historical rather than epic," finding "miniature epic" "paradox," and translating Dryden's terms "Satyre" and "a Picture to the Wast" as incompletion, one commentator observes himself with whimsical incredulity come to a Polonius-inspired conclusion: "we can say that the poem is an occasional, polemical, historical, satirical, panegyrical, truncated, narrative, allegorical poem" (Ramsey 95–96). Others add dramatic technique, biblical typology, and Cowleyan ode with similar uneasiness (McFadden 238, 244; Rothstein 17–19). And some find that the mixed-form theory leads only to dead-end exasperation, or to detection of a cryptic self-serving Dryden, or to canonical rejection of the work.[6]

Inevitably many differing views of the form of *Absalom and Achitophel* have produced great variation in the perceived divisions of the work. The classical-oration theory demarcated six. Dryden's twentieth-century editors found eleven. Other commentators have variously discerned two, three (in two differing patterns), four (in three differing patterns), and five.[7]

More than anything else, Johnson's charge of "defective" structure has prompted study of the form of *Absalom and Achitophel* and has affected the course of that study. Johnson objected to an allegory broken when "Charles could not run continually parallel with David" and to "an unpleasing disproportion between the beginning and the end" (Johnson 1: 436–37). This latter objection, which has stirred most comment, was caused, in Johnson's view, by a sudden fairy-tale kind of conclusion, which was necessitated by the impossibility of Dryden's completing a parallel between the biblical and the contemporary fates of Absalom and Achitophel and of Monmouth and Shaftesbury, respectively. Johnson's view has received support from some who find the work artistically roughened through allusion to historical circumstance uncoincident with biblical narrative, and it has met simultaneously and more often with opposition from others who see in Dryden's use of very particular historical incident, figure, and act dialectical and artistic warrant for a sudden ending.[8]

When Johnson's view enters larger contexts, namely the century's extensive treatments of Dryden's mind and art, the critical result is a discounting of genre as essential to discernment of the form of *Absalom and Achi-*

tophel. Early in the century one commentator with obvious reluctance tagged the work *epyllion.* Another had no trouble regarding it as "a poem so conceived as to be whatever Dryden had the talent to make it." A third let biblical and English history fuse into "*a tertium quid*" of indeterminate overarching form. A fourth saw that much of Dryden's art in *Absalom and Achitophel,* while it suggests various frames, lies "close to the surface." A fifth recognized that a "union of myth and dialectic" displaced a narrative conceptualization of the poem. Noting that the poet had applied the conceptual interpretation of history proper and of *biographia* to his material rather than strictly annalistic narrative, a sixth saw Dryden manage at will the whole store of accumulated English literary machinery with restricted technical allegiance to none of it in particular.[9] Together these studies have led to what a recent commentator has noted: namely a Dryden, in *Absalom and Achitophel,* "prescient . . . of the decay of the strict system of genre" (McKeon 39; cf. Lord 190, Fisch 258–59). Genre disappears from scholarly concern as the key to discriminating the form of *Absalom and Achitophel.*

2

Form in this work might be found in the generative moment or act or decision impelling it. For Dryden the writer, form existed before and after *Absalom and Achitophel*—say, in the preface to *Annus Mirabilis* in 1667, in *The Parallel betwixt Painting and Poetry* in 1695—somewhere in the rhetorical triad of Invention, Disposition, and Elocution. The "first happiness of the Poet's imagination," he averred in the earlier work,

> is properly Invention, or finding of the thought; the second is Fancy, or the variation, deriving or moulding of that thought, as the judgment represents it proper to the subject; the third is Elocution, or the Art of clothing and adorning that thought so found and varied, in apt, significant and sounding words: the quickness of the Imagination is seen in the Invention, the fertility in the Fancy, and the accuracy in the Expression.

There is a generative form in Invention and an instrumental form in Disposition, the former being absolutely decisive. Once Invention occurs, all relevant elements collect in embryo, awaiting instrumental Disposition. Of "Invention" Dryden wrote with passionate concern in *The Parallel betwixt Painting and Poetry* that

> no Rule ever was or ever can be given how to compass it. . . . How to improve it, many Books can teach us; how to obtain it, none; that nothing can be done without it, all agree. . . . Without Invention a Painter is but a Copier, and a Poet but a Plagiary of others.
>
> (1: 53. 23–30; 20: 61. 17–18, 22–24; 20: 62. 1–2)

Generative form is the embryonic conceptual impulse. It gives the author Archimedean leverage. It supplies energy, courage, confidence, anticipation. It is the heart of ancient and Renaissance Invention; for there, rather than in Disposition, which executes the generative form, is where the fundamental formal decision and die are cast.

3

What, then, might be the form, particularly the generative, the more difficult and challenging to perceive, of *Absalom and Achitophel?* Three primal Drydenian impulses inform and govern his crafting powers in this work; and I shall put these as questions, because we are upon one of the most difficult facts to document: the incitement of genius.

First, if Sir Edward Seymour, probably the most powerful immediate adviser to the King in the spring and summer of 1681, asked Dryden to write something to support the King and his administration in the Exclusion Crisis, did the generative form of his response take the shape of a risky witty bold order, by a very minor but articulate subject, to the King of England: "Don't be stupid about anything or anyone, including yourself"?[10] Second, Dryden, who possessed on record the most articulate dialectical intelligence in Restoration England, a mind which while advancing one position simultaneously gave its counters full rein for epistemological testing—such a Dryden perforce always gave more than was called for by an assignment. Did his response in *Absalom and Achitophel* take its generative form from a potent sentiment articulated a decade later in his Dedication of *Amphitryon:* "there is a Pride," he there remarked, "of doing more than is expected from us, and more than others would have done" (15: 223. 19–20)? Third: Could Dryden simply not give up, say, as Shakespeare's Cordelia did in the face of Lear's soul-sinking invincibly naive opening question to his daughters, a question that she needed eighty years to answer? Did Dryden, instead, actually aspire to move a nation's mind from torpor to alertness at one stroke? The most astounding opening ten lines in literature (known to me) have nonplussing hints of an affirmative answer:

> In pious times, e'r Priest-craft did begin,
> Before Polygamy was made a sin;
> When man, on many, multiply'd his kind,
> E'r one to one was, cursedly, confind:
> When Nature prompted, and no law deny'd
> Promiscuous use of Concubine and Bride;
> Then, Israel's Monarch, after Heaven's own heart,
> His vigorous warmth did, variously, impart

> To Wives and Slaves: And, wide as his Command,
> Scatter'd his Maker's Image through the Land.
>   (2: 5. 1–10)

These lines lift the reader—the Restoration specimen and any other in a species that so far has not demonstrably mutated—into a dizzying house of mirrors. Dryden's contemporary Puritans are disarmed by a biblical double-cross. Charles II is simultaneously glorified and arraigned by association with the grandest Hebrew king, who also pulled one of the most heinous tricks in history in order to secure Bathsheba. And while welded to David, Charles is simultaneously associated with the radically foiled diplomatic trick of Restoration history: the acquisition of a barren queen as presumed wife and fertile perpetuator of the Stuart line for one of the age's most innovative regal seducers. Wielding the accumulated English linguistic power of tens of thousands of heroic couplets, Dryden with eight sardonic plosive *p*'s reduces the Puritan outrage over unspeakable depravity to a postlapsarian cipher (cf. Price 53); with thirteen playfully inexorable *m*'s he parades before the nation Charles II's irresponsible sexual frivolity, which distracted him from conducting exact statecraft in an international jungle. Thirteen times was often enough to draw down on Dryden, a hundred times over, the nose-slitting service performed on Sir John Coventry for daring in Parliament to scoff at Charles's amours, to say nothing of Dryden's effecting eight re-runs of the spectacle with the eight *p*'s reconsidered, or of Dryden's call, through the last two *m*'s, to the real Judeo-Christian God to stand up. Through five rhymes he deploys unresolved human contradictions or conflicts across the David/Charles spectacle of character and kingship: eschatological dialectic in "begin"/"sin"; the ethical/psychological/institutional one/many contradictory tensions in human development in "kind"/"confind"; individual and sociopolitical organization of the life force, sex, in "deny'd"/"Bride"; the tension between the vision of God and denial thereof by each member of the race in "heart"/"impart"; and the 99 per cent deadweight of daily human yielding to visionless impulse and casual nature of unorganized intellect and unaroused conceptualization in "Command"/"Land." Above it all, Charles II and David fuse into a momentarily sensed, profoundly flawed nature and race, among whom no one can throw the first stone accurately, except Dryden, who has the wit to strike down all pretenses to strength. In ten lines he has brought all to a puzzled but forward-peering standstill.

Did Dryden really aim to drive his readers, ranging from Puritan to King, into preternatural sensitivity so that they would probe to the outermost reaches of meaning and tone *every line to follow?* Given any one of these three generative forms, interlinked and simultaneously generating as one the art of *Absalom and Achitophel,* there is no structural defect in a work that impels reflection without letup exponentially with every line and segment.[11] The mind of the reader is comprehensively activated by Dryden through dis-

ciplined ad libitum application of the instrumental machinery of epic, allegory, drama, pamphlet, satire, oration, narrative, painting, character, typology, and heroic couplet.[12] That mind is not jarred by an abrupt ending in the
final six lines beginning with "Th' Almighty, nodding, gave Consent," but is
fully stirred to find itself in Dryden's depiction of the November 1681 world
of this "Almighty" of line 1026, shadowed by the "Maker" of line 10 whose
"Image" was "Scatter'd . . . through the Land" by a fused David/Charles,
"*Israel's* Monarch, after Heaven's own heart." A formal narrative ending (pro-
leptic at the very most) is here almost nonexistent; it is a minimal cognitive
effect, a serviceable metaphor on the surface, among many integrated literary
elements fired as one to create a larger ending. Dryden has gone for activa-
tion of his reader's intelligence until it comprehensively circles about and
oscillates back and forth at all angles across the issue of 1681. What must be
done by the England of November 1681 is pragmatic preservation of life
through retention of a flawed but self-conscious succession. And that succession, now in the trappings of Charles II, must be seen by Dryden's readers
against the temporarily receding spectacle of the antecedent, but still-to-be,
problematic behavior of the race and of Charles II.[13] Dryden used his inextin-
guishable wit to take great risks to make that clear.

<h1 style="text-align:center">4</h1>

The form impelled and represented by Dryden's opening ten lines is a continuous, kaleidoscopic multidimensionality that is purposefully adapted, defying
further identification. To account for its perpetual dialectical-artistic motion
would require line by line explication. Here selective example must suffice to
show the coalesced operation of parts and shadows of pre-eminent seventeenth-
century literary forms and to explain Dryden's refusal to limn any one as predominant.

To make a selective demonstration possible, it is necessary to indicate
discursively movable "sections" in *Absalom and Achitophel.* (While this step
seems reductive in light of the total artistic/intellectual apprehension
glimpsed above, it is actually unavoidable, given the chronological element in
cognition in linguistic art and discourse, which is temporally paced or com-
plotted.) Including transitions, these are (1) 1–42, the nonplussing preamble
and the character of Absalom/Monmouth, constituting an unprecedented *in
medias res;* (2) 43–84, the historical character of the Jews/English; (3) 85–149,
a kind of historical painting of the Popish Plot; (4) 150–229, the spherically
endless character of Achitophel/Shaftesbury; (5) 230–302, Achitophel's first,
rhetorically comprehensive, epical/historical/dramatic temptation speech; (6)
303–72, Absalom's response, a speech of cosmically tottering weakness; (7)
373–476, Achitophel's second temptation speech, with its rhetoric of multiple-

design and unyielding triumph; (8) 477–681, the marshaling and manipulation, broadly and subliminally by Achitophel/Shaftesbury, of the malcontents—economic, political, constitutional, ecclesiastical, civic, conformist, social—each delineated mainly via character; (9) 682–758, the depiction, suggestive of historical painting, of the progress of Absalom/Monmouth, managed by Achitophel/Shaftesbury, through the countryside; (10) 759–810, the presiding intelligence's, or speaker's, overt normative dialectical exposition of political and constitutional issues and of his position, founded on pragmatic patching of flawed monarchy; (11) 811—932, the parade of the king's loyal followers—religious, parliamentary, philosophical—depicted via character; (12) 933—1031, David/Charles II's speech from the throne betokening control, confirmed by an epic and apocalyptic, comprehensively stylized Divinity.

This division of the poem might seem remarkably to support the widely considered epic theory of the form of *Absalom and Achitophel*. Besides epical signs like the powerful Miltonic echo in line 373, Achitophel as Satan, Dryden's desire to write an epic here surfacing under severe time constraint (heretofore noted in critical commentary), the division provides the classical and Miltonic twelve-multiple segmentation. It invites consideration of the resemblance to the epic marshaling of the hosts in (8) and (11); a reminiscence of the epic descent into the underworld in the immersion in irrationality and instability of characters in (8); the epical resort to speeches at fateful junctures in (5), (6), (7), (9), and (12); the epical thrust of the audience *in medias res* in (1); and the epic setting of a civilization teetering ominously on the brink of disaster and oblivion during the English Exclusion Crisis spread across (1) through (12).

But it is instructive to notice now that the poem cannot be an epic, not only because of the blurring of epic outline by other forms (cf. below), but because of what for Dryden's audience could be fatally misleading philosophic signals inherent in epic. While suggesting itself often in Dryden's kaleidoscopic commandeering of detail, epic is not the informing or holding frame of *Absalom and Achitophel*. The poem cannot sustain its immediate urgency or advise its audience on unfinished unpredictable business with an epic. For the epic historically represented deep and problematic evaluation of a perceived cultural/historical fait accompli to affirm courage and character for encounters with current challenges, tribulations, and dilemma. Monmouth still wanders loose; the King has not yet proven that he has the staying power for his early 1681 resolve; Shaftesbury is yet to be tried, as it happens, within a week, given the way the publication date of *Absalom and Achitophel* has turned out (Harth, "Legends" 13–29); and, as an imponderable potential in this real 1681 world, all three are depicted as having varyingly good and bad capacities not yet played out. To a point the situation appears epic, but the here and now is so radically dangerous that any distraction from the daily perils of reality—a distraction, say, through pat identification of grave unidentified uncertainties with the formal vision of epic, however reaffirmative or problematic—could spell disaster.

For the seventeenth century, as much as for us in the twentieth, epic theory will not accommodate the elements of other forms that operate in *Absalom and Achitophel*. At the same time, no one of them, in whole or in part, is the organically recognizable form of the poem. Aside from harnessing the emotional, psychological, and apocalyptic energy of Milton's temptation scene in *Paradise Lost,* sections (5), (6), and (7) underscore the real and potential chaos shadowed in the Shaftesbury/Monmouth crowd-dazzling ploy in the late 1670s of the progress in the countryside (9). Like Shakespeare, Dryden believed in a logic of event—an instigating moment under certain circumstances leading to a point of no return or crisis, in its turn heading towards either disaster or relieved resolution. When Absalom/Monmouth tilts (as a result of Achitophel/Shaftesbury's consummate Iago-like improvisatory manipulation) into irresistible and irresponsible ambition, the English world of the late 1670s and 1681 lists into the Exclusion Crisis. But because in late 1681 the outcome has not yet neatly evolved, as in a play however persuasively crafted, into either tragedy or comedy, *Absalom and Achitophel* cannot go on as a play. Instead, Dryden can hit his readers' intellectual nerves with one of the most sharply honed piercing instruments out of the dramatic equipment of at least three cultures, the crisis.

Similarly Dryden incorporated another form exploited since antiquity. Twenty years earlier—with the nation in the foreground and Charles II in the background for the first two-thirds of the poem, reversed in the last third of the poem—Dryden in *Astraea Redux* had to convince both audiences that he accepted the swift-as-dreams arrival of the Restoration and its settlement. To do so, he used what he then knew best, the classical oration (Maurer, "Structure" 13–20). In 1681, with the stakes as high as personal, national, and cultural survival, he had at his disposal mastery of much more than the classical oration. In conjunction with other forms he deployed rhetoric for maximum enhancement: he underscored Achitophel/Shaftesbury's tireless intelligence applying a massive persuasive rhetoric to tempt Absalom/Monmouth, and he lost no opportunities in the whole paced performance of the poem to cut with rhetorical sensibility into the mind of the nation and its king.[14]

Second only to the heroic couplet in concentration, ubiquity, and variegated exploitation of form in seventeenth-century English sophisticated writing was the character, which probed psychology in the program of Baconian induction to command the Renaissance explosion of empirical knowledge.[15] Much of England's fate in the constitutional crises hinged on the motive and personality of individual politicians; but Dryden's sense that time was running out precluded designing the character as a static portrait, however incisive, or *Absalom and Achitophel* as a succession of static portraits, however arresting in juxtaposition. Instead, they became part of mounting urgency through location in not just one, but three forms biased towards a chronological march—drama, epic, allegory—and they simultaneously gave Dryden the swiftest expository mode for identifying fundamental incentive. Thus, in his character of Achitophel/Shaftesbury, Dryden dwells on elaborating the makeup, not of a simplistic villain, but of perhaps the most brilliant politician in England, who risks heading the country into disaster just to see whether he can get it back out, "to boast his Wit" (2: 10. 162). At the same time Dryden conveys the inexorable movement of ominous events by implanting the character in three different narrative exigencies rooted in the passing English scene: through relation, within the character form, of the traits to the prime mesmerizing spectacle of the day ("The wish'd occasion of the Plot he takes" [2: 11.208]); through the lingering vignette of the preceding section (3) on the escalating Popish-Plot fear and hysteria, and through the Shakespeare-like shift in scene to the following section (5), Achitophel in action in a speech tempting Absalom.

What gives the amalgam of *Absalom and Achitophel* a homogeneity, an undiminished energy and momentum, an intellectual carry-over, and a multiplicitous restatement with simultaneous substantive expansion is the unflagging creative power and intellectual infection of every heroic couplet. The apparent discontinuity of forms and parts (but all maneuvered into place alongside one another), because of its peculiar elucidating power, changes to a seamless continuity and a resonating whole. Sustained creative perception and advance inhere together in the recurring need to see the whole in the assigned world of each couplet. Picked and directed by Dryden's incentive to ward off disaster, all the couplets cognitively ignite one another. Thus, via the character, Dryden cuts deeply and quickly into Achitophel/Shaftesbury's makeup until we see Shaftesbury's tireless brilliance fascinated by itself, satisfied only by most fateful, self-imposed challenges.

Dryden's preoccupation widens suddenly into his famous observation about the connection between genius and madness: "Great Wits are sure to Madness near ally'd;/And thin Partitions do their Bounds divide" (2: 10. 163–64; see Wallerstein 445–71). The couplet is rendered unforgettable in a construction that acts out a marvel of time: chronological discovery synchronous with chronological cognition. The first half line conveys a starkly simple subject of inherently overwhelming interest, "Great Wits," and a predicate of arresting confidence, "are sure," arousing irresistible anticipation of the second half line, "to Madness near ally'd"—all in dramatically concentrated milliseconds. The first half line of the second line is in graphically elaborative, immediately consequential cross-pattern with the second half line of the first line, allowing a sudden transfixing glimpse into the powerful brain, "And thin Partitions." The second half line of the second line, in a contrasting cross-pattern that recalls the first half line, depicts the awesome result: disjointed disarray of potent mind "do[es] their Bounds divide." To keep thought perpetual, the rhyme words "ally'd and "divide" point endlessly to the significance of radical devastation.

While this analysis slows the swift inevitability of Dryden's statement, it shows how the couplet achieves indelibility, why it resonates throughout *Absalom and Achitophel* and beyond. It anneals varying complementary segments across the whole of *Absalom and Achitophel:* for example, unified intellectual power in Achitophel (4) with immature instability of ambition in Absalom (1, 6, 9); the chaotic self-centeredness of the malcontents (7) with the responsible intelligence of the King's supporters (11); the frivolous and politically explosive sexual carnival of Charles II (1) with his intellectual and administrative capability (11); the irrational whims of the masses (2) with the dialectical search for healing security (10). And this phenomenon is the direct or subliminal reinforcement and augmentation of but one couplet out of 503 (plus eight triplets and one hemistich, demanding related scrutiny). The couplets achieve this grand blend within sections, in transitions of crucial cunning, and across the whole poem.

5

Under the relentless pressure of events, not least of them the King's order at his back, Dryden realized that the intellectual and cultural preservative capacity of each of the forms known to him was inadequate. While *Absalom and Achitophel* has strongly suggested that it is lodged to achieve its end— now in one form, now in another, in forms attractive and useful to the Renaissance and Restoration—it is not in form any of them. It displays no form fully or consistently. Nor could any form carry for Dryden the urgency and meaning of the moment: England will end if it does not find universal or strategically placed rational competence to get it through the crisis. Any of the traditional forms could substantively mislead or distract readers with apparent solutions too pat, however subtle and profound, for the magnitude of a peril of continually shifting contours in an unknown congeries of events. Dryden's generative power subjected the forms to a fission and produced an amalgam of something authoritatively and appropriately fire-new. When he was tapped by Seymour or by Charles II to do his job, he had no recourse but to the open universe of his wits, which consisted of every literary art he knew, freely reconsidered and redeployed. Confronted with pitiless amorality (at least) of *Realpolitik,* he produced a brilliantly terminal moral reproof of Shaftesbury, the toughest subtlest Restoration politician (ready to wield *Scandalum Magnatum,* it should be remembered); of Monmouth, the King's darling offspring who got away with murder; and of Charles II, the fluctuating center of sovereign mortal power. In producing the astonishingly undiluted product of *Absalom and Achitophel,* John Dryden kept his head then and, so far as I can tell, for good.

Works Cited

Bloom, Edward A., and Lillian D. *Satire's Persuasive Voice.* Ithaca: Cornell UP, 1979.

Boyce, Benjamin. *The Polemic Character 1640–1661: A Chapter in English Literary History.* 1955. New York: Octagon, 1969.

———. *The Theophrasian Character in England to 1642.* Cambridge: Harvard UP, 1947.

Brodwin, Leonara Leet. "Miltonic Allusion in *Absalom and Achitophel:* Its Function in the Political Satire." *Journal of English and Germanic Philology* 68 (1969): 24–44.

Brower, Reuben A. "An Allusion to Europe: Dryden and Tradition." *ELH* 19 (1952): 38–48.

Brown, Wallace C. "Dramatic Tension in Neoclassic Satire." *College English* 6 (1945): 263–69.

Budick, Sanford. *Poetry of Civilization: Mythopoeic Displacement in the Verse of Milton, Dryden, Pope, and Johnson.* New Haven: Yale UP, 1974.

Cable, Chester H. "*Absalom and Achitophel* as Epic Satire." *Studies in Honor of John Wilcox.* Ed. A. Dayle Wallace and Woodburn O. Ross. Detroit: Wayne State UP, 1958. 51–60.

Chapple, J. A. V. *Dryden's Earl of Shaftesbury.* Hull: U of Hull P, 1973.

Conlon, Michael J. "The Rhetoric of *Kairos* in Dryden's *Absalom and Achitophel.*" *Rhetorics of Order/Ordering Rhetorics in English Neoclassical Literature.* Ed. J. Douglas Canfield and J. Paul Hunter. Newark: U of Delaware P, 1989. 85–97.

Copeland, Edward. "*Absalom and Achitophel* and *The Banqueting House Ceiling:* 'The Great Relation.'" *Eighteenth-Century Life* 11 (1987): 22–40.

Cousins, A. D. "Heroic Satire: Dryden and the Defence of Later Stuart Kingship." *Southern Review* 13 (1980): 170–87.

DeArmond, Anna Janney. "Some Aspects of Character-Writing in the Period of the Restoration." *Delaware Notes,* 16th ser. (1943): 55–89.

Dryden, John. *The Works of John Dryden.* Ed. H. T. Swedenberg, Jr., Alan Roper, et al. Berkeley: U of California P, 1956–. 20 vols.

Dyson, A. E., and Julian Lovelock. *Masterful Images: English Poetry from Metaphysicals to Romantics.* New York: Harper, 1976.

Ellis, Frank H. "'Legends no Histories' Part the Second: The Ending of *Absalom and Achitophel.*" *Modern Philology* 85 (1988): 393–407.

Emslie, McD. "Dryden's Couplets: Wit and Conversation." *Essays in Criticism* 11 (1961): 264–73.

Feder, Lillian. "John Dryden's Use of Classical Rhetoric." *PMLA* 69 (1954): 1258–78.

Ferry, Anne Davidson. *Milton and the Miltonic Dryden.* Cambridge: Harvard UP, 1968.

Fisch, Harold. *Jerusalem and Albion: The Hebraic Factor in Seventeenth-Century Literature.* New York: Schocken, 1964.

French, A. L. "Dryden, Marvell and Political Poetry." *SEL* 8 (1968): 397–413.

Griffin, Dustin. "Satiric Closure." *Genre* 18 (1985): 173–89.

Guilhamet, Leon M. "Dryden's Debasement of Scripture in *Absalom and Achitophel.*" *SEL* 9 (1969): 395–413.

———. *Satire and the Transformation of Genre.* Philadelphia: U of Pennsylvania P, 1987.

Hagstrum, Jean H. *The Sister Arts: The Tradition of Literary Pictorialism and English Poetry from Dryden to Gray.* Chicago: U of Chicago P, 1958.

Harth, Phillip. "Dryden in 1678–1681: the Literary and Historical Perspectives." *The Golden & the Brazen World: Papers in Literature and History, 1650–1800.* Ed. John M. Wallace. Berkeley: U of California P, 1985. 55–77.

———. "Legends No Histories: The Case of *Absalom and Achitophel.*" *Studies in Eighteenth-Century Culture* 4 (1975): 13–29.

Hoffman, Arthur W. *John Dryden's Imagery.* Gainesville: U of Florida P, 1962.

Hopkins, David. *John Dryden.* Cambridge: Cambridge UP, 1986.

———, and Tom Mason. eds. *The Beauties of Dryden.* Bristol: Bristol Classical, 1982.

Jack, Ian. *Augustan Satire: Intention and Idiom in English Poetry 1660–1750* 1952. London: Oxford UP, 1957.

Johnson, Samuel. *Lives of the English Poets.* Ed. George Birkbeck Hill. 3 vols. Oxford: Clarendon, 1905.

Korshin, Paul J. "Probability and Character in the Eighteenth Century." *Probability, Time, and Space in Eighteenth-Century Literature.* Ed. Paula R. Backscheider. New York: AMS, 1979. 63–77.

Levine, George R. "Dryden's 'Inarticulate Poesy': Music and the Davidic King in *Absalom and Achitophel.*" *Eighteenth-Century Studies* 1 (1968): 291–312.

Lewalski, Barbara Kiefer. " 'David's Troubles Remembred': An Analogue to 'Absalom and Achitophel.' " *Notes and Queries* 11 (1964): 340–43.

———. "The Scope and Function of Biblical Allusion in *Absalom and Achitophel.*" *English Language Notes* 3 (1965): 29–35.

Lewis, C. S. *Rehabilitations and Other Essays.* London: Oxford UP, 1939.

Lord, George de F. " 'Absalom and Achitophel' and Dryden's Political Cosmos." *Writers and their Background: John Dryden.* Ed. Earl Miner. London: Bell, 1972. 156–90.

Maresca, Thomas E. *Epic to Novel.* Columbus: Ohio State UP, 1974.

Marshall, W. Gerald. "Classical Oratory and the Major Addresses in Dryden's *Absalom and Achitophel.*" *Restoration* 4 (1980): 71–80.

Maurer, A. E. Wallace. "The Structure of Dryden's *Astraea Redux.*" *PLL* 2 (1966): 13–20.

———. "Who Prompted Dryden to Write *Absalom and Achitophel?*" *Philological Quarterly* 40 (1961): 130–38.

Miner, Earl. *Dryden's Poetry.* Bloomington: Indiana UP, 1967.

Moore, John Robert. "Milton among the Augustans: The Infernal Council." *Studies in Philology* 48 (1951): 15–25.

Mullin, Joseph E. "The Occasion, Form, Structure, and Design of John Dryden's *MacFlecknoe:* A Varronian Satire." Ph.D. diss., Ohio State University, 1967.

McFadden, George. *Dryden The Public Writer 1660–1685.* Princeton: Princeton UP, 1978.

McHenry, Robert W., Jr. "Dryden's History: The Case of Slingsby Bethel." *Huntington Library Quarterly* 47 (1984). 253–69.

———. *Contexts 3: Absalom and Achitophel.* Hamden, CT: Shoe String, 1986.

McKeon, Michael. "Historicizing *Absalom and Achitophel.*" *The New Eighteenth Century: Theory, Politics, English Literature.* Ed. Felicity Nussbaum and Laura Brown. New York: Methuen, 1987. 23–40.

Peterson, R. G. "Larger Manners and Events: Sallust and Virgil in *Absalom and Achitophel.*" *PMLA* 82 (1967): 236–44.

Price, Martin. *To the Palace of Wisdom: Studies in Order and Energy from Dryden to Blake.* Garden City: Doubleday, 1964.

Ramsey, Paul. *The Art of John Dryden.* Lexington: U of Kentucky P, 1969.

Randolph, Mary Claire. "The Structural Design of the Formal Verse Satire." *Philological Quarterly* 21 (1942): 368–84.

Rivers, Isabel. *The Poetry of Conservatism: 1660–1745.* Cambridge: Rivers, 1973.

Robinson, K. E. "A Reading of *Absalom and Achitophel.*" *Yearbook of English Studies* 6 (1976): 53–62.

Roper, Alan. *Dryden's Poetic Kingdoms.* London: Routledge, 1965.

Rothstein, Eric. *Restoration and Eighteenth-Century Poetry 1660–1780.* London: Routledge, 1981.

Schakel, Peter J. "Dryden's *Discourse* and 'Bi-Partite Structure' in the Design of Formal Verse Satire." *English Language Notes* 21 (June 1984): 33–41.

Schilling, Bernard. *Dryden and the Conservative Myth: A Reading of Absalom and Achitophel.* New Haven: Yale UP, 1961.

Seidel, Michael. *Satiric Inheritance: Rabelais to Sterne.* Princeton: Princeton UP, 1979.

Smith, David Nichol. *Characters from the Histories & Memoirs of the Seventeenth Century.* Oxford: Clarendon, 1920.

Terr, Leonard B. "Tragic Satire from Jonson to Pope: the Vituperative and Elegiac Phases, and Their Relationships to the Neoclassical Pictorial Tradition." Ph.D. diss., Brown University, 1971.

Thomas, W. K. *The Crafting of* Absalom and Achitophel: *Dryden's "Pen for a Party."* Waterloo, Ont.: Wilfrid Laurier UP, 1978.

Tyson, Gerald P. "Dryden's Dramatic Essay." *Ariel* 4 (January 1973): 72–86.

Van Doren, Mark. *John Dryden: A Study of His Poetry.* 3rd ed. New York: Holt, 1946.

Verrall, A. W. *Lectures on Dryden.* 1914. New York: Russell, 1963.

Wallerstein, Ruth. "To Madness Near Allied: Shaftesbury and His Place in the Design and Thought of *Absalom and Achitophel.*" *Huntington Library Quarterly* 6 (1943): 445–71.

Wedgewood, C. V. *Poetry and Politics under the Stuarts.* Cambridge: Cambridge UP, 1960.

Weinbrot, Howard D. " 'Nature's Holy Bands' in *Absalom and Achitophel:* Fathers and Sons, Satire and Change." *Modern Philology* 85 (1988): 373–92.

———. "The Pattern of Formal Verse Satire in the Restoration and the Eighteenth Century." *PMLA* 80 (1965): 394–401.

Winters, Yvor. *Forms of Discovery: Critical & Historical Essays on the Forms of the Short Poem in English.* Denver: Swallow, 1967.

Worcester, David. *The Art of Satire.* 1940. New York: Russell, 1960.

Zwicker, Steven N. *Politics and Language in Dryden's Poetry: The Arts of Disguise.* Princeton: Princeton UP, 1984.

Notes

1.   Verrall 59, 61; Ferry 26–40. For the epic-form theory in its ascendant, see Worcester 158; Lewalski, " 'David's Troubles' " 341n6; Maresca 3.

2.   Thomas 177–213. For less specifically demarcated applications of the classical oration to *Absalom and Achitophel,* see Feder 1258–78; Bloom 59, 72, 81, 82; and Marshall 71–80. See also, below, n. 13.

3.   For Dryden's knowledge of painting and painters, see commentary on Dryden's translation of Du Fresnoy's *De Arte Graphica* and on Dryden's "The Parallel betwixt Painting and Poetry" (20: 345–49).

4.   On the general influence of satire, see Wedgewood 400–01 and n.49; Peterson 236–37, 244; Brower 45–48. On the detectable influence of formal satire, see for background Randolph 368–84; for application, Schakel 38, 40, 41; Weinbrot, "The Pattern" 400 and n.49. For a claim that formal satire dominates, see Cousins 178. On English adaptation of satire, see Jack 99, 76. On satire and chaos, see Seidel xii; Guilhamet, *Satire* 6–7, 13–17, 84, 99.

5.   Dryden recalled "Satyre" (2: 3. 22–23) as applied selectively (e.g., to Absalom and Zimri), not organically, as a considerable, but not pervasive, literary resource in the work (2: 5. 6). His identification of *Absalom and Achitophel* with Varronian satire in his *Discourse of Satire* (1693) was genial speculative analogizing, for no Varro was extant, only hypothesizing at two removes, Cicero to Casaubon to Dryden 4: 46. 1–48. 20; (see also 4: 526, 558–61).

6.   Ramsey 125; Zwicker 89; Lewis 8; Winters 126; French 404, 413. Mention should be made here of perceived formal designs of music in *Absalom and Achitophel:* fugal fantasia and pervasive harmonizing resonance in the *figura* of David as musician (Levine 291–312).

7.   Thomas 117–213; Dryden 2:233–34; Brodwin 30–41; Ellis 399, 400; Mullin 71–73; Lewalski, "The Scope" 30–34; Peterson 237; Cousins 178–79; and Copeland 34–36.

8.   For support of Johnson's view, see French 399–413; Hopkins 89; Brodwin 42–44. For disagreement with Johnson, see Cable 51; Lord 188; Moore 23; Lewalski, "The Scope" 30,

34; Guilhamet, "Dryden's Debasement" 410–11; Robinson 56–62; McHenry, "Dryden's History" 254, 268–69, and *Contexts* 1–2; and Griffin 176.

9.   In the order alluded to in the text, the works are Verrall 59; Schilling 283, 306, 138, 46; Hoffman 73, 89–90; Roper 14; Budick 89–90, 94–98, 100–05; Miner 110, 141–42, 125 (see also 17: 271. 26–17: 277. 13 and 17: 435–40).

10.   For Seymour, see Maurer, "Who Prompted" 130–38. For Charles as Dryden's audience, the circumspection between them, and Dryden's bent for conveying advice obliquely to Charles, see Dyson and Lovelock 83; Harth, "Legends" 26, and "Dryden in 1678–1681" 75; Rivers 134; Weinbrot, " 'Nature's Holy Bands' " 373–92.

11.   Cf. Brown 263; Jack 76; Emslie 264, 272; Terr 214.

12.   The scale of Dryden's powers led Chapple (19) to Frank Kermode's remark: " '[W]antonness in strength is a mark of the absolutely mature Shakespeare, as perhaps of all poets."

13.   Conlon 85–97 argues (a) that Dryden depicted Charles II exercising his prerogative, within the limits fixed by England's Polybian mixed constitution, at the right time during the Exclusion Crisis when he dissolved the Oxford parliament on 28 March 1681 and (b) that Dryden published the poem at the right time during the Crisis. In crisis, timing is all (the rhetoric of *Kairos*). I would argue that the ultimate Kairos of *Absalom and Achitophel* is Dryden's daring to put publicly—c. 17 November 1681—the rules of behavior to King Charles: viz., "the *persona publica* of the king" must subject "the fallible and embattled person of David" (Conlon 93) to the strictest government, under penalty of disaster to king, constitution, and nation.

14.   See the groundwork done on rhetoric in Dryden by the commentators referred to in n. 2, above.

15.   For studies of the character and its branchings in seventeenth-century England, see DeArmond 55–89; Boyce, *The Theophrastan Character;* Boyce, *The Polemic Character;* Smith, *Characters;* Van Doren 149–69; Tyson 72–86; and Korshin 63–77.

"Nature's Holy Bands" in
Absalom and Achitophel:
Fathers and Sons, Satire and Change

HOWARD D. WEINBROT

The opening lines of *Absalom and Achitophel* long have been considered an *apologia pro regis libidine*. Here is a sophisticated exchange between men of the world, one of whom happened to be the divinely appointed gentleman king whose actions were applauded by the poet, his well-connected readers, and God.[1] Attacks on Charles's private life, the argument runs, were both irrelevant and a stalking horse for attacks on his kingship. During the last several years, however, a few students of the poem have objected to this interpretation. In criticism as in politics vocal minorities may be heard without being listened to. In 1971 A. E. Dyson and Julian Lovelock expressed surprise that "some critics have sought to excuse the censure of the King" either as a rhetorical device "or even worse, as a celebration of the King's humanity."[2] Nonetheless, in 1976 K. E. Robinson rightly complained of the continuing "critical orthodoxy" that absolved Charles of responsibility for his sexual actions.[3] As recently as 1981 Jerome Donnelly lamented that "the most widely accepted readings of *Absalom and Achitophel* view Dryden's attitude toward Charles "as one of almost unreserved admiration."[4] Each of the two latter revisionists also shares a corollary of his skepticism—King Charles as King David must evolve into a better person if he is to become the better monarch capable of speaking lines God sanctions.[5]

These studies have been strengthened by another salutary trend, one perhaps related to the new interest in family history during the Restoration and the eighteenth century. Donnelly has amplified scattered remarks of others and made plain that as a culpable father Charles must acknowledge a superior model before he can improve. This movement, in turn, has served to relocate the poem's decidedly mixed genre, which long had been confidently placed within the heroic kind,[6] its hero, after all, was king by divine right, a

Howard D. Weinbrot, " 'Nature's Holy Bands' in *Absalom and Achitophel:* Fathers and Sons, Satire and Change." Originally published in *Modern Philology,* Volume 85, No. 4 (1988):373–392. Printed by permission.

type of Christ, emblem of grace, and natural enemy of the forces of Satan and Chaos ranked against him. The hypothesis, or assumption, of genre was a function of the hypothesis of royal character—or vice versa as the case may be. With an assumption of a dominant satiric mode, however, different questions suggest themselves. These include the nature of characterization and the placement of characters, and ask how the endangered king becomes the enlightened secure king. They include the role of satiric norms and ask what model or models would allow that king to change, so that both political sides can agree on civic standards and avoid civil war. They also include questions concerning rhetoric, which ask how the narrator can be an admitted royalist while claiming to be a moderate and hoping to persuade Whigs, and how he can criticize the king whose favor he must gain. Finally, such questions ask what external, contemporary evidence from history, politics, theology, or paper wars might substantiate whatever answers one finds.

I propose, then, to enlarge upon and synthesize happy trends in Dryden criticism, and to suggest ways of rethinking some assumptions and conclusions regarding his greatest poem.

I

The patriarchal basis of Charles's power was of course central to royalist theory of divine right. Dryden, however, largely avoids Filmer's dogmatic insistence on Adam's paternal kingship, either to preserve his own appearance of moderation or to avoid a suspect argument. Locke observes that Filmer's putative biblical theory ignores the mother's authority, though the Bible gave equal weight to her in establishing parental power over children.[7]

Dryden nonetheless knew that both Whigs and Tories believed in "Natures Holy Bands" (line 339). Shaftesbury seeks fortune for his son, and Locke argues that "Reverence, Acknowledgement, Respect and Honour . . . is always due from Children to their Parents."[8] Though there are limits on each side's power, by "the Law of God and Nature" even the adult offspring must always seek his parents' welfare. Locke's remarks well support Gordon Schochet's view that there is an "underlying patriarchalism" in much Whig political thought:

> God having made the Parents Instruments in his great design of continuing the Race of Mankind, and the occasions of Life to their Children, as he hath laid on them an obligation to nourish, preserve, and bring up their Off-spring; So he has laid on the Children a perpetual Obligation of *honouring their Parents,* which containing in it an inward esteem and reverence to be shewn by all outward Expressions, ties up the Child from any thing that may ever injure or affront, disturb, or endanger the Happiness or Life of those, from whom he

received his; and engages him in all actions of defence, relief, assistance, and comfort of those, by whose means he entered into being, and has been made capable of any enjoyments of life. From this Obligation no State, no Freedom, can absolve Children.[9]

Dryden's family setting thus recalls the obligations of child to parent shared by each "party," even though circumstances made that setting more attractive to royalists. No one in the early 1680s could forget that Charles II was endangered in part because he was the son of the beheaded Charles I. Samuel Pordage's *Azaria and Hushai* (January 17, 1682) laments "The Scandal of a curs'd Conspiracy, / Against our King and Father to rebell" (p. 14).[10] On July 18, 1683, the author of *A Congratulatory Pindaric Poem, For His Majesties Safe Deliverance from This Hellish and True Plot,* says that the king was victimized "For that great Crime of his, of being his Father's Son" (p. 3). The author of *An Answer written on Sight, by a Loyal Hand* (September 14, 1683) pleads to the Whigs: "Though *CHARLES* the Father you did Murther, / Forbear the Son, and Plot no further." Shortly thereafter the evoker of *Sylla's Ghost: A Satyr Against Ambition* (October 4, 1683) makes a similar point. Lord Grey wishes to kill Charles II "For none other Crime than this alone, / For being his Glorious Martyr'd Father's Son" (p. 8; see also p. 12). On January 7, 1684, *The Recanting Whig* wonders how he can atone for all he has done "To a Martyr'd Fathers too much injur'd Son."

The perpetrators of such wickedness found analogues in Phaethon, Icarus, Satan, Catiline, Brutus, Cromwell, and vipers. Accordingly, Monmouth's opponents easily roused emotion against an illegitimate son suspected of seeking the death of his generous king and father. Dryden raises the problem while avoiding the charge:

> Some thought they God's Anointed meant to Slay
> By Guns, invented since full many a day:
> Our Author swears it not; but who can know
> How far the Devil and the *Jebusites* may go?
> [Lines 130–33]

Others were less oblique. The writer of *A Lash to Disloyalty* (August 13, 1683) berates "Insatiate *Monmouth!*" for seeking "thy Fathers Death" and "Royal Father murdered" (p. 1) to gain the crown beyond his birth. Long after the Exclusion Crisis, Charles Hopkins could explore the natural anger evoked by two simultaneous ugly crimes. A faithful subject in the *Female Warrior* (1700) warns: "On your own Head a double Guilt you bring, / Warring against a Father and a King" (p. 23). Such wars and the way to resolve them form one of the bases of *Absalom and Achitophel;* they also provide its narrator with his bond both to the king and to any reader sensitive to domestic or national family structures.

The poem as rhetorical document thus begins with its address to the reader. Dryden affirms his moderation, his association with the reasonable "honest Party," and his dissociation from the violent fringes of either side. Moderation does not mean indecision, for the introduction plainly aligns the speaker with the king's party and personality. Dryden's own affection for Absalom ingratiates him with the king, whose forgiving temper the speaker here imitates. Like the king, he has "endeavour'd to commit" the faults of extenuation, palliation, and indulgence: "*David* himself, cou'd not be more tender of the Young-man's Life, than I would be of his Reputation" (pp. 3–4).

Such alignment signals Dryden's wish to make his art a model for life in at least two senses. He does not conclude the biblical story because he could not "shew *Absalom* Unfortunate." Indeed, he would prefer to rewrite history and reconcile Absalom and David: "And, who knows but this may come to pass" for "There seems, yet, to be room left for a Composure." But, he warns, the alternative is reality, pity, and the *Ense rescindendum,* the surgeon's work turned to the hangman's, "which I wish not to my very enemies." Far better, Dryden hopes, to allow his "good natur'd Errour" of forgiving Absalom as Charles forgives Monmouth. "God is infinitely merciful; and his Vicegerent is only not so because he is not Infinite" (pp. 4–5). The king's poet, Dryden might have added, is not as merciful as that vicegerent only because he is, as it were, even less infinite than the king, several of whose values as benevolent, forgiving, but potentially stern monarch he shares. The king soon must become the chastiser of vice he prefers not to be. Like his sovereign, Dryden can ameliorate the sting of his satire; like his sovereign, he can convince those who abuse his kindness that he can be severe as well as gentle (p. 3).

Alliance with the king's mercy and filial piety allows Dryden room respectfully to satirize the king himself. Dryden wished that the Absalom outside of the poem would change upon seeing his conduct impartially portrayed, but he allows David the opportunity to change within the poem and so makes his key statement regarding satire only after he has bonded himself to the king. "The true end of *Satyre,* is the amendment of Vices by correction. And he who writes Honestly, is no more an Enemy to the Offendour than the Physician to the Patient, when he prescribes harsh Remedies to an inveterate Disease" (p. 5). On the principle of *ad exemplum regis,* a sick king makes a sick nation; if the king's vices are amended Absalom's can be as well. Dryden's introduction thus lays out his overt and covert satiric design. The latter must be deftly implemented or the narrator will squander the good will presumably gained in his association with the king. Dryden meets this problem in the poem's deservedly famous opening lines, which are not an "apology" or "insinuated condonement of . . . promiscuity" in the king's private life as they have been called.[11] Rather, they lay out a theory of causation: unacceptable conduct breeds unacceptable conduct.

II

Dryden lacked the occasion to savage Charles for his royal lust, as Rochester did in "A Satyr on Charles II" (1674):

> Poor prince! thy prick, like thy buffoons at Court,
> Will govern thee because it makes thee sport.
> . . . .
> Though safety, law, religion, life lay on 't,
> 'Twould break through all to make its way to cunt.[12]

Dryden nonetheless granted both the point of such attacks and their implicit compliment to the monarch's sexual exploits. One could do worse than the blame by praise of telling Charles II that he himself was infinitely virile, though attached to a barren wife, "A Soyl ungratefull to the Tiller's care" (line 12).

But Charles is to blame. He listens to nature's prompting, not to the restraints of law (line 5); he forsakes concubines and bride through indiscriminate sexual use (lines 6, 9); he forsakes the Judaeo-Christian God of design and imitates a deity who thoughtlessly "Scatter'd his Maker's Image through the Land" (line 10). One such "image" is Absalom himself, who shares his father's strengths and weaknesses. Absalom too is born for love, is naturally pleasing and graceful, and is given everything he wishes in spite of violating the law. Accordingly, "With secret Joy indulgent *David* view'd / His Youthfull Image in his Son renew'd" (lines 31–32).

Parallel and comparison and contrast are among Dryden's typical modes of proceeding in *Absalom and Achitophel*. He thus shows how Israel shares Absalom's image, but without the physical charm of the wayward youth. His movements are "all accompanied with grace" (line 29); Israel tries "th' extent and stretch of grace" (line 46). David "To all [Absalom's] wishes Nothing . . . deny'd" (line 33); Israel is "God's pamper'd people . . . debauch'd with ease" (line 47). Absalom is guilty of "Some warm excesses which the Law forbore" (line 37) including murder (line 39); Israel "No King could govern, nor no God could please" (line 48), and no nation is "by Laws less circumscrib'd and bound" (line 54). Israel regards David as "An Idoll Monarch which their hands had made" (line 64); Absalom later accepts Achitophel's view that "the People have a Right Supreme / To make their Kings; for Kings are made for them" (lines 409–10). The Israelites' murmurings and Absalom's sedition, illegitimate complaints and an illegitimate son, are unified by an illegitimate leader: "*Achitophel* still wants a Chief, and none / Was found so fit as Warlike *Absalon*" (lines 220–21) who, in turn, would be made a vassal to the crowd and accept "Kingly power . . . ebbing out" (line 226). David has literally created his own revolution, as his own worst traits, made attractive through engaging presence, in turn encourage the nation's worst traits and lend coherence to chaos. If "The true end of *Satyre* is the amendment of Vices by correction," the poem must show David corrected or Israel ruined.

The image of a guilty king was readily available in the biblical story which, together with some of its commentaries, portrays the morally irregular David as hardly the type of Christ he too often has been called. Shortly before Dryden's poem appeared, for example, the author of *Absalom's Conspiracy: Or, The Tragedy of Treason* (July 1, 1680) made plain that "The king was careless, drown'd in his Pleasures."[13] Bishop Simon Patrick's account of David's adultery with Bathsheba and virtual murder of Uriah, her husband and his loyal officer, includes words like crime, idleness, sloth, sin, guilt, foul, vile, and corrupt. Patrick shows that David's "very Nature was altered, and become base and degenerate; now he had given himself up to Sensuality." His consequent marriage to Bathsheba *"was evil in the eyes* of God."[14] By 1697 Pierre Bayle summarized much of the received awareness of David's uncertain virtue. He caused his own grief, for "his Indulgence to his Children was excessive, and he himself was the first that suffered for it." Had he punished, "as he ought," Absalom's murder of Amnon, "he would not have run the Hazard of being entirely dethroned." Alas, Bayle laments of the varied miseries in David's private and public life, "What Scandal is here given to pious Souls, to see so much Infamy in the Family of this King!"[15]

Hostile readers clearly saw that Dryden invoked the tradition of David as the fallible paragon and attacked this strategy to discredit a popular poem. On December 10, 1681, Henry Care's *Towser the Second: A Bull-Dog* replied to *Absalom and Achitophel* and labeled Dryden a mad dog menacing or biting everyone, including "our Royal *CHARLES,* / And his two Mistresses." Four days later "A Person of Honour" published his *Poetical Reflections on a Late Poem Entituled Absalom and Achitophel.* He complained that Dryden's poem was "a Capital or National Libel." The king as portrayed is "a broad figure of scandalous inclinations" whose "irregularities" render him more "the property of Parasites and Vice, than suitable to the accomplishments of so excellent a Prince." Worse yet, Dryden darkens David's "sanctity in spite of illuminations from Holy Writ" (*Poetical Reflections,* sigs. B1r-v). The author of *A Key (with the Whip) To open the Mystery and Iniquity of . . . Absalom and Achitophel* (January 13, 1682) bitterly charged Dryden with committing "scandalum magnatum *yea of Majesty itself"* (verso of dedication) and with sparing "Nor Queen, nor King, in thy pernicious Book" (p. 25). On April 6, 1682, Elkanah Settle made a similar point in his *Absalom Senior: Or Achitophel Transpros'd.* Dryden's poem has *"this one unpardonable Fault, That the Lash is more against a* David, *than an* Achitophel." This "unmannerly Boldness" both attacks "the publick Justice of the Nation" and affronts "even the Throne itself" (sig. A2r). By July 24 of the same year another hostile poet issued *A Satyr to His Muse: By the Author of Absalom and Achitophel* which records the "Whoring life" of David, "By whom *Uriah* was so basely Slain" (p. 4).[16]

These respondents hoped further to taint Charles by their assumed outrage and to taint Dryden's poem by confusing the part with the whole. They enhance the scandal by denying it and imply that a loyal poet is unconscionable to write such stuff and that the unlawful David is not countered by the new David under God's law. Such remarks show that David's virtue was perceived as very fragile indeed. In the earlier phase of *Absalom and Achitophel,* then, David makes his own rebellion by propagating his own lawlessness in his lawless son and lawless nation. How he remedies that situation is in part a function of other fathers and sons who join the narrator in two essential activities: in general, by establishing increasingly assured and numerous public voices of reason, restraint, and law to which the king as father of his nation listens and from which he grows; and in particular, by establishing through Ormond and Ossory the normative relationship between father and son that also serves as an instructive paradigm for the king. Along the way Dryden allows Absalom and Achitophel to discredit themselves through their words, political theory, and Miltonic context and suggests equally unpleasant biblical contexts for Achitophel's other colleagues. Phillip Harth has demonstrated that Dryden could not have hoped to influence Shaftesbury's trial;[17] but he could have hoped to influence consequent attitudes toward the incorrigible Shaftesbury and the corrigible king, and he certainly hoped that Monmouth would draw the appropriate inference and take the appropriate side.

Dryden's hope was shared by the admiring author of *Absalom's IX Worthies: Or, A Key to a late Book or Poem* (March 10, 1682): "Thy Lines will make young *Absalon* relent, / And though 'tis hard *Achitophel* repent." With the general reconciliation, tearful, protective, "Godlike *David*" fully recognizes that he "owes his Son and Subjects to thy Verse" (sig. A1v). The author of *Good News in Bad Times; Or, Absalom's Return to David's Bosome* (November 30, 1683) also sees the demise of the Whigs, the reform of Monmouth, the intercession of York on his behalf, and the consequent reunion of father and son and subject and monarch. Though these reunions were fanciful, in the enclosed world of Dryden's poem the king can reform after he watches a salutary filial relationship and its links to the divine, and listens to salutary prophetic advice.

III

Achitophel produces a son after his own image, "a shapeless Lump, like Anarchy" (line 172); he also wishes to produce his twin by becoming Absalom's surrogate father and supplying values and the royal birth that David denies him. Achitophel has refused "his Age the needful hours of Rest," punished "a Body which he could not please" and now is "Bankrupt of Life" (lines 166–68). He thus steals from David's nest while implicitly admitting to the defects of age he attributes to David. Achitophel's first speech shows his own apparent power: he elevates Absalom to the level of prince, likens him to Christ in his nativity, and calls him a second Moses leading his people to freedom in the promised land. He is, finally, a "*Saviour*" and "Royal Youth" (lines 240, 250) who must accept Heaven's invitation to be king. To do so he must also accept Achitophel's breaking of international alliances, shaking of public pillars of support, usurping of titles, inverting of order that makes treason safe and the profane sacred, and substituting the people for the crown as a source of power. Achitophel debases David in the proportion that he elevates Absalom, turning David into Lucifer. The monarch "like the Prince of Angels from his height, / Comes tumbling downward with diminish'd light" (lines 273–74). Achitophel also replaces divine order with fortune and chance as he strips David of all his friends—including the son whose duty and gratitude obliged him to defend, relieve, assist, and comfort his father.

Substitution of fathers is another way in which Dryden taps Tory and Whig paternal feelings. Algernon Sidney was one of the many Whig theorists who argued that "No man can be my father but he that did beget me; and it is absurd to say I owe that duty to one who is not my father, which I owe to my father, as to say, he did beget me, who did not beget me; for the obligation that arises from benefits can only be to him that conferred them"—as Achitophel did not so confer to Absalom.[18]

In spite of this misalliance, Dryden's narrator again joins his royal master in attenuating, excusing, and praising Absalom. Some of that credit is due to a young man of such sound familial and political perception that he ably refutes Achitophel and, in the process, condemns himself from his own mouth. Absalom also shows why, in the best sense, he is not his father's son, for he finally refuses to extend the benefit of the doubt to his father that his father extended to him. Dryden reminds us of this difference of behavior through repetition of the same phrase. The father calls the son's murderous act "a Just Revenge for injur'd Fame" (line 40); the son tells Achitophel, "What Millions has he Pardon'd of his Foes, / Whom Just Revenge did to his Wrath expose" (lines 323–24). This son, though, later blames his father who "Exalts his Enemies, his Freinds destroys" (line 711). Absalom's surrender to Achitophel's values is signaled by repeated personal pronouns and by abuse of family ties:

> Why should I then Repine at Heavens Decree;
> Which gives me no Pretence to Royalty?
> Yet oh that Fate Propitiously Enclind,
> Had rais'd my Birth, or had debas'd my Mind;
> To my large Soul, not all her Treasure lent,
> And then Betray'd it to a mean Descent.
> I find, I find my mounting Spirits Bold,
> And *David*'s part disdains my Mothers Mold.

> Why am I Scanted by a Niggard Birth?
> My Soul Disclaims the Kindred of her Earth:
> And, made for Empire, Whispers me within;
> Desire of Greatness is a Godlike Sin.
> [Lines 361–72]

The emphasis on *I, me,* and *my* removes the mask of community interest; the insult to his mother is both humanly offensive and a violation of Whig family dogma; and the last line signals his change of divine analogy. Before falling, Absalom said of his father's mercy also extended to his son: "His Crime is God's beloved Attribute" (line 328). Now the crime has become Absalom's and is the devil's, not God's, in the self-praise and unwitting self-condemnation in "Desire of Greatness is a Godlike Sin." The excessive mercy of David becomes the excessive ambition of Absalom, a change Achitophel notices; his increase in satanic rhetoric is signaled by the Miltonic inversion of "Him Staggering so when Hells dire Agent found" (line 373).

Achitophel's fresh forces of argument include an extreme statement of the contract theory of government, which he turns into family theory. "The People have a Right Supreme / To make their Kings; for Kings are made for them" (lines 409–10). The people have become the patriarchs, and the king is the son who must obey. Filmer's *Patriarcha* has become Achitophel's, but with a change in the cast of characters.

Achitophel also discredits the filial bond between father and son and, again in violation of Whig theory, labels it mere paternal self-love:

> Nor let his Love Enchant your generous Mind;
> 'Tis Natures trick to Propagate her Kind.
> Our fond Begetters, who would never dye,
> Love but themselves in their Posterity.
> [Lines 423–26]

Even that love is questionable. If David loves his "Darling Son" (line 433) why cheat him of his birthright? James will be given a crown he does not deserve, will reverse his brother's vice, and will meditate revenge. Under such conditions nature herself must continue to be redefined. "Natures Holy Bands" that restrain the son from harming his father now become "Natures Eldest law" (line 458) of self-defense and Achitophel's defense of violent revolution. Achitophel also uses another metaphor of retreat from civilized repression, one perhaps drawn from the biblical Absalom's humiliating and incestuous seduction of his father's concubines. To "Commit a pleasing Rape upon the Crown" is at once to possess prince and law (lines 474–76). The virile scatterer of his image has become like one of his own slaves or concubines; he is a passive woman "Secure" (line 475) under the weight of the new values of Achitophel's new royal son.

IV

Achitophel unites several other factions behind that son. Zimri, Shimei, and Corah are the leading players and share several overlapping functions. Each serves internal poetic and structural needs. As the Duke of Buckingham, Zimri parallels Barzillai, the Duke of Ormond, who begins the loyalist catalog. Zimri is "all Mankinds Epitome" (line 546) in contrast to Amiel, Edward Seymour, who elicits the wise words of Commons, "*Israel*'s Tribes in small" (line 906). As one of the "Princes of the Land" (line 543) he has at least a metaphoric title that Achitophel bestows on Absalom as "Auspicious Prince" (line 230). Discrediting such a leader thus discredits much of the movement he represents. He is demonstrably incoherent, unreliable, unpredictable, dubiously sane, and "always in the wrong" (line 547). So is Shimei. Bethel's reputation for republican cruelty during the civil wars and his self-involved acquisition of money contrast with David's mercy and varied generosity;[19] and his biblical support of Absalom and cursing of David and his servants contrast with David's temperance and refusal to allow usurpation. Corah, in turn, is ugly in body and spirit, at once recalling Achitophel's ugly son and contrasting with David's beautiful son. His body is an emblem of the cause of which Absalom should be wary.

These characters also amplify the theme of improper paternity associated with an evil plot. Like the Whigs, Zimri embodies political and moral disorder, instability, and ultimate infertility. Within a month he

> Was Chymist, Fidler, States-Man, and Buffoon:
> Then all for Women, Painting, Rhiming, Drinking;
> Besides ten thousand freaks that dy'd in thinking.
> [Lines 550–52]

As Jerome Donnelly has suggested, the dead freaks may recall Buckingham's notorious liaison with the Countess of Shrewsbury, which generated an illegitimate "child who died shortly after birth."[20] Buckingham's insufficient procreation contrasts with Charles's amplitude, just as his desire to lead the opposition contrasts with Achitophel's ability to do so. Zimri is "wicked but in will, of means bereft" (line 567) and is associated with impotence of which Charles is free.

He also is free from a sexual weakness associated with Oates, who was discharged from the Royal Navy for sodomy, and parallels Buckingham's undisciplined heterosexual lust and incomplete paternity. Numerous attacks on Oates equated his sexual deviance with his political deviance. Such scandalous and abusive things, as Narcissus Luttrell called them,[21] included John Dean's *Oates's Bug {gering} Bug{gering} Boarding School, at Camberwell* (March 8, 1684) which showed the schoolmaster using three hundred boys and reviving a Turkish seraglio in his nominal place of youthful education. Thereafter, *The Sodomite, or the Venison Doctor, with his Brace of Aldermen-Stags* (September 13, 1684), characterized Oates's more mature taste and its monstrous consequences. We hear

> how a *Doctor* had Defil'd
> Two *Aldermen,* and got 'em both with Child,
> Who Long'd for *Venison,* but were beguil'd.
> The *Pasty* lost, they could no longer tarry,
> With *two Abortive Births, & shapes* as vary,
> They fell in *Labour,* and of both Miscarry.

Dryden's poem assumes an educable audience, one main part of which is David and Absalom. The portraits thus allow them to objectify their own state—Absalom's cause in Oates's ugly body, David's unbridled sexuality in ducal philandering and infant death. This device allows its own expansion and warning evoked by the biblical characters. One part of the Zimri tale, for instance, also is addressed to Absalom and makes plain that in rebellion not even a pretender is safe. In 1 Kings 16:11 Zimri kills King Elah and so exterminates his line that "he left him not one that pisseth against a wall, neither of his kinsfolk, nor of his friends." When Zimri's short reign is threatened by Omri and his troops, Zimri incinerates himself in the king's palace. Bishop Patrick's concise comment on Zimri as a traitor and usurper "abandoned by God" places him in a relevant historical context: "So *Saradanapalus* ended his Life" (2:424). David also is warned through his biblical opposition. Shimei is an emblem of deserved punishment deservedly inflicted. David patiently suffers Shimei's insults, Bishop Patrick observes, not "out of meer Greatness of Spirit" that disdains baseness, "but acknowledges the Justice of them, and bears them with a singular Patience, out of Humility, and Reverence to God, who had so ordered it." Moreover, "what were the Revilings of a Stranger, to the murderous Intentions of a Son? And how could he withstand God, who inflicted this Punishment upon him for his Sins?" (2 Sam. 16:10–11; Patrick, 2:325). On this interpretation, David again makes his own world and must make another before he can improve. And here too Shimei is useful, for he represents himself as God's prophet and thus, Patrick says following Grotius, is free from "the Respect that is to be used to Kings, in not giving them publick Reproaches," for "this alone could make it lawful to speak evil of the King, if God, in a special manner enjoined it" (2 Sam. 16:10; Patrick, 2:325). The false prophet Shimei, we shall see, contrasts with the true prophet Nathan just as the false corrector of the king, Bethel, contrasts with the true correctors, the loyal representatives of church, Lords, and Commons. But these men can appear in the poem only after Shimei has been inflicted on David, and he has seen what he has wrought.

Perhaps of greatest importance, however, is the three enemies' shared trait of defeat by David. They have shown David the fruits of his folly; they also show him the fruits of patience, fidelity to God, and the ultimate triumph of the state's justice when supported by God's power. Accordingly, Numbers 25 enlarges upon Zimri's own threat to himself. He wishes to be chief and thinks himself above the law, blatantly takes a woman in contempt of Moses' and of God's authority when Israel had begun its repentance, and induces his own and the woman's death by Phineas's javelin of God's justice: "So the Plague was stayed from the Children of Israel" (Num. 25:8). As Bishop Patrick says, the story "argues *Zimri* to have been very impudently wicked, who thought himself so great a Man, that no Judge durst meddle with him" (1:676). Commentary on Shimei also is instructive. Dryden complains that "During his Office, Treason was no Crime" (line 597) and that he packed juries to liberate the like-minded from secular law: "For Laws are only made to Punish those, / Who serve the King, and to protect his Foes" (lines 610–11). As 2 Samuel demonstrates, however, such triumphs over law are brief and ineffectual, for divine power and justice protect the anointed. Though Shimei curses David and would have killed him if he could, "all the Mighty Men were on [David's] right hand, and on his left," and so, Patrick observes, "*Shimei*'s Rage was little less than Madness; for he could not hurt *David,* but might have been immediately killed himself" (2:324). He is not killed only because David does not allow the eager Abishai to act: "There was admirable Discipline observed in this small Army, none of which durst stir without *David*'s Order, or Leave" (2 Sam. 16:9; Patrick, 2:325). Shimei's illusory power is twice brought home—first in 2 Samuel 23, when the now triumphant David agrees to spare him, and finally in 1 Kings 2:44–46, when David's son Solomon executes Shimei: "The Lord shall return thy wickedness upon thine own head" (44). Temporal power fails before the restored state's power replete with divine justice.

Corah's death supplies the third such lesson. Dryden recalls Corah's biblical relevance by describing Oates's "*Moses*'s Face" (line 649)—that is, his challenge to the authority of Moses and his brother Aaron as God's chosen priests. Oates's "Zeal to heav'n, made him his Prince despise" (line 672); his analogue Corah defies Moses and accuses him of duplicity, arbitrary acts, and usurpation of authority. Like the other characters this one also tells us about the benevolent adversary. Moses is generous and forgiving toward his people, intervening on behalf of the wavering congregation, in fulfilled hopes that God will distinguish between the seducer and the seduced. The merciful God encourages merciful Moses, who in turn encourages a wavering people to make the right choice. Like Jotham in the poem, some Israelites choose the wrong side and are allowed to change, as David himself must. Furthermore, Corah's actions evoke a brief speech from Moses that is a relevant if distant analogue to David's at the end of *Absalom and Achitophel.* Bishop Patrick's paraphrase upon Num. 16:28 sounds like a comment upon the restoration of Charles and the later Exclusion Crisis: "I have been commissioned by *God* to do all the things with which those Men find fault; particularly to take upon me the Government of them, and to put *Aaron* and his Family into the Priesthood, and make the *Levites* only their Ministers. . . . It was none of my own device or contrivance: I did it not out of an ambitious desire to be great myself, or out of private affection to my Brother" (1:623).

The consequences are plain. Corah and his allies are swallowed up by the earth, though Corah may have been struck by God's lightning; the priesthood of Moses and Aaron is confirmed; and the destroyed false priests become "A Monument of GOD's Displeasure against those that affront his Ministers; to give Warning unto all Posterity not to follow their pernicious Courses" (Num. 26:10; Patrick, 1:680). God's law and power again are allied with those loyal to him—however much they waver—and again smite the unbelieving. To receive such authority, the teacher must abjure "private affection" and act as if he actually accepted the governance of his people—as thus far in the poem David has not.

A king in name only can be replaced by a king in name only. The poem's internal logic drives toward a necessary inference: the nation requires a new king, but he should be the old David, not the new Absalom. That young man was changed by listening to Achitophel's bad advice; David must change by listening to others' better advice. His ability to do so at once defines his prudent humanity and confirms his divine anointing. The process starts with the poem's own narrator.

V

Dryden had been both indulgent and forgiving toward Absalom; but that tone and strategy change as Dryden juxtaposes the hated Corah as Absalom's friend, with the hitherto acted upon youth who now deludes the people, does Achitophel's work and lies about David. Absalom "forsakes the Court" (line 683), but he tells the people that he was banished for them (line 700). He was forgiven for murder, but he claims to be "Expos'd a prey to Arbitrary laws" (line 701). He pretends to wish that, Christlike, he "alone cou'd be undone" (line 702) on their behalf, yet he seeks the throne to which he is not entitled. He threatens his king and father with civil war, while he insists that such war would be his father's fault (lines 715, 720). As Achitophel's voice in Absalom's body, he also accepts the new genealogy that Achitophel had offered. Achitophel called him savior (line 240); the crowd "their young *Messiah* bless" (line 728) and make him the "Guardian God" of every new consecrated house he enters (lines 735–36). Accordingly, Absalom not Achitophel becomes associated with the devil or with other rebels who soared too high against paternal advice. He runs from east to west showing his glories, "And, like the Sun, the promis'd land survays. / Fame runs before him, as the morning Star" (lines 732–33). The morning star is Lucifer, and the young man trying to be like the kingly sun is Phaethon, who stole Apollo's chariot and would have set the world on fire if Zeus had not destroyed him with a thunderbolt. (Some versions of the myth include quarrels regarding Phaethon's legitimacy and Apollo's, or Helios', wrongful indulgence of his handsome son's wish.) Here indeed would be an *Ense rescindendum* if Absalom continued his adventure.

The narrator thus encourages us and his monarch to think less well of his potentially murderous son and begins the poem's and the monarch's new direction. Irony, urbane banter, apparent flattery of phallic prowess, and the give-and-take of debate and dialectic—all these disappear with the narrator's answer to his own question, whose key pronoun counters the egoism of Absalom's first-person singular: "What shall we think!" (line 759). Dryden, the ally of the indulgent father, becomes the ally of the embattled king in need of political theory and of instruction regarding his son. He may join with the crowds and their representatives, madly rebellious, threatening "To Murther Monarchs for Imagin'd crimes" (line 790), threatening kingship and orderly government, and turning the apparent solidity of a Lockean contract into the actuality of the Hobbesian "Nature's state; where all have Right to all" (line 794). The nature of Charles's sexual lust and the nature of holy bands between father and son, and even nature as the self-serving law of self-defense, becomes the nature of life nasty, brutish, and short. Dryden's political coda implies nearly as much about proper fatherhood as it tells about proper kingship. It also supplies the benevolent transition to the king's small party, as the Miltonic context changes from Satan to Abdiel.

Barzillai, the Duke of Ormond, as paragon of the family, begins the catalog of worthies and immediately brings the "Relief" (line 811) that besieged David requires—namely, the satiric norm of proper relationship between father and son that denotes the proper relationship between king and subject, one explicit in Barzillai's role in 2 Sam. 17:27 and 19:31–39. The several elegies on Ossory include the unsigned *A Second Elegy on that Incomparable Heroe, Thomas Earl of Ossory* (1680) which suggests that link. Ormond is secure in his greatness, not because of his own worth and pure virtue, "No nor in *Charles* his great Affection; / But only, 'cause he had so great a Son." That son also supports and learns from the true royal line.

> Thanks mighty *Hector* of our second *Troy*,
> Thanks for *Astyanax* thy hopeful *Boy*,
> Young *James*, who influenc'd with *Charles* his Care,
> May shortly prove in *Valour* too thine *Heir*.

Dryden himself included the father in more tactful ways, for his Ormond as mighty Hector was valuable not only for his son but also as a model of the old virtues insufficiently practiced either by the court or country party. The aristocrats Absalom and Achitophel support rebellion to sink the nation and raise themselves; Barzillai opposed rebels, suffered for and with his king, and knew him when he was "Godlike" (line 823) in more than propagation. Barzillai's eight legitimate sons offer a silent rebuke of Charles's eight illegitimate sons. In seeking a crown, Absalom thus is merely "Made Drunk with Honour" (line 312) falsely bestowed by Achitophel; Barzillai is more genuinely "crown'd with Honour" (line 818). Achitophel's son was deformed; Absalom's "motions [were] all accompanied with grace"; and Barzillai's son is "with every Grace adorn'd" (line 831). One of these graces was protecting his father from the threats of Buckingham and Shaftesbury, in obvious contrast to Absalom as agent of those threats.[22] The narrator accordingly uses the word "honour" three times for that un-Absalom-like man who "All parts fulfill'd of Subject and of Son" (line 836). Absalom runs from east to west to promote himself; Barzillai's son runs in a "Narrow Circle, but of Pow'r Divine, / Scanted in Space, but perfect in thy Line!" (lines 838–39). In contrast, David's divinity was one of lust (line 19), and his line was therefore imperfect and destructive. David's son Absalom won renown in war and threatens to use his skills against his father (lines 23–24, 456–60, 715–20) and against the uncle under whom he once had bravely fought; Barzillai's son also wins renown loyally fighting under James and for David (lines 840–45). Israel is all too worthy of the rebellious Absalom it resembles, "But *Israel* was unworthy of [Ossory's] Name" (line 846), and God takes him to His own world. Even there he serves his king, for "From thence thy kindred legions mayst thou bring / To aid the guardian Angel of thy King" (lines 852–53). The warm tribute to Barzillai also is a loving corrective for David, who can see the ongoing value to him, to the state, and to heaven in the man whose "Fruitful Issue" (line 829) benefited the nation, the family, and the father. David has seen the consequences of his own actions in his son, has heard his poet and free subject offer correctives on his behalf, and now sees that the old values of Barzillai remain models for royal conduct.

Dryden encourages this return to order through other vignettes of faithful individuals from the church, Lords, and Commons. In so doing he furthers another essential and one hopeful movement. Again we see the example of proper sons nurturing proper goals in support of the state, as Absalom did not:

> The Prophets Sons by such example led,
> To Learning and to Loyalty were bred:
> For *Colleges* on bounteous Kings depend,
> And never Rebell was to Arts a friend.
> [Lines 870–73]

As the poem progresses, David seems to respond to this poetic reeducation and now becomes less indulgent toward Absalom. Adriel's loyal service is rewarded with honors "That from his disobedient Son were torn" (line 881). "Sharp judging Adriel" himself, in fact, reinforces the image of the poet and the other respectful critics of a king bound by law. Adriel is "True to his Prince; but not a Slave of State" (lines 877, 879). Immediately thereafter, perhaps like the poet who once praised Cromwell, both the father and the son see the possibility of change and its consequences for the state. Jotham

> onely try'd
> The worse awhile, then chose the better side;
> Nor chose alone, but turn'd the balance too;
> So much the weight of one brave man can doe.[23]
> [Lines 884–87]

This return to order is epitomized in two other ways—Amiel in the Sanhedrin ably and loyally represents "*Israel*'s Tribes" and can "speak a Loyal Nation's Sense" (lines 906, 905). Israel, once "a Headstrong, Moody, Murmuring race" (line 45), is becoming verbally and intellectually coherent. We see the return of the sober moderate men—and of their rhyme words (line 885)—who previously had "Inclin'd the Ballance to the better side" (line 76) before Absalom subjected himself to Achitophel and anarchy. David and Israel are being educated together, as loyalists unite and perform their own role in government and in correcting the king and nation.

Earlier, Dryden had been spokesman for that nation's best values. Now he prudently allows his superiors to speak directly to the king on behalf of the three estates they represent:

> These Ills they saw, and as their Duty bound,
> They shew'd the King the danger of the Wound:
> That no Concessions from the Throne woud please,
> But Lenitives fomented the Disease:
> That *Absalom,* ambitious of the Crown,
> Was made the Lure to draw the People down:
> That false *Achitophel's* pernitious Hate,
> Had turn'd the Plot to Ruine Church and State:
> The Council violent, the Rabble worse:
> That *Shimei* taught *Jerusalem* to Curse.
> [Lines 923–32]

Here too Dryden may be calling upon the less attractive parts of the biblical David, who must be reminded of his duties as God's anointed and be made to suffer through his children. In 2 Samuel 12, God sends the prophet Nathan to instruct David through a parable of a rich man taking a poor man's lamb and slaying it for his own company. The tale angers David, who declares that such a man must make fourfold restitution and die: "And Nathan said unto David, Thou art the Man" (line 7); David grieves, admits his guilt, and is spared by God, though he loses his infant child borne by Bathsheba and later loses his sons Amnon, Absalom, and Adonijah.

This cautionary tale of sin, punishment, loss of children, repentance, and a message brought from God's true prophet is clear enough, especially when set against the public railings of the false prophet Corah. In 1680 Nathan already had been pressed into poetic service as "God's dread Prophet" to warn the patricidal, rebellious Absalom that God shall destroy him, for "Rebells to Fathers doubly meritt Hell."[24] The apposite commentary, however, relates Dryden's narrator and David's dutiful advisors to Nathan the prophet, each of whom fulfilled his duty by telling the king unpleasant but necessary truths. Bishop Patrick said of Nathan's parable and its relevance for modern kings: "This was a prudent and respectful way of awakening *David*, . . . Which was so managed, that the Prophet did not condemn *David*, but made him condemn himself. And many have very pertinently observed from hence, that there is never more use of Wisdom and Discretion, than in the Contrivance of Reprehension; especially of Princes and great Persons." Moreover, Patrick says glossing Nathan's statement "Thou art the Man," reproofs "of Men in Authority are to be managed very mannerly." The content should "be plain and downright; so that they may be made sensible of their Guilt," guilt aggravated because of "the Obligations he had to God; who had preferred him to the highest Dignity, when he was in a low, and sometimes desperate Condition" (2:307–8). David's deserved punishment, Patrick argues, comes from divine, not secular, law. Upon the death of his illegitimate son, David thus prays in the synagogue and thanks God "for the Pardon of his Sin. . . . He acknowledged also the Justice of God and did not complain of his Severity. He submitted to his holy Will, and beseeched him, perhaps, that the remaining Afflictions might be moderated and made profitable to him" (2:309). The tangible sign of this repentance is the legitimate son of David and Bathsheba, Solomon, whom God loved and made famous: "Such is the wonderful Goodness of God to truly penitent Sinners; who . . . thereby incline the divine Goodness to shew further Mercy to them" (2:310). As with much else in the poem's biblical and English history, this context is suggestive rather than congruent. Nonetheless, the evoked figure of Nathan as a genuine prophet superior to Corah allows David to see himself and declare his own guilt. Nathan thereby reinforces Dryden's role as an instigating narrator who transfers authority to the ministers appropriately counseling the king.

In the "Life of Dryden" Johnson complains that David's speech is more the product of romance than of logical structure: "Who can forbear to think of an enchanted castle, with a wide moat and lofty battlements, walls of marble and gates of brass, which vanishes at once into air when the destined knight blows his horn before it?"[25] Had the vanishing been "at once" it indeed would have been romantic; but as I hope to have shown, David's speech is carefully prepared and culminates the varied lessons set before him, not the least of which is his own responsibility in making the world and the son that threaten to destroy him. If David is to survive, he must correct and restore himself. Like Barzillai he must be a good father to a well-tutored loyal son; like Jotham he may try the worse awhile but must then choose the better side and bring others with him; like the poet he must understand and speak political sense so that his subjects can know what they should think. As a result of all this, he will again become like the David who had been enthusiastically restored. David demonstrates that he has learned the lessons of Dryden's Nathan-surrogates.[26]

VI

David's speech immediately signals his change and the consequent change of those who depend on him—the patient, indulgent, pagan parent of disruption abjures his earlier fault. The king who had been "inspir'd by some diviner Lust" (line 19) to beget Absalom now speaks "from his Royal Throne by Heav'n inspir'd" (line 936). The king who had been godlike (line 14) in procreating, now is godlike in speaking with God's voice to a subdued audience: "The God-like *David* spoke: with awfull fear / His Train their Maker in their Master hear" (lines 937–38). The speech's genealogy and function insure that it is the only one in the poem that allows neither reply nor exchange. Such a metamorphosis, we recall, is based firmly on royal acceptance and correction of errors—one of which is the improper perception of his son and his people. David thus recognizes that his mercy has been taken for weakness because "So much the Father did the King asswage" (line 942). With his return to kingship, he also returns to manhood and shifts the image of sexual and political weakness to Absalom. Achitophel would use Absalom to shake "The Pillars of the publick Safety" (line 176); David insists that "Kings are the publick Pillars of the State" and that if his "Young *Samson*" wants "To shake the Column, let him share the Fall" (lines 953, 955–57). Moreover, these words imply that as king, David himself may be forced to break nature's holy bands if his son threatens the state. Indeed, in the second edition David speaks four new lines in which he shares Dryden's wish that Absalom reject Achitophel and again be his own "Darling Son" (line 433). As father to his nation, David must eliminate rebels who threaten the public peace. Hence, godlike King David, with the power of justice, says of Absalom:

> But oh that yet he would repent and live!
> How easie 'tis for Parents to forgive!
> With how few Tears a Pardon might be won
> From Nature, pleading for a Darling Son!
> [Lines 957–60]

God, not Achitophel or the people, makes kings, and the agent of God knows the true heir to his throne: "*Esau*'s Hands suite ill with *Jacob*'s Voice" (line 982).

That allusion to Gen. 27:22 has wider implications than are usually seen, for the rejected son Esau at first angrily plans to find his brother and violently regain his birthright. Their mother Rebecca, who instigated the substitution, urges Jacob's flight to her brother until Esau is mollified. Over the years Jacob honors and loves God, is richly rewarded, and upon again meeting his equally well fortuned brother, sends him generous presents. After Jacob wrestles all night with the angel of God, he gains the confidence to face Esau: "And Esau ran to meet him, and embraced him, and fell on his neck, and kissed him, and they wept," and, Jacob adds, "I have seen thy face, as though I had seen the face of God, and thou wast pleased with me" (Gen. 33:4, 10). The tale of Esau and Jacob begins with usurpation and ends with forgiveness and reconciliation between man and man and man and God. As Bishop Patrick says, "For *Esau*'s Kind Reception of him he could not but look upon as a Token of the Divine Favour towards him" (1:117–18). Evocation of Esau thus comments upon David's plea to Absalom: "But oh that yet he would repent and live!"

If Absalom rejects such a model, he will be subject to the rigors of the law, not to David's native mercy. The poem begins with a world in which "no law deny'd" (line 5) David's lust; it then characterizes an unappreciative nation freer from law's limits than any other (line 54). Thereafter, it details several attempted violations of law. Achitophel urges Absalom "To pass your doubtfull Title into Law" (line 408) and usurp his father's role and throne; this would distort "Natures Eldest Law" (line 458) of self-defense into potential patricide and regicide; and it would threaten to turn the source of law into the source of lawlessness if the king is successfully seized by his enemies (line 476). These men can "make Treason law" (line 582) and free their allies "from Humane Laws" (line 609). In David's final speech, however, divine law augments such corrected human law, as David subjects himself and his nation to hitherto deficient regulation and order. He reforms himself as well as his world: "The Law shall still direct my peacefull Sway, / And the same Law teach Rebels to Obey" (lines 991–92). But his questions suggest both a similarity to the narrator and a wrenching from his normal pattern. Severity is an act of will rather than unguided inclination:

> Oh that my Power to Saving were confin'd:
> Why am I forc'd, like Heav'n, against my mind,
> To make Examples of another Kind?
> Must I at length the Sword of Justice draw?
> O curst Effects of necessary Law!
> [Lines 999–1003]

These effects were drawn out by his enemies, of course including Absalom and Achitophel, who could neither accept nor understand mercy. Hence, "Law they require, let Law then show her Face" (line 1006)—that is, to tempt death with the sword that Dryden had hoped need not be used.

We have seen the examples of fathers and sons who serve as negative models and then, in the example of Barzillai, the satiric norm that begins the poem's final movement toward David's corrected vision. Dryden uses another image of parent and offspring to show the self-consuming nature of rebellion. The female viper was thought to have bitten off the male's head, which he put in her mouth in order to fertilize her eggs. To revenge their father's considerable discomfort, the adult offspring destroy their own mother (perhaps as Absalom had also tried to do), an analogue well adapted to the future David predicts for his plotters:

> Against themselves their Witnesses will Swear,
> Till Viper-like their Mother Plot they tear:
> And suck for Nutriment that bloody gore
> Which was their principle of Life before.
> [Lines 1012–15]

The civil war his enemies wished on him redounds upon themselves, as "on my Foes, my Foes shall do me Right" (line 1017).

The final couplet of David's speech is both an obvious and subtle sign of his victory, and of his response to the portrait Dryden has encouraged him to see in the poem. Earlier, Achitophel evoked Absalom's wavering answer to his temptation and encouraged his vice: "Him Staggering so when Hell's dire Agent Found, / While fainting Vertue scarce maintain'd her Ground" (lines 373–74). David absorbs those rhyme words and transforms them in his victory on behalf of law, God's agent and Absalom's and Israel's father: "For Lawfull Pow'r is still Superiour found / When long driven back, at length it stands the ground" (lines 1024–25)—as follow'd by the epic tag "He said."

Given such a dispensation Dryden needs, finally, to give "external" warrant for David's change from misplaced mercy and pagan licentiousness, to law and divine approbation. He does so by characterizing God's nod of "Consent" and voice of thunder—the consent presumably both to David's and the plotters' transformation. Paradoxically, that transformation is shown through a twenty-one-year-old event, so that the poem's conclusion is simultaneously forward and backward looking. By reverting to his old self he reverts to the image Achitophel had tried to erase:

> He is not now, as when on *Jordan's* Sand
> The Joyfull People throng'd to see him Land,
> Cov'ring the *Beach,* and blackning all the *Strand.*
> [Lines 270–72]

The king is indeed even greater, for he creates new time that peacefully extends far into the future by recreating the David and the obedient Israel of the past, as nation and monarch again are one:

> Once more the Godlike *David* was Restor'd,
> And willing Nations knew their Lawfull Lord.
> [Lines 1030–31]

They know their king because both he and Israel have restored themselves. David becomes a true father once he becomes an obedient son to the true God, whose will he carries out by helping to defeat the Belials and Beelzebubs of the world, a contest that far surpasses anything in the secular Virgilian associations of a distant Jove who merely aids Aeneas' imperial expansion.[27]

Absalom and Achitophel, then, exploits assumptions shared by Whigs and Tories—the honor and love due from the son to the father, and the violation of those duties by the title characters. The poem also makes plain that however much it sides with the king, part of its greatness as a satire is in its willingness respectfully to place blame where it belongs. By so doing, Dryden also shows that David is not an unswerving absolute monarch, but a great man and king able to change and again be known to his God and nation. David's vices are amended by Dryden's friendly, physician-like healing satire which, at a crucial point, yields to the experienced seconding ministers' voices and then to David's. In the poem, at least, David's wisdom affirms Dryden's view of satire. Absalom and Achitophel could neither read nor respond so well. Shaftesbury died in exile in Holland; Monmouth was executed after a foolish rebellion against James II in 1685. Contrary to Dryden's hopes, the devil was not saved, and the sick disciple was not spared a fatal *Ense rescindendum.* The real triumph of Dryden's poem, though, is the gradual education of the restored father and king, as nature's holy bands become bands between king and country and king and God, and a world is regained.

Notes

1.   For some studies celebrating this point of view, see Bernard Schilling, *Dryden and the Conservative Myth* (New Haven, Conn., 1961), pp. 48, 281; Alan Roper, *Dryden's Poetic Kingdoms* (New York, 1965), pp. 185–86, 191; Earl Miner, *Dryden's Poetry* (Bloomington, Ind., 1967), pp. 115–22; Leon Guilhamet, "Dryden's Debasement of Scripture in *Absalom and Achitophel,*" *Studies in English Literature* 9 (1969): 409; Bruce King, "*Absalom and Achitophel:* A Revaluation," in *Dryden's Mind and Art,* ed. Bruce King (New York, 1970), pp. 68–69; Steven N. Zwicker, *Dryden's Political Poetry: The Typology of King and Nation* (Providence, R.I., 1972), p. 88; George deForest Lord, "*Absalom and Achitophel* and Dryden's Political Cosmos," in *Writers and Their Background: John Dryden,* ed. Earl Miner (London, 1972), p. 171; Thomas E. Maresca, "The Context of Dryden's *Absalom and Achitophel,*" *ELH* 41 (1974): 341; Steven N. Zwicker, *Politics and Language in Dryden's Poetry: The Arts of Disguise* (Princeton, N.J., 1984), p. 93. In addition to the antidotes cited below, see George McFadden's valuable and suggestive chapter on *Absalom and Achitophel* in *Dryden the Public Writer, 1660–1685* (Princeton, N.J., 1978), pp. 227–64.

2.   A. E. Dyson and Julian Lovelock, "Beyond the Polemics: A Dialogue on the Opening of *Absalom and Achitophel*," Critical Survey 5 (1971): 145.

3.   K. E. Robinson, "A Reading of Absalom and Achitophel," *Yearbook of English Studies* 6 (1976): 53.

4.   Jerome Donnelly, "Fathers and Sons: The Normative Basis of Dryden's *Absalom and Achitophel*," *Papers on Language and Literature* 17 (1981): 363. See also Roper, p. 193; Maresca, pp. 347, 349, 357; Sanford Budick, *Poetry of Civilization: Mythopoetic Displacement in . . . Dryden, Pope, and Johnson* (New Haven, Conn., 1975), pp. 88–90.

5.   See Robinson, p. 54, and Donnelly, pp. 375, 376–79. Donnelly's essay is most insistent, and most useful, on the poem's filial structure.

6.   Barbara Lewalski's distant judgment remains largely accurate: "There is now general critical agreement in referring *Absalom and Achitophel* to the heroic genre despite the elements of satire and wit" (*"David's Troubles Remembered:* An Analogue to *Absalom and Achitophel*," *Notes and Queries,* N.S., vol. 11 [1964], n. 6). Steven Zwicker has more recently argued that the poem's genre is a "confusion" of epic, satire, prophecy, and history (*Politics and Language in Dryden's Poetry,* pp. 88–89, and pp. 220–21, n. 9).

7.   John Locke, *Two Treatises of Government,* ed. Peter Laslett, 2d ed. (Cambridge, 1967), p. 198, treatise 1, chap. 6, sec. 55. Praise of matriarchal authority may also have alluded to Queen Elizabeth as an alternative to Stuart patriarchy. See Larry Carver, "*Absalom and Achitophel* and the Father Hero," in *The English Hero, 1660–1800,* ed. Robert Folkenflik (Newark, Del., 1982), p. 36, and pp. 44–45, n. 3. H. T. Swedenberg, Jr., observes that Dryden's own passage on government does not employ Filmer's arguments (*The Works of John Dryden,* vol. 2, *Poems, 1681–1684,* ed. H. T. Swedenberg, Jr. [Berkeley and Los Angeles, 1972], p. 271). This is the text from which I quote *Absalom and Achitophel,* cited parenthetically in the text.

8.   Locke, *Two Treatises,* p. 226; treatise 2, chap. 9, sec. 90.

9.   Ibid., pp. 329–30, treatise 2, chap. 6, sec. 66; and see Gordon Schochet, *Patriarchalism in Political Thought . . . Especially in Seventeenth-Century England* (Oxford, 1975), p. 201, with specific reference to James Tyrrell.

10.   Here and elsewhere, dates cited are those by Narcissus Luttrell, whose annotated copies I have seen or have found recorded in Hugh Macdonald's *John Dryden: A Bibliography of Early Editions and of Drydeniana* (Oxford, 1939). Pordage's attack on *Absalom and Achitophel* here refers to the Popish Plot; the others in this paragraph refer to the Rye House Plot.

11.   Roper, pp. 186, 191.

12.   *The Complete Poems of John Wilmot, Earl of Rochester,* ed. David M. Vieth (New Haven, Conn., 1968), pp. 60–61, lines 14–15, 18–19. For some other attacks on Charles's seminal generosity and its consequences, see *Poems on Affairs of State: Augustan Satirical Verse . . . 1660–1678,* ed. George deForest Lord (New Haven, Conn., 1963), 1:228–29, 243–44, 278; *Poems on Affairs of State . . . 1678–1681,* ed. Elias F. Mengel, Jr. (New Haven, Conn., 1965), 2:147, 155–56, 158 (in the latter two he is called "Priapus"), 200, 202, 208, 220–21; *Poems on Affairs of State . . . 1682–1685* (New Haven, Conn., 1968), ed. Howard H. Schless, 3:30–31, 253, 478–79, 567. The Restoration's energetic vulgarity toward its monarchs renders suspect—and in my judgment denies—the anachronistic theory of "the king's two bodies," which absolves the monarch of responsibility for his personal actions. That medieval theory of kingship often is used in support of *Absalom and Achitophel's* presumed apology for Charles's behavior.

13.   The text of *Absalom's Conspiracy: Or, The Tragedy of Treason* is reproduced in *The Works of John Dryden,* ed. Walter Scott (London, 1808), 9:205–7, p. 206 for this quotation.

14.   Simon Patrick, *A Commentary upon the Historical Books of the Old Testament* (1694), 5th ed. (London, 1738), 2:306. Subsequent citations are given in the text. For some relevant aspects of these books, see Thomas Jemielty, "Divine Derision and Scorn: The Hebrew Prophets as Satirists," *Cithara* 25 (1985): 47–68.

15.   *The Dictionary Historical and Critical of Mr. Peter Bayle* (1697), trans. Pierre des Maizeaux, 2d ed. (London, 1735), 2:607–8, n. F. For further discussion, see Raymond-Jean Frontain and Jan Wojcik, eds., *The David Myth in Western Literature* (West Lafayette, Ind., 1980), and Allan J. Gedalof's informative review of this volume in *Eighteenth-Century Studies* 15 (1982): 356–59.

16.   Attacks on Dryden are discussed by Hugh Macdonald, "The Attacks on Dryden," in *Essential Articles for the Study of John Dryden,* ed. H. T. Swedenberg, Jr. (Hamden, Conn., 1966), pp. 22–53; Macdonald, *John Dryden: A Bibliography,* passim; and John Robert Sweney, "Political Attacks on Dryden, 1681–1683" (Ph.D. diss., University of Wisconsin–Madison, 1968).

17.   Phillip Harth, "Legends no Histories: The Case of *Absalom and Achitophel,*" in *Studies in Eighteenth-Century Culture,* ed. O. M. Brack, Jr. (Madison, Wis., 1975), 14:13–29. Harth also notes Dryden's attempts to influence external action ("Dryden's Public Voices," in *New Homage to John Dryden,* ed. Alan Roper [Los Angeles, 1983], pp. 6–7, 13–14, 18). In the preface to his translation of the *Aeneid* (1697), Dryden himself insists on the poet's educational function for his ruler. He there uses the familiar argument that the idealized portrait of Aeneas was designed to educate the cruel Augustus into the true manners of a prince. See "Dedication of the Aeneis," in *Essays of John Dryden,* ed. W. P. Ker (New York, 1961), 2:174.

18.   As quoted in Schochet (n. 9 above), p. 196, with comparable references cited by Locke, Tyrrell, and Thomas Hunt in n. 16. For a royalist version, see John Wilson, *A Discourse of Monarchy* (London, 1684): "the people had no more right to chuse their Kings, than to chuse their Fathers" (p. 15).

19.   For a relevant summary of Bethel's reputation, see Swedenberg, ed. (n. 7 above), pp. 262–63.

20.   Donnelly (n. 4 above), p. 371.

21.   He calls *The Sodomite* "An abusive thing on Oates, Pilkington, & c" and *Dr. Oates Last Farewell to England* (together with "fourscore Bums to Attend his Sir-Reverence") a "scandalous libell." Each annotated work is at the William Andrews Clark Memorial Library in Los Angeles.

22.   For the relevant sons, see Scott's *The Works of John Dryden* (n. 13 above), 9:250, 298; and for Ossory's defense of his father, see 9:295–97. For other parallels and contrasts in the poem, see Eric Rothstein, *The Routledge History of English Poetry,* vol. 3, *Restoration and Eighteenth Century Poetry, 1660–1780* (Boston and London, 1981), pp. 17–18.

23.   Barbara Lewalski observes that Jotham is from "the period of the Judges" rather than of David; Sanford Budick adds that Jotham parallels Dryden himself (Lewalski, "The Scope and Function of Biblical Allusion in *Absalom and Achitophel,*" *English Language Notes* 3[1965]: 34, and Budick [n. 4 above], p. 87).

24.   As quoted in Howard H. Schless, "Dryden's *Absalom and Achitophel* and *A Dialogue between Nathan and Absolome,*" *Philological Quarterly* 40 (1961): 141.

25.   Samuel Johnson, *Lives of the Poets,* ed. George Birkbeck Hill (Oxford, 1905), 1:437.

26.   Dustin Griffin provides an attractive revisionist discussion of the final speech in "Dryden's Charles: The Ending of *Absalom and Achitophel,*" *Philological Quarterly* 57 (1978): 359–82.

27.   For the traditional view of Virgilian association with *Aeneid* 9.106 and 10.115, see Lord (n. 1 above), p. 187.

Writing/Reading/Remembering:
Dryden and the Poetics of Memory

DAVID B. MORRIS

"Is memory no more than a container for the thoughts of thinking, or does thinking itself reside in memory?"

—Heidegger

Five years ago, after something more than a decade in the classroom, I resigned my position as Professor of English and abruptly stopped teaching. This otherwise insignificant event at least provided an impulse for the present inquiry. As I began to reflect upon my years of teaching, about the unstable bond between teacher and student, a bizarre and disconcerting image appeared in my first draft. I felt so disturbed at what I had written that I instantly crossed it out. The passage, impressionistically, pictured the student and teacher as two spent heavyweights in the final round, leaning into each other, head to head, pounding away with every ounce of remaining strength.

This alarming image drew, I suspect, upon childhood memories of a famous painting by George Wesley Bellows in which two almost gladiatorial prizefighters strain—in the raw, yellowed haze of postclassical combat—to batter each other into unconsciousness. What I quickly recognized in my phallocentric parody of normal student/teacher relations was a forced self-exposure and mutual exhaustion, not to mention unavoidable conflict, that I recall from the closing weeks of those apparently endless semesters when the energy required for teaching and for learning simply depletes its reserves, when we are thrown back upon whatever bare skills we possess. ("The boxers will bring to the fight everything that is themselves," writes Joyce Carol Oates, "and everything will be exposed—including secrets about themselves they cannot fully realize.") No doubt my pugilistic memory exposes ambivalent emotions about the classroom, as I will not deny. More to the point: the image reminded me, by its inaccuracies as well as by its aptness, that memory always confronts us with substitutions. How is it possible to remember an

David B. Morris, "Writing/Reading/Remembering: Dryden and the Poetics of Memory." Reprinted, with minor changes, from *Teaching Eighteenth-Century Poetry*, ed. Chris Fox, *AMS Studies in the Eighteenth Century*, no. 12 (1990), pp. 119–145. Reprinted by permission of AMS Press.

extended and complex event—say, a dozen years of teaching—without the radical tropes that compress, distort, and represent something ultimately unrecoverable?

Everyday episodes of forgetting, like my misremembered years as a teacher, indicate how slippery our hold is on the past, yet we tend to dismiss such slippage as an exception that demonstrates, indirectly, the general truthfulness of memory. It seems probable, however, that the slips and skids of imperfect remembering suggest a truth about the *normal* operations of memory. From this perspective, memory would not operate on the now popular model of an archive or computer, where separate entries may be deposited, stored, and retrieved intact. Instead, we would recognize that nothing ever comes out of memory exactly as it goes in. Everything is colored, foreshortened, connected, distanced, changed. No one is likely to program a mechanical brain capable of performing the countless common acts of remembering that fill our days, from riding a bicycle to finding our way home in the dark. It seems that any material image—archive, theater, wax tablet, printed page, computer—tends to distort as much as it reveals about the mysterious processes we call memory.

Dryden is a poet who especially invites us to think about the intimate relations among remembering, writing, and reading. Memory, in fact, offers such a rich field for students of Dryden that the main problem lies in finding a way to focus discussion.

In this essay I want to discuss his attractive, much-praised, brief elegy "To the Memory of Mr. Oldham." It provides an introduction to Dryden that fairly represents his maturest art, that does not require lengthy excursions into seventeenth-century political and religious history, and that allows us to examine specific poetic techniques (allusion, metaphor, irony, parallelism) which help generate both power and meaning in his more ambitious works. My aim, however, is not to provide yet another explication of Dryden's poem or to pursue traditional questions of interpretation, except as they bear upon the subject of memory. Further, I am not engaged in a strictly thematic reading, where memory might emerge as the long-hidden key to Dryden's poem, unlocking its secret unities or latent contradictions. Memory, I want to claim, is not the poem's central theme or subject but rather its major action.

What I am proposing is that "To Oldham"—itself a typically occasional work (first published in the posthumous *Remains of Mr. John Oldham in Verse and Prose* [1684])—offers an occasion for us to meditate upon the role of memory in Dryden's work and in our own literary experience as readers of Dryden. The act of remembering involves a basic human biological endowment—a power, like vision, that directly and indirectly shapes our experience of the world. We also need to consider memory, however, as (like reason) a natural endowment which is reshaped and revalued in different historical periods. Thus it is important to understand both how seventeenth-century writers thought about memory and how memory endows us with powers upon which thinking and writing and reading in any age ultimately depend.

One good way to approach "To Oldham" is to read it aloud. Short-term memory binds the poem together even through such typical neoclassical resources as alliteration and rhyme, which depend upon sounds that linger, however briefly, in the reader's mind. Here is the entire poem:

> Farewel, too little and too lately known,
> Whom I began to think and call my own;
> For sure our Souls were near ally'd; and thine
> Cast in the same Poetick mould with mine.
> One common Note on either Lyre did strike,
> And Knaves and Fools we both abhorr'd alike:
> To the same Goal did both our Studies drive,
> The last set out the soonest did arrive.
> Thus *Nisus* fell upon the slippery place,
> While his young Friend perform'd and won the Race.
> O early ripe! to thy abundant store
> What could advancing Age have added more?
> It might (what Nature never gives the young)
> Have taught the numbers of thy native Tongue.
> But Satyr needs not those, and Wit will shine
> Through the harsh cadence of a rugged line:
> A noble Error, and but seldom made,
> When Poets are by too much force betray'd.
> Thy generous fruits, though gather'd ere their prime
> Still shew'd a quickness; and maturing time
> But mellows what we write to the dull sweets of Rime.
> Once more, hail and farewel; farewel thou young,
> But ah too short, *Marcellus* of our Tongue;
> Thy Brows with Ivy, and with Laurels bound;
> But Fate and gloomy Night encompass thee around.

It is not entirely conventional that Dryden should choose the "Lyre" as an emblem of poetry. Both "Alexander's Feast" (subtitled "The Power of Music") and his "Song for St. Cecilia's Day" remind us how far Dryden associated poetry with the musical repetitions and variations that transform the written text into an echoing chamber of sound where each successive line interweaves past with present and with still other repetitions and variations to come. Silent reading frustrates the auditory memory on which Dryden's musical techniques so often depend.

The continuous operations of memory that suffuse any act of reading remain mostly hidden from consciousness, unnoticed. Similarly, memory is so far from occupying the center of attention in Dryden's poem that the excellent critical studies of "To Oldham"—by Earl Miner, Arthur W. Hoffman,

Dustin H. Griffin, and Peter M. Sacks, among others—scarcely mention it. Thus, before we return to an explicit discussion of memory, it will be useful to look briefly at the critical consensus regarding the poem. The most crucial insight on which critics of the poem agree (explicitly or tacitly) is that Dryden's elegy takes Dryden—as much as Oldham—for its main subject. The poem develops through a parallelism that contrasts *two* poetic careers: one cut short, the other (to cite Dryden's metaphors) mellow and mature. Dryden of course contrives the comparison as a tribute to Oldham, emphasizing both Oldham's promise and achievement. (Oldham—author of the somewhat reckless and violent *Satyrs upon the Jesuits* [1681]—had died in 1683, at age thirty.) Still, the point of the tribute requires that we contemplate two careers and two poets. Dryden's presence is important in part because we should recognize the tribute as composed not just by a fellow poet but by the poet laureate. This is praise from Caesar.

It might be helpful to think of "To Oldham" as in various ways a transitional work. When he wrote it Dryden was entering his mid-fifties. He had a distinguished career behind him (including *All For Love, Mac Flecknoe, The Medall,* and *Religio Laici*), but—perhaps even more remarkable—he had an equally distinguished career ahead (including his "Ode to the Memory of Mrs. Anne Killigrew," *The Hind and the Panther, Don Sebastian,* his unheralded masterpiece the *Fables,* and his brilliant translations of Juvenal, Persius, and, above all, Virgil). Dryden was thus writing "To Oldham" at a period in his own career when the theater, satire, and contemporary political events, which had provided the major occasions and motives for his writing, no longer preoccupied him. At such a time it is not surprising that Oldham's early death might prompt an aging poet's reflections on the interconnected Keatsian themes of creative power, art, and loss.

Dryden's elegy generates a subliminal drama from the continuous pressure it exerts to close an uncloseable gap. In effect, the poem strives to overcome the distance separating Dryden from Oldham: their souls are described as "near ally'd" and as cast from an identical "Poetick mould." Through its classical allusions, the poem also links Dryden and Oldham in the relation of friends and describes each as participating in the same race, seeking the same goal. Yet Dryden manages to indicate—through his own performance as elegist—just how great a distance separates the mature poet from his young, erring, and now-deceased fellow satirist. Thus we should not ignore the strains implicit in his allusion to the Virgilian episode concerning Nisus and Euryalus, where Dryden's flattering parallel nonetheless fails to overcome an unresolvable residue of difference.

The strained praise in Dryden's analogy indirectly exposes his dilemma as poet. That is, in Dryden's retelling, the goal toward which both poets run is death, a dubious prize to be sure. Nisus/Dryden—who both gains fame and eludes death—is strangely represented as the loser, whereas Euryalus/Oldham, in securing victory, loses both life and fame. Further, the repeated imagery associating poetic creation with natural cycles of growth and decay in part undermines its own praise of Oldham's abundance. The poem leaves us in doubt whether Oldham's poetic fruits were "early ripe" (ripe but early) or gathered "ere their prime" (not yet fully ripe). This is not a major contradiction. The difference, however, should not be silently disregarded or ingeniously denied, because the poem contains similar disharmonies it cannot entirely resolve or overcome.

The strains of an imperfectly resolved difficulty belong not just to Dryden's description of Oldham but to his own self-portrait as well. For example, we cannot conveniently forget what stage follows ripeness in the cycles of nature:

> And so, from hour to hour we ripe and ripe,
> And then from hour to hour we rot and rot;
> And thereby hangs a tale.

Because he links poetic genius so closely with the fruitfulness of nature, Dryden's description of his own "dull sweets of Rime" (modest and ironic but hardly unequivocal) reminds us that ripeness quickly passes into over-ripe decline and frost-bitten decay. Poets like Oldham who die young are fortunate, Dryden may imply, in not witnessing the inevitable decline of their art. "To Oldham" might be said to struggle with the knowledge of Dryden's own observation on the difference between older and younger poets: "'Tis Natures Law in Love and Wit," he wrote late in his career, "That Youth shou'd Reign, and with'ring Age submit."

Dryden in his mid-fifties was not exactly withering. Like Yeats, he produced work in his old age that reveals undiminished and even intensified creative powers. Nonetheless, his own metaphors and pronouncements betray a sense of his uneasiness with the normal relation between poetry and advancing age. It thus seems quite likely that in Oldham's death Dryden also recognizes intimations of his own mortality; the melancholy tone of the poem, at any rate, cannot rely solely upon Oldham for its depth. In remembering Oldham, Dryden is also remembering himself—but not solely in a mood of self-congratulation. Indeed, the seventeenth-century was strongly connected to the ancient tradition of *memento mori,* within which the highest philosophical and theological function of memory was to remind us that we must die.

The process of remembering—while it returns Dryden to an implicit recognition of his own mortality—centers of course on the figure of Oldham. Our interest in Dryden's presence within the poem thus must not interfere with the poem's explicit attention to Oldham. In fact, Dryden succeeds so thoroughly in focusing upon Oldham that the elegy accomplishes something quite rare. It not merely celebrates or perpetuates but in a sense *creates* the memory of the person it describes. Oldham, although briefly notorious in his own time, by no means demonstrated the literary skills that promise an extended fame. Dryden's strategy is to transform Oldham's limitations from a liability to an asset: failures that would normally cause him to be forgotten now will make him remembered. At Dryden's hands, Oldham becomes a prototype of the young poet whose promise is unnaturally cut short by death. Here is something mere praise—especially praise that whitewashes defects—cannot achieve. Dryden in effect creates for Oldham a unique place within literary history or mythology. We tend to remember Oldham, like Chatterton, not because we read his works but because his portrait has been sketched—transformed into an archetype—by a far greater poet.

Memory, as Augustan poets often claim, is not merely the vehicle of fame but also—through a conventional metonymy—an image of fame. In writing his elegy to Oldham's "Memory," Dryden was addressing a wraith already in the process of rapid decomposition. Even with Dryden's help, Oldham is not a writer whom nonspecialists have much occasion to recall. Still, Dryden's poem effectively removes Oldham's memory from a strictly private realm—where it would perish utterly—and supplies something like a new, public, and lasting memory. The important point is that memory is where neoclassical poets tend to locate the quest for permanence. Memory thus becomes, as we will see, a territory to be claimed, colonized, fought over, yielded, or conquered. It is a space with multiple uses, an Indes. Remembering Oldham is not for Dryden an act of pure, disinterested justice. Dryden's memorial to Oldham is, like all memories, a substitution or trope, but it is more. It is also a conscious effort to reshape the past, not in order to falsify the past but to bring out what Dryden sees as its hidden or rapidly deteriorating truth, which may be no more (and no less) finally than the truth of desire: how we want or need to think—or can't help thinking—of a realm that is already lost.

My procedure for thinking about memory in Dryden's work is to reverse the normal relations between the visible and the unseen. In the language of painting, I want to examine the ground instead of the figure. The reversal I am proposing here assumes that foundations—because they support everything else—often disappear into the common light of what goes without saying. Truly elemental experiences are so crucial to our ways of understanding the world—sight, for example, or upright posture—that we tend not to question them unless something goes terribly wrong. Memory, I want to argue, is similarly fundamental to Augustan poetics. In probing the usually neglected process of remembrance at work in the elegy to Oldham, we are undertaking an inquiry into the unthought basis of Dryden's thought.

Dryden leaves us in no doubt concerning the conventional view of Augustan poetry. It is, as everyone knows, a poetry of wit. Dryden unambiguously explains this position in the Preface to *Annus Mirabilis* (1666): "The composition of all Poems is or ought to be of wit, and wit . . . is no other than the faculty of imagination in the writer, which, like a nimble Spaniel, beats over and ranges through the field of Memory, till it springs the Quarry it hunted after; or, without metaphor, which searches over all the memory for the species or Idea's of those things which it designs to represent." It is of course the nimble spaniel that has for generations preoccupied scholars of Dryden—and with good reason. Wit is not only the explicit subject of Dryden's passage but also commands attention because it became a focus of debate after the Restoration. Wit-wouds and True-wits crowded the theater; critics and clerics declaimed against the alliance that linked wit with ribaldry and irreligion; libertines and courtiers daily invented fresh modes of witty scandal. Wit, in short, was a value in dispute: visible, controversial, supreme. What would happen, however, if the nimble-footed spaniel in Dryden's metaphor suddenly discovered that the ground beneath its paws had somehow utterly dropped away?

The picture of Dryden's nimble spaniel racing frantically above an abyss might remind us how far seventeenth-century writers constructed an aesthetics built upon memory. Memory is the ground on which everything else takes place. As Hobbes put it in a famous genealogy: "Time and Education begets experience; Experience begets memory; Memory begets Judgement and Fancy: Judgment begets the strength and structure, and Fancy begets the ornaments of a Poem. The Ancients therefore fabled not absurdly in making memory the Mother of the Muses." The biblical begat-formula (perhaps the most prosaic of Old Testament devices) serves for Hobbes to demystify accounts of poetry that associate the poet with divine inspiration. Memory thus provides a secular alternative to religious claims for inner light or enthusiasm as a source of poetic creation. Indeed, the Augustan belief that poetry is an art of imitation makes memory into a summarizing metaphor for the poetic process. "Memory," as Hobbes concludes in tracing the origin of all poetic creation, "is the World (though not really, yet so as in a looking glass)."

The mirror is of course the traditional emblem of poetry as the imitation of nature. Hobbes's use of the mirror as a metaphor for the operation of memory suggests how far memory and poetry seemed interpenetrating (almost interchangeable) concepts. In a period when imitation most often implied a deep familiarity with previous literary works and generic models, Hobbes certainly meant to include writing and painting (art as well as nature) in the world that the poet perceives when gazing into the looking-glass of memory. What may be most remarkable is the completeness with which Hobbes has allowed remembrance to take over the creation of poetry. Without memory, Hobbes sees human experience as draining away into nothingness: fancy and judgment stare vacantly into the void.

The mirror is not the only powerful metaphor that suggests an indispensable connection between memory and neoclassical writing. Seventeenth-century theorists frequently return to the image of the wax tablet or seal: impressions are fixed within the mind much as a sealing ring stamps its shape into a piece of wax. This image has the benefit of conforming to seventeenth-century theories regarding the physiology of mind. External impressions, either weak or strong, will register faintly or distinctly depending on whether the brain receiving them is, in Galenic terms, moist, hot, dry, or cold. Yet like Hobbes's mirror this traditional image for memory has the disadvantage of representing memory as entirely passive, as if the mind in the act of remembering were merely acted upon. Cartesian and similarly mechanistic theories also tended to reduce memory to a bustle of passiveness, in which animal spirits race from, say, eye to brain with the apathy of clockwork. They all reflect how much seventeenth-century theorists were *unable* to say about memory.

Probably the most important metaphor employed in seventeenth-century discussions of memory is so fundamental to modern thought that it does not seem a figurative expression but almost a literal description. It is the metaphor of printing. We should not be surprised that printing would infiltrate seventeenth-century discourse on memory. We have recently begun to appreciate the extent to which printing—although a much earlier invention—plays a vastly changed role in shaping both literary production and human thought after the Restoration. Here is how Marius d'Assigny describes the process of remembering in his mostly derivative treatise *The Art of Memory* (1697):

> Now there are four natural Motions observable in Memory; First, the Motion of the Spirits, which convey the Species or Ideas from the thinking Faculty to that of Memory. Secondly, the Formation or Reception of those Ideas, and the fixing or *imprinting* them into the Fancy. Thirdly, a returning back of those Spirits from the memorative Faculty to the rational. Fourthly, that Action by which the thinking Faculty reviews what is treasured up in Memory, which indeed is the very Act of Memory [italics added].

As d'Assigny describes it, the memory is a kind of book or (in another common and compatible image) treasury. Ideas and images are printed and stored in the mind for subsequent reflection just as words are imprinted in a text, where they may be reviewed at leisure.

We may wonder exactly what kind of book this is which the mind prints for its own recollection. No seventeenth-century theorist will provide a very detailed description. Yet despite an absence of details the metaphor of printing offered an apparently satisfying way to account for a process that we too discuss metaphorically, through the technology of computers. Remembering thus gave rise to a consistent (if unobtrusive) vocabulary of books and bookmaking. Memory in fact is the metaphoric book—stocked with the contents of numerous libraries—from which neoclassical writers typically construct their literal books. When the king asked Samuel Johnson if he was then writing a new work, Johnson replied that "he had pretty well told the world what he knew, and must now read to acquire more knowledge." Memory is the suppressed middle term between reading books and writing books.

The metaphor of memory as book helps to complicate other seventeenth-century images that characterize the act of remembering as basically passive. It reminds us that seventeenth-century writers also stress the active attention required to fix ideas and images in the memory. Further, as d'Assigny emphasizes in his fourfold division of memory into successive motions, the process of remembering both begins and concludes with a collaboration that requires assistance from what he calls "the thinking Faculty." Memory for d'Assigny consists in an "Action"—or, more precisely, a series of related actions. Most important, the final, culminating action ("which indeed is the very Act of Memory") does not resemble so much the printing of a book as the act of reading it.

The activity of reading as a metaphor for remembrance finds support in other metaphoric descriptions which represent memory as a dynamic process. Locke, too, insists that in memory the mind is often (as he puts it) *"more than barely passive."* Emotion, will, and understanding all for Locke maintain underground communication with the memory, thus transforming the mental terrain that Dryden described as an inert field into a scene of sudden motion. "The Mind," Locke writes of memory, "very often sets it self on work in search of some hidden *Idea,* and turns, as it were, the Eye of the Soul upon it; though sometimes too they start up in our Minds of their own accord, and offer themselves to the Understanding; and very often are rouzed and tumbled out of their dark Cells, into open Day-light, by some turbulent and tempestuous Passion." My point is not to extract from such sources a perfectly consistent metaphoric landscape of remembering. Rather, the diversity of metaphors and of descriptive images should prevent us from wrongly attributing to Dryden's age only a rigid, single, and reductive vision of memory as simply a passive medium for receiving impressions, like a mirror or block of wax. Remembering is also, if haltingly, described as an active, complex, multi-dimensional process that continually overruns the limits of a single metaphor.

The complexity of seventeenth-century metaphors and theories not only encompasses modern distinctions between short-term and long-term memory but also includes nuances borrowed from scholastic philosophy and ultimately from Aristotle's *De memoria.* Different commentators use slightly different terms, but most agree in dividing memory into three distinct modes. *Recognition* (a power humankind shares with the animals) refers to the ability to identify objects or events that we have encountered before. *Reminiscence* refers to the specifically human power of calling former ideas or images back into the mind. *Recollection* (also restricted to humans) refers to our capacity for recovering impressions that have been temporarily blotted out by forgetfulness. Other classifications might subsume these differences. Jean Starobinski, for example, has argued that Montaigne—who refers to his diary as a "memory of paper"—normally distinguishes between the two related terms *souvenance* and *mémoire,* employing *mémoire* mainly to signify "what is learned from books." Thus, according to Starobinski, Montaigne requires a separate word to refer to the personal reminiscences that fill his essays. Dryden does not observe such linguistic niceness. It remains true, however, that personal reminiscence is not a major resource for Dryden's work. Although we learn an astonishing amount about Pope's domestic world—his dogs, dinners, gardens, neighbors, habits, and desires—Dryden in his poems tells us next to nothing about his private affairs or household life. Memory for Dryden meditates upon a larger past.

As we will see, the functions that memory performs in Dryden's work assume, at their outer limits, the proportions of a world-building act of mind. In this sense, memory constructs (not just reflects) both the world that is known and the poet whose knowledge utterly depends upon memory's stabilizing power. This significance was as clear to the philosopher Locke—for whom memory (consciousness of a personal past) helps to constitute the basis of human identity—as to the clergyman d'Assigny. "*Memory,*" writes Locke, "in an intellectual Creature, is necessary in the next degree to Perception. It is of so great moment, that where it is wanting, all the rest of our Faculties are in a great measure useless." D'Assigny, warming to his theme, grows even bolder in his praise of memory:

> All other Abilities of the Mind borrow from hence their Beauty, Ornaments, and Perfections, as from a common Treasury: And the other Capacities and Faculties of the Soul are useless without this. For to what purpose is Knowledg and Understanding, if we want Memory to preserve and use it? What signify all other Spiritual Gifts, if they are lost as soon as they are obtained? It is Memory alone that enriches the Mind, that preserves what Labour and Industry collect, which supply this Noble and Heavenly Being with those Divine Excellencies, by which it is prepared for a Glorious Immortality. In a word, there can be neither Knowledg, neither Arts nor Sciences, without Memory: Nor can there be any improvement of Mankind, either in respect of the present Welfare, or future Happiness, without the Assistance and Influence of this Supernatural Ability. Memory is the Mother of Wisdom, the common Nurse of Knowledg and Vertue. . . .

Dryden's conscious commitment to improving and refining modern English poetry inescapably required—in the contexts of seventeenth-century thought—a poetics of memory that builds upon the past it constructs and preserves. For Dryden, the best way to understand the present and the future was quite simply to remember them.

While seventeenth-century theories can emphasize the importance attributed to memory, there is a resource closer at hand to help us understand the different functions that memory plays in Dryden's work. The experience of modern students who are very likely reading "To Oldham" for the first time can provide useful insights into the repeated acts of remembering that Dryden requires. Memory, we might say, is not only the major action of the poem but also a major action of the reader. Examining the role of memory in the reader's experience can teach us where and why the process of reading comes to a halt—where it encounters such impediments as superimpose on the poem (even on such a translucent poem as "To Oldham") dark patches of incomprehension: moments when the attention fails or meaning unravels. What happens to the reading process, we might ask, when modern students encounter the puzzling lines "farewel thou young, / But ah too short, *Marcellus* of our Tongue"?

Marcellus—like Nisus—is unlikely to show up in standardized quizzes designed to test cultural literacy. It is understandable to me that students today might not know what it means to call someone a "*Marcellus* of our Tongue." The significance of pausing here to examine an interruption in the reading process lies in what it may imply about the commonplace neoclassical practice of allusion. We need to imagine our own momentary incomprehension abruptly reversed. As we read, suppose that the lines did more than simply make sense. Suppose the lines were suddenly flooded with surplus meaning, an excess that confronts us with more than we can understand. It is a mistake to regard Dryden's allusion to Marcellus as just another ornate reference to the classics, the sign of a world we have lost. If we think about how we read, allusion becomes a local instance of a much larger process that opens the neoclassical poem to a continuous influx of memory.

Critics who have thought hard about the place of allusion in neoclassical poetry—Reuben Brower, Earl Wasserman, Christopher Ricks—emphasize its potential for greatly enriching the poetic line. (As Brower aptly says: "The allusive mode is for Dryden what the symbolic metaphor was for the Metaphysicals.") A quick detour through standard footnotes cannot adequately resolve the question of what it means for Dryden to call Oldham the "*Marcellus* of our Tongue." When we return to Dryden's likely source in Virgil, it turns out that there are *two* Marcelluses or Marcelli. Walking side-by-side in the underworld is Marcellus the younger (the short-lived, adopted nephew of the emperor Augustus) and also his heroic namesake (Marcus Claudius Marcellus, who captured Syracuse during the Second Punic War and fully earned his sobriquet "the sword of Rome"). Certainly a poem that unites Oldham with Dryden might well find uses for a compound allusion linking a younger man whose promise was cut short with an older hero who won lasting fame. Dryden's earlier Virgilian allusion to the friendship of Nisus and Euryalus similarly links two heroic figures, one older, one younger, and at least lends plausibility to a reading that recognizes *two* Marcelluses. Yet even readers who decide that Dryden alludes solely to the younger Marcellus might wish to consider the following question. In a poem that repeatedly asks us to remember pairs rather than single figures, in a poem that directly compares Oldham to the short-lived, adopted nephew of Augustus, who in the regions of English poetry might bear comparison with the emperor himself? Samuel Johnson answered the question when he described Dryden in *Lives of the English Poets* by adapting the praise that Suetonius had applied to Augustus as the rebuilder of Rome: "He found [the language] brick, and left it marble."

Allusion, I want to suggest, adds more than complexity of reference, for Dryden could complicate his lines through other equally effective means. Allusion is the sign of memory: where memory recedes in importance, allusion also recedes. The complications of allusion add to the poem a not-always-containable inrush of remembrance, because it is only through memory that allusion generates its distinctive power. We can't simply rest in the truism that readers who don't know Virgil won't fully understand "To Oldham." Indeed, Nisus and Euryalus are far more than names to which we can assign a meaning (or even several meanings). They also evoke a range of feeling that cannot be precisely mapped but depends in part on how we remember and respond to their doomed, heroic mission. Is it possible to recall their friendship without also remembering their fate, when after Euryalus falls captive to the Greeks they both perish in Nisus's unsuccessful rescue? Death is something the elegy to Oldham remembers in more than one mood. Although discussions of allusion rarely mention the close bond between memory and emotion, the allusive act of memory in Dryden's poem corresponds to emotional changes in the experience of the reader, where feelings often prove as important as meanings and where meanings often prove inseparable from feelings. Modern research confirms that what we remember correlates directly with emotions originally surrounding a particular impression or event. If we cannot discover the emotional power in neoclassical poetry, perhaps we are not remembering well enough.

Consider another instance in which allusion delicately mixes meaning and emotion: "Once more, hail and farewel." Here, as Dryden moves toward his conclusion, the poem recalls its opening word ("Farewel") and repeats its initial gesture of separation. Oldham of course can be addressed now nowhere else except in memory. Farewells, however, are especially curious social and linguistic events—"performatives" that (like marriage vows) initiate a change of condition. Saying goodbye is action as well as speech. Farewells, we might say, are departures that paradoxically imply a still lingering point of contact, a bond not yet completely broken, speech not yet reduced to silence. They are echoing, repetitive, reverberating events—often said again and again—even as Dryden's conclusion echoes its own melancholy note ("Once more, hail and farewel; farewel . . ."). Yet surely there is a recognizable difference between farewells spoken in the confidence of seeing someone again and what we might call final farewells. Dryden's elegy clearly belongs to the occasion (modern as well as Roman) when we say farewell for the last time. It is a moment when what is said is somehow said forever: a present acutely conscious of its changed relation to past and future. What is spoken in effect consigns the past to a period no longer continuous with the present. Such farewells are in the nature of a futureless severance.

It is possible, however, that memory might deepen or redeem even such moments of stony farewell. I find I am incapable of reading the words with which Dryden begins his final farewell without hearing the *ave atque vale* of Catullus. The echo seems to me unmistakable, although some readers are not so sure. What for me gives significance to this allusive moment—what argues most persuasively for its status as allusion—is a fact that commentators pass over in silence. The emotion generated by Catullus's poem (no. 101) owes much to its occasion: the death of his brother. Brotherhood is the repeated theme of the moving final couplet:

> accipe fraterno multum manantia fletu,
>   atque in perpetuum, frater, ave atque vale.
> (Accept these offerings, with many brotherly tears,
>   And forever, brother, hail and farewell.)

It is the resonant noun *frater* that drops out of Dryden's line to Oldham, but which of course in dropping out—like the gaps carved by time in a classical frieze—creates a sense of its absence.

Its absence is appropriate, of course, in the literal sense that Dryden and Oldham were not linked by birth. Yet the poem also emphasizes that they are, as poets, intimately related. Dryden in fact employs kinship, especially the ties linking fathers and sons, as his consistent metaphor for expressing literary relationships ("Milton was the poetical son of Spenser, and Mr. Waller of Fairfax; for we have our lineal descents and clans as well as other families"). Christopher Ricks points out that Dryden naturally found the word "brother" coming to his pen when writing of poetic emulation and of poetic lineage. How fitting, then, that Dryden's final "hail and farewel" should draw its emotional resonance from a recollection of the classical bond that unites Oldham and Dryden—through Catullus—in the closeness of brothers. Remembering Oldham is for Dryden inseparable from remembering a great poem in which Catullus remembers his own dead brother, before speech yields to an unending silence. Dryden's act of memory typifies a poetics that celebrates—rather than disguises or denies—a kinship with other writers, employing such relations in order to build up meaning and to deepen emotion.

Memory, understood less as a poetic theme than as a human action, extends its importance throughout Dryden's work, where allusion serves as simply the most obvious example of how remembering both complicates and enriches the poet's voice, as if the reader were hearing at least two voices, simultaneously ancient and modern. Some of the wider implications of Dryden's poetics of memory are evident in the very last line of the elegy "To Oldham": "But Fate and gloomy Night encompass thee around." Footnotes—or a good recollection of Virgil—can tell us that Dryden's line almost exactly translates a verse from the *Aeneid* describing the unfortunate early death of Marcellus.

Whatever this echo contributes to our interpretation, it alters the poem dramatically by adding a "double-voiced" conclusion in which Dryden and Virgil now speak completely in unison. The climax, however, is surprisingly anticlimactic. As memory allows us to hear this double note of grief, what consolation (if any) can we find in the image of the dead poet Oldham surrounded by the darkness of a classical underworld?

The poem's refusal to supply an uplifting Christian consolation remains for me its most daring act of remembrance. Poems, of course, remember other poems in numerous ways, indirect as well as explicit. For example, in its lucid neoclassical surface "To Oldham" indirectly—as if through a law of opposites—recalls Dryden's earlier baroque/metaphysical/Cowleyan elegy "Upon the Death of the Lord Hastings" (1649), where lucidity is nowhere to be found. In effect, "To Oldham" might be said to remember its ornate predecessor in the act of rejecting its model. Yet the somewhat juvenile elegy to Lord Hastings is not the only predecessor that "To Oldham" calls to mind. In defining a counter-tradition of the English elegy (leading directly to a new elegiac mode in Pope and in Johnson) Dryden's poem includes echoes linking it to the greatest of all seventeenth-century elegies, Milton's "Lycidas." "Lycidas," too, concerns the death of a young poet, but its highly ornate style and its Christianized mythology and—above all—its rapturous final consolation ("So *Lycidas,* sunk low, but mounted high, / Through the dear might of him that walk'd the waves / . . . hears the unexpressive nuptial Song, / In the blest Kingdoms meek of joy and love") reminds us of what Dryden has so severely refused or denied. For Dryden, John Oldham belongs to a very different world of death than does Milton's shepherd-hero, Edward King. Memory lets us know exactly what is *not* being promised or performed. It allows us to understand "To Oldham" in all its calculated differences.

Dryden's characteristic act as poet involves understanding the present by establishing its relation to a remembered past. It may seem redundant to characterize the past as remembered, but Dryden and his age—because of their deep interest in ancient Greek and Roman literatures—recognize that vast tracts of intervening time simply disappear into darkness. *Mac Flecknoe* (1682) repeatedly emphasizes this wasteland of unremembered backwardness, just barely visible in such emblems as the "Nursery" near the site of Shadwell's throne: a "Monument of vanisht minds." Time is understood as containing a kind of black hole into which things keep disappearing, never to be seen again, like the blank space (from Ireland to Barbadoes) that constitutes Shadwell's appropriate empire. There is more than amusing parody of Sybilline possession in the gesture that precedes Flecknoe's prophetic commands to his son:

> The *Syre* then shook the honours of his head,
> And from his brows damps of oblivion shed
> Full on the filial dullness. . . .

In a passage whose Miltonic syntax deliberately remembers the relation between heavenly Father and Son, Dryden's rich metaphor of poetic kinship now perversely links mock-father to mock-son, emphasizing that the remembered past achieves its fragile permanence only in a continuous struggle against "oblivion." Pope will develop with even greater urgency the theme that poetry is engaged in a powerful contest between memory and forgetfulness. The past for Augustan writers is not simply out there behind us—preserved in books and accessible to thought. Memory (even though Dryden wouldn't put it this way) *makes* the past. Writing that slips through the cracks in memory effectively ceases to exist, swallowed up by the darkness surrounding Dryden's portrait of Oldham.

The power of memory to clarify the present by placing it in close relation to the remembered past is brilliantly employed by Dryden in *Absalom and Achitophel.* Here again to understand the present means fundamentally to remember it. In his *Life of Plutarch,* Dryden—who served as historiographer royal and (as Achsah Guibbory shows) saw at least five different patterns at work in human history, from cyclical recurrence to providential design—described a familiarity with the past as a kind of mental telescope:

> 'Tis, if you will pardon the similitude, a Prospective-Glass carrying your Soul to a vast distance, and taking in the farthest objects of Antiquity. It informs the understanding by the memory: It helps us to judge of what will happen, by shewing us the like revolutions of former times. For Mankind being the same in all ages, agitated by the same passions, and mov'd to action by the same interests, nothing can come to pass, but some President [*sic*] of the like nature has already been produc'd, so that having the causes before our eyes, we cannot easily be deceiv'd in the effects, if we have Judgment enough but to draw the parallel.

"It informs the understanding by the memory": which is to say, memory serves as an indispensable guide to action and to understanding in the present. Caught up in the turmoil of unfinished contemporary events, fearful that social chaos will accompany this latest threat to the lawful continuity of monarchical succession, Dryden in 1681 employs the telescope of memory in order to make sense of the world he inhabits. Memory, in supplying the parallel between the Exclusion Crisis and the biblical story of Absalom's rebellion, thus uncovers a pattern that clarifies an otherwise unknowable swirl of dangerous political circumstances. This act of memory is no mere exercise in antiquarian curiosity. Dryden's poem directly intervenes in the contemporary events it describes, seeking to shape the present and the future by revealing the design inscribed but hidden in a distant past.

Dryden's intervention in the political events of his time can remind us—as we see repeatedly today—that memory is profoundly ideological. That is, the past we recall is very often a past already constructed for us. The rewriting of history in totalitarian states simply reveals more clearly what goes on around us daily, as we sort through the myths and official lies, recovering and discarding fragments of our own social and political pasts. In a sense, we create the past we need, and the past we need often depends upon our position within a party or class or state or system of power. Dryden lived at a time when scholars and polemicists were actively creating rival versions of English history in order to validate their competing political ideologies, as J. G. A. Pocock has demonstrated in *The Ancient Constitution and the Feudal Law* (1957). Indeed, when political legitimacy depended on rights of origin, it mattered greatly which version of the past won out, whose memory prevailed. "To Oldham" is not directly involved in the ideological uses of memory that we see in Dryden's overtly political works, but poetry, too, is an arena of power. In selecting Oldham as brother and ally, Dryden is in effect declaring in favor of a heritage from which other writers will find themselves, like Shadwell, rigorously excluded. He seeks to manipulate literary history in ways designed to assure who will be forgotten and who, like Oldham, will be remembered.

Ordinarily we tend to experience time as continuous: past, present, and future weave together in a seamless unity, or so it appears. As semester followed semester for thirteen years, my past and future tended to flow into one another, which is what lends significance to the rare moments of absolute rupture. Memory contributes to a general connectedness in which both time and human identity seem fundamentally coherent. (Neurologist Oliver Sacks in one of his clinical tales describes a patient whose memory had stopped thirty years earlier: he was referred to Sacks with a transfer note that read "Helpless, demented, confused, and disoriented.") This specific function of memory in creating a sense of coherence and connectedness can help us grasp a crucially important feature of Dryden's writing. Dryden most often views the present as a transitional moment that separates—far more obviously than it links—two radically different orders of time. The present for Dryden is represented as an unstable vantage point for surveying a fixed past now rapidly receding and a future whose outlines are still unsure.

Modern readers may be confused by Dryden's immersion in contemporary events and by his range of classical reference, but they are nonetheless well situated to understand how he repeatedly depicts the present as a moment of abrupt transition. In its opening lines, "To my Dear Friend Mr. Congreve" (1694) dramatizes the moment of transition with special vividness:

> Well then; the promis'd hour is come at last;
> The present Age of Wit obscures the past. . . .

Six years later, in the year of his death, Dryden still views time as somehow breaking apart, disjoining:

'Tis well an Old Age is out,
And Time to begin a New.

But it was not simply the turn of the century that inspired Dryden's vision of an unstable, transitional present. In his well-known essay *Of Dramatick Poesie* (1668) Dryden directly associates the return of Charles II with a new era of literary production. ("With the restoration of our happiness, we see reviv'd Poesie lifting up its head, & already shaking off the rubbish which lay so heavy on it.") In fact, his very early "Heroique Stanzas" (1659) on the death of Cromwell similarly reads the present as a time of transition—"He made us *Freemen* of the *Continent* / Whom Nature did like Captives treat before"—just as "Astraea Redux" (1660) celebrates another radical break between past and future:

> And now times whiter Series is begun
> Which in soft Centuries shall smoothly run. . . .

Dryden has been persuasively associated with a "conservative myth": a vision that resists innovation and celebrates a continuity with the values attributed to a nostalgic past. Yet we need also to understand how far Dryden's vision of the future is consistently prophetic. He recalls the past, we might say, not in order to relive it but to foretell a future which decisively transcends it.

The prophetic function of memory for Dryden is nowhere clearer than in his most circumstantial and unrefracted engagement with the immediacy of what the Russian theorist M. M. Bakhtin has called "unfinished contemporary time." *Annus Mirabilis* (1666)—which locates its main subjects in episodes so contemporary that embers from the Great Fire were still smoldering as Dryden wrote—stands as supreme testament to Dryden's vision of the present as transitional. In a city now charred and desolate, he foresees a new order emerging from the ashes, an order he anticipates in large part because he understands the present through the telescopic memory of biblical prophecy, Roman history, and the work of select previous writers from Horace and Virgil to Sir William Davenant. Readers who may not regularly find their way to *Annus Mirabilis* should not miss the significance of Dryden's similarly prophetic conclusion to *Absalom and Achitophel:* "Henceforth a Series of new time began. . . ."

Memory, as such examples show, serves Dryden as an instrument which not only connects us to the past but also releases us from its potentially deadening grip. Memory permits us to imagine something better, while establishing the foundation for any improvement. It permits us to evade the consequences of a world doomed endlessly to repeat its mistakes. Thus, with timely understanding, Shaftesbury and Monmouth may yet remember and avoid the grisly fates of their biblical prototypes. "Yet this I Prophecy": so writes Dryden as he looks forward from the transitional moment dramatized at the beginning of his poem "To Mr. Congreve." This typically prophetic stance—so hard to reconcile with the staid Dryden of our textbooks and anthologies—draws its power not from divine inspiration or from inner light but from a rigorous and continuous act of memory. Remembering the past is for Dryden no exercise in nostalgia. Instead, memory—from the dangerous and unknowable flux of contemporary time—initiates a movement that ultimately shapes the future and allows it to emerge.

Certainly all poets rely upon the resources of memory. Nonetheless, they also differ greatly in what particular modes of remembering they emphasize, from personal reminiscence to the rewriting of social or literary history. They differ, too, in what specific acts of memory they demand from readers and in what values they assign to remembering as a poetic resource. It is thus possible to construct an inquiry that would ask what very different relations to memory characterize individual poets from Dryden to Wordsworth. Although Wordsworth clearly announces the primacy of imagination, his emphasis upon emotion "recollected" in tranquillity raises questions that seem not only unanswered but unasked concerning the Romantic uses of memory. For example, how is recollecting an emotion different from recollecting an image or idea or event? Coleridge compared the power of imagination to "moonlight or sunset diffused over a known and familiar landscape." Does memory thus play an important role in allowing us to *recognize* the uncanny changes that imagination performs? Is imagination perhaps powerless in the absence of memory?

A full historical study of memory will help greatly in illuminating the different modes of writing—the different constructions of the past—that intervene between Dryden and Wordsworth. In Dryden's time, memory held an importance in the thinking about thinking that it has not regained until the present day. Memorizing was a principal tool and activity of education; rhyme and sententiousness were defended explicitly for their moral value in permitting ease of recall. "We frequently fall into error and folly," wrote Samuel Johnson, "not because the true principles of action are not known, but because, for a time, they are not remembered; and he may therefore be justly numbered among the benefactors of mankind, who contracts the great rules of life into short sentences, that may be easily impressed on the memory, and taught by frequent recollection to recur habitually to the mind" (*Rambler* no. 175). Remembering was held to possess an ethical, cognitive, and aesthetic value we are just beginning to rediscover. Thus Heidegger saw as a central issue facing modern philosophy the dilemma he called the "forgetting of being." Dryden's elegy "To the Memory of Mr. Oldham" is not only a memorial to Oldham but also—if we choose to remember it thus—a testament to the momentous powers of memory.

Postscript

During the past months I returned to teaching for a single term as a Visiting Professor. I was astonished at how deeply I enjoyed this return to the classroom. My experience was so pleasurable, I believe, partly because it consisted entirely of teaching, with no other responsibilities to a department or institution. This uncommon opportunity, however, also reminds me that memories are far from transparent in their meaning. They belong, as Freud taught us, to complicated conscious and nonconscious structures of interpretation. Initially, it seemed obvious to me that those troublesome, battling figures in my memory represented the student and teacher. Now I am not so sure. Within the department and university, my energies as a teacher were frequently spent in opposing policies that struck me as wrongheaded and in pushing for change. Thus I can think of vice-presidents, deans, department chairs, and colleagues who might well reappear within memory cast as opponents. For me the struggle within the institution seemed mainly a struggle *against* the institution. The boxing ring, I now see, is an apt metaphor for conflicts far less rewarding than the spirited dialogue that, at our best moments, unites student and teacher in a struggle to understand.

Selected Bibliography

Brower, Reuben Arthur. *Alexander Pope: The Poetry of Allusion.* Oxford: Clarendon Press, 1959.
Catullus. *Carmina.* Ed. R. A. B. Mynors. Oxford: Clarendon Press, 1958.
d'Assigny, Marius. *The Art of Memory* (1697). Introduced by Michael V. DePorte. New York: AMS Press, 1985.
Coleridge, Samuel Taylor. *Biographia Literaria* (1817). Ed. John Shawcross. 2 vols. Oxford: Clarendon Press, 1907.
Dryden, John. *The Works of John Dryden.* Ed. Edward Niles Hooker, H. T. Swedenberg *et al.* 20 vols. (projected). Berkeley: University of California Press, 1956– .
Griffin, Dustin. "Dryden's 'Oldham' and the Perils of Writing." *Modern Language Quarterly* 37 (1976): 133–150.
Guibbory, Achsah. *The Map of Time: Seventeenth-Century English Literature and Ideas of Pattern in History.* Urbana: University of Illinois Press, 1986.
Heidegger, Martin. *What Is Called Thinking?* (1954). Tr. J. Glenn Gray. New York: Harper & Row, 1968.
Hobbes, Thomas. *The Answer of Mr Hobbes to Sr Will. D'Avenant's "Preface" Before "Gondibert"* (1650). In *Critical Essays of the Seventeenth Century.* Ed. J. E. Spingarn. 3 vols. 1907; rpt. Bloomington: Indiana University Press, 1957.
Hoffman, Arthur W. *John Dryden's Imagery.* Gainesville: University of Florida Press, 1962.
King, Bruce. " 'Lycidas' and 'Oldham.' " *Études anglaises* 19 (1966): 60–63.
Locke, John. *An Essay concerning Human Understanding* (1690). Ed. Peter H. Nidditch. Oxford: Clarendon Press, 1975.
Mell, Donald C., Jr. "Dryden and the Transformation of the Classical." *Papers on Language and Literature* 17 (1981): 146–163.
Miner, Earl. *Dryden's Poetry.* Bloomington: Indiana University Press, 1967.

————. "The Poetics of the Critical Act: Dryden's Dealings with Rivals and Predecessors." In *Evidence in Literary Scholarship: Essays in Memory of James Marshall Osborn.* Ed. René Wellek and Alvaro Ribeiro. Oxford: Clarendon Press, 1979. Pp. 45–62.

Oates, Joyce Carol. *On Boxing.* Garden City, NY: Doubleday, 1987.

Peterson, R. G. "The Unavailing Gift: Dryden's Roman Farewell to Mr. Oldham." *Modern Philology* 66 (1968–69): 232–236.

Pocock, J. G. A. *The Ancient Constitution and The Feudal Law.* Cambridge: Cambridge University Press, 1957.

Ricks, Christopher. "Allusion: The Poet as Heir." *Studies in the Eighteenth Century III: Papers presented at the Third David Nichol Smith Memorial Seminar.* Ed. R. F. Brissenden and J. C. Eade. Toronto: University of Toronto Press, 1976. Pp. 209–240.

Rosenfield, Israel. *The Invention of Memory: A New View of the Brain.* New York: Basic Books, 1988.

Sacks, Oliver. *The Man Who Mistook His Wife for a Hat and Other Clinical Tales.* New York: Simon & Schuster, 1985.

Sacks, Peter M. *The English Elegy: Studies in the Genre from Spenser to Yeats.* Baltimore, MD: The Johns Hopkins University Press, 1985.

Sitter, John E. "Mother, Memory, Muse and Poetry After Pope." *ELH* 44 (1977): 312–336.

Starobinski, Jean. *Montaigne in Motion* (1982). Tr. Arthur Goldhammer. Chicago: University of Chicago Press, 1985.

Wasserman, Earl R. "The Limits of Allusion in *The Rape of the Lock.*" *Journal of English and Germanic Philology* 65 (1966): 425–444.

The Paradoxes of Tender Conscience

STEVEN N. ZWICKER

Toward the end of Dryden's *Hind and the Panther,* in that elaborate and mysterious exchange of aviary fables that comprises much of part 3 of the poem, the Hind introduces the person of James II disguised as a "Plain good Man."[1] For the Hind the allegory is transparent because in this age, "So few deserve the name of Plain and Good" (3.906). James has appeared briefly before in the poem, and rather more conventionally, roaring and shaking his mane as the British lion (1.289, 304). But in the longest portrait of the king, this protector of hapless Roman Catholics, proclaimer of Toleration, and patron of the recently converted laureate is displayed neither in the glory of military exploit,[2] nor in the conventional imagery of Stuart panegyric, nor even in the language of piety and wisdom so prominent in the dissenters' thankful addresses for the Toleration,[3] but rather in the dress of a blunt and gullible farmer of domestic poultry. Even allowing for the fabular character of the poem as a whole and for the idiom of the Panther's particular fable which the Hind is about to engage and contest, the decision to cast James II as the barnyard landlord is puzzling. More than one of Dryden's contemporaries remarked the embarrassing oddity of the portrait, contrasting the slack and effeminate character of this panegyric with the strength of the laureate's earlier praise of Oliver Cromwell.[4] Perhaps in a poem that turns on mysteries, we ought not to be wholly surprised by the turn of this portrait, but it remains a rather large puzzle deposited near the poem's oracular conclusion. To cite Burnet's remark that James was noted neither for wit nor fancy, does not, I think, solve the rhetorical mystery of the portrait;[5] nor does it explain the portrait's function to suggest, on the evidence of the poem, that Dryden needed to keep the portrait simple and restrained.[6] The laureate had not, up to this point, been known either for the realism or restraint of his Stuart panegyrics, and the spring of 1687 seems an odd moment for Dryden to begin experimenting with paradoxical encomia: strength of mind figured as gullibility, imperial sovereignty as barnyard sway.

But the puzzles and paradoxes of *The Hind and the Panther* hardly begin in part 3. They are present where we have learned most immediately to

Steven N. Zwicker, "The Paradoxes of Tender Conscience." Originally published in *ELH,* Volume 63 (1996), pp. 851–69. Copyright © The Johns Hopkins University Press. Printed by permission.

expect this poet to begin unfolding the characteristic modes of his work: the prefatory address to the reader. Here we discover that Dryden composed the poem "during the last Winter and the beginning of this Spring" (468, l. 58), and that two weeks before it was finished, and in a disconcerting surprise to the poet, James issued his Declaration of Indulgence. Dryden distances the Declaration from his poem, claiming that if he had "so soon" expected the Declaration, he would have spared himself "the labour of writing many things which are contain'd in the third part of it" (II, 468, lines 61–62). But neither Dryden's first readers, a number of whom shrewdly and maliciously combed over Dryden's text looking for just such problems,[7] nor more recent and more sympathetic students,[8] have been able to identify what about part 3 was rendered superfluous by the Declaration. As we might expect, the puzzles that Dryden flagged in the Preface are only the beginning.

The Declaration was a surprise, so this idealist tells us, because he had clung that spring to "some hope, that the Church of England might have been perswaded to have taken off the Penal Lawes and the Test, which was one Design of the Poem when I propos'd to my self the writing of it" (468, ll. 63–65). Setting aside the poet's "surprise" in April of 1687 (and how many other well-placed apologists of the court could have been surprised by the London Declaration of April 4?),[9] we might wonder exactly what in the poet's exhaustive and abusive handling of the origins, character, and conscience of the Anglican confession, or the motives and tactics of its prelates and parliamentarians could possibly have been received as persuasion to take "off the Penal Lawes and the Test"? Of course the rhetorical feints of Dryden's prefaces, deeply complicit though they may be with his poems and plays, do not always yield their guidance in a straightforward manner. Nevertheless it is difficult to locate a plausible field of rhetorical action, to say nothing of a coherent program for Dryden's poem, if we allow the ameliorative and persuasive work the poet avers along with the satiric commonplaces he also acknowledges in the Preface. If the poem had been commissioned or (to allow the poet the fiction that he composed the twenty-five hundred and ninety-two lines of this allegorical defense of Roman Catholic theology entirely of his own volition) simply dreamed up in order to prepare the Anglicans for a repeal of the Penal Laws—itself an odd program for Dryden to undertake in his privacy and laicy—[10] then the regime of insults prepared for the history of Protestant reform and the character of the present Anglican Church is hard to rationalize. On the other hand, if the poem were intended to play a role in the public celebration of the Toleration and the courting of dissent, then the wicked portraits of the sectaries that open *The Hind and the Panther* seem to contradict the ameliorative work of the king's Declaration itself. Either way, the paradoxical twinning of persuasion and abuse is difficult to compass. Contradictions might be resolved simply enough by arguing the fundamental incoherence of the text,[11] but before taking refuge under that cover I want to suggest that paradox and contradiction, rather than unintended consequences of the poet's political and intellectual dilemmas and circumstances, were central to Dryden's expressive and argumentative modes in *The Hind and the Panther.*

Most simply, paradox allowed Dryden to celebrate the mysteries of Christianity and ally them with the institutional tenets and practices of Roman Catholicism. Paradox also allowed Dryden to soften the obvious contradictions between the language and spiritual program of toleration and the closeting, politicking, and bullying of this king and his closest advisors. But there was more personal work for paradox in *The Hind and the Panther;* the poet aimed not only to represent the mysteries of his new faith and resolve the contradictions of the new regime; he needed also to compass or at least to acknowledge the contradictions within his own political and spiritual experience of Roman Catholicism. In that complex arena, paradox might play a crucial role, allowing Dryden to reflect on if not wholly to reconcile discrepancies between his desire (indeed, his active campaign) for preferment and the program of denial and spiritual elevation which his conversion more or less demanded. Paradox might even be used to rationalize the specific failures of patronage which the poet had experienced in the early spring of 1686–87, for in the decision to cast James II not as the warrior king or wise benefactor of private conscience but as the blunt and gullible farmer of domestic poultry, the poet discovered a way to figure private disappointments into the court's public and surprising embrace of sectarian dissent.

That Dryden had a lot of work to do seems obvious from the circumstances in which he found himself as convert and spokesman for an increasingly isolated and unpopular regime as well as from the spectacle of the poem's ambitions: its array of fictions and fables, its intricate allegories and satires, its elaborate symbols and dark prophetic sounds. But not everything about the poem is mystery. Certain elements of the poem's performance were easy enough to discern: it was designed and can be read as part of the court's effort if not to persuade its Anglican audience of the general beneficence of a Toleration, then to extort sectarian support for that Toleration, and to urge, in a solemn and spiritualized manner, the mysteries and eternity of the Catholic communion. The poem also attempts to bolster the spiritual integrity of its author and his royal patron, two actors in the drama of Toleration who needed a lot of support in the area of spiritual integrity. The public idioms of the poem—its vocabulary and images, its strategies of attack, its defensive and celebratory moves—illustrate the resources available to the court in representing the policy of Toleration, and they are used with immense, indeed dazzling skill. But the poem has more to display than the linguistic armory of a high-grade publicist, and indeed it displays quite other and what seem rather private matters as the poet goes about official polemical work. The poem reveals not only Dryden's vulnerability and dilemmas as courtier and convert but also the general contradictions of a Roman Catholic Toleration and the nation's troubled and doubtful mood in the spring of

1687, when Anglicans, Catholics, and sectaries alike watched the twists and turns of James's efforts to remove the Penal Laws and, failing that, to nullify those laws through the Declaration itself.

The central literary device of Dryden's poem is a beast fable in which the Hind and the Panther are, respectively, the Roman Catholic and Anglican communions, and the dissenters are variously styled bears, apes, boars, foxes, and wolves. But not every character in *The Hind and the Panther* turns out to be a beast, and Dryden must have reflected on the limitations of the fabulist's mode as he faced the difficulty of representing the spiritual magnanimity of James II and Roman Catholic kingship while integrating the traditional images of magistracy and authority with the ostensible program of Toleration: mildness, the denial of persecution, the abhorring of constraints in matters of the spirit, the repealing of the sanguinary laws, and the celebration of conscience, that kingdom where every man is absolute.[12] To these various ends, James appears in *The Hind and the Panther,* as we have seen, as a slightly dim-witted chicken farmer: blunt, slow, and preoccupied with the care of his domestic poultry. There is perhaps something wry about framing a beast fable in which the narrating beasts tell their own fables, discoursing subtly of theology, and humans wander naïvely in the allegorical landscape. But why, we might wonder, does Dryden arrange the fabling so that the Panther is allowed a complex literary narrative while the Hind, the voice of institutional Roman Catholicism and hence memory, continuity, and cultural authority, is given a fable that ends up in the barnyard? In the answer to that question lies, I believe, an exposition of the disparate and at points contradictory aims and desires of Dryden's poem, of the difficult and indeed dangerous character of James's pursuit of Toleration, and of the circumstances in which both the laureate and his patron discovered themselves once James had decided to abandon parliament and statute by going down the road of proclamations and declarations to embrace dissent, including, to John Evelyn's horror, the Family of Love.[13]

In the concluding episode of the poem, the Hind and the Panther retire from their theological debate—what Swift called Dryden's "compleat Abstract of sixteen thousand Schoolmen from Scotus to Bellarmin"[14]—to while away the evening in fables. There is more than a touch of the Chinese puzzle about this part of the poem as the beasts purport to instruct one another with mysteries and enigmas. Here, among a host of other puzzles (like what exactly Dryden is predicting about the fate of both Anglicans and Roman Catholics when King Buzzard—read either William III, or Gilbert Burnet, or perhaps both, or perhaps neither—gets ready to dine),[15] Dryden sets his contrasting tales.

To the Panther Dryden gives an elaborate and eerie fable full of the heavy weather of natural disaster and political doom. As interesting as the tale itself is the brief coda in which the Panther makes an excursus on Roman Catholicism by way of an application of *The Aeneid* to contemporary religious politics, a reading of James's intrusion of Roman Catholicism into England as Aeneas's invasion of Latium:

> Methinks such terms of proferr'd peace you bring
> As once Aeneas to th'Italian King:
> By long possession all the land is mine,
> You strangers come with your intruding line,
> To share my sceptre, which you call to join.
>
> (3.766–70)

The allegory involves a complex and clever application of Virgilian materials to the politics of English Catholic rule, and though we recognize the Panther's distortion of Virgil—she is narrating Aeneas's story from Turnus's point of view and thereby ironically and unwittingly confessing the fated triumph of Roman (or rather Roman Catholic) empire—the application itself demands wit and economy. The Panther's literary and exegetical sophistication stands in sharp contrast to the Hind's own barnyard tale. If the Panther's triumph is a Pyrrhic victory, it nevertheless casts the Hind's own fable rather into the shade, for even the reader's correction of the Panther's misreading involves an intricate response to and rewriting of the Panther's Virgil. We cannot help noting that the Panther's allegorizing of Virgil looks oddly like the reading of antiquity in which the ventriloquist himself would soon engage as he translated Virgil's Roman politics into a more contemporary idiom.[16] Dryden no doubt meant for his readers to reject the Panther's Virgil, but he seems to have enjoyed writing these lines; and we can hardly miss the mocking and slightly savage tone of the Panther's speech as she marks the intrusive presence of popish practices:

> But still you bring your exil'd gods along;
> And will endeavour in succeeding space,
> Those household Poppits on our hearths to place.
>
> (3.778–80)

Are we wrong to hear an echo of the Anglican laureate's earlier pleasures when he ridiculed that religion whose gods were recommended by their taste? But how much sarcasm could Dryden allow himself in a poem where the convert insisted that Roman Catholicism had made a specialty, at least in England, of highminded suffering (cf. 3.135–138)? The rhetorical palette had been narrowed, and Dryden alludes in the poem itself to some of the difficulties of accepting such discipline (cf. 1.72–77; 3.12–15; 3.298–305). Of course, Dryden understood, now as before, the rhetoric of fair play, and he ingenuously avers in the Preface to *The Hind and the Panther* that he has made use only of the "Common Places of Satyr, whether true or false, which are urg'd by the Members of one Church against the other. At which I hope no Reader of either Party will be scandaliz'd; because they are not of my Invention" (469–470, ll. 102–104). Dryden is an old hand at disclaiming the credit as satirist he so fully deserved, though at this late date he must have wondered if there could still be any advantage to invoking the rhetoric of fair-mindedness. He could not have expected nor did he receive, "either fair War, or even so much as fair Quarter from a Reader of the opposite Party" (467, ll. 1–2); indeed, how much fair quarter could he have expected from readers of his own party or who exactly might have belonged to that party in the spring of 1687?

Having allowed the full reflexivity of the passage, it remains a puzzle that both as fabulist and exegete Dryden should allow the Panther's literary triumph. Perhaps barnyard simplicity is meant to express both the innocence and the mysteries of the Roman confession, an institution marked, for most of Dryden's audience, rather by equivocation and intrigue than naveté. The setting of the Hind's fable may be an attempt to express the essential simplicity of that form of belief which makes the embrace of elemental mysteries its central spiritual concern. What could be at once simpler and more mysterious than transubstantiation? And the Panther's vexing of Virgil's text might itself be understood as a symptom of the spiritual and intellectual equivocations of Anglicanism. The Hind's attack on reformation exegesis focuses exactly on such detortion of texts, and Dryden may be noting, through the Panther's application of Virgil, how reflexive is the subversion of texts to Reformation spirituality, how complicit in the loss of exegetical authority is the undermining of spiritual control enacted by those "diff'ring Doctours" and jarring sects.

And yet the barnyard remains an odd location for the Hind's tale; nor does the problem become simpler when we gaze directly into her fable. The self-conscious design of the whole episode allows Dryden to raise questions about the rhetoric of fables, signs, and dreams and to distinguish their expressive from their prophetic character. To the Hind, the Panther's threatening fable seems less a prophecy of the fate of English Catholicism than a revelation of the malice and slandering character of the reformed church, a character long since derived from Martin Luther and now borne out in the barbarity of the Penal Laws. The Hind invites us to see in the malice of the Panther the art and intent of a rapacious Anglican Church:

> But, through your parable I plainly see
> The bloudy laws, the crowds barbarity:
> The sun-shine that offends the purblind sight,
> Had some their wishes, it wou'd soon be night.
> (3.657–60)

But might we not at the same time apply the Hind's skeptical reading of fable as character to her own story, and most particularly to her barnyard portrait of the king? Reading Anglican politics out of the idiom of the Panther's fable is rather different from inferring the intentions, restraints, and equivocations of the poet by analyzing the Hind's language as she sketches James's character. And suggestions of James II's naïveté could easily be turned to strategic purpose; but the portrait seems to go beyond mere naïveté:

> A Plain good Man, whose Name is understood,
> (So few deserve the name of Plain and Good)
> Of three fair lineal Lordships stood possess'd
> And liv'd, as reason was, upon the best;
> Inur'd to hardships from his early Youth,
> Much had he done, and suffer'd for his truth:
> At Land, and Sea, in many a doubtfull Fight,
> Was never known a more advent'rous Knight,
> Who oftner drew his Sword, and always for the right.
>   As Fortune wou'd (his fortune came tho' late)
> He took Possession of his just Estate:
> Nor rack'd his Tenants with increase of Rent,
> Nor liv'd too sparing, nor too largely spent;
> But overlook'd his Hinds, their Pay was just,
> And ready, for he scorn'd to go on trust:
> Slow to resolve, but in performance quick;
> So true, that he was awkard at a trick.
> For little Souls on little shifts rely,
> And coward Arts of mean Expedients try:
> The noble Mind will dare do anything but lye.
> False Friends, (his deadliest foes,) could find no way
> But shows of honest bluntness to betray;
> That unsuspected plainness he believ'd,
> He look'd into Himself, and was deceiv'd.
> Some lucky Planet sure attends his Birth,
> Or Heav'n wou'd make a Miracle on Earth;
> For prosp'rous Honesty is seldom seen:
> To bear so dead a weight, and yet to win.
> It looks as Fate with Nature's Law would strive,
> To shew Plain dealing once an age may thrive:
> And, when so tough a frame she could not bend,
> Exceeded her Commission to befriend.
>
> (3.906–37)

There is ample precedent for pastoral allegories of spiritual vigilance; Marvell's account of Lord Fairfax weeding ambition and tilling conscience springs most immediately to mind. But Dryden's barnyard scene does not suggest spiritual pastoralism, nor is self-regulation its most obvious theme. Slowness, gullibility, and blunt honesty are the cardinal virtues in this portrait. James's vaunted military career is acknowledged—"At Land, and Sea, in many a doubtfull Fight, / Was never known a more advent'rous Knight, / Who oftner drew his Sword, and always for the right"—but the triplet seems rather to diminish than to dignify the "advent'rous Knight," a figure more likely from romance than epic. If Dryden is remembering Chaucer here, the allusion is more likely to the Squire than the Knight, the tone ever so delicately suggesting a send-up of James's military career, a slightly mocking appropriation of a standard topic of praise in panegyrics for this prince; even "many a doubtfull fight" allows doubtfulness to slide in two directions. And while Dryden claims moderation and charity for the king, a language that celebrates bluntness, rigidity, and the dead weight of honesty constitutes a curious panegyric idiom.

James had come to the throne declaring his devotion to the preservation of his subjects in their properties, the perfect enjoyment, that is, of their religion and their estates. The panegyrics that celebrated James's accession dwell on the sanctity of his word. Surely in the wake of a Declaration that was immediately construed as a threat to those properties, Dryden's reiteration of the innocence and integrity of the king's word would not be amiss. The portrait's central claim is for the king's naïveté, his gullible simplicity. But there are other arguments posed within the portrait and other interests competing with the polemical character of naïve simplicity. Stubborn rigidity and bluntness accord very well with what we know by anecdote and report of James's character and intellect, and Dryden seems quite happy to seize on James's dullness and stubbornness and flaunt them as virtues. We might be reminded here of the strategy he so brilliantly deployed at the opening of *Absalom and Achitophel*, making central to his argument the very defect of Charles II's character from which the Exclusion Crisis sprang.

Although the brewing crisis over James's kingship did not wholly derive from a failure of wit, James's very dullness could shield him from the charges of intrigue and duplicity which so troubled the reigns of Stuart kings. What nicer exposition of wit and duplicity than Charles II's negotiation of two different Treaties of Dover, one public and unexceptionable, the other a private betrayal of the nation to France and to Roman Catholicism. The revocation of the Edict of Nantes in October of 1685 was an unfortunately timed reminder of the murderous duplicity of Roman Catholic kingship.[17] And English Protestants had been alarmed not only by that warning; they had also learned, in the spring of 1686, of the Catholic massacre of Waldensians when Victor Amadeus II of Savoy moved against the Huguenots to strike a "blow for Catholic uniformity" in Europe.[18] In such a context, at once domestic and international, evidence of the innocence and integrity of the English king's word might best be plucked not from the bloated imagery of panegyrics and proclamations but from those very defects of the king's person that had been the occasion of wit at his expense. How more neatly than by praising James's barnyard simplicity could the king's laureate perform the integrity of his client?

But the political innocence of the Declaration of Indulgence was only part of Dryden's program in the poem as a whole and more particularly in this curious portrait of the reigning monarch. The laureate needed not only to assert the innocence of the king's wit; he needed at the same time to suggest the integrity of his own wit: the purity of his conscience and the constancy of his service. From the moment his conversion was rumored, Dryden was reviled for the meanness and calculation of his spiritual life. This conversion excited memories of earlier change, and while it may not have been a surprise, it must nevertheless have been a nasty reminder of that vulnerability for Dryden to discover his elegy on Cromwell reprinted in 1687 under the title, *A Poem Upon the Death of the Late Usurper, Oliver Cromwel. By the Author of The H – – – d and the P – – – r.*[19] But it need not have been malice that led some to assume, late in 1685 or in 1686, that the fifty-five-year-old laureate might indeed have fixed his worldly hopes on compliance with the king's religion and on the vigor of James's regime. Dryden had long been attached to York's circle; he had served as a brilliant advocate of the crown in the war against Exclusion, and had long defended the duke and both duchesses of York. Within months of James's coronation, Dryden's conversion was known and it naturally raised speculation over compliance and gain.

But by the spring of 1687 Dryden was no longer a fresh convert, and the Roman Catholic monarch had been on the throne for two years. What had Dryden to show for his new religion? In the four months directly preceding the poem's publication he was twice disappointed in his quest for university sinecure. Nor were these most recent quests Dryden's only bid for preferment after James's accession, nor were the disappointments a matter only for private ruefulness. Rumors of the quests and the denials were widely and no doubt maliciously circulated, and in composing his own self-defense, Dryden dramatizes the "suff'ring from ill tongues" he bore (3.304). We might be tempted to calculate the depth of such injury from the very unguarded denial that Dryden has the Hind issue on his own behalf:

> Now for my converts, who you say unfed
> Have follow'd me for miracles of bread,
> Judge not by hear-say, but observe at least,
> If since their change, their loaves have been increast.
> The Lyon buyes no Converts, if he did,
> Beasts wou'd be sold as fast as he cou'd bid.
> (3.221–26)

It could not have been an altogether happy denial that the Hind issued for Dryden. The failure of patronage thrust him into a dilemma of paradoxes; the very thing that Dryden was charged with was what he in fact had sought, and the very proof of the innocence of his intention was the failure to secure patronage, a proof that must have felt like a bitter and ungrateful vindication. Ungrateful or not, it was the only one he had.

In a passage dated April 16, 1687, the moment of confluence between private quest and public Declaration, Roger Morrice, the Presbyterian diarist, records in detail one such quest and its psychological consequences. Morrice notes that by that April Dryden had long since "declared" his new religion; now, looking toward preferment and specifically at the presidency of Magdalen College, a post vacated by the death of Henry Clerke on March 24, Dryden "united all the interest that he could possibly make any manner of way, which he had to be great, to get that Presidantship, which is a very desirable preferment and had great hopes of obtaining it; but at last had this final answer that place was not to be given to him that had Declared but to one that was yet to Declare, which sarcastick denyall has made him very pensive and melancholy, and will be reflected upon him as well as the missing of the place, and he will be hereupon exposed throughout the town."[20]

There had been earlier rumors of quests and possible preferments—Eton College, Trinity College, Dublin[21]—but if Dryden were playing the odds, waiting for just the right office to fall into his lap, then he missed his bet. It was one thing to be dismissed as a calculating cynic, quite another to be caught out as a fool, and not exactly as a holy fool either. Perhaps such failure suggested the naïveté of his quest, but the poet now had a complicated set of perceptions and feelings to manage. For the failure of patronage was a humiliation not at the hand of his enemies, though it clearly enough played into their hands, but from a patron whom he had so long served. In the 1690s Dryden indulges some rueful remarks on the quality of Stuart gratitude; perhaps ruefulness was already to be found counterpointed against assertions of humility and steadfast faith.

If we return to the Hind's portrait, we might now entertain the possibility that the figure is strategic and expressive in several ways. The portrait is not I think a unitary performance, but one moving simultaneously in several directions, and perhaps not all of the directions under very exact control. The image of James II perhaps doth protest too much the dependable simplicity of the king; in so protesting the image asserts a programmatic defense of James's honesty. At the same time it releases Dryden's frustration over James's folly and Dryden's anger at the ingratitude of his very integrity: this lion buys no converts, nor have the loaves of those who have "follow'd" the king been increased. "Follow'd" surely means obeyed the king's example in his conversion to Rome, but perhaps, in the context of the barnyard fable, the word also allows a slightly humiliating image of the converts following after the landlord as he trails crumbs for their feed. If there is frustration directed outward at the king, there is perhaps as well some frustration swallowed by the poet over his own naïve participation in the drama that was collapsing around him at the very moment he was writing this poem. Is there then some odd and strategic alignment of patron and poet, now coupled in their honesty and simplicity, the king in his naïve expectations for the Toleration and the poet in his own naïveté over preferment? And both alike victims of suspicion and ill will?

Perhaps too the portrait assuages the disappointments of conversion, allowing the poet to get his own back under very difficult circumstances. Dryden had long ago learned how to answer and how highmindedly to look beyond the insults of vindictive detractors. But what was one to do if detraction came from the putative source of benefits, humiliation from the hand that by any reasonable calculation should have been the source of rewards? Students of *The Hind and the Panther* have long appreciated Dryden's apprehension over the direction of the forward party at James's court; and we can feel apprehension at a number of moments in the poem. But something other and perhaps more difficult to manage than political anxiety is also displayed in this text. Little wonder that sarcastic denial would have made the poet pensive and melancholy; the record is, I believe, available for inspection in *The Hind and the Panther,* and nowhere more clearly than in the humiliating allegory of James II and his flock. The allegory inverts majesty and records the parsimony of Roman Catholic patronage. It also gave Dryden a way to turn his disappointments into an emblem of the larger paradoxes and follies written into James's unlikely embrace of dissent and strategy of Toleration, the paradox, that is, of liberty of conscience from a prince and a church known rather for bigotry and inquisition than humility and toleration, and the folly of abandoning old allies for the cultivation of the most unlikely of new friends. The king's nomination for the Presidency of Magdalen College went not to the laureate who had long served James's interests and who had converted to the king's religion, but to one Anthony Farmer, a man of "disorderly and scandalous character,"[22] who had not even "Declared" when the king's Mandamus ordering his election had been sent down.[23] This was the candidate handpicked by a king who would neglect the obligations of gratitude in order to force his will on a resentful college. What I am suggesting is that the mixed motives and mixed modes of this text project both the ironies and paradoxes in which the poet was caught and the larger puzzles and paradoxes of the moment itself and especially of the king's strategy of turning his back on the traditional Stuart alliance with the Anglican hierarchy and its longstanding strategy of quashing dissent. James I had declared "no bishop, no king"; Charles I had gone to the scaffold as a martyr of the Anglican Church; Charles II had acquiesced in the Clarendon Code; and James's own staunchly Anglican Parliament had voted him a huge supply at his accession. Now, frustrated in his designs to staff the army, the universities, and his government with Roman Catholics, James turned away from old loyalties and traditional ties of gratitude to seek alliance with the likes of the Anabaptists of Oxford, the Independents of Gloucester, and the Nonconformists of York.

What could this king have had in mind? Those who observed the maneuverings of the court in the spring of 1687, Halifax prominent among them, knew only too well that James's embrace of dissent was driven by the politics of strategic alliance.[24] By cobbling together an alliance of the Roman Catholic court and a variety of dissenter communities, James hoped to out-maneuver the Anglicans. And Dryden's Preface to *The Hind and the Panther* makes the political *quid pro quo* almost embarrassingly explicit:

> This Indulgence being granted to all the Sects, it ought in reason to be expected, that they should both receive it, and receive it thankfully. . . . to refuse the Benefit, and adhere to those whom they have esteem'd their Persecu-tors, what is it else, but publickly to own that they suffer'd not before for Con-science sake; but only out of Pride and Obstinacy to separate from a Church for those Impositions, which they now judge may be lawfully obey'd? . . . Of the receiving this Toleration thankfully, I shall say no more, than that they ought, and I doubt not they will consider from what hands they receiv'd it. 'Tis not from a Cyrus, a Heathen Prince, and a Foreigner, but from a Christian King, their Native Sovereign: who expects a Return in Specie from them; that the Kindness which He has Graciously shown them, may be retaliated on those of his own perswasion.
>
> (468, ll. 40–55)

Could the domineering and impatient language, the expectations and threats, be less veiled? James expected a "Return in Specie" from this motley theolog-ical crew, these wolves, foxes, bears, buffoon apes, graceless Athanasians, and blaspheming Socinians.

The official language of James's Declaration belongs wholly to the king-dom of conscience, and the Addresses from Dissenters are equally high-toned and gracious. Dryden's poem allows us to see a rather different face of Tolera-tion: its paradoxical strategy of embracing, with the sharp edge of threat quite explicit, the former enemies of the Stuart polity while abandoning old friends. The course was dangerous, a revolutionary coup against entrenched and propertied interests that would not likely produce a stable alliance for the court. What it produced was a stable alliance between old enemies and for-mer allies of that court, and a fairly swift resolution, in the persons of James's daughter and son-in-law, to the threats of Roman Catholicism.

Of the unlikeliness of the alliance between Roman Catholicism and dis-sent, Dryden's poem makes its own brilliant and damaging case. From the court's point of view the Anglicans, stubbornly unmoveable on the Penal Laws, might be quite properly charged with self-interest and greed;[25] but what chicken farmer in his right mind would give shelter to foxes and wolves? At first glance it seems very peculiar indeed that the groups James had reached out to embrace should be so sharply treated in the satirical sketches with which Dryden opens his poem. Why, if we are looking from inside the court, would the laureate be hired to insult the very groups to whom the King was extending his most gracious and most Christian hand? Dryden's aim was to make certain that Dissenters not resolve to bite the hand that fed them, turning away from the proffered Toleration in some putative and high-minded display of allegiance to the principles of reformed religion.[26] But Dryden understood the deeper contradictions of seeking new alliances and abandoning old loyalties, and his portrait of James in all his dimness and rigidity is at once a vindication of the slow-witted integrity of the King's word and an expression of his own anger and exasperation over James's violation of the principle of gratitude, that linchpin of early modern politics.

On the face of it Dryden's poem is and ought to be an orchestration of James's religious policies. In part 1 Dryden warns the king's new clients that the court is mindful of the past, that James, or at least his laureate, has not forgotten exactly with whom he was now treating. Such a two-pronged approach is quite plausible: the king takes the high ground, his laureate unveils the sharp edge of satire. In part 2 Dryden vindicates the theology of the Roman Catholic Church, elevating both its mysteries and the inviolability of the oral tradition—an argument, I believe, on behalf both of the eternal mysteries of authority and the sanctity of Declaration.

In part 3 the poet turns to the equally mysterious matter of fable, and here the paradoxes and mysteries of his poem most exactly suggest the instability and dangers of a Roman Catholic Toleration as well as the folly and galling short-sightedness of this king's policies on benefits and gratitude. For we come, late in part 3 and without any real preparation, upon the barnyard exegesis of the person and character of this most Christian king, not a Cyrus or a foreign monarch but a native sovereign. And yet in Dryden's hands, James II is not revealed, to quote the language of the dissenters's Declarations so actively solicited by the court, in the glory of his "Divine Bounty" (*London Gazette*, no. 2240) and "Princely Pity," (*London Gazette*, no. 2238) or in the solicitude of his fatherly compassion, or in the infinite capacity of his "Royal and Intelligent Heart" (*London Gazette*, no. 2251), least of all in the visible "Blossoming" of the king's "celebrated Wisdom" (*London Gazette*, no. 2258).

There was at least one customer at the court who would have been difficult to persuade of the "celebrated Wisdom" of James II. Dryden turned rather pointedly away from the rhetoric of addresses of thanksgiving. For his years of service, the laureate had some reason to hope not only for the spiritual rewards of the Roman Catholic communion but also for more tangible signs of the king's gratitude. What he was now told was that the office of the Presidency of Magdalen College was not to be given "to him that had Declared but to one that was yet to Declare." In the winter and early spring of 1686–87 he was hopeful that proper benefits might indeed flow; but by April he had been given a particularly bitter pill to swallow. And so we come, in part 3 of his poem, to Dryden's representation of the policy and politics of Toleration, to the portrait of James as the blunt, slow-witted farmer of domestic poultry, a man "So true, that he was awkard at a trick." Dryden's line allows an odd admission to hover over the portrait—not that James's integrity knew no tricks, but that it rendered him awkward in their performance. It was as open an expression of resentment as circumstances, and indeed as the poet himself, would allow. What could he now do, having, in his conversion to Rome, burned what bridges remained behind him?

The prospects must have been bitter to contemplate. But through the considerable power of his mysterious poem Dryden was able to project more than his own gall. Part of the irony and disappointment is fairly well hidden, folded into the idiom of the Hind's curious and disturbing fable. But the disappointment in the king's rigid and single-minded pursuit of his political program and what Dryden judged a particularly foolish embrace of dissent was not only personal gall. It expressed as well what it felt like for all those driven by the politics of Roman Catholic Toleration down a path of willfull political confrontation and parliamentary defiance, a path that some could remember had once ended in civil war and that must have looked, in the spring of 1687, to be headed to similar places. The gloomy conclusion of the Hind's fable, with its images of tyranny, tumult, and bloody confusion, indicates vividly enough the sense of doom that attended the politics of this particular king's Toleration. Dryden was caught inside the web, and he felt the full force of both personal and institutional doubts and contradictions. He had been pushed away from its center, but he could hardly break from the court, for he had nowhere else to turn. The poem he spun out of the calculations and disappointments of the moment offers us a guarded and difficult but also a singular and a penetrating look at this Roman Catholic Toleration, in all its contradictions, and as it appeared not from the outside, but from near the very center of that court, not near enough to reap the benefits its laureate felt were his due, but too close, at least by association, to deny his complicity with the regime.

In memory of Edith Baras Burke

Notes

1. *The Poems of John Dryden,* ed. by James Kinsley, 4 vols. (Oxford, 1958), II, 526; all subsequent citations are to this edition. References to the poem will be to part and line numbers, and references to the Preface will be to page and line numbers; both will be included parenthetically in my text.

2. The tradition of representing James, both as duke of York and as king, in the figure of military exploit began early and provided a continuous idiom for verbal and visual iconography. In portraits by Wissing, Gascars, Cooper, and Lely, and in a number of anonymous portraits, James is depicted in full armor, with helmets, batons of command, land battles, and naval engagements providing the emblematic counterpoint to the armed portrait figure. For early prose and verse panegyrics, see Richard Flecknoe, *Heroick Portraits with other Miscellany Pieces* (London, 1660), C1r-C2r, "The Portrait of the Dukes of York and Glocester, under the Names of Castor and Pollux," "But whilest all other extreams in him are temper'd in the mean,

his Valour and Courtesie admits no mean at all; for in the Field (i' th' face of the enemy) the furious North winde that blows down whole Forrests before it, and leaves nothing but Ruine behinde, is not more fierce nor terrible . . ."; and [Thomas Ireland], *Speeches Spoken to the King and Queen, Duke and Duchesse of York in Christ Church-Hall, Oxford, Sept. 29, 1663* (London, 1663), 7: "To the Duke of York," "But to remove all fears, behold here stands / A Prince That bears Protection in his Hands; / Who in his Infancy to Conquest bent, / Did in his Cradle apprehend a Tent; / And since by mighty deeds of War hath shewn / The Dons a Courage which they ne're durst own; / Whose Arm alone appearing their relief / Made him at once their succour and their grief."

      Dryden's own rendering of James as martial hero began in *Annus Mirabilis* and reached an apogee in *Threnodia Augustalis* where James is celebrated as "Alcides" (l. 447) and the "Martial Ancus," (l. 466) and his accession hailed, "A Warlike Prince ascends the Regal State" (l. 429).

      3.   The London Declaration was issued on April 4, 1687 and the dissenters's "Addresses" of thanks started appearing in the *London Gazette* of April 14–18; as Earl Miner notes in his commentary on *The Hind and the Panther,* over one hundred addresses had appeared by the beginning of September 1687, and they continued until September of 1688; see *The Works of John Dryden,* ed. H. T. Swedenberg, Jr., et al. 20 vols (Berkeley and Los Angeles, 1956—), III (1969), ed. by Earl Miner, 349.

      4.   See *The Revolter* (London, 1687), 23, "When he comes to the Panegyrick upon his present Majesty, where he had so transcending a Subject, and ought tho it had been by way of Digression, to have expended the whole Treasure of his Genius. Heaven's! what a difference there is between the feminine Encomiums of Mr. D. the Romanist, upon his present Majesty, and the ranting Raptures of Mr. D. the Independent upon a Monster of a Tyrant, as if the very Noise of Olivers silver Prize had inspir'd him."

      5.   Kinsley, *The Poems,* IV, 1987, glosses 3.906–14, by quoting Gilbert Burnet on the Duke of York, "I go next to the duke; he has not the king's wit nor quickness, but that is made up by great application and industry. . . . He has naturally a candour and a justice in his temper very great, and is a firm friend, but a heavy enemy. . . . He understands business better than is generally believed, for though he is not a man of wit or fancy, yet he generally judges well when things are laid before him. . . ."

      6.   Miner, *The Works,* III, 441, "It was necessary to make James seem simple and trustworthy; beyond that, Dryden never had the enthusiasm for him that he did for Charles."

      7.   For the contemporary attacks on *The Hind and the Panther,* see Hugh Macdonald, *John Dryden: A Bibliography of Early Editions and of Drydeniana* (Oxford, 1939), 44–47 and 253 ff.

      8.   Miner, *The Works,* III, 350, acknowledges that "the problem of possible last-minute revisions is . . . difficult to solve," but suggests that there were last-minute changes in the portrait of the Buzzard (part 3, 1120–1194); Kinsley, *The Poems,* IV, 1968, cites Scott's thesis that the portrait of the Doves, more virulent than Dryden's portrait of the Panther, was written after the Declaration; Kinsley also suggests that ll. 811–12, 892–7, and 1233–55 were added after the Declaration. James Winn, *John Dryden and His World* (New Haven, 1987), 423, allows that Dryden "evidently made some adjustments in his poem to reflect this change of policy [James's issuing of the Declaration]," but then argues that the poem "could not easily be altered to accommodate new events," and declines to identify what changes Dryden made or what Dryden might have thought was rendered superfluous by the king's Declaration. Phillip Harth in *Contexts of Dryden's Thought* (Chicago, 1968), 50 n., apparently believes that the king's Declaration "caught [Dryden] by surprise . . . as he admits later in the preface," that this preface alone reflects Dryden's attempt "to fit his poem" to the king's new policy, and that Dryden's original aim, to "isolate the Dissenters without exception and to appeal to the Anglicans to form an alliance with the Catholics," is reflected in *The Hind and the Panther.* What this hypothesis fails to address is how the poem's sustained attack on Anglican greed, intolerance,

and political inconstancy constitutes a strategy of appeal to the Anglicans and an invitation to ally with the Catholics.

9.   In Edinburgh on February 17 James issued a "Proclamation for the Universal Liberty of Conscience"; the Edinburgh "Proclamation" was printed in the *London Gazette* (no. 2221) of February 28 to March 3. John Evelyn noted the "Proclamation" in his diary entry of March 2, see *The Diary of John Evelyn,* edited by E. S. de Beer, 6 vols. (Oxford, 1955) IV, 539; see also, *An Astrological Diary of the Seventeenth Century: Samuel Jeake of Rye, 1652–1699,* edited with an Introduction by Michael Hunter and Annabel Gregory (Oxford, 1988), 183, entry for March 23, "News also per Gazette of somethings preparatory to the Declaration for Liberty of Conscience. News per letter that hopes began to rise," and for April 11, "Enclosed also in his Letter I received King James's Declaration for Liberty of Conscience."

10.   On the privacy of *The Hind and the Panther,* see the Preface, "'Tis not for any Private Man to Censure the Proceedings of a Foreign Prince: but, without suspicion of Flattery, I may praise our own. . . . As for the Poem in general, I will only thus far satisfie the Reader: That it was neither impos'd on me, nor so much as the Subject given me by any man" (Kinsley, *The Poems,* II, 468, ll. 30–31, 56–57.)

11.   See, for example, Winn, *John Dryden and His World,* 423, 427, who writes of *The Hind and the Panther* as Dryden's "fascinating, risk-taking failure," and argues that its lack of unity and coherence was the "inevitable consequence of trying to do too many things at once. . . . In *The Hind and the Panther,* he was betrayed by too many inventions, too many styles, too many conflicting purposes."

12.   See the language of Dryden's Preface, *The Poems,* II, 468, ll. 35–37, "Conscience is the Royalty and Prerogative of every Private man. He is absolute in his own Breast, and accountable to no Earthly Power, for that which passes only betwixt God and Him."

13.   John Evelyn, *The Diaries,* IV, 554.

14.   *A Tale of a Tub,* ed. A. C. Guthkelch and D. Nichol Smith, (Oxford, 1920), 69.

15.   On the identity of the Buzzard, see the commentary by Miner, *The Works,* III, 440, 449–50; Zwicker, *Politics and Language in Dryden's Poetry* (Princeton, 1984), 156–157; and Annabel Patterson, *Fables of Power: Aesopian Writing and Political History* (Durham, N. C., 1991), 104–105, who rejects the ambiguity of the reference as an intentional confusion but does not, in turn, solve the riddle of the twin reference.

16.   On Dryden's interpretation of the contemporary meaning of Virgil's circumstance and the politics of Dryden's translation of the *Aeneis,* see Zwicker, *Politics and Language,* 177–205.

17.   Evelyn, *The Diary,* IV, 484; and on Louis XIV and the Duke of Savoy, *The Diary,* IV, 511, [May 9, 1686], "The Duke of Savoy, instigated by the French <king>, put to the sword many of his protestant subjects: No faith in Princes."

18.   See J. F. Bosher, "The Franco-Catholic Danger, 1660–1715," *History,* vol. 79, No. 255 (February 1994), 5–30.

19.   Macdonald, *Bibliography,* 6 [item 3e].

20.   Roger Morrice, "Entring Books," 3 folio ms. vols., (Dr. Williams's Library [14 Gordon Square, London, WC1], vol. 2, 93.

21.   See Roswell G. Ham, "Dryden and the Colleges," *MLN* vol. 49 (May, 1934), 324–332.

22.   *Magdalen College and James II, 1686–1688: A Series of Documents,* collected and edited by J. R. Bloxam (Oxford, 1886), x.

23.   *Magdalen College and James II,* vii–xiv, 36–42.

24.   See Halifax's *Letter to a Dissenter* (London, 1687), 2, "Consider that notwithstanding the smooth Language which is now put on to engage you, these new Friends did not make you their Choice, but their Refuge: They have ever made their first Courtships to the Church of England, and when they were rejected there, they made their Application to you in the second place."

25.   On Dryden's own address to Anglican greed and inconstancy, see David Bywaters, *Dryden in Revolutionary England* (Berkeley and Los Angeles, 1991), 14–22.

26.   On the potential for alliance between Anglicans and Dissenters in the wake of the king's Toleration see M. Goldie and J. Spurr, "Politics and the Restoration Parish: Edward Fowler and the Struggle for St Giles Cripplegate," *The English Historical Review,* CIX [No. 432, June 1994], 595, "In 1687 James II ousted the Tories and liberated the Dissenters, with predictable effects on civic and parish life. . . . Although a deep enemy of James II's Catholicism, Fowler saw that James's reign was good 'in one respect,' for it forced Anglicans and Dissenters 'to be united in affection, and to have more charity for each other,' so that 1688 'was the most comfortable year, that ever fell within my memory.' "

Dryden and the Birth of Hercules

James D. Garrison

I

The unique character of Dryden's *Amphitryon* is nowhere more evident than in the prophetic conclusion, where Jupiter reveals his divinity and promises Hercules to the world.[1] In both of Dryden's acknowledged sources the prophecy looks inward to the mythical plot, providing a resolution to the conflicts caused by the intervention of the gods in the affairs of men. In Dryden, on the other hand, Jupiter finally brushes aside these same conflicts, looks away from the demands of the plot, and articulates a vision that collapses the distinction between the world of the play and the world shared by Dryden and his audience. In effect, Dryden transforms the inherited prophecy from a more (Plautus) or less (Molière) satisfactory justification of the ways of Jupiter to man into a severe indictment of the contemporary world. As a consequence, for all its affinities with the Amphitryon plays of Plautus and Molière, Dryden's version of the legend has ultimately a very different effect from either of theirs.

The audience of Plautus' *Amphitruo* can never be in doubt of a happy ending. Although it includes extended scenes of human suffering, the Roman play reconciles suffering with comedy through a pervasive dramatic irony that allows the audience to share the vision of the gods and thus to laugh even when the human characters appeal for help to their unknown tormentors. The function of Jupiter's prophecy is, then, to disclose to the long-suffering protagonist the pattern of divine beneficence already revealed to the audience. In this disclosure the divine imposture is acknowledged and the twinning trick explained, as a new set of twins emerges. Perceived by Amphitryon as evidence of divine favor ("di me seruant"), the twins Iphicles and Hercules signify reconciliation between gods and men.[2] Hercules, here an instrument of concord, also makes possible the renewed domestic harmony of Amphitryon and Alcmena, who are promised perpetual glory in compensa-

Reprinted from "Dryden and the Birth of Hercules," by James D. Garrison, appearing in *Studies in Philology*, Vol. 77 (2). Copyright © 1980 by the University of North Carolina Press. Used by permission of the author and publisher.

tion for temporary suffering. Obediently acknowledging divine authority and goodness ("faciam ita ut iubes"), Amphitryon responds to Jupiter's prophecy by preparing to rush inside to communicate his joy to Alcmena.[3] The play ends on an unambiguously happy note: the gods are good, men obedient.

No such assurance is available at the conclusion of Molière's *Amphitryon*, a version of the legend more polished in its comedy and yet darker in its implications.[4] Here the fiction of doubling is presented and perceived rather as a fiction of division. Amphitryon, divided against himself, separated from his wife, and alienated from his god, faces a tragic dilemma without ever acquiring tragic stature—not even when he confronts Jupiter with his sword. Alcmena, more nearly tragic in scale than her husband, challenges Jupiter not with a sword but rather with her mind, refusing to accept the god's distinction between *époux* and *amant* and accepting only with great reluctance his distinction—and it is a distinction central to classical French tragedy— between *gloire* and *amour*. It is against this background of potentially tragic division that the comedy proceeds. Indeed, the theme of division is reflected in the dual design of the comic plot: the Sosia Cléanthis-Mercury episodes counterpoint the Amphitryon-Alcmena Jupiter action with such significant precision that two resolutions are required. If the first ending, where Mercury justifies himself to Sosia, is comically satisfactory, the resolution to the main plot, where Jupiter justifies his ways to Amphitryon, is left doubtful and ambiguous. Promised immortal glory, this Amphitryon (in sharp contrast to his grateful Roman ancestor) is enigmatically silent, causing Jupiter to transform his promise into a warning, almost into a threat.

> Tu peux hardiment te flatter
> De ces espérances données.
> C'est un crime que d'en douter:
> Les paroles de Jupiter
> Sont des arrêts des destinées.[5]

Amphitryon, whose state of mind is obliquely reflected in Jupiter's verb "douter," remains apparently unreconciled to divine providence and shows no signs of seeking reunion with his wife. The prophecy of Molière's Jupiter, although more elaborate and extensive than that of his Roman counterpart, is finally less satisfactory. The same promise that elicits an affirmation of faith from Plautus' Amphitryon elicits from Molière's protagonist literally nothing.

Thus juxtaposed, the prophetic conclusions of Dryden's sources can be seen to differ in details that characterize each author's individual interpretation of the legend. When set next to Dryden's ending, however, the prophecies of Plautus and Molière begin to look more similar. Following Molière quite closely down to Sosia's interruption ("*Jupiter* . . . knows how to gild a bitter pill"), Dryden thereafter drastically alters divine motivation and enlarges the scope of the vision.[6] Abandoning the attempt to conciliate and compensate the injured Amphitryon, Dryden's Jupiter concentrates on the future of Hercules, who is portrayed not as an agent of reconciliation but rather as a heroic reformer in a post-heroic world.

> From this auspicious Night, shall rise an Heir,
> Great, like his Sire, and like his Mother, fair:
> Wrongs to redress, and Tyrants to disseize;
> Born for a World, that wants a *Hercules.*
> Monsters, and Monster-men he shall ingage,
> And toil, and struggle, through an Impious Age.
> Peace to his Labours, shall at length succeed;
> And murm'ring Men, unwilling to be freed,
> Shall be compell'd to Happiness, by need.[7]

If this is a coherent vision of the world, it is also a vision gratuitously complex given both the immediate context of the plot and the larger context of the dramatic tradition in which the play exists. At issue here is the meaning of heroism in an age of impiety, and the complexity of Dryden's treatment becomes immediately evident when we try to understand the significance of the word "wants" in the second couplet. Any initial impulse to understand this verb to mean "desires" is checked by the succeeding lines, where it becomes obvious that the world most emphatically does not desire such a hero. We are left, then, with "wants" in the sense of "lacks" and with the added implication of "needs," suggested by the very last word of the passage. But this is not simply a world without a hero. It is also a world in which the very idea of heroism has become problematical.[8] Hercules' opposition is more than traditional enough ("Monsters," "Monster-men," "Tyrants"), but the indecisive verbs that define his relationship to the world ("disseize," "ingage," "toil," "struggle") emphasize difficulty with little promise of recognition, appreciation, or triumph. If there is any optimism at all in this prospect, it must be found in the concluding triplet. But even this prediction of success is expressed largely in the passive voice and is seriously complicated by the uneasy, almost oxymoronic relationship between compulsion and freedom that success here entails. Unnecessary to resolve the plot, this complex vision transforms the instantaneous happiness of Plautus' ending and the uncertain happiness of Molière's into a happiness contingent upon the future success of the promised hero. And success is defined in terms that make its achievement problematical, if not, in fact, logically impossible.

This severe conclusion, hardly conceivable as an ending in either Plautus or Molière, has (to my knowledge) no parallel in any antecedent version of the play that Dryden might have known. And yet these lines are not original. They can be traced to Pindar's laudatory analogy between Chromius and Hercules in the first Nemean Ode. As translated by Abraham Cowley, stanza VIII of the Pindaric ode includes Tiresias' vision of the future of Hercules.

> When wise Tiresias this beginning knew,
>   He told with ease the things t'ensue,
> From what *Monsters* he should free
> The *Earth,* the *Ayr,* and *Sea.*
> What mighty *Tyrants* he should slay,
> Greater *Monsters* far then *They.*[9]

The context and prophetic significance of this passage, the reiterated emphasis on *"Monsters,"* the reference to *"Tyrants,"* the idea of freedom, are together
sufficient to suggest Cowley's translation as Dryden's source. Even so, however, the differences between the two prophecies are perhaps more revealing
than the similarities. Dryden borrows the crucial nouns (notably transforming the second *"Monsters"* into "Monster-men"), but passes over the decisive
verb "slay" in favor of the unusual "disseize" and incorporates the other
strong verb "free" into a passive construction, "unwilling to be freed." In
effect, Tiresias' Hercules confronts a world simpler than that of Jupiter's hero;
Tiresias' prophecy is genuinely confident and assured (he forecasts "with
ease"), whereas Jupiter's vision seems more doubtful with each successive
reading. Cowley, then, provides the framework and vocabulary of Jupiter's
prophecy, but it is Dryden himself who renders the prophecy problematical.
Just how problematical can be seen by placing the prophecy in the context of
Dryden's public poetry, especially the poetry from the reign of James II.

II

Dryden's final laureate poem, published on the eve of the Revolution that
sent James to Saint-Germain, calls into question the prophecies that had
dominated the conclusions of his public poems since 1660.[10] No longer able
to envision transcendence of the trial that is history, he now anticipates a
future undifferentiated from the past: "Nor yet conclude all fiery *Trials* past, /
For Heav'n will exercise us to the last."[11] Inevitably a reminder that in the
poems of the 1660's (literally so in *Annus Mirabilis*) Dryden *had* viewed "all
fiery *Trials* past," this implicit repudiation of the earlier prophecies discloses
an idea of history revised in the light of the political conflicts of the 1670's
and 80's. Whereas the Restoration poems combine cyclical and progressive
ideas of history in order to idealize the future, the later poems combine cyclical and regressive concepts to show the nation moving away from the past
ideal of the Restoration, the recovery of which becomes the new focus of
prophecy. This restricted vision is first evident in the conclusion to *Absalom
and Achitophel:*

> Henceforth a Series of new time began,
> The mighty Years in long Procession ran:

> Once more the Godlike *David* was Restor'd,
> And willing Nations knew their Lawfull Lord.[12]

This prophecy of the restoration of the Restoration, replete with echoes of *Astraea Redux,* is itself echoed in the more hesitatingly contingent prophecy that concludes *Threnodia Augustalis.*[13] Here, moreover, Dryden incorporates into his increasingly pessimistic vision an extended allusion to the birth of Hercules, an allusion derived from Cowley's Pindar and later modified for service in *Britannia Rediviva.* It is in these two poems from the reign of James II that we can discover the lineage and contemporary significance of the prophecy that closes *Amphitryon.*

In *Threnodia Augustalis* Dryden shapes the Hercules allusion to celebrate James, whose career describes an ascendant curve leading to the throne, just as, "by degrees" Hercules "rose to *Jove's* Imperial Seat."[14] The identification of monarch with hero allows for the further identification of the "Monsters" confronted by Hercules with the political opposition confronted by James.

> Like his, our Hero's Infancy was try'd;
> Betimes the Furies did their Snakes provide;
> And, to his Infant Arms oppose
> His Father's Rebels, and his Brother's Foes;
> The more opprest the higher still he rose:
> Those were the Preludes of his Fate,
> That form'd his Manhood, to subdue
> The *Hydra* of the many-headed, hissing Crew.
> (*Threnodia Augustalis,* 457–64)

Although the details of this elaborate analogy are not all historically decipherable, the general framework of political reference is clear enough. Born into an inescapably hostile environment, James proves his Herculean greatness by triumphing over the "Rebels" and "Foes" sent by the "Furies" against him. Individual heroism can "subdue" the monster of faction and rebellion, but cannot (Dryden's carefully limited verb suggests) render the institution of monarchy immune to future attacks by this popular hydra. Far from implying such immunity, the prophecy that concludes the poem rests precariously on the voluntarily "amended Vows of *English* Loyalty" (*Threnodia Augustalis,* 505). To secure the future, Dryden prescribes to the subjects of the new king a test of loyalty that is also a test of faith in divine providence. "Faith is a Christian's and a Subject's Test, / Oh give them to believe, and they are surely blest" (*Threnodia Augustalis,* 502–3). Dryden's prophecy—and the national future—hang by the thread of faith.

Shortly before this thread was irreversibly severed by the Revolution, Dryden again invoked Hercules in his poem on the birth of the Prince of Wales.

> For see the Dragon winged on his way,
> To watch the Travail, and devour the Prey.
> Or, if Allusions may not rise so high,
> Thus, when *Alcides* rais'd his Infant Cry,
> The Snakes besieg'd his Young Divinity:
> But vainly with their forked Tongues they threat;
> For Opposition makes a Heroe Great.
> To needful Succour all the Good will run;
> And *Jove* assert the Godhead of his Son.
> *(Britannia Rediviva, 52–60)*

Casting the so-called "warming-pan baby" in the role of Hercules, Dryden emphasizes the divine rather than the heroic nature of the son of Jove and thus implicitly reiterates the necessity of faith. But a future dependent on the faith of monsters offers no more promise than a future dependent on the heroism of an infant. This passage, which adds the dragon of Biblical *Revelation* to the snakes of classical myth, serves finally to create rather than to dispel apprehension, and thus further restricts the already limited optimism conveyed by *Threnodia Augustalis*. Instead of optimism, the succeeding lines present a decidedly negative vision of the future.

> The Manna falls, yet that Coelestial Bread
> Like *Jews* you munch, and murmure while you feed.
> May not your Fortune be like theirs, Exil'd,
> Yet forty Years to wander in the Wild.
> *(Britannia Rediviva, 65–8)*.

Directly addressed to the people ("you"), this admonitory allusion to one of Dryden's favorite Old Testament passages echoes *Absalom and Achitophel* and *Threnodia Augustalis* while anticipating *Amphitryon*.[15] Like the "Monsters" and "Monster-men" of Jupiter's prophecy, the "murm'ring Men, unwilling to be freed" can be traced to representations of the English people ("a Headstrong, Moody, Murmuring race") in Dryden's later public poetry. By giving to Jupiter the resonant language of the later political poems, Dryden lends contemporary, local significance to the *Amphitryon* prophecy without destroying its universality.

If the "Monsters" of Cowley's Pindaric translation are thus particularized for Dryden by such phrases as "The *Hydra* of the many-headed, hissing Crew" and "The Dragon winged on his way," both of which refer to a rebellious people, the "Tyrants" of Tiresias' prophecy also reach *Amphitryon* via the public poetry of the reign of James II. In *Threnodia Augustalis* James is urged to emulate the virtues of his deceased brother, described as "Intrepid, pious, merciful, and brave" (*Threnodia Augustalis,* 206). After three years of observing James as king, however, Dryden sharply restricts his list of expected monarchical virtues, concentrating in *Britannia Rediviva* on the ideal of justice.

> Some Kings the name of Conq'rours have assum'd,
> Some to be Great, some to be Gods presum'd;
> But boundless pow'r, and arbitrary Lust
> Made Tyrants still abhor the Name of Just;
> They shun'd the praise this Godlike Virtue gives,
> And fear'd a Title, that reproach'd their Lives.
> (Britannia Rediviva, 339–44)

Defined positively as a "Godlike Virtue," justice is also defined negatively by reference to "Tyrants." Extending this implicit warning, Dryden concludes his poem by prescribing a test for the king, a test of monarchical justice that parallels the test of popular faith closing *Threnodia Augustalis*. "But Justice is Heav'ns self, so strictly He, / That cou'd it fail, the God-head cou'd not be" (*Britannia Rediviva*, 355–6).

The virtues of faith and justice express in the poems from the reign of James II the reciprocal duties of subject to king and king to subject. Royal justice and public faith are the ideals on which Dryden's later prophecies depend; the accomplishment of those prophecies—the restoration of the "pious times" briefly celebrated in the opening of *Absalom and Achitophel*—is thus contingent on mutual fulfillment of the obligations expressed by these ideals. The prophecy that closes *Amphitryon* signals the failure of such idealism and marks the progress of "an Impious Age." It is into a world of perverted ideals—men become monsters, monarchs become tyrants—that Dryden again introduces Hercules, whose task is nothing less than to reverse the direction of history. That this is an impossible task, suggested by the terms of the prophecy itself, Dryden confirms in the vision that concludes *Eleonora*, published two years after *Amphitryon* and four years after the Revolution.

> Let this suffice: Nor thou, great Saint, refuse
> This humble Tribute of no vulgar Muse:
> Who, not by Cares, or Wants, or Age deprest,
> Stems a wild Deluge with a dauntless brest:
> And dares to sing thy Praises, in a Clime
> Where Vice triumphs, and Vertue is a Crime:
> Where ev'n to draw the Picture of thy Mind,
> Is Satyr on the most of Humane Kind:
> Take it, while yet 'tis Praise; before my rage
> Unsafely just, break loose on this bad Age;
> So bad, that thou thy self had'st no defence,
> From Vice, but barely by departing hence.[16]

A desperate vision indeed, this passage offers no hope that history can be reversed and, by allusion to the poems of the 1660's, denies the possibility of a second Restoration.[17]

The implicit identification of Eleonora with Astraea at the end of this passage defines "this bad Age" in terms of the classical myth of degenerative history as popularized by Ovid in the first book of the *Metamorphoses*. Dryden's own translation of the first book of Ovid, prepared for inclusion in the miscellany of 1693, advances the evolution of prophecy in his poetry and helps to explain the particular significance of Jupiter's vision of "an Impious Age" in *Amphitryon*. The translation invites us to see "impiety" as the defining characteristic of the Ovidian Iron Age.

> To this came next in course, the Brazen Age:
> A Warlike Offspring, prompt to Bloody Rage,
> Not Impious yet—[18]

Translating Ovid's *scelerata* as "Impious," Dryden thus marks the transition from bronze to iron. After a sequence of particularizing descriptions that emphasize violence and avarice, Dryden concludes his account of the Iron Age by repeating the ideal of piety and placing it in a context of abstractions loosely translated from the Latin. Ovid had written:

> victa iacet pietas, et virgo caede madentis
> ultima caelestum terras Astraea reliquit.[19]

Dryden retains the central importance of *pietas*, renders Astraea abstractly as "Justice," and adds to this complex of exiled ideals, "Faith."

> Faith flies, and Piety in Exile mourns;
> And Justice, here opprest, to Heav'n returns.
> (*The First Book of Ovid's Metamorphoses*, 191–2)

The Iron Age, then, is "an Impious Age," and impiety is contextually defined by the departure of Faith and Justice, precisely the ideals that provide the contingent basis of prophecy in *Threnodia Augustalis* and *Britannia Rediviva*. This definition of "an Impious Age," indeed this entire context, becomes particularly relevant to *Amphitryon* when we recall two related facts: (1) as Margaret Merzbach has shown, Dryden was well aware of Thomas Heywood's dramatization of the birth of Hercules in his play entitled *The Silver Age*,[20] and (2) Act IV of *Amphitryon* ends with Mercury's soliloquy portraying "Our Iron Age." To see how Dryden makes Mercury's indictment stick, we can consider more generally the nature of the play itself.

III

Traditionally perceived either in relation to Plautus or Molière or in relation to the conventions of the Restoration theater, *Amphitryon* is readily classified as comedy. Since Dryden himself so described the play in his preface, this designation is secure against even the sharpest changes in critical fashion. It should be, for *Amphitryon* is a richly comic play that entertained audiences for a century after its first run and has retained since then the power to amuse readers who are unlikely ever to see a production. Nevertheless, it is notable that most discussions of the play refuse to be confined by Dryden's generic description and escape in such diverse directions as opera, farce, tragi-comedy, and satire.[21] It is the satiric dimension of the play that I believe has been most seriously underemphasized and, when discussed, most often misapprehended. The prophetic ending and its context challenge us to consider the possibility of satire in the play, if only to understand why this world needs a reformer of Hercules' proportions. To answer this question will also be to understand why Dryden has wrenched the legend of Amphitryon from its place in Heywood's silver age and relocated it in an age of iron and impiety.

Insofar as criticism has explored the possibility of satire in *Amphitryon,* it has been to say that Dryden here gently attacks Charles II and his courtiers. In this view the philandering Jupiter is identified with the philandering Stuart king, who was unable to benefit from the corrective force of the satire, having been buried five years earlier. This identification is expressed with most conviction by Frank Harper Moore. "Dryden by his treatment of the amorous activities of Jupiter ridicules the similar activities of Charles II and his courtiers."[22] Why in 1690 Dryden should be concerned with the sexual activities of Charles II Moore does not explain, although he does comment on the appropriateness of the poet's satiric vehicle. "In this myth of the amorous Jupiter, Dryden had hit upon an eminently satisfactory vehicle, both safe and suitably elevated, for a retrospectively satirical expression of his revised and disillusioned view of the 'conversation' of Charles II and his courtiers."[23] John Loftis, who endorses this view with some hesitation, finds "affectionate criticism of the late King . . . in the vein of half-disguised topical allusion recurrent in the play."[24] Satire of Charles II, however safe or affectionate, strikes me as decidedly irrelevant in 1690, and I wish to suggest that the "topical allusion recurrent in the play" has at once more immediate and more enduring significance.

The political language of the play, pervasively evident in the opening scene, justifies the general identification of god and king, even if it does not encourage us to specify the king as Charles II. The analogy between god and king was, in fact, a convention that Dryden had adopted repeatedly in his public poetry, most pointedly in *Astraea Redux.*

> Thus when the bold *Typhoeus* scal'd the Sky,
> And forc'd great *Jove* from his own Heaven to fly,
> (What King, what Crown from Treasons reach is free,
> If *Jove* and *Heaven* can violated be?)[25]

Similarly conventional in the political verse of Dryden and his contemporaries, however, is another analogy, also important in *Amphitryon,* that defines the relationship between king and subject in domestic terms: king as husband, subject as wife. Hence, to stick with the example of *Astraea Redux:*

> We sigh'd to hear the fair *Iberian* Bride
> Must grow a Lilie to the Lilies side,
> While Our cross Stars deny'd us *Charles* his Bed
> Whom Our first Flames and Virgin Love did wed.
> (*Astraea Redux,* 17–20)

This triple analogy, god/king/husband: man/subject/wife, is given succint expression shortly after *Amphitryon* in Dryden's celebration of Eleonora's conjugal virtues.

> Love and Obedience to her Lord she bore,
> She much obey'd him, but she lov'd him more.
> Not aw'd to Duty by superior sway;
> But taught by his Indulgence to obey.
> Thus we love God as Author of our good;
> So Subjects love just Kings, or so they shou'd.
> (*Eleonora,* 176–81)

Against this background it can be shown that, in *Amphitryon,* the domestic analogy complicates the divine analogy in such a way as to suggest a pattern of allusion, not to the conditions of 1660–1685, but rather to the political situation after the Revolution of 1688.

Sosia's reference to "this dismal Revolution in our Family" (3.1.349–50) should alert us to the allusive potential of some remarkable (and yet so far unremarked) passages in Dryden's play. In the most important such passage Dryden adds a political dimension to the distinction between husband and lover, advanced by Jupiter.

> In me (my charming Mistris) you behold
> A Lover that disdains a Lawful Title;
> Such as of Monarchs to successive Thrones:
> The Generous Lover holds by force of Arms;
> And claims his Crown by Conquest.[26]

Transforming Molière's apolitical distinction, Dryden here updates *Absalom and Achitophel* to match the conditions of post-revolution England. Achitophel, it will be recalled, had argued against "a Successive Title, Long, and Dark, / Drawn from the Mouldy Rolls of *Noah's* Ark," and had urged Absalom to "Commit a pleasing Rape upon the Crown."[27] By 1690 the "Crown" had in fact been gained "by Conquest," if not precisely "by force of Arms," and the English throne was occupied by a "Monarch" without "a Lawful Title." For a moment, then, we are invited to see in the Jupiter-Alcmena-

Amphitryon triangle an allusion to the political struggle between William (false Amphitryon) and James (true Amphitryon), vying to occupy the bed of England (Alcmena). This strand of allusion, which conveniently accounts for the negative portrayal of Jupiter, is picked up not only in the confrontation between Amphitryon and Alcmena but also in the climactic scene where Amphitryon is forcibly restrained from attacking his rival, "Thou base Usurper of my Name, and Bed" (5.1.144). In such a line as this it is perhaps easy to see William III in the false Amphitryon but difficult to see how such a topical allusion informs our understanding of the play as a whole. In fact, however, there is no real difficulty here, because the context that invites us to see the topicality of the triangle in the first place also provides the key to its meaning. In the public poetry of James II's reign, Dryden had identified the true monarch with the virtue of justice and the loyal subject with the virtue of faith, and it is by emphasis on these specific human qualities that the topical allusions became meaningful in the play.

Before the final scene, Amphitryon and Alcmena are on stage together but once. The confrontation in 3.1 results in mutual alienation precipitated by the prior intervention of Jupiter, whose presence is felt throughout the scene, especially when Amphitryon complains "Of all that prodigality of Kindness, / Giv'n to another, and usurp'd from me" (3.1.293–4). Whatever political allusiveness there may be here is absorbed by the dramatic tension of the scene, which Dryden carefully structures as a trial. As the scene unfolds, accusation is made, witnesses are called, physical evidence is introduced, and judgment is rendered. It is, clearly, Alcmena who is on trial, accused of adultery and arraigned before Amphitryon, who appears as both prosecutor and judge. His verdict, "Perfidious Woman" (3.1.290), signifies a rupture between husband and wife: through the intervention of the impostor-usurper, his justice and her faith have become incompatible, even mutually exclusive. The antagonism of Amphitryon (king-husband) and Alcmena (subject-wife) thus confirms by analogy the topical significance of the scene, while elevating our concern from the topical to the ideal.

In the mouth of Jupiter, however, the ideals of justice and faith become the subjects of jest. After the husband-wife confrontation, Jupiter reappears in the role of Amphitryon, whose behavior he attempts to defend in order to reinstate himself with Alcmena.

> Can you forsake me, for so small a fault?
> 'Twas but a Jest, perhaps too far pursu'd:
> 'Twas but at most, a Trial of your Faith . . .
> (4.1.21–3)

This casual parallelism between a "Jest" and a "Trial" perfectly characterizes the nature of the play, in which serious issues are given a comic setting. Jupiter's jest is, moreover, consistent in tone and style with his earlier appeal to Alcmena, urging her to violate her oath to Phaedra: "Forswear thy self; for *Jupiter* but laughs / At Lovers Perjuries" (1.2.146–7). The contrast between Jupiter's jocular use of the word "Perjuries" and Amphitryon's outraged use of the word "Perfidious" defines the essential difference between these two pretenders to Alcmena's bed. These words signal the perversion of justice and faith that occurs in the play. Encouraged by Jupiter, this process of perversion infuriates Amphitryon.

Amphitryon and his wife become, in fact, aliens in this version of the play that bears his name. Displaced from the center of the action by the addition of a third plot, husband and wife are idealists in a world that ultimately has no use for ideals. Their resultant frustration and rage, emotions vigorously expressed in several scenes, add an alloy to the comedy that may even make them unsympathetic to the audience, especially when they vent their anger against each other. However comic the play, the dilemma of Amphitryon and Alcmena is tragic; and yet even their tragedy is thoroughly frustrated by a world that cannot believe in the ideals, including faith and justice, that make tragedy possible. The originality of Dryden's play ultimately derives from this limitation, a limitation that begins to explain the significance of Jupiter's prophecy: the heroism of a Hercules is necessary to make room for idealism in the world. Should Hercules succeed in his encounters with "Tyrants" and "murm'ring Men," justice and faith—and hence "pious times"—would be restored. The prophecy is, in effect, a reassertion in negative terms of the contingent prophecies that conclude *Threnodia Augustalis* and *Britannia Rediviva*. To see why the prophecy must now be offered in negative terms, to see why the future of idealism is so problematical, we can turn to the only plot of the play original with Dryden. The carefully designed and thematically related roles of Phaedra and Gripus are finally decisive in making Dryden's play at once unique and universal.

IV

The Jupiter-Alcmena-Amphitryon triangle admits of topical interpretation but does not insist on it. The confrontation between Alcmena and Amphitryon, entirely contained and comprehensible in its classical setting, does not require allegorical explanation; many readers may even prefer to ignore the allusive potential of Dryden's similes. But consider the parallel confrontation between Phaedra and Gripus in 5.1.

GRIP.:   Thou very mercenary Mistress!

PHAED.:   Thou most mercenary Magistrate!

GRIP.:   Thou Seller of thy self!

PHAED.:   Thou Seller of other People: thou Weathercock of Government: that when the Wind blows for the Subject, point'st to Priviledge; and when it changes for the Soveraign, veers to Prerogative.

(5.1.10–16)

This passage not only admits of a topical interpretation, it demands one. Phaedra's description of Gripus has nothing to do with the situation in Thebes, but a great deal to do with seventeenth-century English politics. In such a passage as this (and there are others like it), Dryden makes no effort at all to render his original creations historically appropriate to the classical setting of the play. On the contrary, the significance of the Phaedra-Gripus plot lies precisely in its disjointed relationship to the traditional materials of the Amphitryon legend. The satire of Dryden's play emerges less from its topical allusions than from the discordances between its inherited and added plots. By imposing Phaedra and Gripus on the world of Alcmena and Amphitryon, Dryden places his own stamp on a very traditional fiction, and yet the effect of Dryden's originality is ultimately to universalize the satire of his play.

The discordance between old and new is strongly evident in the trial scene discussed above. While Amphitryon and Alcmena contend in lofty blank verse, Phaedra interjects occasional prose comments that seem to come from an utterly different realm. Nor is this discrepancy simply a matter of "high" versus "low" characters. Aligning herself with the contemporary English audience, Phaedra becomes a modern spectator of the action of a classical play.

This is as good sport for me as an Examination of a great Belly before a Magistrate.

(3.1.271–2)

The reductive nature of this aside not only confirms the judicial character of the scene and Phaedra's modern perspective on it, but it also reveals her total inability to grasp or even care about the seriousness of the action before her. She does not belong on the same stage with Alcmena any more than the citizen's wife belongs on the stage of Beaumont and Fletcher's *The Knight of the Burning Pestle*. And yet she is there, and (like the citizen's wife) she imposes her values upon the action. Called to witness to Alcmena's faith, Phaedra defines her sense of values unmistakably:

ALCM.:   Speak, *Phaedra;* Was he here?

PHAED.:   You know, Madam, I am but a Chamber-maid; and by my place, I am to forget all that was done overnight in Love-Matters, —unless my Master please to rub up my Memory with another Diamond.

(3.1.200–4)

For Phaedra, faith has no reality as an absolute value; its importance can be understood only by reference to a monetary scale. As an intruder upon a familiar plot, Phaedra comes from a domain of relative values whose only absolute is gold itself. Her "Hand open to receive" (1.2.173) pushes the play away from both comedy and tragedy toward satire.

Phaedra, as "seller" of herself, thus represents the perversion of Alcmena's ideal faith; Gripus even more obviously represents the perversion of ideal justice. This "mercenary Magistrate" and "seller of other people" is the perfect suitor of Phaedra.

> MER.: [Gripus] sells Justice as he uses, fleeces the Rich Rebells, and hangs up the Poor.
>
> PHAED.: Then while he has Money he may make love to me.
>
> (2.2.123–5)

In effect, both of Dryden's original characters worship the same god, and Jupiter is well aware that he is not it.

> when I made
> This Gold, I made a greater God than *Jove*
> And gave my own Omnipotence away.
> (3.1.580–2)

The longer the play continues the more valid this conclusion becomes. At first we are likely to wonder what Phaedra and Gripus are doing in a play about the birth of Hercules; by the end, however, we should be wondering what idealists like Amphitryon and Alcmena are doing in a world finally dominated by the relative values of Phaedra and Gripus.

As worshippers of gold, Phaedra and Gripus can be quite at home in a world where truth itself varies in accordance with material self-interest. Amphitryon and Alcmena, on the other hand, discover that efforts to assert the truth repeatedly end in accusations of falsehood. This process of contradiction culminates in Alcmena's attempt to distinguish instinctively the true Amphitryon from the false.

> ALCM.: Farewell my needless fear; it cannot be:
> This is a Case too nice for vulgar sight:
> But let me come; my Heart will guide my Eyes
> To point, and tremble to its proper choice.
> [*Seeing* Amphitryon, *goes to him.*
> There neither was, nor is, but one *Amphitryon*;
> And I am onely his. —[*Goes to take him by the Hand.*
>
> AMPH.: *pushing her away from him.* Away, Adultress!
>
> (5.1.255–61)

Alcmena touchingly asserts the truth of the heart (faith) and is repulsed by Amphitryon's assertion of the truth of the senses (justice). One truth contradicts the other, thus validating the conclusion that Sosia has already drawn from his own experience: "I never saw any good that came of telling truth" (3.1.335). In the world of this play self-interest ("good") can be protected or extended only by ignoring the truth. Witness not only Sosia, but also Phaedra, who earlier faces the same dilemma as Alcmena.

PHAED.:   Which of you two is *Sosia?* For t'other must be the Devil.

SOSIA.:   You had best ask him that has play'd the Devil with my back and sides.

MERC.:   You had best ask him who gave you the gold Gobblet?

PHAED.:   No, that's already given: but he shall be my *Sosia,* that will give me such another.

MERC.:   I find you have been Interloping, Sirrah.

SOSIA.:   No, indeed, Sir; I onely promised her a gold Thimble: which was as much as comes to my proportion of being *Sosia.*

PHAED.:   This is no *Sosia* for my money: beat him away t' other *Sosia:* he grows insufferable.

(4.1.408–19)

Clearly, Dryden has added this parallel scene (it has no counterpart in Plautus or Molière) to define the difference between the world of Alcmena and the world of Phaedra, the one governed by ideals, the other by self-interest. It is, moreover, Phaedra's world that prevails, as Dryden follows Molière in portraying the parade of characters who opt in favor of *l'Amphitryon où l'on dine.*

It is Mercury, then, who makes Dryden's satire explicit and universal.

> Such Bargain-loves, as I with *Phaedra* treat,
> Are all the Leagues and Friendships of the Great:
> All seek their Ends; and each wou'd other cheat.
> They only seem to hate, and seem to love;
> But Int'rest is the point on which they move.
> Their Friends are Foes; and Foes are Friends agen;
> And, in their turns, are Knaves, and Honest Men.
> Our Iron Age is grown an Age of Gold:
> 'Tis who bids most; for all Men wou'd be sold.
> (4.1.549–57)

A conventional topic of Roman satire, the assault on gold's dominion aligns Dryden with such English predecessors as Jonson and such followers as Pope. Although Dryden does not approach the apocalyptic vision of Pope, the voice of Jupiter at the close of *Amphitryon* sounds decidedly like the voice of Jupiter on the verge of destroying the world in *Metamorphoses.* In Dryden's version:

> The Clamours of this vile degenerate Age,
> The Cries of Orphans, and th' Oppressor's Rage
> Had reach'd the Stars; I will descend . . .
> (*The First Book of Ovid's Metamorphoses,* 274–6)

Discovering on descent a world as corrupt as that envisioned at the end of *Amphitryon,* Jupiter concludes:

> Mankind's a Monster, and th' Ungodly times
> Confed'rate into guilt, are sworn to Crimes.
> (*The First Book of Ovid's Metamorphoses,* 323–4)

At the conclusion of his play, Dryden thus dismisses the Jupiter of Plautus and invokes instead the Jupiter of Ovid to condemn an age whose impiety is exposed most emphatically in the new plot. Worshipfully kissing her gold goblet. Phaedra locates the moral center of the play in phrases reminiscent of *Volpone:* "Now *Jupiter,* of his Mercy, let me kiss thee, O thou dear Metal" (4.1.103).

In an age such as this, when "all Men wou'd be sold," the future of heroism is problematical at best. The specific future outlined for Hercules—to reform the world—is especially problematical because a world without idealism inevitably denies reform a goal. Like Alcmena and Amphitryon, Hercules must face the limiting conditions imposed by those who aspire to nothing beyond self-interest; to a world preoccupied in the manner of Phaedra, justice and faith are finally irrelevant. The conditions that make Herculean reform necessary also make it impossible.[28]

Internally explicable by reference to the satiric design of the superimposed plot involving Phaedra and Gripus, and externally explicable by reference to the prophecies of Dryden's non-dramatic poetry, Dryden's concluding departure from Plautus and Molière is a rejection of the optimistic vision that characterizes the poems of the 1660's. Dryden's poems on the Restoration are governed by a belief that such virtues as faith and justice are (or can become) the shared ideals of the political community; his post-Revolution poems portray instead the artist, saint, martyr, hero isolated from his culture precisely by a commitment to ideals. And the highest ideal of all is piety, which Dryden explores most fully in the *Aeneis* and the *Fables,* poems selected and adapted for "an Impious Age." *Amphitryon,* itself a careful adaptation of a classic, is a perfect introduction to Dryden's later career.

Notes

    1.   Although the details of the Amphitryon legend vary from one version to the next, the basic story can be briefly summarized. "Zeus, wishing to have a son who should be a pow-

erful protector of both mortals and Immortals, descended one night to the city of Thebes where he assumed the appearance of Amphitryon and lay with Amphitryon's wife, Alcmene. Shortly afterward Amphitryon himself returned from a victorious expedition and took his wife in his arms. From the two successive unions Alcmena conceived twins: Hercules and Iphicles." *New Larousse Encyclopedia of Mythology,* ed. Felix Guirand, trans. Richard Aldington and Delano Ames (London and New York, 1968), p. 169. For discussion of the many dramatic interpretations of this durable legend, see L. R. Shero, "Alcmena and Amphitryon in Ancient and Modern Drama," *Transactions of the American Philological Association,* LXXXVII (1956), 192–238; Orjan Lindberger, *The Transformations of Amphitryon* (Stockholm, 1956); C. D. N. Costa, "The Amphitryo Theme," *Roman Drama,* eds. T. A. Dorey and Donald R. Dudley (London, 1965), pp. 87–122; Charles E. Passage and James H. Mantinband, *Amphitryon: Three Plays in New Verse Translations* (Chapel Hill, 1974). For discussion of Hercules as hero, with specific reference to Dryden, see Eugene M. Waith, *The Herculean Hero in Marlowe, Chapman, Shakespeare, and Dryden* (New York and London, 1962).

    2.   Amphitryon actually recognizes the twins as evidence of divine favor even before Jupiter discloses the significance of Hercules' birth. See Plautus, *Amphitruo,* ed. W. B. Sedgwick (Manchester, 1960), 5.1.1089. (For the sake of consistency and convenience, I shall refer to the various characters in the Amphitryon story by their names as commonly rendered in English. Hence, Amphitryon rather than Amphitruo, Alcmena rather than Alcumena or Alcmène, etc.)

    3.   *Amphitruo,* 5.3.1144–5. The conclusion thus fulfills the implicit promise Jupiter had earlier made to Alcmena.

> uerum irae si quae forte eueniunt huiusmodi
> inter eos, rusum si reuentum in gratiam est,
> bis tanto amici sunt inter se quam prius.

The anticipated doubling of affection is symbolically confirmed by the birth of the twins. *Amphitruo,* 3.2.941–3.

    4.   For discussion of the ending of Molière's play, see Lionel Gossman, *Men and Masks: A Study of Molière* (Baltimore, 1963), pp. 32–4; Jacques Scherer, "Dualités d'*Amphitryon,*" *Molière: Stage and Study,* eds. W. D. Howarth and Merlin Thomas (Oxford, 1973), pp. 185–97; especially pp. 196–7; Judd D. Hubert, *Molière and the Comedy of Intellect* (Berkeley and Los Angeles, 1962), pp. 162–89.

    5.   Molière, *Amphitryon,* 3.10, *Oeuvres complètes,* ed. Maurice Rat, Bibliothèque de la Pléiade (Paris, 1956), p. 295.

    6.   The similarity between the prophecies in Molière and Dryden down to Sosia's interruption has been noted by Earl Miner in *The Works of John Dryden,* XV, eds. Miner and George R. Gutfey (Berkeley and Los Angeles, 1976), 494–5. For comparative discussion of Dryden and Molière, see Alexander L. Bondurant, "The Amphitruo of Plautus, Molière's Amphitryon, and the Amphitryon of Dryden," *SR,* XXXIII (1925), 455–68; Ned Bliss Allen, *The Sources of Dryden's Comedies* (Ann Arbor, 1935), pp. 210–39, 277–81; John Wilcox, *The Relation of Molière to Restoration Comedy* (New York, 1938), pp. 35–46, 105–26; Thomas E. Barden, "Dryden's Aims in *Amphitryon,*" *Costerus,* IX (1973), 1–8; Frank J. Kearful, "Molière among the English: 1660–1737," *Molière and the Commonwealth of Letters: Patrimony and Posterity,* eds. Roger Johnson, Jr., Editha S. Neumann, and Guy T. Trail (Jackson, Mississippi, 1975), pp. 199–217. As Professor Miner has indicated, Dryden's use of Molière in *Amphitryon* has received considerable attention (for additional references, see Miner, p. 465), although evaluations of their comparative achievement have varied widely. Montague Summers expresses a clear preference for Dryden. "*Amphitryon* is a very delightful comedy, and it is no disparagement to the genius of Molière when we say how vastly it has been improved by Dryden, who has combined in his own inimitable way episodes of the liveliest humour and scenes of the most brilliant wit with passages of passionate poetry and soft amorous beauty." *Dryden: The Dramatic Works,* ed. Sum-

mers (London, 1932), VI, 142–3. Implicitly endorsing the more cautious preference for Dryden voiced by George Saintsbury ("in the life and bustle proper to comedy Dryden excels both his formidable predecessors"), Miner ranks *Amphitryon* very high in the canon of Dryden's plays. "With *All For Love* and *Don Sebastian,* it is at the peak of Dryden's achievement as a playwright. The three plays together show that it is humanity, and Dryden's questions about man, that provide the basis of his dramatic greatness" (p. 472). It is worth noting, however, that Charles Passage and James Mantinband prefer Molière, denying to Dryden's version the very quality that Miner stresses. "What the play lacks," they say, "is humanity" (p. 196). Similarly disparaging views are held by others, including Lindberger, pp. 99–101 (see below note 21) and Sedgwick, p. 9. Of the charges leveled against Dryden's play, its alleged "coarseness" has been the most often reiterated. As Robert D. Hume has remarked, *Amphitryon* "is a distinctly unrefined play: the indelicacy is not extraordinary, but the speech is racy, coarse, and colloquial: Dryden eschews the courtly polish which so pleases manners-comedy critics." Hume, *The Development of English Drama in the Late Seventeenth Century* (Oxford, 1976), p. 383.

7. *Amphitryon,* 5.1.413–21, *The Works of John Dryden,* XV, 316. All subsequent citations from the play will be repeated from the California edition and identified in the text by act, scene, and line numbers.

8. This is a problem of real importance in Dryden's later career. For an excellent discussion, see Michael West, "Dryden's Ambivalence as a Translator of Heroic Themes," *HLQ,* XXXVI (1973), 347–66, especially the consideration of *Amphitryon,* pp. 357–8.

9. Cowley, *The First Nemean Ode of Pindar,* ll. 113–18, *The English Writings of Abraham Cowley,* ed. A. R. Waller (Cambridge, England, 1905), p. 174.

10. For discussion of the prophetic mode in Dryden's poetry, its context, and its significance as an index to his views of his age in relation to history, see Earl Miner, "Dryden and the Issue of Human Progress," *PQ,* XL (1961), 120–9; Steven N. Zwicker, *Dryden's Political Poetry: The Typology of King and Nation* (Providence, 1972), especially pp. 61–83; Achsah Guibbory, "Dryden's Views of History," *PQ,* LII (1973), 187–204; Michael McKeon, *Politics and Poetry in Restoration England: The Case of Dryden's* Annus Mirabilis (Cambridge, Mass. and London, 1975), pp. 190–266.

11. *Britannia Rediviva,* ll. 267–8, *The Poems of John Dryden,* ed. James Kinsley (Oxford, 1958), II, 548. All citations from Dryden's poetry will be repeated from the Kinsley edition; after the initial citation of a poem, all references will be identified in the text by title and line numbers.

12. *Absalom and Achitophel,* ll. 1028–31, *Poems,* I, 243.

13. Compare *Astraea Redux,* ll. 246–9, 292–5, *Poems,* I, 22–3, and *Threnodia Augustalis,* ll. 506–17, *Poems,* I, 456.

14. *Threnodia Augustalis,* l. 455, *Poems,* I, 454.

15. Compare *Absalom and Achitophel,* l. 45, *Poems,* I, 218, and *Threnodia Augustalis,* ll. 425–8, *Poems,* I, 454.

16. *Eleonora,* ll. 359–70, *Poems,* II, 594.

17. See in particular the flood image in *Astraea Redux,* l. 134, *Poems,* l. 19, and in *To His Sacred Majesty,* ll. 1–4, *Poems,* I, 24. In the latter poem the phrase a "wild Deluge" is specifically used to refer metaphorically to the rebellion and to identify Charles II with Noah.

18. *The First Book of Ovid's Metamorphoses,* ll. 160–2, *Poems,* II, 804.

19. Ovid, *Metamorphoses,* I, 149–50, *Ovid: Metamorphoses,* ed. and trans. Frank Justus Miller, The Loeb Classical Library (Cambridge, Mass. and London, 1916), p. 12.

20. Margaret Merzbach, "The Third Source of Dryden's *Amphitryon,*" *Anglia,* LXXIII (1955), 213–4.

21. Considering Purcell's contribution to Dryden's play, Lindberger writes: "When Dryden's *Amphitryon* is analysed as spoken drama the result must be that the piece is found to be mainly an imitation of Molière, reaching neither in theatrical nor literary respect the level of its model, even though here and there it has witty or poetically brilliant elements. From a historical point of view such an evaluation is not entirely just. The contemporary impression of

the play was to a large extent determined by its being apprehended as opera" (p. 101). Hume, on the other hand, unhesitatingly defines the play as farce. "Dryden's delightful *Amphitryon* (October 1690) is a greatly underrated play. The reasons for its neglect are several. First, it is a farce" (p. 383). John Loftis, meanwhile, discusses the "structural pattern of the play, which approximates to the pattern of tragicomedies more closely than may at first appear." Loftis, "Dryden's Comedies," *John Dryden,* ed. Earl Miner (Athens, Ohio, 1972), p. 54. Finally, Passage and Mantinband raise the possibility of satire. "And if the author's purpose was the castigation of vice by merciless depiction of vice, then the Amphitryon scenario was not the proper vehicle for his purpose. The vices of gods in whom neither the author nor the audience believed cannot make for effective satire" (p. 196).

22.   Frank Harper Moore, *The Nobler Pleasure: Dryden's Comedy in Theory and Practice* (Chapel Hill, 1963), p. 198.

23.   Moore, p. 209.

24.   Loftis, p. 54.

25.   *Astraea Redux,* ll. 37–40, *Poems,* I, 17.

26.   2.2.83–7. In his headnote, Miner discusses the style of this passage, but does not comment on its political significance (pp. 467–8).

27.   *Absalom and Achitophel,* ll. 301–2, 474, *Poems,* I, 224–9. Although the parallels between the speeches of Jupiter and Achitophel are not extensive or even very precise the general similarity of vocabulary is still remarkable given the difference in context.

28.   In his very helpful discussion of Renaissance interpretations of the Herculean hero, Waith writes: "Hercules is both the great individual and the selfless benefactor. He is pitted against a cruel world, whose monsters he is obliged to combat, yet fighting for himself he also saves the world. . . . Renaissance depictions of Hercules often seem . . . to stress unselfishness and glorious individuality almost equally, with the implication, perhaps, that the two need not conflict in an ideal world" (p. 43). In Dryden's *Amphitryon* we can see the break-up of this particular vision of an ideal world. There is nothing in Dryden's play to suggest that the Hercules whose birth is prophesied by Jupiter will be either a "glorious individual" or a savior of the world. Denying the possibility of heroism, the world refuses to be saved.

Educating the Senses:
Empiricism in Dryden's *King Arthur*

ERIC JAGER

[Love] blinds the Wise, gives Eye-sight to the Blind.
—"Palamon and Arcite"[1]

In his late semi-opera *King Arthur* (1691), Dryden dramatizes several problems related to the empiricist philosophy that arose in the latter half of the seventeenth century in England, including the reliability of the senses as a basis for knowledge, the scientific distrust of poetic language and the imagination, and the effects of blindness and recovery of sight upon sense experience.[2] In the play, Arthur undergoes an education in which he learns to distrust both the senses and mere words. Blind Emmeline, who receives her sight during the play, anticipates what came to be called Molyneux's Question: does the subject have to *learn* how to see? Dryden's "empiricist" drama draws away from a purely sensory epistemology, at the same time that it invokes ironically the prevailing distrust of poetic language, and parallels (or anticipates) certain refinements in sensory psychology.

In *Leviathan* (1651), Hobbes enunciates the cardinal empiricist tenet that all human knowledge is derived from the senses, but the question of whether the senses can deceive is left in some uncertainty.[3] Hobbes speaks confidently of "the knowledge of Fact," which "is originally, Sense"; he even refers to sense experience as *"Absolute Knowledge."*[4] But already in his *Humane Nature* (1650) Hobbes had employed a distinction (corresponding to Boyle's and Locke's later one between primary and secondary qualities) entailing that the senses are *always* in some degree deceived: *"whatsoever Accidents* or Qualities our Senses make us think there be in the *World,* they be *not* there, but are *Seeming* and *Apparitions*only: the Things that really *are* in the World without us, are those *Motions* by which these Seemings are caused."[5] Hobbes calls this "the *great Deception of Sense.* . . ." If Hobbes's empiricism reduces all ideas ultimately to sense experience, it also casts doubt upon the ability of the senses to provide true knowledge.

Eric Jager, "Educating the Senses: Empiricism in Dryden's *King Arthur.*" First printed in *Restoration,* vol. 11 (1987), pp. 107–116. Reprinted by permission.

Dryden's familiarity with Hobbes's doctrines is well-known.[6] Especially noteworthy are the "Hobbist ideas of appetite, fancy, and imagination" enunciated by Lucifer in *The State of Innocence* (1677), a work that anticipates *King Arthur* in several ways, not least in being an opera.[7] Dryden's treatment of Hobbes's ideas is various; he will use what he finds acceptable or convenient, while disputing or casting doubt upon what he does not.[8] In *King Arthur,* Dryden admits the fundamental relation of the senses to knowledge, but he also dramatizes the capacity of the senses to deceive. The potential danger of the senses is conveyed most clearly in the education of Arthur, who goes from unquestioning dependence upon what he sees and hears to a cautious skepticism about appearances.

Because of her blindness, Emmeline initially seems more susceptible to perceptual error than Arthur, who is in full possession of his senses. Emmeline's first words establish her dependence upon an abnormally limited sense experience: "Oh Father, Father, I am sure you're here; / Because I see your Voice" (I, p. 249). Her father has in fact departed, but the sightless girl does not know this and is corrected by Arthur: "No, thou mistak'st thy hearing for thy sight; / He's gone, my *Emmeline.*" And when Arthur goes on to compare Emmeline's eyes to a "Star-like Night, dark only to thy self," Emmeline further reveals the limitations of her perception:

> What is this Heav'n, and Stars, and Night, and Day,
> To which you thus compare my Eyes and me?
> I understand you, when you say you love:
> For, when my Father clasps my Hand in his,
> That's cold, and I can feel it hard and wrinkl'd;
> But when you grasp it, then I sigh and pant,
> And something smarts, and tickles at my Heart.

Emmeline's sightless love may seem less empirical than Arthur's, but as a type of "Love, Born Blind" Emmeline can hardly represent the Neoplatonic ideal, for which sight is the main vehicle of love. Emmeline's love is every bit as empirical as Arthur's own, though it is based on audile and tactile rather than visual perception. Emmeline not only relies too confidently upon her limited senses; unaware of the limits imposed by her blindness, she mistakenly believes that in touching (as in hearing) she also sees:

EM.:   Then 'tis my Hand that sees, and that's all one:
        For is not seeing, touching with your Eyes?
ARTH.: No, for I see at distance, where I touch not.

(I, p. 250)

Emmeline even believes that she could recognize Arthur by his kisses alone, though she has only fantasized about this experience:

> For surely I have seen him in my Sleep,
> And then, methought, he put his Mouth to mine,
> And eat a thousand Kisses on my Lips;
> Sure by his Kissing I cou'd find him out
> Among a thousand Angels in the Sky.
>
> (II, p. 258)

But when Arthur condescendingly corrects Emmeline's limited and confused sense experience, he betrays his own vulnerability to his senses. His avowal that colors—mere secondary qualities—"produce" his love suggests an unquestioning trust in appearances (or what Hobbes called "Seemings"):

> I view the lovely Features of your Face;
> Your Lips Carnation, your dark shaded Eye-brows,
> Black Eyes, And Snowwhite Forehead; all the Colours
> That make your Beauty, and produce my Love.
>
> (I, p. 250)

Arthur's words foreshadow his nearly fatal mistake in the enchanted grove, where he sees Emmeline's "lovely Features" and "Colours" looking out at him, though the apparent Emmeline is a fraud. For now, however, Arthur is certain of his own knowledge in his role as Emmeline's teacher, and answers her objections self-confidently:

> EM.: Nay, then, you do not love on equal terms:
> I love you dearly, without all these helps:
> I cannot see your Lips Carnation,
> Your shaded Eye-brows, nor your Milk-white Eyes.
>
> ARTH.: You still mistake.
>
> EM.: Indeed I thought you had a Nose and Eyes,
> And such a Face as mine; have not Men Faces?
>
> ARTH.: Oh, none like yours, so excellently fair.
>
> EM.: Then wou'd I had no Face; for I wou'd be
> Just such a one as you.
>
> ARTH.: Alas, 'tis vain to instruct your Innocence,
> You have no Notion of Light or Colours.

Arthur's love is more dependent upon the senses than Emmeline's, which is sustained "without all these helps." Emmeline may have "no Notion of Light or Colours," but Arthur forgets that a love based on "Colours" is susceptible to illusion. Dodging Emmeline's charge of unequal love, Arthur pedantically points out her error ("You still mistake"), sidestepping the more serious problem of affections based solely upon sense experience.

The education of Arthur's senses takes place during his sally into enemy territory. Merlin warns him to "Remember well, that all is but Illusion" (IV, p. 275). Left to himself, Arthur trusts in his senses to the point of doubting Merlin's warning:

> No Danger yet, I see no Walls of Fire,
> No City of the Fiends, with Forms obscene,
> To grin from far, on Flaming Battlements.
> This is indeed the Grove I shou'd destroy;
> But where's the Horrour? Sure the Prophet err'd.

The insinuation of "*Soft Musick*" (s.d.) puts Arthur on his guard; as "Wonders" unfold before his eyes, "all delightful," he suspects "a Trap, for my Unwary Feet." Since Arthur imagines his dangers as violent and apocalyptic—"With Fire or Water, let him wage his War" (IV, p. 276)—the sirens take him by surprise. The "Lazie Pleasure" Arthur feels at this encounter is hardly the "Horrour" he had expected, and he admits that he could "stay, and well be Couzen'd here."[9] But Merlin's remembered advice enables him to see through these "Fair Illusions." Certain of the difference between his love for Emmeline and his attraction to these fantasies, he goes on to the enchanted grove:

> And what are these Fantastick Fairy Joys,
> To Love like mine? False Joys, false Welcomes all.
>
> (IV, p. 277)

The enchanted grove recalls scenes in Virgil, Dante, Spenser, and Tasso, but its principal reference is to Genesis 3.[10] The motif of man's temptation by woman hardly needs reinforcement by the characters' initials (Arthur/Adam, Emmeline/Eve), or by Arthur's direct self-comparison to his "Grand-sire" Adam (IV, p. 278), but significantly Dryden also invokes the psychological allegory of the Fall, a commonplace from Chaucer to Milton, in which reason (man) capitulates to the senses (woman).[11] Dryden had used this gendered allegory advantageously in *The State of Innocence,* where (following Milton's version) the tempter is made to whisper "Delusive dreams" into the ear of the sleeping Eve, and Adam is warned by Gabriel that "Ills from within, thy reason must prevent."[12] Upon seeing "Emmeline" break out of the tree, Arthur hastily concludes, "'Tis she." The apparition causes Arthur to hesitate between what reason has told him and what his senses seem to say:

> O never, never, to be ended Charm,
> At least by me; yet all may be Illusion.
> Break up, ye thickning Foggs, and filmy Mists,
> All that be-lye my Sight, and cheat my Sense.
> For Reason still pronounces, 'tis not she.

The "Foggs" and "Mists" deluding Arthur's senses eventually overthrow his reason, as the seductive fantasy presents itself as the reward of "Faithful Passion." Arthur hesitates again—"O Love! O *Merlin!* Whom should I believe?"—and then gives in, invoking as he does so the fall of Adam:

> By thy leave, Reason, here I throw thee off.
> . . . .
> If, falling for the first Created Fair,
> Was *Adam*'s Fault, great Grandsire I forgive thee,
> *Eden* was lost, as all thy Sons wou'd loose it.

Only Philidel's intervention ("Hold, poor deluded Mortal, hold thy Hand" [IV, p. 279]) saves Arthur. With her wand, Philidel reveals the "Fiend" underlying the "Infernal Paint" of the apparition, and the peril of Arthur's trust in his senses becomes clear.[13] Of the enchanted wood Arthur had originally asked, "[W]here's the Horrour?" Now he confesses, upon discovering his error, that "Horrour seizes me"—a moment of both peripeteia and moral recognition. Arthur's experience with the false Emmeline has shown him that he can be cozened by his senses—that his love for the true Emmeline has been based on "Colours" impossible to distinguish from "Infernal Paint." The Arthur who thought that Emmeline had "no Notion of Light or Colours" has learned that Merlin's warning, "all is but Illusion," refers to sense experience in general.

II

Hobbes, Sprat, Locke and other representatives of the scientific movement in the seventeenth century distrusted the imagination and "poetic" language.[14] Dryden, who himself had joined the Royal Society in 1662, circumscribed poetry in its relation to knowledge when he pronounced, in his "Apology for Heroique Poetry and Poetique Licence" (1677), that one should be *"pleas'd with the Image, without being couzen'd by the Fiction."*[15] Significantly, the Apology appears as a Preface to *The State of Innocence,* which shows Lucifer rejoicing when human reason sleeps

> but Mimic fancy wakes;
> Supply's her parts, and wild Idea's takes
> From words and things, ill-sorted, and mis-joyn'd;
> The Anarchie of thought and Chaos of the mind:
> Hence dreams confus'd and various may arise;
> These will I set before the Woman's eyes.[16]

Although Dryden's assignment of Hobbesian theory to Lucifer may not be wholly approving, Dryden's psychological theory has been seen as keeping pace with the developing empiricist tradition and has been linked with Locke and even (anticipatorily) with Addison.[17] In any case, by the time of Locke's *Essay* (1689), imagination and reason had undergone a "rigorous separation of function," and poetic language was receiving severe philosophical censure.[18] The contemporaneous *King Arthur* dramatizes the imagination's susceptibility to verbal conceits and fictions but does so in the ironic manner of poetry, which must deceive in order to undeceive.

Both Arthur and Emmeline show themselves as susceptible to verbal illusions, though each is vulnerable to a different sort. Again, despite Emmeline's blindness, it is Arthur whose deceived imagination has the more serious consequences. Blind Emmeline falls into the sorts of absurdities proscribed by the philosophers. Many of these, however, are poetic conceits arising from an atypical organization of sense experience, and some are actually powerful—if unusual—images. For instance, Emmeline's characterization of the trumpet as having "an angry, fighting face" accords well with the martial purpose of its sounding. And her surmise that

> This Devil Trumpet vexes 'em, and then
> They feel about, for one anothers Faces;
> And so they meet, and kill
>
> (I, p. 251)

not only expresses the relation of martial music to the feelings but also suggests palpably the man-to-man violence of battle. Emmeline's fancy even employs the terminology of vision with uncanny effect when she wishes Arthur safety in battle:

> My Heart, and Vows, go with him to the Fight:
> May every Foe be that, which they call blind,
> And none of all their Swords have Eyes to find him.

That "which they call blind" is beyond Emmeline's conception precisely because she *is* blind, but she assimilates sight's action at a distance to the threat of the sword, producing a powerful animation of that weapon. Though swords do not literally have eyes, Emmeline's belief that Arthur's eyes can "see my Naked Legs and Feet / Quite through my Cloaths" (I.250) enables her to extend the threat of eyesight to a martial application (in terms that also link the penetrative male "gaze" to the phallic sword). Because the figure of speech arises from Emmeline's actual (if flawed) sensory experience, it speaks as powerfully as any commonsense statement.

But Dryden also shows that blindness limits Emmeline's imagination. For instance, Emmeline avows to Matilda concerning Arthur that

> He must be made of the most precious things:
> And I believe his Mouth, and Eyes, and Cheeks,
> And Nose, and all his Face, are made of Gold.
>
> (II, p. 258)

Matilda's protest only elicits Emmeline's elaboration upon the conceit:

EM.:   Yet I must know him better: Of all Colours,
       Tell me which is the purest, and the softest.

MAT.: They say 'tis Black.

EM.:   Why then, since Gold is hard, and yet is precious,
       His Face must all be made of soft, black Gold.

Emmeline has experienced gold as a hard substance considered to have great value, but not as a color. Therefore she mistakenly conjoins her ideas of gold with her ideas of black, the latter being associated in her mind (at Matilda's prompting) with purity and softness. The absurdity that results—technically, a catachresis—might offend the philosophers, but Emmeline's many such "errors" do not occasion the risks that Arthur's imagination gets him into.[19]

Arthur's censure of Emmeline's imaginative absurdities, "thou mistak'st thy hearing for thy sight," may be taken as an advance judgment upon his own susceptibility to words. In the first instance, Arthur listens credulously to Grimbald's fictitious account of Oswald's escape. Dressed *"in the Habit of a Shepherd"* (s.d., II, p. 256), Grimbald deceives Arthur's eyes, but most of all his ears:

Here, this way, *Britons,* follow *Oswald*'s flight;
This Evening as I whistl'd out my Dog,
To drive my straggling Flock, and pitch'd my Fold,
I saw him dropping Sweat, o'er labour'd, stiff,
Make faintly as he could, to yonder Dell.

The descriptive details, set within an apparently casual parenthesis, supply the listener's imagination with a palpable and entirely plausible scene. The account of Oswald's physical condition, apparently gratuitous, fills out this deceiving fiction in a similarly convincing way. Dryden is tipping his hand, showing that poetry can deceive, that it sometimes lies because it *does* affirm. The imaginary scene conveyed by words to Arthur's mind convinces him that in following Grimbald's suggestions he will indeed "follow *Oswald*'s flight." Arthur trusts wholeheartedly in what he hears and sees: "I thank thee, Shepherd; / Expect Reward, lead on, we follow thee."

As in the enchanted grove, it is Philidel who sounds the alarm, counterposing a cautious skepticism to Grimbald's deceit: *"Trust 'em not, for they'll deceive ye."* Because both choruses of spirits, false and true, commit their utterance to song, the status of poetry remains equivocal, and its operation upon the mind remains equally fraught with either truth or falsehood:

CHOR. PHIL. SPIR.:   Hither this way, this way bend.

CHOR. GRIM. SPIR.:   This way, this way bend.

The truth wins only by sheer insistence, so that finally Grimbald yeilds and Arthur declares that "the Cheat is plain" (II, p. 257). The entire scene testifies to poetry's power of embodying truth or lies, and to the susceptibility of the imagination to convincingly staged fictions.[20] In Purcell's setting, the evil chorus's canonic *imitation* of what the good chorus sings dramatizes the problem thoroughly. Arthur learns that there are more serious ways than Emmeline's verbal mix-ups to mistake one's hearing for one's sight. And the audience listening to and viewing *King Arthur* is ironically reminded that they must yield their imaginations to the fiction in order to partake of its meaning. In his Epistle Dedicatory, Dryden accordingly values "the parts of the Airy and Earthy Spirits, and that Fairy kind of writing, which depends only upon the Force of Imagination . . ."[21]

III

In 1688, William Molyneux wrote to Locke and proposed a question remarkably similar to one dramatized by Dryden's Emmeline:

> A Man, being born blind, and having a Globe and a Cube, nigh of the same bignes [sic], Committed into his Hands, and being taught or Told, which is Called the Globe, and which the Cube, so as easily to distinguish them by his Touch or Feeling; Then both being taken from Him, and Laid on a Table, Let us suppose his Sight Restored to Him; Whether he Could, by his sight, and before he touch them, know which is the Globe and which the Cube?[22]

Locke at first ignored Molyneux's inquiry but included it, with a reply (negative, in accord with Molyneux's own hypothesis), in the second edition of his *Essay* (1694).[23] Dryden could have had no knowledge of Molyneux's Question until after having produced *King Arthur*. But had he read the first edition of the *Essay,* available as early as 1689, he would have encountered a related suggestion in Locke's famous reference to the blind man and the sound of the trumpet:

> A studious blind Man, who had mightily beat his Head about visible Objects, and made use of the explication of his Books and Friends, to understand those names of Light, and Colours, which often came in his way; bragg'd one day, That he now understood what Scarlet signified. Upon which his Friend demanding, what Scarlet was? the blind Man answered, It was like the Sound of a Trumpet.[24]

The blind man's synaesthetic terminology is very much like Emmeline's, who in fact discusses the sound of trumpets early in the play:

> . . . I can tell you how the sound on't looks.
> It looks as if it had an angry fighting Face.[25]
> (I, p. 250)

What came to be known as Molyneux's Question—whether a person with newly restored sight would be able to name or identify objects known to him previously by touch alone—is dramatized when Emmeline receives her sight. Not until the early part of the next century did cataract operations confirm Molyneux's hypothesis, but Dryden's rendering of Emmeline's experience is consistent with both contemporary theory and later experimental discovery.[26]

When magical drops from Merlin's vial have been applied to Emmeline's eyes to "let in Knowledge by another sense" (III, p. 267), she is shown a mirror and fails to recognize herself:

> EM.: What's this?
> It holds a Face within it: Oh sweet Face;
> It draws the Mouth, and Smiles, and looks upon me;
> And talks; but yet I cannot hear it Speak:
> The pretty thing is Dumb.
>
> MAT.: The pretty thing
> You see within the Glass, is you.
>
> EM.: What, am I two? Is this another me?
>
> (III, pp. 267–68)

Emmeline's new visual experience still needs to be coordinated with her other sense experience; until then, the world and self she sees remain alien to the familiar experience of her other senses. The personal terms applied to herself ("I" and "me") contrast with the impersonal terms applied to the image in the mirror ("it" and "thing"), bespeaking Emmeline's dissociation of her tactile and audile sense of self from her visual image. Emmeline's terms anticipate not only Molyneux's Question but also the modern (psychoanalytic) concept of "the mirror stage," the phase of cognitive development in which "the child discovers his 'self' by identifying with the image he perceives in a mirror."[27]

Self-recognition turns to self-love, and Emmeline recapitulates the Narcissus myth by conceiving a vain affection for her own image, embracing and kissing it ("I Love it; let me Kiss my to'ther Self. / Alas I've kiss'd it Dead" [III, p. 268]). Further dramatizing Molyneux's Question, Emmeline next must learn to associate Arthur's face, first imaged in her mirror, with her prior experience of his person (touch of hand, sound of voice):

> EM.: Ha! What art thou, with a new kind of Face,
> And other Cloaths, a Noble Creature too;

> But taller, bigger, fiercer in thy Look;
> Of a Comptrolling Eye, Majestick make?

MAT.:   Do you not know him, Madam?

EM.:   Is't a Man?

ARTH.:   Yes, and the most unhappy of my kind,
> If you have chang'd your Love.

EM.:   My dearest Lord!
> Was my Soul Blind; and cou'd not that look out,
> To know you e're you Spoke?

Only when Arthur speaks does Emmeline recognize him, associating his familiar voice with his unfamiliar face. The implied answer to her question (analogous to Molyneux's) about the "Soul"—"cou'd not that look out, / To know you, e're you Spoke?"—is negative. Neoplatonism runs up against a skeptical empiricism that reduces all ideas to sense experience. Emmeline's talk of a "Soul" that apprehends knowledge apart from the senses may betray Dryden's sympathies for an older psychology; but in fact Dryden shows Emmeline as unable to recognize Arthur until her previous sense experience has informed her untrained vision. Arthur's face, before he speaks, is as unrecognizable to her as the cube and sphere are to Molyneux's hypothetical subject. Whether or not Dryden knew of Molyneux's Question, his *a priori* answer to it is consistent with Molyneux's own, with Locke's, and with Berkeley's after them—all of whom postulated, before eye operations confirmed them to be right, that seeing is a *learned* experience.[28]

How comfortable Dryden felt with the empiricist direction of philosophy in his day is hard to know. Clearly he disputes the deterministic implications of Hobbes's cosmology, and his use of Hobbes's sensory psychology is sometimes tinged with irony, as when it is propounded by Lucifer as a prelude to the Fall.[29] Dryden still uses the Neoplatonic vocabulary increasingly under scientific pressure in his day, but on the other hand he readily uses empiricist terminology when it is to purpose, and constructs in *King Arthur* a dramatic action that affirms, in Emmeline's failure to recognize Arthur, the developing refinements of the sensory psychology. Yet again, Dryden dramatizes the inadequacy of sense experience to true knowledge, showing Arthur's own blindness to the folly of trusting appearances. Finally, in what amounts to a delightful equivocation, Dryden constructs a poetic fiction that variously dramatizes the capacity of poetic language to deceive its audience. Thus poetry assists the education of the senses even as it uses the senses to "deceive."[30]

Notes

1.   "Palamon and Arcite" 2.354, ed. James Kinsley, *The Poems and Fables of John Dryden* (London: Oxford UP, 1970), p. 568.

2. *King Arthur; or, The British Worthy, A Dramatick Opera,* ed. Montague Summers, in *Dryden: The Dramatic Works,* vol. 6 (London: Nonesuch, 1932), 231–89, with textual and explanatory notes, 500–502, 553–64. Parenthetical citations refer to act and page.

3. "For there is no conception in a mans mind, which hath not at first, totally, or by parts, been begotten upon the organs of Sense," *Leviathan* 1.1, ed. C. B. Macpherson (Harmondsworth: Pelican, 1968)," p. 85.

4. *Leviathan* 1.7, 9; pp. 131, 147.

5. *Humane Nature: Or the Fundamental Elements of Policy,* in *Hobbs's Tripos, in Three Discourses,* 3rd ed. (London, 1684), ch. 2, par. 10; p. 10. Robert Boyle, *The Origine of Formes and Qualities* (Oxford, 1666), Pt. 6 ("The Theoricall Part"), p. 43. John Locke, *An Essay concerning Humane Understanding,* 4th and later eds.; cited from the 5th ed. (London, 1706), bk. 2, ch. 8, par. 10; p. 75. Locke's additions are distinguished in the edition by Alexander Campbell Fraser (2 vols., 1894; rpt. New York: Dover, 1959).

6. See Louis I. Bredvold, *The Intellectual Milieu of John Dryden,* University of Michigan Publications, Language and Literature, vol. 12 (Ann Arbor: U of Michigan P, 1934), pp. 65–69. For an argument against Hobbesian influence upon Dryden, see John A. Winterbottom, "The Place of Hobbesian Ideas in Dryden's Tragedies," *JEGP* 57 (1958), 665–83.

7. *The State of Innocence and Fall of Man: An Opera,* ed. Montague Summers, *Dryden: The Dramatic Works,* vol. 3 (1931), 407–62, as characterized by Bruce King, *Dryden's Major Plays* (Edinburgh: Oliver and Boyd, 1966), p. 104.

8. Jackson I. Cope, "Dryden *vs.* Hobbes: An Adaptation from the Platonists," *JEGP* 57 (1958), 444–48, discusses Dryden's irony in using Hobbes's ideas.

9. Cf. Eve, "We have been cozen'd," in *The State of Innocence* (Act V, p. 453), and the discussion of Locke and language below.

10. *Aeneid* 3.19–48; *Inferno* 13.22–45; *The Faerie Queene* 2.12.42; *Gerusalemme Liberata* 18.32, 37.

11. *The Parson's Tale* X(I).330–35, in *The Riverside Chaucer,* ed. Larry D. Benson (Boston: Houghton Mifflin, 1987), p. 297. Milton, *Paradise Lost* 9.1127–31.

12. Act IV, p. 444. Cf. "His Passion cast a Mist before his Sense" until "Reason resum'd her Place, and Passion fled" ("Palamon and Arcite" 2.334, 349; Kinsley, p. 568).

13. Elsewhere Dryden humorously suggests that Eve "learn'd to paint" after the Fall ("To Sir Godfrey Kneller," line 92; Kinsley, p. 498), a similar association of cosmetics with deception.

14. See Basil Willey, *The Seventeenth Century Background* (London: Chatto and Windus, 1934), ch. 10, and Edward Pechter, *Dryden's Classical Theory of Literature* (London: Cambridge UP, 1975), ch. 5.

15. "Apology," ed. Summers, *Dryden: The Dramatic Works,* 3:421. On Dryden and the Royal Society, see Bredvold, *Intellectual Milieu,* pp. 48–50; and Phillip Harth, *Contexts of Dryden's Thought* (Chicago: U of Chicago P, 1968), p. 15 and n.

16. *The State of Innocence,* Act III, p. 440.

17. Willey, *Seventeenth Century Background,* pp. 216–18, discusses Dryden briefly in connection with Hobbes. See also King, *Dryden's Major Plays,* ch. 6, and Pechter's claim that Addison "defines clearly a position towards which Dryden's innovations were tending" (*Dryden's Classical Theory,* p. 114).

18. Pechter, *Dryden's Classical Theory,* p. 141. Cf. Locke, *Essay* 3.10.34: "all the artificial and figurative application of Words Eloquence hath invented, are for nothing else, but to insinuate wrong *Ideas,* move the Passions, and thereby mislead the Judgment; and so indeed are perfect cheat . . ." (1st ed., p. 251; facsimile rpt. Menston, Yorkshire: Scolar Press, 1970). Locke's *Essay* appeared in 1689, though the title-page is dated 1690; see prefatory note in facsimile reprint cited above. A French abridgement of Locke's *Essay* was published in the *Bibliothèque Universelle et Historique* 8 (1688), 49–142; see Hendrika Johanna Reesink, *L'Angleterre et la littérature anglaise dans les trois plus anciens périodiques français de Hollande de 1684 à 1709* (Zutphen: Thieme, 1931), p. 231 (item no. 388).

19. In the tradition of formal rhetoric, catachresis (*abusio*) is defined as "the inexact use of a like and kindred word in place of the precise and proper one" (*Rhetorica ad Herennium* 4.33.45; ed. Harry Caplan, Loeb Classical Library [London: Heinemann, 1954], pp. 342–43).

20. Compare Locke's description of metaphorical language as "cheat," quoted in note 18.

21. "Epistle," ed. Summers, *Dryden: The Dramatic Works* 6:242. Arthur is again deceived by words in the enchanted grove, when the false Emmeline recounts how "Fierce *Osmond* clos'd me in this bleeding Bark, [etc.]" (Act IV, p. 278).

22. *The Correspondence of John Locke,* ed. E. S. De Beer, vol. 3 (Oxford: Clarendon, 1978), pp. 482–83. For a history of the matter, see Michael J. Morgan, *Molyneux's Question* (Cambridge: Cambridge UP, 1977), and K. Theodore Hoppen, *The Common Scientist in the Seventeenth Century: A Study of the Dublin Philosophical Society 1683–1708* (Charlottesville: U of Virginia P, 1970), pp. 172–75, with references.

23. Locke, *Essay* 2.9.8; see note in Fraser's edition, 1:186. Molyneux wrote to Locke a second time in 1692/93; for details of the correspondence, see Wolfgang von Leyden, *Seventeenth-Century Metaphysics: An Examination of Some Main Concepts and Theories* (London: Duckworth, 1968), p. 277n, and editor's note in Locke, *Correspondence, 3:*482.

24. Locke, *Essay* 3.4.11; p. 199.

25. Other editors imply a more general anecdotal background to the story: "In imitation of the blind man, who said that 'red resembled the sound of a trumpet' " (Walter Scott and George Saintsbury, eds., *The Works of John Dryden,* vol. 8 [Edinburgh, 1882], 146n). Cf. Dryden's "Apology for Heroique Poetry and Poetique Licence": "*'Tis just as reasonable as to conclude there is no day, because a blind Man cannot distinguish of Light and Colours?*" (ed. Summers, *Dryden: The Dramatic Works,* 3:419).

26. On cataract surgery, see Morgan, *Molyneux's Question,* ch. 2.

27. See Jacques Lacan, "Le stade du miroir comme formateur de la fonction du Je," *Écrits 1* (Paris: Seuil, 1966), pp. 89–97. Definition from Jonathan Culler, "The Mirror Stage," *High Romantic Argument: Essays for M. H. Abrams,* ed. Lawrence Lipking (Ithaca: Cornell UP, 1981), p. 150. See also Emmeline's self-description as "an Infant of the World" (III, p. 267).

28. For Locke and Molyneux's verdicts, see reference in note 23. George Berkeley, *An Essay towards a New Theory of Vision,* 2nd ed. (Dublin, 1709), Sects. 41–42; pp. 44–45.

29. See King, *Dryden's Major Plays,* ch. 6.

30. I am indebted to Professor James A. Winn for reading this article in draft and making many valuable suggestions.

The Ironies of Dryden's "Alexander's Feast; or the Power of Musique": Text and Contexts

ROBERT P. MACCUBBIN

Though universally regarded by the eighteenth century as the greatest English specimen of the grand, or Pindaric, ode, and though praised in almost reverential terms after it was set to music by Handel in 1736, Dryden's "Alexander's Feast; or The Power of Musique. An Ode, in Honour of St. Cecilia's Day" (1697) is today generally regarded as ironic in its treatment of the Macedonian King and/or the musician Timotheus.[1] Even though its ironic tenor is now apparently assumed, the "Ode" has never been rigorously examined by reference to the contexts that informed it: namely, baroque theories about music's effects, legends of ancient musical modes, and the figure of Alexander in history, tradition and baroque art—as well as, of course, the annual St. Cecilia Day celebrations.

During the seventeenth century the Platonic explanation of musical effects on the innately harmonic soul was supplanted by empirical study of the more mundane operation of sound impulses on the body. George Sandys, Descartes, Robert Boyle, Kenelme Digby, Abraham Cowley and John Wallis—whose works were certainly known to Dryden—agreed that music creates vibrations of air which strike the ear and are transmitted to the brain, exciting the passions so immediately that reason has little time to prevent the resultant bodily motions corresponding to the passions.[2] To Descartes and his successors each passion was thought to effect a characteristic visible external bodily reaction: for example, "gestures of the eyes and face, changes of color, tremblings, languishing, swouning, laughter, tears, groans, and sighs."[3]

Thus, Dryden's Alexander, celebrating at Persepolis the defeat of Darius, reacts without rational reflection to the music of Timotheus, which moves him through a series of passions depicted by Dryden according to their external bodily signs, such as "glowing cheeks . . . ardent eyes."[4] The tearful Alexander sighs as he contemplates the death of his vanquished foe:

Robert P. MacCubbin, "The Ironies of Dryden's 'Alexander's Feast; or the Power of Musique': Text and Contexts." This article originally appeared in *Music and Literature*, a special issue of *Mosaic: A Journal for the Interdisciplinary Study of Literature*, Guest edited by W. John Rempel and Ursula M. Rempel, Volume 18/4, Fall 1985, pp. 33–47. Reprinted by permission.

> With down-cast Looks the joyless Victor sate,
>   Revolveing in his alter'd Soul
>   The various Turns of Chance below;
>   And, now and then, a Sigh he stole;
>   And Tears began to flow.
>
>   (ll. 84–88)

And in the next stanza, "unable to conceal his Pain," a passion which Descartes too had associated with that of love, Alexander gazes on his lovely consort, Thais, and continues to sigh until sinking senseless upon her breast.

Not only could music arouse the passions, but baroque music conventionalized certain rhythms, keys and graces as the scientifically correct ones for arousing particular passions. By using music, therefore, Timotheus not only prevents the operation of Alexander's reason, but knowingly moves Alexander through a succession of emotions by varying pitch, rhythm and volume:

> The trembling Notes ascend the Sky,
>   And Heav'nly Joys inspire. (ll. 23–24)
> . . . .
> The Master saw the Madness rise:
> His glowing Cheeks, his ardent Eyes;
> And while He Heav'n and Earth defy'd
> Chang'd his Hand, and check'd his Pride.
>   He chose a Mournful Muse
>   Soft Pity to infuse: (ll. 69–74)
> . . . .
> Now strike the Golden Lyre again:
> A lowder yet, and yet a lowder Strain.
>   (ll. 123–24)

The baroque era—which rationally examined acoustics and music's mathematical proportions, which found scientific reasons for sounds' being pleasing or unpleasing, and which declared the passions to be distinguishable, separable and expressible motions of the soul—saw a natural relation between certain sounds and certain passions, and therefore anxiously sought to determine what aspects and kinds of music were most effective in moving the passions.[5] Harmony or rhythm? Polyphony or monody?[6] The learned and subtle Timotheus perceives the effects of monody and rhythm as well as the consanguinity of different passions and different musical modes:

> The Mighty Master smil'd to see,
> That Love was in the next Degree:
> 'Twas but a Kindred-Sound to move;
> For Pity melts the Mind to Love.

> Softly sweet, in *Lydian* Measures,
> Soon he sooth'd his Soul to Pleasures.
>
> (ll. 93–98)

As important as "measures" were to the baroque musician, however, they were generally considered most successful when they danced opposite a poetic text. For fullest effect, therefore, Timotheus sings as he plays his lyre (and later as he plays his flute!—impossible even in music hall). Singing first a song of Alexander's lineage, then songs of bacchic joy, the sad fate of Darius, the futility of war and honor, and finally a song of revenge, Timotheus, an ancient bard using the ancient musical modes, also uses baroque scientific method, joining rhythms and words to create effects unequalled by either alone. More importantly, however, the effective strains of Timotheus, though originally prompting the gentle passions of pity and love (though the latter is qualified, as we shall see), ultimately urge the drunken mob vengefully to burn down Persepolis. The occasion for which the ode was written—the annual 22 November music festival in honor of the patron saint of music, Cecilia[7]—would lead us to expect an unambiguous honoring of music, but here a pagan bard subverts the traditional Christian humanist expectation that artistic (and scientific?) powers ought to operate for the good. Baroque musical theory seems to be abused by the occasional bard, who is, moreover, ironically analogous to the official state poet, the laureate.

Accounts of the distinctive emotional effects of the ancient modes, exemplified by tales of their usage, were readily available, especially after the appearance of Marcus Meibomius' *Antiquae Musicae Auctores Septem* (Amsterdam, 1652) and Caspar Bartholini's *De Tibiis Veterum* (Rome, 1677), both packed with such tales reiterated frequently thereafter: tales of Orpheus, Amphion and Arion; or Achilles' fierceness' being allayed by the harp, Asclepides' reducing seditious multitudes to temperance and reason, Pythagoras' stopping a young man's fury, David's curing Saul, and Timotheus' enflaming and then appeasing Alexander the Great.

Four of the five prime sources for the life of Alexander the Great—Plutarch's *Lives,* Justin's *History of the World from the Assyrian Monarchy down to the Time of Augustus Caesar,* Diodorus of Sicily's *Library of History,* and Arrian's *Anabasis of Alexander*—do not even mention the Timotheus episode; and the fifth—Quintus Curtius Rufus' *History of the Life and Death of Alexander the Great*—mentions only the effects of the warlike Phrygian mode. Nevertheless, the Timotheus/Alexander tale, together with those about Orpheus and David, formed a tonic triad as the most important instances of ancient musical effects. So well-known was the tale that in his "Preface" to Robert South's *Musica Incantans,* James Gibbs begins a long section on the history of music's powers with the observation: "The Story of Alexander and Timotheus is commonly known. . . ."[8] Not troubling to repeat it, Gibbs classifies the tale with others in which a young man distracted by the Phrygian is restored by a gentler mode. The St. Cecilia odes by Samuel Wesley (1691), Theophilus Parsons (1693) and Peter Motteux (1695), though not using the Timotheus tale, emphasized its moral—the cessation of discordant passions in general and the resolution of war into peace. This was a moral of hope amidst the jarring strife of King William's reign until the peace of September 1697.

So pervasive was the influence of the Timotheus tale and its moral that in 1749 Richard Brocklesby distorted a tale in Plutarch's *Morals* to make it agree with the Timotheus one.[9] In his "Second Oration Concerning the Fortune or Virtue of Alexander the Great," Plutarch described Antigenides' playing in the Harmatian[10] mode to Alexander, who "was so transported and warm'd for battle by the charms of the lofty air, that leaping from his seat all in his clattering armore, he began to lay at those who stood next him."[11] Brocklesby, a physician, recounted this tale because he wished to demonstrate the pernicious medical consequences of anger. Although he cites Plutarch's "Oration" as his source, because he also wished to demonstrate a cure for anger, to Plutarch's account he adds the restorative ending from the Timotheus tale.

Plutarch was not alone in describing Alexander's being excited to arms by music. Jean Freinshemius, for example, in his summaries of the lost first two books of Quintus Curtius Rufus, said Alexander especially favored Timotheus among musicians because of his ability to excite him with the Phrygian mode.[12] The legend that music drove Ericus, King of Denmark, to fury was frequently used to reinforce faith in the Timotheus tale, or was described as a mere retelling of it; and like the accounts by Plutarch and Freinshemius, it ended in violence.[13] In his "Preface" to South's *Musica,* Gibbs translates the whole account from Saxo Grammaticus' *Historae Danicae,* XII:

> It happened, that among several musicians that attended the king at supper, there was one most eminent artist, who, upon a dispute about the force of musick, being ask'd whether it was in the power of his art to provoke a man to rage and fury, affirm'd it possible, and being afterwards question'd, whether he knew the way or method of such a performance, confess'd he did: Whereupon the king, being curious to try the experiment, desir'd, and at last by threats compell'd him to use his utmost endeavors to perform what he pretended to. The musician perceiving no way of declining the undertaking, order'd that all arms and dangerous instruments should be remov'd out of the room, and that several persons, placed out of the sound of his musick, as soon as they heard any extraordinary noise, should break open the doors, to prevent what mischief might happen. And this being accordingly done, he began so grave a strain, that it presently fill'd the hearers with sadness, and lull'd their spirits into a deep satisfaction: After he had thus play'd a convenient time, by a brisker and more sprightly sort of musick; he rais'd them from their dullness to a chearful temper, so that being cured of their melancholy they were now dancing for joy:

At last running over a confus'd division with a most violent quickness, he made them so impatient, that they fill'd the House with clamours, such an absolute power had the variety of sounds over the affections of their mind.

As those outside rushed in, the king grabbed a sword and slew four guards. The greater resemblance of "Alexander's Feast" to the violent Ericus tale than to the traditional version of the Timotheus tale is obvious: instead of having a destructive urge calmed by music, Alexander, having been first moved to pity and love is, in the dramatic climax of the poem, driven to an apocalyptic and fanatical "zeal to destroy" (l. 147). Dryden's drastic departure from traditional legend[14] is one of the poem's fundamental shaping ironies, and it may have had satiric political ramifications inasmuch as the poem was performed hard on the heels of peace.

By reversing the traditional order of Alexander's musically effected moods, Dryden's ode, which may be an allusive soured statement on the militarism of King William emphasizes the worst of Alexander's passionate excesses, and obscures his virtues, which according to Plutarch included judgment, compassion and determination. Judgment is entirely lacking in the ode; compassion takes up all of stanza III only to be obliterated by the spirit of vengeance; and Alexander's determination, encouraged by Timotheus' music, is misused to destructive ends.

In both Rufus' and Plutarch's "Life," Alexander's compassion is most notable when he visits Darius' despairing mother, wife and children, and of all the Alexander subjects in renaissance and baroque painting, this was by far the most popular.[15] In 1661, as he began to rule personally, Mazarin having died, Louis XIV commissioned Charles LeBrun to do an Alexander painting on any subject, the result being the "Tent of Darius," a lengthy description of which was soon to be found in André Felibien's *Receuil de Descriptions de Peintures et d'Autres Ouvrages faits pour Le Roy* (Paris, 1689). This, the most famous and frequently alluded to of any of the baroque representations of Alexander, is called by Donald Posner a "lesson in formalized gallantry, in the ethic of royalty," that is, in not just compassion, but self-control as well.[16]

Another of Alexander's virtues, the magnanimity expressed toward the conquered Porus—and portrayed in Racine's *Alexandre le Grand* (1665), dedicated to the new Alexander, Louis XIV—was perhaps an amplification of the compassion and self-control expressed in LeBrun's painting. Both the play and the painting, later to become one of a series of five allegories of Louis as Alexander, were "a statement of the ideological premises of Louis' reign," that is, says Posner, "the just and undeniable triumph of unlimited ambition through inherent, monarchical virtue" (p. 224). Dryden almost certainly knew Racine's play, and because of his keen interest in painting probably knew Felibien's flattering commentary and LeBrun's paintings as engraved by Gerhard Edelinck and Gerard Audran for the *Cabinet du Roi* volumes sent out to all the world in glorification of Louis. But Dryden's Alexander, lacking self-control and magnanimity, is much closer to the Alexander of Nathaniel Lee's heroic tragedy, *The Rival Queens* (1677), for which Dryden wrote several commendatory verses. Richard Steele's complaint against *The Rival Queens* illuminates Lee's intentions, of which Dryden apparently approved: "instead of representing that hero in the glorious character of generosity and chastity in his treatment of the beauteous family of Darius, he is drawn all along as a monster of lust or of cruelty, as if the way to raise him to the degree of an hero were to make his character as little like that of a worthy man as possible" (*The Tatler,* #191 [June 27–29, 1710]).[17]

Like Lee's Alexander, Dryden's can be judged by his falling short of Louis XIV, who at least in French art was the grandest model of baroque heroism. The fame of LeBrun's allegories almost guarantees that a comparison would have been made, and that the result would be denigration of the inferior example. Not only has Dryden rearranged the Timotheus tale to emphasize Alexander's natural inclination to anger, moreover; he has rearranged the chronology of Alexander's life by placing the Darius episode *before* the burning of Persepolis; and in so doing Dryden has placed in the most emphatic position that episode traditionally demonstrative of Alexander's worst excesses.

The two rearrangements—of the Timotheus tale and of the chronology of Alexander's life—may have had satiric political ramifications, especially when one considers that the poem was performed only two months after the Treaty of Ryswick. By the Treaty, England's Alexander had triumphed over France's Darius. No more could Louis be compared to Alexander without irony. But if "Alexander's Feast" alludes to William's Protestant victories, the Catholic Dryden's distress was even more severe than has been suspected. Until 1701 peace was to reign in Europe. Is Dryden, the deposed Jacobite poet laureate, contrarily prophesying resumption of hostilities, the blame for which would be the monomaniacal passion of a madman urged on by a perverse court and a flunky laureate? To answer that question one needs to consider that Dryden would not have dared to make a comparison of Alexander and William in a public, occasional poem—unless the comparison were allusive enough to escape prosecution. It escaped not only prosecution, however; for if it was a satire on William, as two recent critics argue,[18] such historically specific satire may have escaped "all the town" that so esteemed the poem.

Nevertheless, since 1688 William's detractors and defenders alike had occasionally compared him to Alexander, though more frequently to Caesar; so such an analogy would not have been unique to Dryden. Furthermore, the St. Cecilia odes of Shadwell (1690), Wesley (1691), Nicholas Brady (1692), Motteux (1695), and the anonymous "Ode" for 1696[19] mention war (some only because Dryden had done so in his admired and therefore imitated 1687 "Song for St. Cecilia's Day"), and Shadwell's and Wesley's odes make quite apparent that the occasional ode for St. Cecilia's day was considered a legitimate political forum. Such usage by Dryden, therefore, would not have been unique. Intriguingly, the obscure and heretofore unnoticed 1696 "Ode," performed at the height of international hostility, is the only St. Cecilia ode besides Dryden's in which the dramatic conclusion prefatory to the Grand Chorus is a warrior's excitation to destructiveness:

> The trembling Slave, tho pale with Fears,
> When the loud Trumpet's Voice he hears
> Feels a strange Fire his Soul invade,
> Collects his new-born Courage to his Aid.
>   The warlike Notes impart
> Strength to his Limbs, and Boldness to his Heart.
> Dauntless to fight he goes,
> Stalks thro the Field, and swells to meet his Foes.

As in "Alexander's Feast," the musical excitation to destructiveness is prefaced by an account of music's ability to soothe the warrior's passions. That pattern of emotions, so appropriate in 1696, hardly seems so a year later, after the Treaty of Ryswick.

Whatever the political ramifications of the ode, however, they seem not so pervasive or simple as Bessie Proffitt has argued, and I concur with Ruth Smith's assessment that it is dangerous to impose an allegorical politic on such an ambiguous poem.[20] The issues at hand are larger than mere events. Dryden's ingenious manipulations of the entire body of accumulated lore associated with Alexander (and Timotheus) has as its end not the debasement of William, a King almost beneath Dryden's contempt, but a whole mode of baroque glorification and representation in need of ironic exposure.

In the light of these informing contexts, we may now move to the poetic text itself, noting first that Alexander's gradual collapse under the effects of music, love and wine is a decadent parody of Darius' "severe . . . fate" (l. 76)—the perhaps sarcastic periphrasis, "vanquish'd victor" (l. 115), suggesting not only Alexander's ultimate fate, but also a disparaging contrast between Darius' heroic martial death and Alexander's drunken stupor. Similarly disparaging of Alexander are lines implicitly comparing Darius' haunting stare into the lonely blankness of death—"On the bare Earth expos'd He lyes,/With not a Friend to close his Eyes" (ll. 83–84)—and Alexander's rhythmically silly, repetitious and empty staring at his whore: "[He] sigh'd and look'd, sigh'd and look'd,/Sigh'd and look'd, and sigh'd again" (ll. 112–13). He then sank, not onto "bare Earth" but soft bosom.

The draught of love is itself given a twist of irony: the "fair/Who caused . . . [Alexander's] care" is not, as tradition had it, either Statira or Roxanna, the rival queens of Lee's drama, neither of whom was at Persepolis, but Thais, who though an Athenian whore is likened to Alexander's "blooming bride" (l.

10). In a letter to his publisher, Tonson, Dryden directed, "Remember in the Copy of Verses for St. Cecilia, to alter the name of Lais, which is twice there, for Thais; those two ladyes were contemporaryes, which caused that small mistake."[21] According to Pierre Bayle's article on her life in his *Dictionnaire Historique et Critique* (Rotterdam, 1697), Lais was a famous Sicilian courtesan falsely said by Amyot to have been a visitor to Alexander's camp. Whatever the source of Dryden's original error (perhaps Amyot's misunderstanding of Plutarch's *Treatise of Love*), his awareness that Alexander's companion was a whore is certain. Apparently unwilling to accept the irony, or thinking that Dryden had unconsciously erred, John Hughes, in revising the ode in 1711 for musical setting by Thomas Clayton, removed the reference to Thais' being a bride, making only more obvious Dryden's sarcasm.[22]

Dryden also creates irony by re-shaping the formal expectations of the St. Cecilia ode genre. Remembering that many such odes began with an opening "welcome" song or declaration that the day was to be one of public celebration, Dryden begins his poem with a description that appears to be not only a grandly painted baroque victory celebration, but a wedding feast:

> 'Twas at the Royal Feast, for *Persia* won,
>   By *Philip's* Warlike Son:
>   Aloft in awful State
>   The God-like Heroe sate
>   On his Imperial Throne:
>   His valiant Peers were plac'd around;
> Their Brows with Roses and with Myrtles bound.
>   (So shou'd Desert in Arms be Crown'd:)
>   The Lovely *Thais* by his side,
>   Sate like a blooming *Eastern* Bride
>   In Flow'r of Youth and Beauty's Pride.
>   (ll. 1–11)

The royal whore, Thais, is only "like" a bride, however. Furthermore, what appears to be a fitting subject of an epithalamic hymn, the lineage of Alexander, the supposed bridegroom, becomes, in part, an ironic analogue to the accounts in other St. Cecilia odes of God's giving form to matter at Creation:

> The Song began from *Jove;*
> Who left his blissful Seats above,
> (Such is the Pow'r of mighty Love.)
> A Dragon's fiery Form bely'd the God:
> Sublime on Radiant Spires He rode,
>   When He to fair *Olympia* press'd:
> Then, round her slender Waste he curl'd,
> And stamp'd an Image of himself, a Sov'raign of the World.
>   (ll. 25–33)

Jove, assuming a dragon's form that belies his identity, and motivated by "mighty Love," rapes Olympia, thereby creating Alexander, "an Image of himself." In imagery at once reminiscent of the biblical creation of man and of Eve's temptation, Dryden has created an action simultaneously creative and destructive.[23] The language and structure contain other ironies. The rape scene is preceded by the statement that Timotheus' notes will inspire "Heav'nly Joys" (l. 24). And so they do—the heavenly lust of Jove, who because of the ambiguity of Dryden's syntax seems to leave his "blissful Seats above" only after Timotheus' "trembling Notes ascend the Sky" (l. 23). Increasing the damage to Timotheus is the last line of the ode, which praises St. Cecilia for drawing an *angel* down to earth, not the rapacious Jove—an act of incomparably greater merit.

Timotheus, however, is merely playing his role as true-blue poet laureate—flattering Alexander's vanity. According to tradition, Olympia confessed that Alexander was begotten by Jove, after which Alexander demanded to be called Son of Jove. "From this very moment," said Justin, "he became insupportably insolent and haughty, and forgot that affability of behaviour, which had been instilled into him by his Grecian education." Furthermore, continued Rufus, the Macedonians, "reserving a greater show of liberality than other nations, did withstand him more obstinately in his affectation of immortality, than was either expedient for him or them."[24] The response to Timotheus' song of Alexander's begetting, though precisely traditional in declaring Alexander's vanity and his warriors' docility, is uniquely sarcastic:

> The list'ning Crowd admire the lofty Sound,
> A present Deity, they shout around:
> A present Deity the vaulted Roofs rebound.
> > With ravish'd Ears
> > The Monarch hears,
> > Assumes the God,
> > Affects to nod,
> And seems to shake the Spheres.
>
> (ll. 34–41)

The iambic dimeter and such terms as "ravish'd," "Assumes," "Affects" and "seems" make the accolade, "A present Deity," as hollow as its own echo.

Thais, the blushing "bride," and Jove, the dragon—neither figure is what she/he seems to be. And Timotheus and Alexander are not what they ought to be. And none of them sees the implications for the future inherent in the tale of Alexander's being made in Jove's image: that the rape of Olympia is a precursor of later actions by Alexander, specifically the burning down of Persepolis. The destruction of the temple of the Ephesian Diana by fire on the night of Alexander's birth had been interpreted by the magi as a sign that the orient would be destroyed by fire.[25] But foreseen or not, Jove's fiery descent in stanza II is a sign of the firing of "another Troy" in stanza VI. Meanwhile, the mindless revels career with abandon.

Ushered in by trumpets and drums (l. 50), as though a conquering military hero, Bacchus now enters as a triumphant god. Hughes' revision of this stanza drops the military instruments, but five completely new lines reinforce the sense of Bacchus as a conquering general:

> As when, by Tigers drawn, o'er India's Plains he rode,
>   While loud with Conquest and with Wine,
> His jolly Troop around him reel'd along,
>   And taught the vocal Skies to join
>   In this applauding Song.

The analogy between Bacchus and Alexander is in each libretto ironic: Alexander feasts after conquering Persia, and Bacchus enters into Alexander's feast in martial triumph over Alexander himself or as a parody.

In the primary accounts, the abandon at Persepolis was invariably cited as the worst example of Alexander's bacchic excess.[26] During the winter at Persepolis, said Rufus, Alexander's uncontrollable desire for women and feasts defaced his excellent qualities.[27] The accounts by Diodorus and Plutarch fully describe the debauch: "Here Alexander made a sumptuous feast for the entertainment of his friends in commemoration of his victory, and offered magnificent sacrifices to the gods. At this feast were entertained whores, who presented their bodies for hire, where the cups went so high, and the reins so let loose to drunkenness and debauchery, that many were both drunk and mad." At Thais' suggestion they all jumped onto tables to celebrate "a victorious festival to Bacchus. Hereupon, multitudes of fire-brands were presently got together, and all the women that played on musical instruments, which were at the feast, were called for, and then the king, with songs, pipes, and flutes, bravely led the way to this noble expedition, contrived and managed by this whore, Thais. . . ."[28] Plutarch's account varies only slightly, and also regards the burning down of Persepolis as an act of barbaric vengeance.[29] At Persepolis, then, Alexander was at his worst, his self-control entirely dissipated and his will subject to that of a whore and wine, both of which in Dryden's ode are made especially potent by Timotheus' reinforcing musical accompaniment.

None of the earlier St. Cecilia odes is as narrative as "Alexander's Feast," and none uses so specific a setting or so dramatic a personage as does Dryden's theatrical ode. To explain why he chose to represent this luxuriant, barbaric, but dramatic episode in an ode honoring St. Cecilia—who makes an appearance only in the undramatic seventh, and seemingly irrelevant, stanza—we need to examine the circumstances of the St. Cecilia's Day festivals, considering first whether the feast at Persepolis was designed to correspond to the St. Cecilia's feast in Stationers' Hall.

Since 1683, the "Society of Gentlemen, Lovers of Music" had assembled ritualistically on 22 November to address St. Cecilia, attending a divine service of sermon and sacred music in the morning but then retiring to Stationers' Hall later in the day for a secular feast of food and music. Information on the conduct of these affairs is scanty, the fullest being the account in Peter Motteux's *The Gentleman's Journal* for January 1692:

> This feast is one of the genteelist in the world. There are no formalities nor gatherings like at others, and the appearance there is always very splendid. Whilst the company is at table, the hautbois and trumpets play successively. Mr. Showers [John Shore] hath taught the latter of late years to sound with all the softness imaginable; they plaid us some flat tunes, made by Mr. [Godfrey] Finger, with a general applause, it being a thing formerly thought impossible upon an instrument design'd for a sharp key.
>
> (p. 7)

Motteux was one of the stewards of the feast; and his account reads like a public whitewashing of the event, especially in light of the very different account in the "Court Records" of the Company of Stationers: "in consideration of the damage that may be done to the Hall by setting up and fastening to the floors and wainscott scaffolds, tables, and benches. . . . the Hall should not be lett upon that occasion under five pounds" (Book F, fol. 194).[30] The Hall must have been severely mauled in 1693 for the rent to have jumped so sharply—by one hundred fifty percent! The Stationers' apprehension seems to have abated somewhat by the time payment was actually made, but they came down only to £4.0.0. However, in 1698, in reaction to the feast at which Dryden's ode was performed, another escalation of rent was proposed: "they might have the use of the Hall for keeping the . . . Feast offering to pay £5 for the same . . . they makeing good all spoile and damage that may happen . . . to the Hall or any Roomes adjoyning" (Book G, fol. 15).[31] The Company thus protected itself against whatever destruction the celebrants invoked upon themselves. These are intriguing records, urging us to speculate, with a smile, as to the cause of the damage: press of sheer numbers; weight of singers, musicians and instruments; or general mirth and abandon?

Just as in earlier St. Cecilia odes the celebrants were often described as sons of Apollo gathered at the foot of Mt. Parnassus as muses, so here they are gathered around the elevated figures of Alexander, Thais, Timotheus and their choral retinue—all of whom were apparently on scaffolding. The masque qualities of the action, most notably of course the rollicking entrance of Bacchus and his pards (stanza III) and the surging exit of flaming torches (stanza VI), indicate that the text was acted as well as sung. Many lines describe other performed actions; for example, "The Prince, unable to conceal his Pain,/Gaz'd on the Fair," then "sigh'd and look'd," and finally "sunk upon her Breast" (ll. 109–15). And in stanza VI the audience is actually directed to observe performers:

> See the Furies arise!
> See the Snakes that they rear,
> How they hiss in their Hair,
> And the Sparkles that flash from their Eyes!
> Behold a ghastly Band,
> Each a Torch in his Hand!
>
> (ll. 132–37)

Even the use of the passive voice indicates a staging of the action: Timotheus is "plac'd on high/Amid the tuneful Quire" (ll. 20–21). In fact, then, the opening eleven lines describe the stage set and arrangement of the cast as the action begins. The extent to which Dryden has been commenting on, as well as appealing to, the bacchic qualities of the St. Cecilia feast, cannot be established. What is clear, however, is the uniquely dramatic quality of Dryden's ode compared to its predecessors and successors in the genre. But we still have not satisfactorily accounted for the last stanza—the analytical and retrospective epilogue—in which St. Cecilia is finally mentioned.

The dramatic action of the lyric concludes in stanza VI with an unredeeming antimasque, one of the last and most ferocious outbursts of seventeenth-century baroque violence. But its demonic paganism is abruptly de-energized in the final stanza by the narrator's formal apostrophe which places the just-now-concluded action at a safe distance in the past, freezing the action as it was frozen in stanza I:

> Thus, long ago
> 'Ere heaving Bellows learn'd to blow,
> While Organs yet were mute;
> *Timotheus,* to his breathing Flute,
> And sounding Lyre,
> Cou'd swell the Soul to rage, or kindle soft Desire.
>
> (ll. 155–60)

The second and sixth stanzas, which open and close the narrative of Timotheus' role, parody biblical accounts of the creation of man, the Fall and the Apocalypse, and suggest the movement of history. In his earlier "Song for St. Cecilia's Day" (1687), Dryden began with an account of the Creation; then, after depicting both past and present human history, he closed with an account of the Dissolution. Just as in that poem human discord was judged against the spiritual concord of St. Cecilia and the harmony of the macrocosm, so here Alexander's unredeemable history is judged against the redemptive biblical pattern, and Timotheus' pagan lyre and flute are judged against the Christian organ:

> At last Divine *Cecilia* came,
> Inventress of the Vocal Frame;
> The sweet Enthusiast, from her Sacred Store,
> Enlarg'd the former narrow Bounds,
> And added Length to solemn Sounds,
> With Nature's Mother-Wit, and Arts unknown before.
>
> (ll. 161–66)

Timotheus yields the crown, or at least divides it with Cecilia (ll. 167–68); but mere division of honors would seem to prevent a thoroughly Christian reading of the concluding stanza. That, however, is mere paradox: Dryden's point is that Christianity builds upon, but grows out of and improves upon, the pagan world—under the aegis of divine grace.

As in his "Secular Masque" of 1700, Dryden presents us with figures of Mars and Venus, and agrees with Momus' judgment that they are vanities. Similarly, just as the final chorus of the "Secular Masque" indicates optimism that mutability and action may operate for the good, so the final apostrophe of "Alexander's Feast" reminds us that the history of musical art is a progression, not a regression. The Christian possesses "Arts unknown before." And as a progression mimetic of the advent of Christian grace to post-lapsarian man, music ought to be glorified annually, in what must have become by 1697, however, a gloriously secular bash!

Notes

1. In addition to works cited later, see Martin Price, *To the Palace of Wisdom* (Garden City, 1964), pp. 372–73; John Dawson Carl Buck, "The Ascetic's Banquet: The Morality of 'Alexander's Feast,' " *Texas Studies in Literature and Language*, 17 (1975), 573–89; Paul H. Fry, *The Poet's Calling in the English Ode* (New Haven, 1980), pp. 49–62. William A. McIntosh's defense of the romantic, non-ironic Dryden is unconvincing: "Handel and the Muse," *Cithara*, 12 (May 1973), 18–40.

2. Sandys, trans., *Ovid's Metamorphoses* (Oxford, 1632), notes to Bk. X, p. 356; Boyle, "An Essay of the Great Effects of Even Languid and Unheeded Motion," *Works* (London, 1772), V, 18–23; Digby, *Two Treatises: in the one of which, the nature of bodies: in the other, the nature of man's soul, is looked into* (London, 1645), 334–40; Cowley, *Essays, Plays, and Sundry Verses*, ed. A. R. Waller (Cambridge, 1906), I, 275, n. 32; Wallis, "A Letter of Dr. John Wallis, to Mr. Andrew Fletcher; concerning the strange Effects reported to Musick in Former Times, beyond what is to be found in Later Ages" (18 August 1698), *The Royal Society of London: Philosophical Transactions, 1665–1780* (New York, 1963), no. 243, p. 297.

3. Descartes, *The Passions of the Soule* (London, 1650), arts, XIII, XVII, XXXVI–XXXVII.

4. *The Poems and Fables of John Dryden*, ed. James Kinsley (London, 1962), I. 70. All subsequent quotations from Dryden's poems are from this unmodernized text.

5. Scientific studies of music abounded. Besides those by Alexander Malcolm (1721), Marin Mersenne (1623), William Holder (1694), and William Turner (1724), Roger North (ed. John Wilson, 1959), and Thomas Salmon (1672), other studies are mentioned in L. S.

Lloyd, "Musical Theory in the Early *Philosophical Transactions," Notes and Records of the Royal Society in London,* 3 (1941), 149–57; and Edward J. Dent, "The Scientific Study of Music in England," *Mitteilungen der Internationalen Gesellschaft für Musikwissenschaft,* 2 (1930), 83–92. See also Arthur W. Locke, "Descartes and Seventeenth-Century Music," *Music Quarterly,* 21 (1935), 423–31, and Paul Henry Lang, "The Enlightenment and Music," *Eighteenth-Century Studies,* 1 (1967), esp. 96, 102–04.

6. Robert Boyle expressed belief in the special effect not of harmony or timbre, but of rhythm, that aspect of music most resembling motion: see *Works* (London, 1772), pp. v, 181. Isaac Vossius argued that monody, rather than polyphony, was the source of ancient musical effects; see *De Poematum Cantu et Viribus Rhythmi* (Oxford, 1673), pp. 66–74. Others more subtle than Vossius argued against him: Roger North, "Criticism on Isaac Vossius' *De Poematum Cantu*" (BM Add. MS. 32531); Abbé [Jean Baptiste] DuBos, *Critical Reflections on Poetry, Painting and Music,* trans. T. Nugent (London, 1748), I, 365–71.

7. For the festival, see William Henry Husk, *An Account of the Musical Celebrations on St. Cecilia's Day in the Sixteenth, Seventeenth and Eighteenth Centuries. To which is Appended a Collection of Odes on St. Cecilia's Day* (London, 1857).

8. James Gibbs, "Preface" to Robert South's *Musica Incantans: or, the Power of Musick* (London, 1700).

9. Richard Brocklesby, *Reflections of Antient and Modern Musick, with the Application to the Cure of Diseases* (London, 1749), pp. 30–31.

10. On the ethos of each ancient Greek mode, and ancient discussion of the Phrygian vs. the other modes (especially the Dorian) as arousing either martial or religious frenzy, see Warren D. Anderson, *Ethos and Education in Greek Music: The Evidence of Poetry and Philosophy* (Cambridge, Mass., 1966), *passim.*

11. *Plutarch's Morals,* trans. John Phillips (London, 1684), I, 273–74. In the passage just preceding, Plutarch mentions Alexander's erecting a statue of the musician, Aristonicus, in commemoration of his ability to inspire courage, presumably by the Phyrgian mode.

12. *Supplemens de Jean Freinshemius sur Quinte Curce,* trans. DeRyer, in Rufus, *De la Vie et des Actions d'Alexandre le Grand,* trans. De Vaugelas (Paris, 1659), pp. 29–30. The supplements are based upon material in Arrian, Justin, *et al,* so this account may be simply a variant of Plutarch's.

13. See for example Vossius, pp. 58–59; William Derham, *Physico-Theology* . . . (London, 1713), pp. 135–37; Athanasius Kircher, *Musurgia Universalis . . . sive Ars magna Consoni et Dissoni* (Rome, 1650), II, 217.

14. One other critic has noted Dryden's rearrangement of the traditional tale: Douglas Murray, "Dryden's Inversion to Disorder in *Alexander's Feast," The Scriblerian,* 16 (Spring 1984), 182.

15. See, for example, the list of paintings in A. Pigler, *Barockthemen: Eine Auswahl von Verzeichnissen zur Ikonographie des 17. und 18. Jahrhunderts* (Budapest, 1956), vol. II. Antonio Verrio (1639?–1700) did include Alexander in a wall painting for the Hampton Court banqueting house, the subject being taken from Julian the Apostate's *Satire of the Caesars;* but apparently the only English art using the motif of Alexander with Darius' family was an oil on plaster in the inner hall of Shaw Hall, near Flixton in Lancs., done by a follower of Verrio and Louis Laguerre.

16. Donald Posner, "Charles LeBrun's Triumphs of Alexander," *Art Bulletin,* 41 (1959), 236–45.

17. See William M. Peterson, ed., Colley Cibber's *The Rival Queans, with the Humours of Alexander the Great* (Painesville, Ohio, 1965), pp. viii–x, for Augustan ridicule of Alexander as he was represented with pompous bombast. For a denigrating French view, see Nicolas Boileau-Despréaux, *Oeuvres Diverses du Sieur D*** Avec le Traité du Sublime ou du Merveilleux dans le Discours* (Paris, 1683), satire #8.

18.   Bessie Proffitt, "Political Satire in 'Alexander's Feast,' " *Texas Studies in Literature and Language,* 11 (1970), 1307–16; Howard Erskine-Hill, "John Dryden: Poet and Critic," in *Dryden to Johnson,* ed. Roger Lonsdale (London, 1971), pp. 50–51, and "Literature and its Context. II, Scholarship as Humanism," *Essays in Criticism,* 29 (Jan. 1979), 42–43. Also see two essays that argue the possibility that the portrait of Alexander was meant to evoke King William, but that by Darius, Dryden was alluding to James II (not Louis XIV): Alan Roper, *Dryden's Poetic Kingdoms* (New York, 1965), pp. 8–9, 13, 28; and Earl Miner, *Dryden's Poetry* (Bloomington, 1967), p. 273. Inasmuch as both defenders and detractors of William compared him to Alexander the Great, imaginative literature could work both sides of the same street. It is, therefore, all but impossible to determine who perceived Dryden's Alexander in what way.

19.   Both the Motteux 1695 ode and the anonymous ode for 1696 exist in unique broadside copies at the Cheatham Library, Manchester, and are reproduced in my "Critical Study of Odes for St. Cecilia's Day, 1683–1697," unpub. Ph.D. diss. (U. of Illinois, 1968).

20.   Ruth Smith, "The Argument and Context of Dryden's 'Alexander's Feast,' " *Studies in English Literature,* 18 (1978), 465–90.

21.   *The Letters of John Dryden, with Letters Addressed to Him,* ed. Charles E. Ward (Durham, 1942), p. 96.

22.   Hughes's poem, divided into airs, recitatives and duets for musical setting by Clayton, appears in *Poems on Several Occasions* (London, 1725), II, 507–09. A non-holograph ms of the poem is among Hughes's "Poems and Translations" at Harvard. In it, though not in Hughes's hand, are several minor notations for musical performance, some of which appear to be later than others, and some of which have been crossed out.

23.   Dryden may have been consciously using Milton's comparison of Jupiter Ammon (or Jove) and the serpent in *Paradise Lost,* IX, II. 507–09.

24.   Justin, *History of the World* . . . , trans. T[homas] Brown, 2nd edn. (London, 1713), pp. 126–27; Rufus, *The History of . . . Alexander the Great,* trans. "Several Gentlemen of the University of Oxford" (London, 1687), p. 96. Also mentioned in Elijah Fenton's "Observations" in *The Works of Edmund Waller in Prose and Verse* (London, 1720), p. clv.

25.   Freinshemius, *Supplemens,* p. 12.

26.   See also Giovanni Botero, *Observations upon the Lives of Alexander, Caesar, and Scipio* (London, 1602); Henry Purcell, *Catches, Rounds, Two-Part and Three-Part Songs,* ed. W. Barclay Squire and J. A. Fuller-Maitland, *The Works,* vol. 22 (London, 1922), catch #20; Saint-Évremond, *The Works* (London, 1700), I, 115; Cibber, *The Rival Queans,* pp. 17–18.

27.   Rufus, *De la Vie,* pp. 154–56.

28.   Diodorus of Sicily, *The Historical Library,* trans. G. Booth (London, 1814), II, 215–17.

29.   "The Life of Alexander the Great," trans. John Evelyn, in *Plutarch's Lives,* IV, 329–32, 266, 385.

30.   Stationers' Hall "Court Records," as quoted in Charles H. Bikle, "The Odes for St. Cecilia's Day in London (1683–1703)," unpub. Ph.D. diss. (U. of Michigan, 1982) 1:41.

31.   Quoted in Bikle, 1:48. Bikle also notes that on 7 Feb. 1697 the Stationers agreed not to rent the hall "to any person or persons that doe or shall require scaffolding to be had or used therein" ("Court Records," Book G, fol. 3).

Index

◆

The Volume Editor

James Anderson Winn is professor of English and professor of Music at the University of Michigan. He recently completed eight years as the founding Director of the University of Michigan Institute for the Humanities. In addition to books on Pope's letters and the history of the relations between music and poetry, he has written two significant studies of Dryden: *John Dryden and his World* (New Haven: Yale University Press, 1987), now the standard modern biography; and *"When Beauty Fires the Blood": Love and the Arts in the Age of Dryden* (Ann Arbor: University of Michigan Press, 1992), an interpretive study placing Dryden in the context of seventeenth-century ideas about gender and aesthetics.

The General Editor

Zack Bowen is professor of English at the University of Miami. He holds degrees from the University of Pennsylvania (B.A.), Temple University (M.A.), and the State University of New York at Buffalo (Ph.D.). In addition to being general editor of this G. K. Hall series, he is editor of the James Joyce series for the University of Florida Press and the *James Joyce Literary Supplement*. He is author of six books and editor of three others, all on modern British, Irish, and American literature. He has also published more than one hundred monographs, essays, scholarly reviews, and recordings related to literature. He is past president of the James Joyce Society (1977–86), former chair of the Modern Language Association Lowell Prize Committee, and currently president of the International James Joyce Foundation.